Patrick McDermott

BLACKMOUNTAIN

The ancestral townland and home of
Seán Mac Diarmada's cousins

Le gac bea-ġuí
Pádraiz Mac Diarmada

AUSTIN MACAULEY PUBLISHERS™

LONDON • CAMBRIDGE • NEW YORK • SHARJAH

A CIP catalogue record for this title is available from the British Library.

ISBN 9781398403079 (Paperback)
ISBN 9781398401396 (ePub e-book)

www.austinmacauley.com

First Published (2021)
Austin Macauley Publishers Ltd
25 Canada Square
Canary Wharf
London
E14 5LQ

I would like to acknowledge the assistance from my daughter Deirdre Mc Dermott and all my neighbours and friends, many of whom are mentioned in this book, who assisted me in my effort to tell the story of life in Blackmountain in the twentieth century and before.

Contents

Families in Blackmountain during 1930–1950

HOUSE NO. 1

Mc Dermott (Known as the Eddies)

Parents: **Eddie** and Kate.

Children: Baby, Celia, Maggie, Nora, Susan, Rosaleen, Sonny, Jim, Gerald, Keven, Michael.

HOUSE NO. 2

Mc Dermott (Known as the Donalds – Seán Mac Diarmada's people)

Parents: Daniel (known as ould Daniel) and wife (name unknown).

Children: Thomas, John, Beezie, Francie, Mary. (Possibly more.)

HOUSE NO. 3

Moore (Lived by the river on Moore's Hill)

Parents: Christopher and Margaret.

Children: Kit, Jimmy, Nixon, Bob, Susan, Dora, Kate. *(Kit went to the USA. Susan and Dora moved away, not sure where and Kate married Bob Hughdie in Barrs. They were Protestant. Johnny Kilkenny, still with us, claims Mickie Donald Bhig (a cousin of Seán Mac Diarmada) was originally in Moore's place but that he was moved further down Blackmountain to a smaller farm where we knew his son known as Johnny Dermott who was married to Rose Ellen. Johnny died in*

*1950 and Rose Ellen moved into Manorhamilton. Mickie
had two brothers who went to America and weren't heard
about for years until a fellow called Devanney from Glencar
came home and told he saw them. I saw a letter written in
1993 from Mickie to them describing the hard life he had
under the Landlord Aljoe. The three Moores, Bob, Nixon,
and Jimmy who remained at home are central to the John
Donald story.)*

HOUSE NO. 4

Clancy

Parents: Johnny and Mary.

Children: Mary Ellen, Bridget, Kate, Lizzie, Tessie, Paddy, John,
Michael. *(All except Lizzie emigrated to the USA.)*

HOUSE NO. 5

Mc Dermott

Parents: Farrell and Nora (Keaney from Glenfarne).

Children: Farrell, Cormac, Thomas, John, Ann, Bridget and two
girls who died of TB. *(John remained in Blackmountain
and married Ellen O' Rourke from Glenague and they had
two sons John and Denis. John married Mary Mc Morrow
and they had five children – Patrick, Annie, Seán, Hubert
and Denis.)*

HOUSE NO. 6

Walsh

Parents: Owen and Catherine. *(Owen was known as Oweney
Power among the neighbours because he was so strong that
he was able to carry two stones for the brace in the house
from the Barrs' quarry when the man with him failed to
carry his. He was also reputed to have got between the shafts
of a cart in Blacklion where he was selling pigs having the*

loan of a horse from a man who fell out with him and took the horse from him. He is reputed to have pulled it the whole way home. This was the age when physical strength and endurance were in much demand. He was related to Mary Ann Kilkenny (née McManus).)

Children: One son, John.

HOUSE NO. 7

Kilkenny

Parents: Oweney and Ann McDermott from Barrs.

Children: Johnny, Tommy, Paddy and Ann. *(Tommy married Mary Ann Thomas Tady (McManus) and they had five children: Johnny, Paddy, Oweney, Mary Alice, Annie.)*

HOUSE NO. 8

Walsh

Parents: James (cobbler) and Mariah.

Children: One daughter, Lilly. *(Lilly married Jimmy Cormac McSharry and had five children: Maura, Betty, Sarah, Annabelle, Shane. James died first and Mariah and Jimmy died about the same time after which Lilly moved to Camderry where Jimmy's brother lived.)*

HOUSE NO. 9

Walsh

Parents: Tommy and Ann (McSharry).

Children: Tom, Jimmy, Pa, Mary, Margaret (Babby).

HOUSE NO. 10

Clancy

Joe (a bachelor).

HOUSE NO. 11

Parents: Johnny and Rose Ellen. *(Johnny is a cousin of Seán MacDiarmada and is known as Johnny Donald bhig. His father was Mickie Donald Bhig. They had no family but Larry Feeney and Keven Cleary lived with them for a period.)*

HOUSE NO. 12

McMorrow

Parents: Dinny and Anne.

Children: Owen, John (who went to Australia), Maggie, Mary, Patrick, Denis

HOUSE NO. 13

Burns

Parents: Tommy and Ann (Kilkenny).

Children: A large family, all of whom died of TB except Mary who Married Tommy Cullen from Corranmore, Seán MacDiarmada country.

HOUSE NO. 14

McMorrow

Parents: John & Bridget.

Children: Michael Joseph, Thomas Hugh, Charles, Patrick, Mary, John, Martin.

Maps:
Manorhamilton and environs

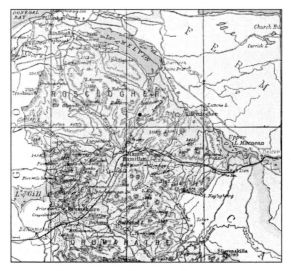

Map of area of Leitrim around Manorhamilton taken from Atlas and cyclopedia of Ireland *(1900), p.181. (Source: Wikimedia Commons.)*

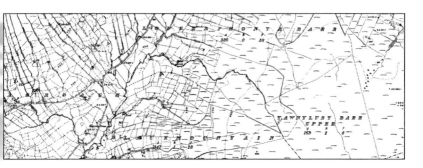

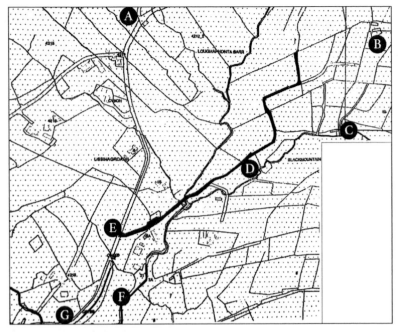

Map of the area of Blackmountain and Lissnagroagh.

Key

A Road to Kiltyclogher.

B Ruins of the ancestral home of Sean Mac Diarmada in Blackmountain. (His cousins John and Bizzie Donald were the last residents).

C Moore's House.

D Laneway into the ruins.

E Jack Hughie Dinny's (Mc Morrow) gateway entrance to Blackmountain.

F Corr na bhfeannóg river.

G Road to Manorhamilton.

Introduction

THERE ARE 640,000 TOWNLANDS IN IRELAND. Most are of Gaelic origin, predate the Norman invasion and have names of Irish origin. However, some townlands, names and boundaries come from Norman manors, plantation divisions, or late creations of the Ordnance Survey. This is the smallest unit of land division in the country, but it is the most important as it is the area where the huge population of over eight million were squeezed in prior to 1847, the year the great famine commenced. It often happened that when a new member got married, he was given a few acres in a corner of the farm and a hastily-built shack to get him started in his new life.

In this book I'm attempting to describe the way of life of such a people in one of those townlands, namely, Blackmountain, which is situated between Manorhamilton and Kiltyclogher, five miles from the former and three miles from the latter, near the old school, Twanyinshinagh, where Hubert McMorrow now lives.

But this is not just any old townland. It is the ancestral townland and home of Seán MacDiarmada's people. Seán, as many know, was the second signatory of the proclamation of the 1916 Rebellion in Ireland, an event which was a watershed not just in Ireland but all over the world. It inspired people everywhere to shake off the yoke of slavery and imperialism and seek independence. Seán has been described as the "mind" of the 1916 Rebellion – that without him the rebellion would not have happened. He recruited and organized those who took part in it.

The Mac Diarmada family in 1890. Sean is in the middle row,
on the extreme left

There was no omen when Patrick Donald McDermott left
Blackmountain at the end of the eighteenth century to start a
new life in Laghty Barr, Corranmore, close to Kiltyclogher and
County Fermanagh that a son of the clan would one day die so
that Ireland might live, as Seán himself put it.

But the emphasis is otherwise than on Seán in this book,
noble though his deeds have been. His relatives who were left
behind in Blackmountain eking a bare living on poor land and
the neighbours among whom they lived is what this book is
about.

I grew up among them in the early years of the twentieth
century and shared their trials and tribulations and engaged in
the daily tasks of subsistence farming. They shaped my early
years. I thank them for that.

I am not making any judgements on a great people who
inhabited my native townland, Blackmountain, and the
surrounding townlands for centuries. Without any preten-
tiousness on my part, I am simply telling the story of their
struggle to survive in a bleak landscape on poor soil in the late
nineteenth and early twentieth century.

I try to place this story in the great onward thrust of the human race towards some destiny which we all hope will be perfect happiness. I deal with the influence of the Catholic Church, the future of agriculture, and the evolutionary process in general which most of us are agreed is carrying us along towards some final destiny which, with our present knowledge, we can only speculate about.

We are all living the mystery, as Dom Mark Patrick Hederman OSB of Glenstall Abbey tells us in his latest book.

I wish to thank all my neighbours who encouraged me to tell their story and are happy to see their names in the story.

A prime purpose of this book is to ensure that the people of Blackmountain will not be forgotten and it is my great wish that all their relatives, wherever they may be, will enjoy reading about their ancestral townland.

The tombstone of Donald and Mary McDermott, Seán's father and mother

Chapter One

Blackmountain in the past

TO LIVE IN IRELAND, ANY PART OF IT, NOT just Leitrim, or specifically Blackmountain, is to be confined by the mérin ditch. This is the boundary fence between farms. "Good fences make good neighbours" is an often-heard dictum in the countryside.

"Any well-to-do farmer," as my mother Mary Hughie Dinny was wont to say, "must be up early in the morning so that everything is alright and that no trespassing is taking place." Those "slounging" in bed – another phrase of hers – would be "ate out of it" if the fences were not up to scratch and the animals would be removed before they got up. Of course, if you were a good tracker you could see the evidence when you'd rise and go out and look about you, but it would be too late then as the damage would be done and since you didn't actually see them thieving you couldn't be dead sure whose stock they were.

The original name of the townland of Blackmountain was Cnoc na raithní (the hill of the fern). Cnoc na ceárta (the hill of the forge) was the Irish name for Moore's land. The folklore is that it was the result of two landlords falling out with one another that brought about the name Blackmountain when one suggested to the other that all he had got was a black mountain. And so the name stuck. We frequently used "Fernhill" when writing home.

Since there was no industry in the country, especially in the Manorhamilton-Glenfarne-Kiltyclocher area – except for a button factory in the former and a few jobs on the railroad and County Council and in Killasnet Creamery – everyone was dependent on their twenty-odd acres and their two to six cows for a living. In the twenties and thirties there was much talk about ditching with the loy (spade) and the graip* (fork) and this was usually done in the winter and early spring. It was heavy work. You had to build up the sods high on one side so that a beast wouldn't be able to climb up. It had to be high enough on the other side so that the beast would balk at throwing himself down. It was a huge task to keep the ditches in good repair and if there was not a good understanding between neighbours there would be continual feuds and recourse to law. Any wealth a man accumulated had to come from the land. There was no other way. Hence the greed for land.

Loy

* These and other Irish terms are explained in the Glossary at the end of the book.

At the end of the nineteenth century the land acts gave more freedom to the landowners, but it was still hardship. The demand note and the receivable order were two documents feared in every house. There was a valuation on every piece of land no matter how poor the quality.

Since the cow was the standard of judgement, it was always a question of how many cows you had. An "eight cows" or "ten cows" place would be considered a big farm. Most people sent milk to the creamery. A creamery cheque of £10 a month would be considered a lot of money, but the snag was the cows milked well for only four or for five months, if even that. People were always "short of grass", as they called it. If it was slow in coming in the spring (and some years it was slower than usual), it compounded the problems. It was said that old hay was old gold so any left over from the previous year came in useful for the following year if you had to keep the cows in longer to give the grass a chance to grow. A lot of people were overstocked and the cows were bare, going out from seven months feeding on poor quality hay with a lot of sprat and rushes in it, with but the odd sheaf of corn for the barest of them. There were no fertilisers of course except for the odd bag of sulphate of ammonia for the potatoes. Grass grew with whatever the sun, the moisture and the weather in general managed to coax out of the reluctant earth. As they used to say, the hens only laid when the birds of the air were laying and the grass only grew when nature answered to the most favourable weather conditions. Were it not that nature kept renewing itself, the people would not have been able to feed themselves.

The one consoling factor was that almost everyone was in the same boat, except that some people did have better quality land and more acreage. Little did they know then that the world would change, and the lot of the farmer would even get worse, if that were possible. Of course, not everyone was equally industrious, and many people failed to grow enough potatoes to feed the family and were in dire straits every spring when they had no potatoes for dinner, not to speak of seed potatoes for the following year. Looking back now, one is inclined to blame them for finding themselves in the lurch, which they frequently were. You'd imagine they should have the foresight and industry to see to it that they would have enough potatoes to see them through the whole year. Now, it wasn't that easy to grow potatoes. Some people hadn't the land for potatoes, as they used to say. There was very little clay land in the Dubh area, so people were depending on patches of moss which were cut-away bog. This was excellent for potatoes and other vegetables, especially cabbage and carrots.

Some of the Dubh people used to go down to John Larry's (McDermott) on the lower road near Thompson's to set their potatoes. They would have been given so many ridges such a length, as they used to describe it. They might have to bring down the cow dung if they had any to spare, which wasn't always the case because there were so many demands for it like top dressing the meadows to increase hay yield. They would have to give so many days' work in lieu of pay. No money changed hands simply because there was no money. Families were big and there was no way of making money because there were no jobs around. The cycle could begin with "putting in" the potatoes, as they called it.

Most people had no horse, so they had to rely on the little black or grey donkey and pardóga (panniers) to put out the manure. The pardóga were usually made of wood/sallies and a bottom that was hinged with two pieces of leather and two loops of wire which could be released to drop the dung. It would be very messy to put the dung out in the ordinary creel because you would have to lift it off and dump it and you would need a second person to hold the other creel or it would topple over. So, the pardóga were the first hydraulic tippers down on the farm.

This job of putting out the dung with the donkeys and pardóga was frequently left to the boys in the family when they came home from school. It was heavy and dirty work, no matter how careful you were, so their hands and clothes would be filthy and often they were barefoot and had oighear (inflamed skin) on their legs so they suffered doing the job of getting the "potatoes in". The better-off people might have a dray for the donkey. This could be pulled along the ground, but it took a strong donkey to pull it, especially if the ground was bumpy. "Between hopping and trotting", another phrase of my mother, they somehow got the work done.

It was said that a good man would cover a hundredweight of seed in a day. It was also said that "a good man" would mow a half-acre of meadow in a day with a scythe. The mowing with the scythe and the coping (turning the sod) with the loy was "brutal hard work". You got blisters on your hands and hacks on your fingers with the wet and cold spring air.

Rural Ireland was exemplified in the townland of Black-mountain, ancestral home of the Seán MacDiarmada clan. The Dubh area generally was just typical of any rural area in Ireland in the late nineteenth century and early twentieth century. Almost everyone was eking a living from the soil. Even as late as 1950 there were 350,000 farmers in the country. This fact helps us to understand the attachment to the land. It was the land that sustained our ancestors during all those thousands of years when they were foragers wandering all over the planet searching for something to eat. And it was still doing that in the early twentieth century. But things were changing; imperceptibly for most people, but nevertheless changing.

Like many others I don't like change. I wanted our rural life to remain static. I thought our neighbours, the Clancys, the Moores, the Donalds, the Eddies and all the others in proximity, would be with us always. Nobody was to die. After all, they had been there for the last twenty years. Hadn't they been there since I was capable of knowing of their presence?

Why should things change? This was the youthful simplicity of my thinking. I can't ever forget them. I witnessed all of them at their daily chores and I sometimes lent a hand. There was something about them – a resilience that gladdened my heart. I carted out the dung for John Donald in April 1953 and my father coped the last potato crop that he ever set. They were never dug and the flattened ridges can still be seen in the garden at the back of the house to this day.

In moments of reverie I can see the contours of all their farms in my mind's eye as clearly as if I was there and all the names of the fields. I often ask myself is this a penance I have to bear for all the sins of my youthful years in that dark townland, Blackmountain, with its back to the sun. Equally, I can visualise all the nearcuts through their lands – down by Eddie's, Hugh Kilkenny's, and across by Bob Nixon's, and over by Tobar and yet again down from the line by Dolan's. Talk about landscape – it's all there in my mind's eye.

Contemplating the future, one has to face the inevitable. The memory of this mountainy people will fade into the annals of history. Their humble abodes will be smothered in blankets of afforestation. No amount of nostalgia will bring them back. Unlike the Blasket islanders off the Kerry coast, whose literary output assured that they wouldn't be forgotten, the people of Blackmountain and surrounding area have no such assurance.

Dubh mountain

Chapter Two

My family

I WAS BORN IN MY GRANNY'S HOUSE ON THE banks of the Corr na bhfeannóg river which rises in Healy's askey at the foot of Thor mountain and winds its way down till it eventually flows into Lough McNean in Glenfarne village. The date was the 27th March 1934. I was christened Patrick Joseph – Patrick, because it was the month of March and the feast day of one of our patron saints, Saint Patrick, was celebrated all over the world on the 17th March; Joseph after the carpenter, Saint Joseph, partner of the Virgin Mary.

My father was known as Wee John, although he was six foot, and his father as Big John, although he was much short of the ideal height, simply because he was his father. His son then had to be Wee John and the name stuck to him although he was destined to grow taller than his father.

My father, Wee John (McDermott), married his neighbour Mary Hughie Dinny (McMorrow), the eldest of 13 in the family of Hughie Dinny Phaidí and Rose Ann Johnny Farrell (also McDermott), whose house was situated just across the river on the banks of the Corr na bhfeannóg river. Wee John picked out the best ewes he had and sold them for seven shillings each, which was reckoned to be a great price. She got a dowry of £175 which was considered a lob of money in those days; the equivalent today would be a big sum.

They got married in January 1933 and this accounts for my appearance in March the following year. The reason I was born in my granny's house was because my mother was back with her mammy while my daddy was reconstructing the house on the hill just across the river. They were certainly close neighbours.

Much of the activity in the Dubh area (Dubh was the generic name for all the townlands in that region) centred on my mother's people, the Hughie Dinny's. And this is how it came about. My grandfather Hughie Dinny Phaidí (McMorrow) from Corranmore, a first cousin of Seán MacDiarmada, married Rose Ann Johnny Farrell (McDermott), my granny, on the banks of the Corr na bhfeannóg river.

Big John McDermott, the author's grandfather

The marriage took place in 1900. Rose Ann was only 16 years. Her uncle said that it was not right to have a young girl about the house unmarried when he had a servant boy named Tommy McGourty. Rose Ann was reared by her Uncle Hughie Farrell largely because she belonged to her father's first family and her uncle had no family of his own. Rose Ann's father Johnny Farrell (McDermott) had married twice, the first time to Kate McLoughlin (Rose Ann's mother) and the second time to Sarah McMorrow from Blackmountain. John Johnny, his son from his first marriage, married a sister of Sarah's called Cecily, so you had a father and a son married to two sisters.

Hughie Farrell was a very progressive and successful farmer, kept his land well and milked good cows. He had a churning machine for making the butter and a nice mare for doing the job. (Mullán creamery wasn't around at this stage.) There was a market for the butter. He was noted for having early spring grass, so much so that people going to the fair in Manorhamilton would often drive in their cattle to get a good feed before they would have to stand up all day in the fair green, too often on empty bellies. Hughie was noted for putting the cows in early for the winter to give the land a chance to recover, as they used to say, and this was how he was able to have early grass in the spring. The manure from the animals was put out as topdressing in the meadows. This made a big difference that you could easily see in the quality of the grass.

Johnny and Hughie Farrell had a brother in Dublin who had a business. His name was Thomas. He had no family either. My mother thought that it was peculiar that neither Hughie nor Thomas had children. When Thomas died all his brothers and sisters got a legacy of four to five hundred which was a considerable amount of money then. This left them all comfortable.

My grandfather Hughie Dinny was a *cliamhain isteach* (he married into the farm). He hailed from Corranmore, birthplace of Seán MacDiarmada, as I have already said. His aunt Mary, sister of his father Dinny Phaidí (McMorrow), was Seán MacDiarmada's mother. Dinny had a shop at the bridge in Corranmore which served all that area to Laughty Bar and out on the Glenfarne road. To have a country shop was to be relatively prosperous. It was said that a yard of a counter was as good as a farm of land and a customer was as good as an extra cow.

The marriage of Hughie and Rose Ann was a watershed in the life of the people in the Dubh area. They would have a family of 13, of whom my mother Mary was the eldest. The fact that Hughie Dinny had some experience of running a shop almost certainly prompted himself and Rose Ann to open a shop in Lisnagroagh where they were living. It was successful and very convenient for all the people in the area, especially for all the people in the townlands of Blackmountain and Lisnagroagh and, indeed, further afield. Since a shopkeeper had everything at cost, as they used to call it, this was a considerable saving for their family of thirteen.

The McMorrow family in 1934: from left, Hughie McMorrow, son of Hughie Dinny; his mother, Rose Ann; Baby, sister; the author's mother Mary with author in her arms; either Annie or Bridid McMorrow

The McMorrows in later life: Brigid Kilbride and Baby at back; her brother Hughie in front; Mary McMorrow, author's mother and sister Maggie

Rose Ann was a very kind, generous woman who never refused anyone, whether they had the money or not. Many people were in no position to pay their bills. They had very little to sell: a nod calf, perhaps, or an occasional pig if they could manage to fatten it on spuds, if they had them, or the few eggs from the hens, if they were laying. That was about it. Everybody had to buy flour if they wanted to have bread. You had to have money for the shop, as they used to say, to get that. You got that on tick, of course, but you expected to have to pay for it someday. Your pride wouldn't let you default, anyhow. Many people were lucky enough to have people in America so the few dollars would come at some stage to clear the bill in Hughie Dinny's, as they used to say.

Hughie Dinny's house and shop

As well as serving the many needs of many poor people in the locality, the shop became the centre of activity and leisure for the Dubh area. All the people gathered around the cart shed adjacent to the shop which acted as a shelter in inclement weather to recount the day's happenings and have a bit of fun. Famous people who came there would include wee Brian (McGourty), John Healy, Francie Dermott, Michael Gilbride, Jimmie Oweney (McMorrow), Sonny in Eddies (McDermott) and Willie Evens. They were often up to mischief, planning escapes to here and there and playing tricks on people. A crowd of them would often head up to "Ould" Tommy Burns in Blackmountain to spend the night with him and his lone surviving daughter Mary. Another character who used to be present on these excursions into the countryside was Biddies Con (Mc Govern) who lived at the bridge now known as Biddie's bridge. One wonders what they would do if there was no shop there.

My father's family consisted of just two boys – John and Denis. My mother sometimes derisively referred to them as the "Cuckoo Family". Between the two of them they re-constructed the house that year, putting blue banger slates on the roof. This meant that we had one of the best houses in the locality, with three rooms upstairs and three downstairs.

Denis Mc Dermott the handiman in Black Mountain, with his mother Ellen O'Rourke

Uncle Denis, who was a wonderful tradesman, was destined to never marry and he remained living in the house after John got married. Not being physically strong, he wasn't able for farming, but he soon developed a talent for almost any kind of handy work: as they used to say, he could turn his hand to anything. He did everything in the wood area from roofing houses to making tables. He even succeeded in harnessing the Corr na bhfeannóg river constructing a rampart, powerhouse and a huge wheel. This meant we had electricity long before the Electricity Supply Board arrived in the area. He had a lathe driven by the water power and here he turned bed posts and spinning wheels which he sold to Vocational Educational Committees all over the country as well as charging batteries for those who could afford a radio. On top of all this, he repaired watches, clocks, guns and all sorts of machinery, including car engines, mowing machines and tractors when they came along. He made horse carts, horseshoes and a host of other jobs. He also made a threshing machine which was used for threshing the corn in the area. They came from far and near for these services. Many little jobs such as hanging scythes and sharpening instruments he did for nothing.

Left: Wee John with author; right: Hubert McDermott and his uncle Jack McMorrow

Annie, Denis and Hubert

There were five children in our family but, unfortunately, three of them were destined to die young. We all got that deadly disease, diphtheria, when young and it swept away my youngest brother, Denis. This was absolutely horrendous. It was to be imprinted on my mind for all time.

Annie, Hubert, Patrick and Seán

Hubert, Seán, Patrick and Wee John

Rose Ann, Annie and Dessie McPartland

I was on Thor mountain searching for our sheep on New Year's Day 1948. It was nothing more than a mere count, looking to see were they all there, where they were "camping", making sure that they had not left the mountain altogether (which was always a possibility, especially for new sheep as we called them) and, when I found them, chasing them in towards the head of our own land, so that they would know from whence they came. This was a very important exercise, otherwise they could disappear down some other person's land in Corranmore, Seán Mac Diarmada country, or in Lacoon on the Barr's side. If that happened you might never see them again. I remember I met Tommy Kilkenny, a neighbour, on the top of Thor and we had a chat and parted. His errand would have been similar to mine.

Sheep are like all creaturehood, they can be helped to form a habit – and the habit to be formed in this instance is to be able to make their way back to their own land after foraging all over the mountain. I arrived home that evening and reported what I saw. The next morning I had a sore throat and from there the tragedy started. Further in the evening I was tired and I lay into bed with my youngest brother, Denis. Soon he was sick and all the other children with him. He was dead within three days. This was unbelievably traumatic for the family. My father cycled into Manorhamilton to get Dr Fitzgerald. She was reluctant to come. Petrol was scarce and rationed. She made all sorts of excuses but eventually decided to come. She diagnosed pneumonia. He was dead within an hour of her leaving and all the other members had sore throats. Then we got Dr Harry O'Carroll (another doctor in Manorhamilton) to see my brother Seán and sister Annie. He said they had diphtheria. As for me I didn't seem to have anything except a slight sore throat. So the question arises. Was I the carrier? I was on the mountain on the 1st January and my brother Denis dies on the 5th January.

Seán and Annie were taken to the hospital in Carrick-in-Shannon and spent several months there lying on their backs with their feet raised. (Hubert, the second youngest in the family, didn't get it at all.) They recovered but had to learn to walk again. You can imagine the anxiety. The lives of all the children were seriously threatened. Diphtheria is a deadly contagious disease.

I can still see my little three-year-old brother Denis sitting on his three-legged stool by the fire at the commencement of his illness and soon after going to bed beginning to breathe heavily and passing away within seconds when his heart failed. Denis, his uncle after whom he was called, made a lovely white coffin for him and he was buried in the family grave in Kilmakerrill graveyard to await the resurrection.

One doesn't easily get over these things, but being young we did eventually manage to leave them behind us. As for our poor parents, one never knows what they had to suffer. My mother was to live to see two of her remaining three sons die soon after her husband. But we know that life has to go on, so we soldiered on – my mother for more than twenty years and, thankfully, I myself am still around, as is my sister Annie. It would appear that I was the one who got the diphtheria first, whether on the mountain or elsewhere, and it also appears that I shook it off, though not before I had passed it on to my little brother.

The author with his brother Hubert in later life.

It was unlikely that I picked up the disease on Thor mountain. It was almost certainly incubating long before that. We had opened a drain in front of the house and it is thought that it was here that the germ was lying.

We had three byres (always "byres" in Leitrim): one at the house, one on the first hill and the third one just before the drains' field. You might wonder what these mountain byres were for. Our neighbours the Clancys, the Moores and John Donald all had a mountain byre. They were used for the cows that could be released easily to graze the adjacent tulaigh and barr which had an abundance of cíob and heather – a not too nourishing diet but very useful when the grass lower down was skint. As my mother used to say, "You could always put a couple stirks on the barr for a while in the summer, but they might find it hard to bull." I well remember how pleasant it was to see our cows eating the cíob and ceannabháin in the bog holes as we were saving the turf as children. There was always the danger that they might bog or fall into a hole, so we had to keep a watchful eye on them. As children we much preferred the bog to the hay. We could play in the soft peat, throw sods of turf at one another and jump bog holes.

I loved Thor mountain. It was an excuse to escape the endless chores around the house. I remember that when we were footing the turf at the shed in the bog, I'd suggest to my mother that I should take a run up the mountain to have a look at the sheep (of course, I was hoping I might bump into Annie McManus at the turf at the end of the Barr's bog road also) and direct them in towards the head of our own land. I was familiar with all the haunts the sheep had on the mountain – the binn, the quarry, leabaidh (where Diarmaid and Gráinne were reputed to have slept), sruthán, McGirril's askey, Thomas Tady's turf, Lackey's bog, etc.

The author with his uncle Stephen

Dubh mountain taken from Wee John's Tulaigh

Chapter Three

Our neighbours

I F YOU WERE TO TAKE THOR MOUNTAIN AS the centre of a circle you could travel around the base clockwise beginning at the Kilty cross where the travellers used to camp in the 'thirties and 'forties, up by the black hollow, past Ms Kilkenny's (ex-N.T.), past Felie's, past old Tawnyinshinagh national school, past Biddie's and down the whole way to Bernie's (Maguire), turning right up the Corranmore road, past Denis Dinny's, past Seán MacDiarmada's house and out on the Glenfarne road, soon again turning right up the Barrs' Line coming out at St Michael's and reaching Kilty Cross again. Within this circle, practically all the farms have some land at the base and some running up to the mountain with the mountain itself as commonage. Few of the farms have more than thirty acres and some are as small as fifteen.

It would be very interesting to know how all the ditching was done and the acreage divided. All the holdings had some green land near the road and then running up the hill towards the mountain, be it Thor, Dubh or Ballaghnabehy Rock, the land got rougher and is mostly cíob and heather. The brae face is called the tulaigh (raised ground) and outside that the area is known as the barr (top) and is invariably heathery with ceann-bhán around. Depending on the lie of the land a small number of holdings had no outlet to the mountain, which meant they had no grazing rights there, although they would have the right of way through different people's land to the bog which was on the head of the farms. It would almost appear that God had ordained it so – how handy it was to have turf on the head of your own land. The land generally was of poor quality but God, as it were, had made sure that these poor people had moss-type land on which they could crop to feed themselves and turf to cook the food and keep them warm.

Now, almost nobody cuts turf on the headlands. That shows how sophisticated the people have become, though the presence of peat there since time immemorial was a Godsend for countless generations. Within an hour you could have an ass load of turf and a sparkling fire radiating heat about the kitchen. In fact, for some people getting turf was the main occupation. There was some hardship when the turf was not saved. The trick was to get them cut early so you got the early good weather if it happened to come as well as the later good weather which didn't always come.

As children we were very interested in our neighbours. Four of our neighbours used the same lane into their houses and Wee John constructed a bridge across the Corr na bhfeannóg river to facilitate the crossing of the river. Prior to this, you had to walk over the riverbed. When there was a flood, it was almost impossible to cross, though huge stones were strategically placed to help you make it across. This was a time when country people had to do everything for themselves so any one with a bit of talent like Wee John stepped into the breach. Not alone was the bridge built, but a big hill out of the river was reduced considerably by cutting it away. This is known as "the cutting" to this day.

Paddy and Lizzie Clancy were our immediate neighbours. Their house was situated on the lane into our house on the banks of a tributary of the Corr na bhfeannóg river. They were very kind and always giving us titbits. My sister Annie and I had to carry water in buckets because there was no water in the houses then. Since the nearest river was at Clancy's, we were continually up and down to the river for buckets of water. And every time we went down we dropped in to see them.

Paddy, like his brother Michael before him, was a great footballer. They both played for Glenfarne. The whole family ended up in America, except for Lizzie who married John McGourty. Times were changing and girls were now less likely to marry into a small holding. All the Eddie Pat Jimmies McDermott (ten of them) emigrated, except Celia who married Breslin in Maguire's bridge in Fermanagh. That was the pattern from now on – in the 1940s, though the war was raging. People like my father Wee John and Jack Hughie Dinny stuck it out. They formed a kind of partnership. My father had a double horse mowing machine and a plough – arguably the two most important pieces of equipment for the industrious farmer – and Jack had, at least, an extra horse.

Lizzie McMorrow and Molly McDermott, cousins

Clancy's and Wee John's were reached by turning right after coming out of the cutting. You went straight ahead to the house of the Moore family. Bob, Nixon, and Jimmy, three bachelor brothers, were what was left of a much larger family. We, as children, loved visiting them. They loved ramblers, as they called them, though they never visited any one themselves. Jimmy the eldest wasn't seen on the road for forty years. Nixon only visited the two sheep fairs in Manorhamilton in August and September each year. Bob, the youngest, did the shopping in Hughie Dinny's. Rose Ann gave him the shopping on tick till Nixon sold the sheep. It wasn't easy to eke out a living in the townland we called Blackmountain.

The three Moores passed away in the the 1950s as did John and Bizzie Donald, Seán MacDiarmada's cousins. I remember that when Jimmy Moore was in Manorhamilton hospital I brought Bob into see him and his last words were: "Make sure that you bring the lad home." Nixon, the good neighbour who made sure that John Donald was put on his cart with the reins in his hands every Friday to go into Manorhamilton to collect his pension, had passed away previously. Bob lingered on for another few years with his sister Kate who had married Bob Hughdie and lived with two sons John James and Roy on the Barrs' line. Thus was the end of two unusual families, two neighbours, one Protestant (the three Moores) and the other Catholic (the Donalds) and they lived in complete harmony for their whole lives, totally oblivious of the great national struggle for the freedom of Ireland. And, except when John Donald took to the road every Friday for his pension, the three Moores were but rarely seen in public (Jimmy not in forty years). But we all loved them and enjoyed visiting them. Their one great attribute was that they accepted everything that life threw at them without any moaning.

Noel and Josie Cullen, the two children of Johnny and Bizzie Cullen from Mooneenagear, the highest house on the mountain, used to visit the three Moores almost daily. I used to see them passing when I was foddering in the mountain byre. When the sheep were being killed by dogs and Nixon used to put them in our bog shed, he often used to carry Noel around on his back. John Healy who lived on the line claimed there were fairies on the stretch between Moore's and Johnny Cullen's because he used to see lights at two o'clock in the morning there, but that was Nixon leaving them home after visiting. (That just shows that there is a natural explanation for many things which seem preternatural or even supernatural.)

On the lane up to Moore's you branched off to the left to get to John Donald McDermott's, the original home of Seán MacDiarmada's family, who will be discussed in the following chapter. Just down from John Donald's in the hollow was Eddie Pat Jimmie's (McDermott). Eddie was married to Kate McDermott and they had 11 children. They were a wonderful family and great workers. Eddie grew everything in a field they called the old bog that sustained the family and he got a job on the County Council. They had to emigrate, of course.

To the right of our house we had another neighbour, Tommy Burns. Ould Burns, as we called him, had two-cow's place, where he lived with his daughter Mary. He lost his wife, Sarah Kilkenny, early in life and had to send his children to the orphanage where all of them except Mary died of the "decline", as they used to call TB. And next to the Burns' was Tommy Kilkenny and his family. Mary was a frequent visitor to our house where she darned socks amongst other things. My mother used to say that she learned these skills from the nuns.

Among the many stories about Ould Burns, here are two. He once sold an old cow during the economic war for a half crown and had to give two pence back as luck money. After a few days the cow made her way back home to Burns' place and the poor old man was so conscientious that he went down to Glenfarne Garda Station to report it to the Garda there. Then there was a famous Mummer's Join (spraoi) held in the house in the 'forties where poteen was on the menu and all hell broke loose. The Francie Georges arrived uninvited and Eugene Oweney James took them on. A right melee broke out. The priest heard about it and that was very serious in those days. Poor Ould Burns was humiliated.

This particular spraoi has gone into the annals of history; at this particular time, it was a mortal sin to have a dance that continued after midnight. Kate Eddie Pat Jimmy (McDermott) was also in trouble. She also held a dance that continued after midnight. These were all occasions of sin and couldn't be tolerated. She also had to face censure.

The highest house on the Blackmountain side of the glen belonged to Johnny Cullen, his wife Bizzie and children Josie and Noel. There was no road to the house. You had to travel through several farms of land to get there. The right of way was up by Paddy Frank Clancy's but you could choose to go up by Tommy Kilkenny's or Joe McGourty's also. Imagine what it was like in the big snow of 1947 which lasted for over six weeks.

Further up Thor mountain Tommy Curneen and his wife Maggie lived. You could make it to their house up the Ballashantra bog road by John Joe McMorrow's. Curneen's farm consisted mainly of bog banks and a couple meadows and a piece of moss for cropping below the house. But these people survived despite all the obstacles.

On the Dubh side, the sunny side, the highest house was Pat Flynn's. You had a great view from this house: you could see the whole way over to Ballaghnabehy. There lived Rosie, her two sons Francie and John James and her two daughters Maggie and Agnes. Agnes married Francie McSharry and John James married Mary Moran. Biddie and other sisters went to America and sent home money to reconstruct the house. My uncle Denis did the roofing. Another son became a priest, Father Peter, and ended up in New Zealand.

Rosie was sister to Oweney James, Jimmy Oweney's father and Mickie James, John Joe McMorrow's father. She was a most amiable and generous person. No sooner would we have arrived up in Granduncle Farrell's meadows to save the hay than she would be out calling us in for tea.

There was always a big spree when Father Peter came home from New Zealand and all the neighbours gathered in. Father Peter said mass in many of the neighbours' houses and I served the masses. There was something very sad that he was ministering so far away.

All these families were our immediate neighbours and we cherished them. The thing that stands out is the huge effort they made to survive. But there was a community awareness and helpfulness. You could call on anyone in an emergency.

Work on the farm was never finished. This didn't seem to bother some people. There was a sense of togetherness among the local community. If your house was situated on a hill you could see what your neighbour was doing all day long and this gave you some sense of belonging. Apart from the main tasks you had to be out and about looking at your cows and keeping the fences in order. Good farmers kept the rushes cut and did bits of reclamation to improve the farm. If it didn't drive you mad it could turn out to be good therapy, helping to keep the mind active and the limbs subtle. And you were your own boss. This meant a lot.

The scene was all these households scattered over the landscape, struggling to survive in a bleak and hostile environment – many with large families. But there was a true sense of belonging among all of them. Didn't they all believe in the same God? Didn't they all attend St Michael's chapel? Didn't they all have the same priest to guide them? Their religion was important to them.

People could not afford to buy meat and some people were rarely seen in Manorhamilton, the only place where you would get meat. Of course, there was no transport. Few people had bicycles, or horses and carts so the desire to walk the five-odd miles into "town", as they called it, was far from the mind of most people. Anyhow, they had no money, so what was the point?

Although people helped one another, one should not conclude that it was so widespread that you would be carried along without much effort on your part by the neighbours. People were usually aware of what their neighbours were doing, but they didn't invade their privacy. All things like births, deaths and marriages were passed along quickly by word of mouth. Apart from the gossip, people instinctively knew that it was important that all this information was passed along.

All the people lived close to one another and depended on one another. As the Irish seanfhocal (proverb) puts it: "*Ar scáth a chéile a mhaireann na daoine*" ("The people live in the shadow of one another"). That puts their dependency succinctly. In order for this to work you must have great respect for the dignity of the human person, so there had to be a great sensitivity in your dealings with your neighbours. This was especially so in sexual matters. Any mistakes in this regard could be difficult to correct and might sour relations badly. Nobody wanted this to happen so great caution was always exercised.

This could almost be regarded as survival instinct. Here you have all these people in close proximity. The houses are certainly much more scattered than they would be in the average urban area, but their knowledge of and dealings with each other are much, much more. They are almost completely dependent on the fruits of the earth for survival. People share everything: if you run out of potatoes you'll get a creel from your neighbour; if you haven't a stripper – a cow that misses calving for a year, but still continues milking – you'll get a five naggin from your neighbour who has.

There was a supportiveness in the country which sustained the people and a watchfulness which kept you on your toes and helped you to present your best side to the public. It is as if you were saying to yourself: *If Mary is able to put up with it and keep laughing, why can't I?*

Every seventh day is a Sunday and you have to go to mass, under pain of mortal sin as it was then. This means you have to shape up and get out early on Sunday morning, milk the cows if they are still milking, do a host of other little jobs and don your best clothes and head for mass, meeting several of the neighbours on the way. This effort is good for the people. It helps to ward off insanity. They know that they will be missed if they do not turn out to mass. It is suspected that there is something really wrong if you are not seen at weekly mass. Religion looms large in people's lives and Sunday observance is almost the barometer of your health. No one wants to be the odd one out, so you make every effort to get to mass. You'll often hear,

"There must be something wrong with Mary; I didn't see her at mass for the last two Sundays."

Naturally, some people see this as suffocating, but, equally, it could be accepted as genuine concern; This is the reality – they are all in it together, whatever "it" is. Going to mass did people a world of good. There was a good chance that the priest might give a good sermon about faith in God and resignation to your station in life. To be able to look beyond this life to a Being who would restore justice and make up for the imbalance in this world has to be of great importance to a people who are struggling to maintain their sanity in a harsh environment in order to eke a bare existence for themselves. The meitheal (group help) is still in vogue. People rally around each other, visit each other, and talk through their problems.

Of course, people are critical of one another but it is not as bad as is sometimes thought. Nor were they too intrusive. They never visited each other's houses without announcing their approach by whistling or making some noise. You'd never dream of looking into your neighbours' byres or at their stock in case they wouldn't be too well fed and they'd be embarrassed. You'd never visit at dinner time because they mightn't have much on the table. There was a great sensitivity about many things. Oftentimes people blame themselves for their poverty. Well-to-do people are looked up to. It is considered a shame to be poor. There has to be something wrong with you if you are not successful. You'd know a lot about where your neighbours were. They might be asking you to take care of things while they'd be away. People didn't make any great secret about many things. You'd hear about their successes, failures and sicknesses.

There was little to be jealous about. One's means of existence was no secret. It was open and transparent. You knew how many cows your neighbour kept. The acreage alone told you that. It took roughly five acres of green, not so green, cíbby and heathery land to feed a cow. And woe betide you if you over-stocked. If the holding extended up the mountain, which the overwhelming number did, you had a portion of green land down towards the road, as they called it. This quality of greenness faded somewhat as you moved up the mountain, first on the tully (from the Irish "tulach", meaning hillock) where you see the first rusty colour of cíob and later on the barr (top) where you meet the purple heather and ceannabhán (bog cotton). This doesn't happen to the same extent in Sligo, where green mountains are a beautiful sight – a fellow from Mayo told me how he looked in wonder and amazement at them the first time he passed through Glencar.

So a person with thirty acres – above the average – might manage six cows if he was industrious (some of them would be the easy-fed Kerry type), took care of his land, put out topdress, cut the rushes (which are a permanent problem) and kept the sheughs (drains) cleaned.

If your calves lived, which they often didn't mainly due to a disease called the cough, you would sell the bulls and keep a heifer or two as replacements. Of course, not many had six cows.

You got your status and your order of merit in the community according to the way you kept your holding, how early you rose, how early or late you were with the seasonal tasks such as putting in the spuds, cutting the turf and saving the hay. Perhaps this told its own story about the mental quality of the people. Those who were depressed tended to rise late, go to the field late and go to bed late, never managing to get out of the cycle.

Poverty has the effect frequently of creating a situation, especially in the farming community, where people see little point in getting going and making an effort. As a farmer you are continually reliant on the weather and too frequently you fail to save your turf and your hay and you end up struggling to feed yourself, never mind the animals. There are no jobs because there are no minerals or natural resources to create any sort of industrial employment.

Frequently, those who strangled themselves working the land just got enough to eat and nothing more. As my mother used to say, "to have a little bit of a roughness" (a little above the bare wants) relative to some neighbours who often went hungry, was wonderful, but that's about all you got for working yourself into the ground.

Both our family (the Wee John Farrells – McDermott) and the Jack Hughie Dinnys (McMorrow) put in a huge effort. We were out early and late in all kinds of weather, saving huge harvests relative to our neighbours, reclaiming land that Francie McSharry (a neighbour) claimed God failed to do. If you put in for hard work, as they called it, you got plenty of it. When all the other neighbours were all long finished with the hay saving, our two families were belting away at it as if our lives depended solely on it. There was always that extra field which could be "cleaned up": "Wouldn't it do it the world of good? It's no good the way it is... The cows would only trample it into the ground if you let them into eat it," and so on.

We, as children, were "mad" about this. Here we are looking at our neighbours' children running around playing with all the hay saved and us being eaten by midges at the backs of hedges in the evenings and the sun sinking – the very time that the midges are at their worst. The story is told about a yank going back to America and telling his friends there is a little thing in Ireland called the midge and if it was as big as an elephant it would eat the devil and his clutch. Flying pismires were another scourge, especially if you were wearing something white. They were supposed to be a sign of bad weather.

The older folk regarded these plagues as a mere hiccup or occupational hazard in their everyday routine and powered on regardless. There was little chance that they would leave the field, especially if there were signs of rain. They used to say: "What harm are a few bites? You'll soon get over them," and they might hand you a bit of cream. The diehards didn't even feel them. Indeed, a lot of it was psychological and depended on your interest in your work. The farmer who was on a high about getting his hay rucked before the rain would suffer anything. Those less interested, and this almost certainly included his own children, seemed to get bitten much more. So much for psychology.

There was even a hierarchy among all the families. This was often based on the quality of the land and how many cows' place they had and what shape they made to farm it; but it was a help if you had a priest in the family or someone like a teacher or a guard. Certain families took up a certain position in the chapel in St Michaels, Upper Glenfarne. Pat Tady, in the Dubh area, was often spoken of as a man of some standing, so also was Hughie Farrell and Brian McGourty. Further afield were the Brennans on the Moor, the John Mcs (McDermott), the John Marys (Cullen) and the Willie McMorrows. Teachers had some status. You had Master Hunt and Miss Kilkenny who taught in Twanyinshinagh for many years and earned a reputation for themselves.

Human nature being what it is, everyone wanted to be well thought of. Stealing was almost unheard of – you could throw your bicycle on the side of the road and get a lift into town from someone luckier than yourself and it would be there when you came back. In court it seemed to mitigate the offence if the judge was assured you came from a "respectable" family. Some of the local papers seemed only too happy to name you in their pages if you were unlucky enough to be convicted of some minor offence like no light on your bicycle or your donkey having turned-up toenails, which was considered cruel, because they weren't pared. So much for poor peasants who probably hadn't had their own toenails "pared".

Great store was laid on owning land. The family farm was an heirloom to be passed on from generation to generation. After all, God only knows how long it has been in the family. It might be frugal living, but the land was yours, at least. God isn't making any more of it.

Of course, farming could be a lonely life. When you went out to those fields you could well be alone if you had no other members of the family around. You had plenty of time to reflect, as we see from Patrick Kavanagh's life on the stony grey soil of Monaghan. If you hadn't newspapers and the radio you didn't know what was going on in the outside world and this could make you uneasy.

Chapter Four

The cousins of Seán
Mac Diarmada

A S I ALREADY MENTIONED, ALL THE FARMS IN
Blackmountain stretched from the Corr na bhfeannóg
river where there was some semblance of greenery. The milk
cows grazed this, though it was very hard to keep the rushes
off it. John Donald McDermott and his sister Bizzie lived in
the ancestral home up to 1955 when they both died after a long
life of hardship on 25 acres (under the cross ditch, as they used
to say) and a third share outside the cross ditch of 39 acres of
heather, seisc and ceannabhán leading up to the base of Thor
mountain and the place we all knew as Healy's askey – the word
comes from the Irish *eascaí*, meaning wet, sedgy bog – a green
oasis where the source of the Corr na bhfeannóg bubbled up,
creating a green patch which always attracted a few sheep.
(You'd often hear sheepmen saying: "I saw four sheep belonging
to Wee John in Healy's askey.") The reason it was called Healy's
askey was because the Healys owned the farm mérining John
Donald and it was between the two farms that the oasis was.

There was a similar oasis called McGirrill's askey over
the Corranmore side of Thor where "teach" (house) Sheáin
Mhic Dhiarmada is now. Seán would no doubt have been aware
of it growing up in Corranmore. Tommy Cullen who married
Mary Burns, our next-door neighbour, left Blackmountain in
1947, the year of the big snow, and moved into McGirrill's
house just down a couple hundred metres from the *eascaí* and
survived the blizzard with five of a family to tell the tale.

Ruins of Seán MacDiarmada's ancestral home

Seán MacDiarmada's house is just down another few hundred metres from this house. This would be the nearcut between the two *eascaí* from the original home to the place where Seán was born. The last resident in Seán's was John James Pat Donald, son of Pat Donald, a brother of Seán. I often saw John James visiting the Blackmountain John Donald who remained in the ancestral home after returning from America where he had an accident with horses. To begin with he was just dragging one leg after the other. His father, Ould Donald, who had the name of being a good stonemason, used to tell him not to be pretending and to pull himself together. However, it got worse and eventually the two legs just completely crossed over one another about halfway up the thigh, but yet he succeeded in walking with the aid of two sticks. This was a most unusual affliction but John Donald dealt with it without the least grumble. I never heard him grumble and as I have written elsewhere, he went about his daily tasks with a determination which was heroic. The determination of this relative of Seán was a salutary lesson to all the neighbours. You'd hear people saying: "What are we complaining about? Look at John Donald. See how he is carrying on with all his disabilities. We should be thankful to almighty God that we have our health."

John Donald's land

John could even make it to the bog a half mile away. Once mounted on the cart kneeling behind the centre board, he could drive the wildest mare imaginable through seven gates out to the county road and into Manorhamilton to collect his pension on Fridays. This was some feat. When he reached the town he would career up and down the main street, still on the cart because he couldn't get off, with glasses rolling around the cart. The people would keep bringing him half ones. When he made it home again – often giving a lift to people walking

– Nixon Moore, one of the three Moore brothers, helped him down from the cart and unshackled the mare. Bizzie then saw to his needs.

The house and byres were well constructed, the stonework much superior to anywhere else in the Blackmountain. They had the name of been good stonemasons. Much of the stones would have come from Thor mountain and the Barr's quarry where Francis and Felix Mc Manus would quarry the Leitrim stone. (Felix, regrettably, is no longer with us. *Ar dheis Dé go raibh a anam dílis*.) At the bottom of the meadows is a waterfall still known as *poll an easa* to the present day, a pleasant reminder that our native tongue was spoken in the Blackmountain all those years ago. To the right of the fireplace there was a recess in the main wall of the house to accommodate a bed which was traditionally used for old people to keep them near the heat. Outside there were three good-sized outhouses which housed the mare and the livestock and built into the bank was a house for the ducks. Attached to the upper gable was another room for storage – all in all a neat arrangement of buildings. As far as the quality of the land goes in the townland, there are some nice level fields on the farm. They had turf banks inside the cross ditch on the 25 acres but usually cut the turf on a bank beside ours on the top of the shared 39 acres.

And as I have written elsewhere (and I have a letter to prove it), I put out the cow dung in 1953 for John and Bizzie in the brae garden and my father, Wee John, the only ploughman in Blackmountain, coped it for them and they were never dug. The flattened ridges are to be seen to this day. I got one pound for my effort.

Both John and Bizzie died within a couple months of one another, John in October 1955 and Bizzie in January 1956, and they are both buried in Kilmakerrill cemetery to await the Resurrection. They were the last residents in the ancestral home of the Seán Mac Diarmada clan. Incidently, both myself and my sister Annie attended to Bizzie after John died and our father Wee John went up every morning to help. She suffered in her last days. We did what we could for her. The idea of calling a doctor never entered our heads. She would be violently against the idea anyhow. I never heard of John having a doctor either. Cold, flu or *galar* (Irish for sickness caused by overeating) they had to get over themselves. And they did many times during their long lives. I heard John Donald say once of a man who had stuffed himself to the point of sickness: "He was damn lucky to have what gave him a *galar*." The local wisdom was to stuff a cold and starve a *galar*. People did not have doctors in those days. Frequently enough, I suppose, it was because they did not have the money, but also because it was a sign of weakness. You might be considered "delicate" and that had a certain stigma attached to it. You had to avoid being stigmatised at all costs. If you were young it might lessen your chances of getting married.

None of us ever managed to photograph John or Bizzie. Bizzie always refused to have her "likeness" taken, as she described it, and so did the three Moores, so there are no photographs of any of them. What a pity! My sister, Annie, told Bizzie she was going to England one of the last times we attended to her just to give her a little comfort in her last days on this earth and Bizzie said, "You'll not be in England till I'll be in Killmakerrill" – the local cemetery. And so it was that the last human being and cousin of Seán MacDiarmada, second signatory of the Proclamation, and last resident of the ancestral home in the townland of Blackmountain, almost certainly never to be inhabited again, departed this world to await the Resurrection. And I am the proud owner of the ancestral home of Clann Mhic Dhiarmada whose son gave his young life, in his own words, "that Ireland might live".

Frank McCourt's acclaimed novel *Angela's Ashes* wouldn't hold a candle in its description of poverty to what John and Bizzie Donald suffered in the ancestral home of Clann Mhic Dhiarmada – a house badly thatched with rushes, propped up at strategic places, the wind blowing under the door, four cows to be attended to night and day, a terrible struggle to save the hay for them, a similar struggle to cut and save turf, John Donald himself badly crippled and only able to move at a snail's pace, inch by inch, with the outer part of his foot to the front because of the intensity of the crossing of the legs – talk of the continual suffering he must have endured, but never once complained. He had, as he explained, to throw the arse away from him before he could put on his trousers because the legs were crossed. He had great difficulty attending to nature's calls and, frequently, if not always, he had to do it in his trousers. One Friday on his weekly trip to Manorhamilton on the horse and cart he said, "All the doctors in the town couldn't make a certain man shit and I have done it twice in my trousers without any help."

On another such trip he gave a lift on the cart to James Edward Evens. James sat dangling his legs on the back of the cart and the cart was tipping up and John told him to move up. "He wasn't doing so," said John, "but when the water came trickling down the cart he wasn't long moving up."

It's hard to imagine how they lived before they got the pension. There was a huge churn in the middle of the floor and they churned the milk. I often took a brash at the churning. My grandmother, Rose Ann Johnny Farrell, bought the butter from them. This would have earned them a few shillings and they might sell an odd calf now and again. So much for the few opportunities they had to get any money. It was said at one time that John Donald was to marry Mary John Biddy (McDermott) but it never happened and she married Patrick Foley from Corranmore. She lived where Margaret McDermott is living now. Her brother John Biddy married Kate Johnny Farrell (McDermott) but he died with the great flu in 1918 and Kate married Eddie Pat Jimmy. (Another McDermott: there were a lot of McDermotts in the area and not related either. My father had to have "F" after his name to distinguish him from the other Johns.)

John got up each morning and, after a feed of stirabout eaten with buttermilk from the ever-present churn in the middle of the kitchen, he inched his way forward with his two sticks to a mound at the gable of the house beside a big ash tree which has just toppled over as I write. You could hear him calling the dog as he spotted sheep trespassing from Thor mountain and then the whistling and shouting started.

Even though John and Bizzie got some help – from our family mostly, but also from the Eddies, as we called them, and the Kilkennys at the hay gathering – it has to be said they were mostly on their own. I'd hazard the guess that a lot of the neighbours never stood in their house nor did they know that they were related to Seán Mac Diarmada. They were in no position to visit anybody, to engage in any of the social activities in the townland, to go to mass, receive communion except when Fr Smith from Kilty visited them, or attend wakes or funerals. You could say they were almost completely isolated from humanity. They had no radio or clock, but John somehow knew when Friday came around, the day for the pension, when Nixon Moore tackled the mare and cart and put him up kneeling behind the centre board and put the reins in his hands and let him off with the wildest mare imaginable. How he was to get to the county road, as they called it, through seven gates didn't seem to enter into the head of Bizzie or Nixon. He had a loop on the tip of a rod to open the gates, but this entailed backing the mare and cart and the danger of entanglement was always present. The mare ran away once and jumped from the bank at the top of the cutting, but this did not daunt John. If we cubs were around we'd run and open the gate for him and he might have thruppence for us.

Bizzie went barefooted summer and winter and I can still see her in my mind's eye carrying two huge buckets of well water from the well constructed by my Uncle Denis down at the rampart where he harnessed the river Corr na bhfeannóg to generate electricity. Whenever I visited the pair of them, I never heard a word of complaint. They went about their daily tasks with a heroism that would earn them a place in the *Guinness Book of Records*. As was said of the Blasket Islanders: "*Ní bheidh a leithéidí arís ann.*"

I have no doubt that they are in the highest seats in Heaven among the greatest of saints. Their earthly sojourn was of the severest kind, but they accepted it with a resignation that could only be in keeping with the highest aspirations of Thomas à Kempis that I heard John reading from *The Imitation of Christ. In iothlainn Dé go gcastar sinn. Suaimhneas Dé da nanamacha.*

Bizzie's well

It's incredible how this man survived to the age of 86. As a young man he was in America and worked horses. He used to describe how you would have to eat at the end of a long ridge when ploughing because you'd be too hungry if you waited to get back. He came home to a small mountainy farm of 25 acres (some of this was just heather, cíob and bog). He had a share in 39 acres outside the cross ditch which was nothing but heather. My mother, Mary Hughie Dinny, used to suggest that people who came home to these poor holdings must have seen a ghost in America. Some people seemed to get enough of America: Patrick Joseph McMorrow of Tawnylust was another who came home to a small holding.

John Donald kept four cows and a mare. Johnny Cullen always turned up for the mowing. And mind you, he could handle the mare. He managed to save the hay, standing up all the time because if he sat down he would not be able to get up. Wee John and family with the help of Tommy Kilkenny and family gathered the hay for him. This was a big day. Bizzie killed a rooster and there was full and plenty around the place.

He had a cousin – Johnny Donald bhig, as he was called, married to Rose Ellen, further down in Blackmountain – but I never saw him call too often. It was this Johnny Donald's father, Micky Donald, who was reputed to have shouted at Seán: "Go home to Corranmore and roast a *ceaist* of potatoes for yourself" (*ceaist* is Irish for potatoes roasted in fire), when he was talking at St Michael's chapel in Upper Glenfarne around 1908.

Two brothers of Micky Donald had emigrated to America around 1880 and he had lost contact with them until a man called Devanney came home from America and told him about meeting them over there. I saw a letter written in 1893 on behalf of Micky to his brothers telling them about the miserable life he had under the landlord Aljoe as a tenant. Micky obviously did not own his land at that stage – just about two cow's place with little greenery which his son Johnny inherited from him. Johnny died in 1950 and his wife, Rose Ellen, moved into Manorhamilton. He had two meadows which Wee John, my father, usually mowed for him. Alan Stephenson occasionally did the job for him. Alan tried to replicate the success my Uncle Denis had in harnessing the Corr na bhfeannóg river for electricity by attempting it at a stream in Hugh McCorduck's land, but he did not succeed, to the laughter of some people. Micky Donald's brothers went under the name of McDermont in America, possibly because they did not know how to spell their name correctly. One of them was killed by the kick of a horse.

So much for the Blackmountain relatives of Seán Mac Diarmada. Of course John Donald and Bizzie had a brother, Francie, who spent some time in America, a sister, Mary, who married in America and a brother, Thomas, who was in the IRC.

Nobody married into any of the homesteads in the townland from the 1930s on. The last two to marry were my father, Wee John, and Tommy Kilkenny in the early 'thirties. That townland with its back to the early sun had run its course. That it produced a son who gave his life that "Ireland might live" was rarely mentioned. Nor that John and Bizzie were the last residents in the ancestral home who had to eke out a living in the thin dauby soil in the most miserable of circumstances.

It appeared that Seán MacDiarmada's own relatives had succumbed to the power of the foe. They knew that they were not free but at least they now owned their land and they could sell it for the first time in their lives. And they were worn out from the struggle. Peace had to be important to them. As I have said elsewhere, that was why even his own relatives were initially against the 1916 Rebellion and certainly his involvement in it. He was called the Corranmore brat by some.

It was easy for England to control the country once the population was suitably divided between the owners and the dispossessed. And gradually, through emigration and then legislation (the land acts) at the end of the nineteenth century which handed over land to tenant farmers, the threat from the dispossessed decreased and the country became stable but conservative, its population insecure and fearful, desperate to hold on to the small improvements in their lot. This would be the reason that initially the people were so much against the 1916 Rising: why disturb the status quo? We are getting on with our lives; they may not be the best; we know we are not free; at least we now own our land and we can sell it if we want to – all a very reasonable train of thought. Wee John had four Uncles in the IRC –two on his father's side and two on his mother's side. Even Seán MacDiarmada had a cousin in the IRC. And as mentioned, Thomas Donald, brother of John Donald and Bizzie Donald, was in the IRC. Of course, diehard republicans wouldn't join the conquerors' police. This had to be a source of division. Divide and conquer is the motto of the cute invader. Some people were even prepared to apostatise for a quiet life. This is, of course, what happens in all walks of life – you get a split. Brendan Behan (author of *The Quare Fellow* among other works) used to suggest at meetings that the first item on the agenda was "the split".

During my years growing up in Blackmountain, from the late 'thirties on, there was little talk of Seán MacDiarmada. I can't recall my grandfather, Hughie Dinny Phaidí, ever mentioning him. He had enough problems rearing a family of 13, of whom my mother Mary Hughie Dinny (as she was known) was the eldest and married to my father, Wee John Farrell. To begin with, the economic war was in full swing and it was soon followed by the Second World War where everything was rationed. They were hungry times. And John Donald and Bizzie had their own struggle to survive in straitened circumstances, especially with John's disablement. I know that their sister Mary visited occasionally from America. Of course, Seán had sisters in America also.

The Seán MacDiarmada memorial

Unlike the other signatories of the Rebellion proclamation, Seán was an ordinary country fellow from a large and poor family in a barren area at the foot of Thor mountain near the Fermanagh border. He put in a huge effort to self-educate and succeeded to a great extent, despite all the difficulties confronting him. Before making it to Dublin, he had been to

Scotland like his brother and he also worked in Belfast. There was a tradition in that part of Leitrim of going to Scotland as there was in Donegal. Glasgow was the usual destination. I had cousins there on my father's side.

When the seven signatories were executed, Seán and Connolly being the last two, the attitude of the Irish nation towards the Rising changed completely. They now became martyrs. But only those of us who were born and reared in the ancestral townland of the family can appreciate the poverty and suffering still existing in the original household for years after the Rising. And now, only Oweney Kilkenny lives to tell the tale. There are surely valuable lessons to be learned from all this. The glorious death of a relative for a noble cause may not put bread in the mouths of their remaining relatives who have to continue in poverty for the remainder of their lives. And such was the case for John and Bizzie in the Blackmountain.

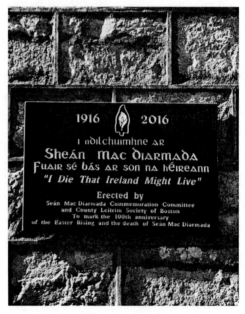

Memorial plaque for Seán MacDiarmada

Chapter Five

Just surviving

THOSE OF US WHO LIVED IN THE EARLIER part of the twentieth century and by the mercy of God are still around, look nostalgically upon our youthful years in the Dubh area of our beloved Leitrim, the poorest county in Ireland. All of us who attended Tawnyinshinagh school together love to look at school photographs of ourselves in our bare feet taken all those years ago. We have happily forgotten the stone bruises on our big toes and heels. If you saw a scholar walking on his/her toes you could be sure that he/she had a stone bruise on the heel and if on the heels you could be equally sure the bruise was on the big toe.

Most of the houses had just three rooms, a kitchen in the middle with a door opening out on the street, as they called it, with perhaps a half-door to keep the pigs and hens from coming in, or even to keep the children from going out and getting lost or being gobbled up by the sow if there was one around. There was the occasional two-roomed house around with perhaps a byre attached to one gable. Often the hens roosted in the byre attached to the house. Inside the kitchen door there was often a horseshoe embedded in the wall to tie the newly-born calf and keep him warm with the heat of the hearth fire. The calf – the fruit of the most precious animal, the cow – was very important. If it was a heifer it may be kept as a replacement and if a bull it might be one of the few means of getting a few bob to buy a few essentials – shoes or clothes principally. Indeed, there were many families who didn't turn over a single penny some years.

Some of the houses were just thrown together and a lot of them had only clay floors which had to harbour germs of some sort. Sanitation and hygiene were generally very poor. While I never heard of any other family getting diphtheria in the neighbourhood, there were many outbreaks of polio. I once brought a "White Father" (African missionary), Father Thomas Kingston – an uncle of my wife – to visit Seán Mac Diarmada's house years after we had the diphtheria and in the course of the visit I brought him to see a woman with a large family. He said he had never seen such poverty even in Africa. That's how it was in those days.

In the nature of things, people had a simple approach to life. They were very happy with simple things. They didn't expect to have anything lavish about their lives. They were told by the priest to be happy with their station in life. Acceptance of the trials and tribulations which life brought them was the order of the day. What made it all bearable was the sameness of the situation for everyone. Getting your fill to eat was what was important. Anything else was a bonus. "People went nowhere," as many used to express it. Into town, Manorhamilton, was as far as some people managed to go during their whole lives – they never made it to Bundoran to give themselves a good wash in the sea. Weddings were usually confined to relatives, unlike now when all and sundry are asked. Wakes and funerals were regarded as obligations based on what happened in the previous generation – if their people had attended wakes and funerals in your house, you felt obliged to go to their occasions.

Survival was the name of the game. They all shared the peat at the head of the farms – Eddie's, Donald's, Moore's, Wee John, Hugh Kilkenny, James Walsh, Paddy Clancy, Tommy Kilkenny, Johnny Donald bhig, Dinny Mcmorrow and Joe Clancy – they all had a turf bank on the head of the land. But what a struggle it was to get the turf saved. There were many years when no turf was saved. If the turf lay on the bank for the winter, the good (as they used to call it) was washed out of them, but they might be got the following year, especially if the good weather came early. They were now called *spadar* (Irish, "sodden turf") that were dried out and as light as feathers, but they'd at least manage to boil a kettle, which in some houses was almost the only used pot on the fire, meaning they rarely ever had a dinner, batch loaf and tea being the main diet. (And, mind you, batch loaf must not be all that bad because many bachelors managed to live to a ripe old age on it.)

The evolutionary process is continuing apace, whether we like it or not. At one time we thought that everything was stationary and we expected things to remain as they were forever. We, as children, thought that somebody would remain at home on the farm to inherit and continue the tradition. We believed that the fire on the hearth had never gone out. It was raked every night by our father or mother before going to bed. You could say that it was a specialised job. It was certainly too important to be left to any of the younger members of the family. It was almost a sacred job to keep the home fire burning. That was what kept continuity in the great chain of eternal society. Heat was life; cold was death; the hearth fire was the centre of all activity. Not only did it boil all the pots and kettles and bake the bread to sustain life, it was faced by everyone and radiated warmth all over the kitchen. Any ramblers or céiliers were told immediately to pull in to the fire. The "raking" consisted of picking out the cinders and shoving the ashes aside, getting six or seven good black turf, putting them lying down in the centre of the hearth and placing the red cinders upon them and covering them all over with plenty of ashes. This would smoulder on well into the next day – you could certainly have a good sleep-in and be sure that it would be lighting. As they used to say, "Sticks are no good for raking, you must have the black turf to have any success."

"There's nothing like your home fire" would be often repeated around the turf fire at night. Another version of this was: "There's nothing to beat your own corner." And how true it was: you mightn't have much, a couple broken chairs, a three-legged creepy stool, a block of ash in the corner maybe, a small form or two, or even a creel turned on its mouth in a pinch when an extra seat was required, but it was yours. The main thing was that there was a good fire in the open hearth and a few spuds around. When you had that, nobody went hungry. And that's what it was all about – not going hungry. It was suspected that there were houses who didn't have that.

Boiling potatoes in the three-legged pot, or baking a cake on the open hearth took some time and effort and some people hadn't the energy or the time for the exercise. It was often said that some people "neglected" or "took no care" of themselves. You were expected to eat anything.

John Donald's house was an exception. It was known as a house for good food. I heard that big Francie often got a mug of tea in Donald's (as they used to say) on his way to the bog barefooted for a creel of turf when the ones he left at home might be hungry. And I can vouch for the good wholesome food myself when gathering the hay with the Tommy Kilkenny's. Bizzie killed the year-old cock for the occasion and we had chicken, soup and barley to beat the band and good floury potatoes. I snigged (as we called pulling the cock with a rope behind the horse) in the hay and Tommy the Butt, as we affectionately called Tommy Kilkenny, built the stack of hay. On this particular occasion we young fellows rushed into the dinner when called by Bizzie and left Tommy up on the stack with no ladder to get down. When he eventually managed to get in, we had all the potatoes eaten and Tommy made Bizzie boil more.

Despite all the apparent hardship, bare feet, rags of clothes and oighered (irritated) legs, people radiated a certain happiness. They loved to bump in to one and other when shopping in Hughie Dinny's or the creamery in Mullaun. They were always anxious to hear the latest bit of news. They managed to smile and greet you laughingly: "How are you? How is all the family? Did Mary come home yet? That's great," and so on when you would give them a bit of good news. Whether sincere or genuine, this exchange worked wonders. As they used to say, "A good laugh is as good as a tonic." And how right they were: doctors recommend it now.

You could always say there was common cause among them. With whatever education was among them, they could see their plight as the hand of God in the human condition. Those who stayed at home felt they had a sacred obligation to be there for all their brothers and sisters who had to take the *bád bán* (emigrant ship) to foreign lands.

In a sense rural life is the real life; anything else seems almost superfluous. What undoubtedly made early man happy was to be able to get food from the earth, be it only berries or whatever. How well you could do this was a measure of your success. Little else mattered, but the supreme being, or whatever it is that is out there, seems to have had much more in mind. There appears to be an onward trust towards something – towards some finality which we are all hoping will be perfect happiness. We may not understand why we are here, from whence we came, or where we are going, or what is expected of us while we are here, but I suggest that many of us strongly suspect that everything will make complete sense in the final analysis. The Christian message is, of course, one of the best, if not the best there is, but even here we have great difficulty in living up to its message, to love one another as Christ loves us.

Anyhow, what is love? Is it a feeling or an intellectual conviction or a mixture of both? Should it mainly be about doing and giving, or is it enough not to do anyone any harm? Everyone thinks he knows and we are continually lectured about it, especially by our priests in their Sunday sermons. But while we are all engaged in this sermonising, there may well be an old person up the road who urgently needs help but nobody goes near him – and such was often the case with John and Bizzie Donald. Of course from a practical point of view, it's not possible to see to everyone's needs. And we excuse ourselves accordingly. We might even ask ourselves, was Christ living in the real world?

There was great familiarity about everything – the hedges, ditches, the black hollow, Feilie's style and the near way down by Hugh Kilkenny's, Tobar, the Blackmountain road, Nan Walshes and a host of other places. You could instantly describe where you met someone to the nearest yard. One absolutely loved to meet someone on the road. It was better than a tonic. People had no opportunities to read newspapers, but they developed a talent for endless conversation and it did them the world of good. They may occasionally have poked fun at one another, but it was all relatively harmless.

Despite all the hardship and the poor quality of life, the affection for the land still existed. Of course, people appreciated that the quantity of land was limited, and it was wonderful to own a strip of the sphere that is circling around on its axis. That was why the price of land continued to rise despite the poor living it gives to any one solely dependent on it. Businesspeople, like builders, who spot the needs of a burgeoning society and make money from supplying those needs, are only too happy to purchase land even though they haven't the slightest notion of farming it. Indeed, they don't bother to set it to anyone who might be foolish enough to want to farm it (and those people are still around).

The great lesson to be learned from all this is that you must have the foresight and confidence to look after yourself – nobody else will do it for you, though you will be hearing plenty about Christian concern for your fellow man. After all, we're only the highest form of creation – just one better than the animals. The animals know but they don't know that they know. Fortunately, or unfortunately, we do, and we have all the advantages and disadvantages which go with it. We are capable of reflection – we can plan ahead (but doesn't the squirrel do that also?) and take precautions about the future. The trouble is that all mankind are vying with each other for scarce resources and some have to lose out.

For millennia the whole emphasis was on food, but not any longer, even though there are millions still starving. Modern invention has made the production of food much easier. Together, a few countries have the means to feed everybody on the planet, but that would upset too many economies. On the one hand, we express this great concern for our fellow man and, on the other hand, we cannot sense out a way to do the obvious – produce the food and give it to them. We are told that the savage loves his native shore even though it may have little to offer him. The extent to which sentiment should rule his life is the great question here. Indeed, this is the great question for all of us. You may have inherited a mountainy farm in the Black Mountain but is it worthwhile trying to live on it?

Chapter Six

Our daily routine

THERE IS SOME SORT OF RESILIENCE IN subsistence farmers. It's hard to put a finger on it, but it's there. When people took to their daily chores every morning, chasing the cows around or dunging the byres as they had to in the winter, they were not thinking of money, though you'd think they would be. The strange thing is that one rarely heard people complaining about lack of money. They seemed to be content if they had enough to feed themselves. Anyhow, it might tell the neighbours that you were lazy and putting in little effort. That would be the ultimate humiliation. Of course, no one wanted to be known for the "poor mouth" – that is, complaining about lack of money and not being able to make ends meet. If these people proved anything it was that you needed very little to survive. Nothing went to waste. Eugene McLoughlin used to boast that his wife could make a dinner out of nothing and Mary Burns claimed that her husband could make chairs out of trees with the most basic of tools.

The routine was that you got up about 8am, lit the fire (it had been raked the night before) and sauntered out to see where the few cows were. If it was hot weather they could be anywhere. One of them could have fallen into a hole or sheugh, might even be thieving in the neighbours' patch or running all over the place with the flies, or taking the shade in some nook or corner, standing in the river battling off the flies with her tail, or whatever. To find them could take an hour or more, even on a relatively small acreage, and you were exhausted when you arrived back at the house – and to make matters worse you still hadn't got anything to eat. If somebody else hadn't risen and set the fire going, you had to do it. This is where the family effort came into to play. A well organised household would make sure that this job was done when the man of the house was out looking for the cows.

You still had to do the milking – take your cans and buckets and three-legged stool and root them out from under the bushes and the flies and try to milk them, getting an odd swish of the tail in the process. It took a couple hours to milk the cows sitting on your hunkers if you couldn't find the three-legged stool. This milking of the cows had to be done by everybody – and in a sense this made it bearable because you knew the other fellow was going through the same drudgery a few fields away from you – you might even exchange a bit of banter across the ditch – but if you didn't get a bit of help from the other members of the family it was tough work, especially since you had to head to Mullán creamery immediately afterwards, wait your turn there, come home, have a bit to eat and go out to the hay or to the bog, as the case might be.

Of course, the family effort was not equal in maintaining the fabric of the average household. If you were willing and able to do the essential chores like milking, the job was left to you. And worse still, the milking was thought to be the natural domain of the woman. She was born into it. After all, wasn't she the nour-isher of the family? Didn't she breast-feed all the family with her own milk and wasn't the cow the natural follow-on? My sister, Annie, was left the job of milking eight cows morning and evening over in the farside, as we called it. This was some task through the wet rushes. She had then to carry the buckets to fill the creamery cans down at the well and make sure that no cow drank any of the buckets. In the earlier years we used to bring the cows home in the evenings and milk them in the byre at home, let them out around the house for the night and drive them to the farside after milking the following morning. This took up a lot of time, but it had the advantage of milking them in the byre, so you were always assured of being dry during the actual milking process. Now you saved time, but at what exposure to the elements in one of the wettest counties in Ireland?

Milking in primitive conditions like this was the order of the day for centuries, but nobody minded because the milk cow was, as they said, next to the human being. Milk was a complete food. You could live on it alone. However, when the suckler cow came on the scene, the people gladly threw the drudgery of the milking aside and accepted the situation. Prior to this a lot of calves died because they did not get enough milk; people wanted to send as much milk as possible to the creamery to get a good creamery cheque. Henceforth, calves rarely died once they made it to the sucking stage, though there could be difficult births, especially if they were too big.

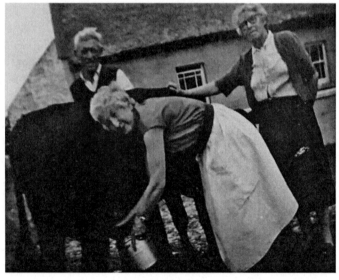

Milking

If you delivered your own milk to the creamery (a time-consuming and exhausting activity in hot weather), which we did, you had to look for the mare which was up in the mountain in a cíoby field, bring her down to the house and tackle her, put her in the van and head to the creamery. In hot weather you were roasted on the van, but it was much better than following an ass with a creamery can and empty creel and a couple stones in it to balance the load. Not many could manage to fill a second can. As Joe Walsh from Clonakilty, County Cork (one-time minister for Agriculture), joked: "Some people brought a second can when one would have done."

Left: butter churn; right: butter spades

Before Mullán creamery came into being, everybody did a churn or two per week and sold whatever butter they could. There were mountain tracks where firkins of butter were carried to the market by foot. Some people never sent milk to the creamery. Even the Hughie Dinnys didn't send milk to the creamery until well into the 'thirties. They had a horse-churning machine (one of the few around) and they were obviously slow to break the routine. (I often heard about the little grey mare who could do the churning herself without anybody driving her, she was so accustomed to it.)

Many's the day I helped to churn myself, especially when the milk went sour and was returned by John Brennan from the creamery. As children we hated it. Pulling the dash up and down was heavy work. We often had to stand up on a stool because we were too small. This gave us more power to handle the dash. John and Bizzie Donald Mc Dermott used to do a big churn every week. I often took a "brash" when I called in to see them. It was considered unlucky not to do so. They might never get the churn finished – it would never turn into butter. Indeed, this sometimes happened if the milk wasn't at the right temperature and they'd have to keep throwing in kettles of boiling water to bring it up to the right heat.

Eventually we got lucky when Uncle Denis decided it was time to mechanise the job and made a contraption for the creamery can which spun inside when it was driven by a small engine. This gave us a welcome respite from the drudgery of the churning. Things changed slowly then.

When you arrived home from the creamery you were exhausted and then you had to follow your father out to the field or up to the bog which meant having to force yourself on. The potatoes, the hay and the turf had to be seen to. These three tasks absorbed the main energies of the subsistence farmer. And for the most part he had only the most primitive implements – the loy, the spade, shovel, graip, scythe. Some people put in a huge effort and others very little. As my mother used to say: "They all got a bit." And of some she used to say: "They'll neither work nor want."

No matter how hard you worked, you didn't see any wage at the end of the week. The best you had to look forward to was a creamery cheque at the end of the month if you were sending milk to the creamery. Some people weren't. It wouldn't be worth their while, they had so little. The cheque only lasted as long as the cows were milking.

The people were worn out by all the physical activity and the walking which was an unavoidable accompaniment of their work. Indeed, things like churning might well be left till night because the daily pressure. As they used to say, "There aren't enough hours in the day to do everything."

People stayed out as long as there was hay to be rucked (cocked), especially if there were signs of rain. To run out of hay during the long winter and early spring, which could be seven months, would be a real calamity. There was a train from Enniskillen to Sligo which was supposed to reach the big bog at eight o'clock in the evening but was usually an hour late. Some people took this as a signal to leave the field and look for the cows for the milking. However, people like my father and Uncle Jack stayed out while there was light. When on the bog we waited for the sun to sink behind John Frank's (McGourty) house on the line. In the month of June this would be close to 11 o'clock.

It was a struggle from when they arose in the morning till they went to bed at night. Their comfort depended on the woman of the house. If she was a good housekeeper, kept the home fire burning (even when the turf was wet), baked the bread in the oven on the open hearth and managed some kind of a dinner, things would be reasonably happy; but if she didn't, things would be pretty miserable. That was the reality in subsistence farming.

There were endless chores to be done each day besides milking the cows, saving the hay, putting in the crop and winning the turf. The hens and ducks had to be let out. You might have to try the ducks to see that they had laid. This meant you had to put your long finger up the rectum to make sure there was no egg there. If there was an egg there you had to keep it in until it laid. The young birds must be watched so that the hawk wouldn't lift them, the turkeys needed special attention, the pigs had to be fed and a whole host of other jobs. All had to be counted, housed at night and the door secured. The fox made the odd siege, just like the hawk. Eternal vigilance was the name of the game.

In many houses it was the mother who kept the household moving and ensured these necessary jobs were done. Without her everything would go awry. She was usually the mainstay of the whole enterprise. The man was usually left to do the heavy work in the fields and liked not to have to bother about these minor tasks, as they often appeared to him.

A lot of farmers could manage to keep a boy (servant boy). My father had one for a while, John McCann, from Glencar. He was a relative on his mother's side. Farrell, the retired IRC Sergeant, had several: Jimmie Gilbride, Stephie Loughlin and a fellow called Ford, to name but a few. It was a status symbol to have a boy. You'd have to have a fair-sized farm to begin with. You'd have to be able to keep six or seven cows at least and you'd need to be regimental and industrious, otherwise, apart from the money, there'd be no point having a boy hanging about the place. Generally, they were treated quite well unlike down south where they frequently slept outside in a barn loft and ate in a separate place and entered by the back door. They were paid £30 to £40 a year, usually at the end of the year, and they took this home with them to help the remainder of the family at home. There was a certain stigma attached to being hired out, as they used to call it. Large families had no other option but to send the eldest children out to hire to earn a few bob to help to feed the others. There was no idle money to be got, you had to work for it. If you were at home you could avoid some work and it could be done by some other members of the family, but this wouldn't happen if you were hired out. You'd hear people talking about the hardship of "working for the stranger", as they often referred to it.

Looking back now, it seems odd that people didn't learn more quickly. Hay, of course, was scarce and it was intended for the cows and not for the sheep. People thought almost anything would do the sheep. They seemed hardy and light in comparison to the cow that was big and awkward and needed a lot of nourishment. Anyhow, the cow was almost sacred like in India; she provided the milk without which no family could survive. Indeed, if you had plenty of milk and potatoes and a good fire you could get along comfortably. But it was amazing how many families couldn't manage this.

During those years at the beginning of the century and up to the sixties, life was largely about putting food on the table. You had to be fairly astute to manage this. To begin with, the weaponry was primitive, the elbow grease necessary to get the gruelling hard work done was massive and if you weren't strong and healthy it was pure torture. I remember seeing old men trying to put in the crop with the loy in tough sinewy ground and it was pitiful. And to make matters worse, the land didn't easily or generously yield up its fruits. You had the weeds, the weather, the pests and the vermin against you.

Because of the primitive tools, it took all of the family to do all of the chores on any farm. Those who had no children to run errands had a tough time of it. Children could do many tasks like going to the bog for an ass load of turf, or to the shop, or bringing in the cows for milking. This left the adults free for the heavier tasks like coping with the loy, mowing with the scythe, or cutting turf with the sleán.

It's no wonder that they used to refer to the "family farm". It certainly was a family effort. It took them all to eke out a living on often marginal-type land. But the sad and inevitable fact was that each member of the family had to emigrate as soon as they reached eighteen and very soon the "old pair", as they became known, were all that were left with no one to look after them in their old age. In many cases, not even the youngest would stay at home and take over the farm.

Many people took pride in their work and kept their holding neat and tidy, which is almost a legal obligation for the basic payments from the EU now. Others made little effort, especially old bachelors who let the roof fall in on them. No matter how successful the family, the place was only suitable for one to remain. There was a time when farms were divided up to enable more than one to remain but this didn't work because the holdings became too small to sustain a family.

People who survived and stayed at home benefited from the death of their neighbours and emigration by extending their holdings. Generally, the eldest son was the inheritor of the farm, though when the others did well abroad he often felt the worse off because he had to continue with the endless chores with little return for all the drudgery.

Living in the North West, one of the wettest areas in the country, was some ordeal. All those wet days sitting in the kitchen or trudging along in drenched fields trying to find the cows to milk them are still ingrained in my memory. Trying to keep those cows alive was the main preoccupation of everybody. I can still hear Maggie Curneen on Balashantra bog shouting after her cows in the mist (and that was what it was mostly, misty) among the turf banks. Years when the hay rotted in the fields brought about a pitiful sight – cows a-lifting in many houses. Terry Rooney from the line said you'd need a helicopter to get to the bog because there was a cow to be lifted in John Joe's (McMorrow) and you'd be called over to give a hand.

Of course the farmer, if they got the basics right, would be much better off than the cottiers, who had only an acre of land, or those who had no land at all, especially in "bad times", as they used to say. Again, this was what made land valuable. The thinking was that you wouldn't starve, at least, if there was some sort of economic collapse, God forbid.

In those houses who made a real effort there was no one idle about the house – not even the young children. Children were kept well out of the way when babies were being born. They were sent out to the hay shed, if they had one, to play. Nothing concentrates the mind like the fear of not being able to keep going – not being able to make ends meet. As they used to say: "When want comes in, love goes out the door." In subsistence farming it is difficult to make hard cash to buy necessities like clothes, shoes and utensils for the house, not to mention paying doctors and other officials or bureaucrats who were often looking for exorbitant sums of money.

We, as a family (the Wee Johns), put in a huge effort. We put in more crop than anybody else, we saved more hay than anybody else and we drained land and made roads through the farm which almost nobody else did. This was some achievement, but at what expense? We were out early and late in all sorts of weathers. We sometimes missed the turf because we were draining land in the spring and were late going to the bog and missed the good weather if it came early. This caused considerable hardship, and the cross-cut (the only one in the area) had to be taken out. Felling alder trees in hail, rain and snow to keep the fire going was the ultimate in drudgery. A tree might have fallen with the wind up at Farrell's mountain byre. This was a legitimate target for the cross-cut. It meant getting the mare harnessed and in the cart and then driving up the most dangerous passage to the mountain byre. It's hard to imagine anything more tortuous than pulling a cross-cut for hours in a cramped position and making slow progress – especially if you are only twelve years old. You had to cut it in suitable lengths and they had to be split with wedges (all expertly made by Uncle Denis in the forge). The trouble was, the alders were full of knots. These were often split on the kitchen floor at night with a sledge. Our house needed much more fuel than the average house because we had to boil big pots of potatoes for pigs (we kept two sows). It has transpired since that, perhaps, there was no need to boil them. The raw potatoes would have done them as much good. Anyhow, as they used to say, potatoes will fatten nothing. They wouldn't make the hens lay either, except when the birds of the air were laying. We had a "crane crook". This meant that you could bake a cake and boil a pot of potatoes at the same time. The average household just kept a small little fire to boil the kettle and bake a cake – that is, they lived "in a small way", as the saying went. It was declared about some people that they could live on the "clippings of tin".

This was the confusing conundrum of rural living in the earlier part of the twentieth century as I experienced it, especially in a county like Leitrim with poor shallow wet soil with the daub near the surface. Francie McSharry described reclamation as "trying to make land where God had failed to do it." If you attempted it, as Wee John did, you got the princely sum of one shilling and six pence in old money per perch. My father bought three extra farms – Moore's, Donald's and Farrell's – and put more hardship on himself and eventually wired them all in. To save up the money to do this was some achievement, because there was no way you would get a loan in those days. He felt he was preparing for the next generation, but this wasn't to be. He signed over his farms to his two sons who departed this world soon after getting married.

People didn't take any holidays. The amount of daily chores made this almost impossible. Some people didn't even make it to Bundoran. But it didn't seem to matter. Anybody willing to work was totally absorbed in their work. The only reward was sitting around a good fire at night (if you had the turf) warming yourself before you went to a cold bed. The only place there was a fire was in the kitchen. A second fire could not be afforded. Open fires consumed a lot of turf.

Tucked away, mostly in sheltering areas because of fear of the wind, all the people in these houses went about their daily chores with what appeared to be an air of stoicism, though I'm sure few of them ever heard of the philosophy. Each family had a history of endurance. They knew their ancestors had seen some hardship and misery. Their effort had to be a family effort. Their children, from the smallest up, were not spared in the struggle. There was something to do for even the youngest in the family. The young birds had to be minded so the hawk wouldn't swoop on then when they were let out to grub around, the turf had to be brought in to keep the fire going, tea had to be carried out to the field where Daddy was working and Hughie Dinny's shop had to be visited for the paraffin oil and tea and sugar. The older children – especially the boys, though girls were not excluded – had to do the nastier tasks like carrying out dung in pardógs for the potato crop. (They might even be asked to cope with the loy.)

However, as in every area of life, something is lost when the family farm disappears. That closely-knit community, that shared responsibility, that dependence on one and another and helpfulness is disappearing too, never to return. But I suppose that's all part of the evolutionary process and we should be happy with it. Wouldn't it be terrible if poor rural communities were fated to remain at subsistence level for the life of the universe while other areas of endeavour forged ahead? Unthinkable! Of course, it could be argued that there are some things from the past that should be preserved forever. Kindness, compassion, helpfulness, cooperativeness, toleration, concern for one and others' well-being and respect for the dignity of the human person are qualities that should always remain with us – and these are more readily available in the rural settling, I think, because of the nature of the enterprise. Let us hope that they will not be entirely forgotten in the brave new world of the microchip and space travel.

The folklore is that people were driven to living in Leitrim during the Ulster Plantation. Certainly, people wouldn't be expected to live on the poor quality land there if they had a choice, so there must have been sort of compulsion or necessity which forced them to cultivate those cíob-covered tulaigh which were so cold that they yielded but little. A piece of heathery land mérining us, known as Burns' heather after the owner, was the scene of 15 men coping with loys in the latter half of the nineteenth century, according to oral tradition.

The simple truth is that historically the production of food is mainly a subsistence-like activity. Initially everybody (every man, woman and child) was involved in it because they had to be. The choice was stark – grow your own food or starve. In ancient Ireland you were paid with cattle. There was no talk of money. Of course, as people began to develop other skills and the production of food became that bit easier, the cuter of them began to move away from the active production of food and the drudgery attached to it, leaving this to the less-well educated; and so it continues to the present day when the EU has decided to give money (the so-called decoupled payments) to farmers and do away with the restrictions which were inconsistent with calling farming and the production of food a business.

Indeed, looking back on all this hardship many of us can see what fools we were to be involved in this nonsense. Those cutter people who lived in a smaller way with less hardship got a bit to eat as well. I think it was in the genes. The Johnny Farrells were hard triers and they didn't spare themselves and despite all the stress and strains some of them lived into a ripe old age.

But, make no mistake about it, in general it was a very happy life; the feeling of fulfilment we got after making thirty rucks of hay and visualizing the cows chewing the cud on a cold snowy night was incomparable to anything else I ever felt at any other period of my life. We might be getting a bare living out of the soil, but it was ours and we loved it and we shared the joys of our little victories with all our neighbours, and we wanted to stay at it forever, but only one member of the family could inherit the holding.

The eldest son was usually the inheritor if he remained at home. In the 'twenties and 'thirties those who had to leave felt aggrieved and a bit envious of the person who was getting the land. It's never easy to leave. The first eighteen years of anyone's life marks you forever; and in those rural areas from which the surplus members had to flee the land, it was never other than painful, though some of them swore they would never be seen back, and for many that's what happened. Indeed, some of them were never heard of again. I often heard it said of someone when chatting around the fire on a cold winter's night: "Nobody knows what happened to him... He never wrote after the father died. Some say that he was killed... God help us... No one knows what is in store for them... Always say three Hail Marys to the Blessed Virgin to protect you, my child," and such like lamentations.

There are a lot of mixed emotions about the land; we see it very poignantly in the writings of Patrick Kavanagh: "The love from my youth you stole... You threw a ditch in my vision... You gave me your clod-conceived," etc. Yet one never forgets all those named fields, hedges and ditches, styles, near cuts, sacred wells, forts and mounds that enthralled your childhood.

Feilie's style, tobar, the black hallow, where all those ghosts were reputed to be seen, gallaí dubh, Biddie's bridge and many others will remain with me forever.

Paddy Clancy, our nextdoor neighbour, and Uncle Jack were coming from a dance in McGivern's hall in Glenfarne when Paddy saw what appeared to be this man in front of them at a place we called the black hollow, near where Ms Kilkenny (NT) used to live. Suddenly, as Paddy described it, he took this huge step in to Hugh Kilkenny's field and disappeared. Jack didn't see him at all. It was suggested that if Paddy put his hand on Jack's shoulder he would have seen him too. The hair stood on Paddy's head and for years afterwards he went up the Black-mountain road to avoid having to pass the black hallow. There were many haunted houses also. Strangely, there is no talk of such things now. Why have all these ghosts disappeared? A good question, no doubt!

Chapter Seven

The people's character

IN GENERAL, PEOPLE WERE SHY AND CLUMSY in gait and behaviour. They didn't feel entitled to much. They almost apologised for their presence. Reading Chekhov about peasants in Russia tells me that this was not peculiar to Leitrim and Blackmountain in the early twentieth century. People in Blackmountain felt the townspeople were much superior to them. You'd hear names like Hugh Dolan, Joe Rooney or Armstrong mentioned (all merchants in Manorhamilton) as if they were gods. It would be considered that these were gentlemen who wore nice clothes, lived in nice houses and were able to send their children away to grand boarding schools in faraway places. One didn't hear about any of these people having to emigrate. There was no point in their comparing themselves to these people. Sometimes their children succeeded in becoming what they called shop boys in their stores: a coveted job in the locality, though it was usually poorly paid.

To all outward appearances the people seemed happy enough – that is, all those who had a bit of land and could make some shape at growing their own produce. Those living in cottages with but an acre of land would be much worse off – that is, until times changed and the odd job cropped up. Then they began to be better off because they had some sort of a job and had a wage, however small. The farmer, in his stupidity, thought it was a climb-down to take a job, like going out to the Council for instance, and he soldiered on to his own detriment and was soon forgotten about when people and successive governments expected him to produce food at uneconomic prices – in reality to do a social service to the nation by providing the one thing, namely food, that nobody could do without, but didn't want to pay for.

It will never be known exactly how the people felt. Those were the days when there was little heard about psychologists, psychoanalysts, psychiatrists or psychotherapists – not that they would be of much help in these circumstances, where hard work was the order of the day. Of course, people had the priest, confession and religion in general which is, arguably, the best of the lot. There are moments of real madness in all our lives. As the saying goes: man is necessarily mad and to be not mad is a form of madness itself. The one thing that madmen lack that sane men have is the ability to be careless, to disregard appearances, to relax and laugh at the world. They can't unbend, as it were, can't do what religion is asking of them – namely, to gamble their whole future on something which seems absurd. As the tailor wisely said in that delightful book *The Tailor and Ansty* by Eric Cross: "The world is only an old blue bag; knock a squeeze out of her while you can." Indeed, it was only because so many of the people in rural Ireland managed to cultivate the mentality of the tailor that they warded off neurosis – which, in effect, is seeing the world as it really is and not being able to do much about it.

Some of the most observant locals had some interesting things to say about the poor land and the struggle to survive in the wet and rain. Mary Ann Kilkenny declared that what ruined the country altogether was the arrival of wellingtons and barbwire. Prior to this people cleaned sheughs, opened drains, made ditches and kept the water flowing, but now they didn't have to do that because the barbwire did the job of blocking animals from thieving and you had your Wellingtons to keep you dry. There was certainly a lot of truth in that statement. No longer did you see people making ditches with the graip and loy. One of the last scenes of ditch-making I saw was Tim Pat Felie (McManus) ditching between himself and Johnny Cullen on the barr. That was probably in the early 1940s.

People in Blackmountain, despite the thousands of years in between, hadn't advanced much further. It was still back-breaking work to eke out a living on the land. But life has to go on wherever you find yourself. It is no mystery as to why the people of Blackmountain found themselves in some of the poorest land in Ireland. They were driven there. Just like in the animal kingdom, the weakest have to accept whatever is given to them. The strongest will always come to the fore.

And so the mystery of life and living will always accompany us. Of course, each individual brings his/her particular outlook to the scene. Nobody knows for sure yet whether we are just pilgrims passing through this valley of tears on our way to eternal bliss, as our Catholic faith tells us. If this is true, nobody has come up with any meaningful explanation as to why we had to be here at all. Could things have been different? After all, if there is an omniscient entity out there somewhere, surely it could have succeeded in giving us eternal happiness from the beginning. Our finite minds cannot fathom the depths of the mystery of our being here at all. And then, accepting the fact that we are, why do some appear to have it so easy and others so difficult?

In the early twentieth century in Blackmountain one couldn't expect them to be philosophising like this about their lives. They knew what they had to do – get out there and hoke the earth to feed themselves. Didn't Patrick Kavanagh do it in the stony grey soil of Monaghan? Didn't his mother tell him that he would be the most independent man in Ireland if he got a bit more land? Of course, not everyone foresaw that new inventions would revolutionise the production of food and without any of the incantations which often accompanied the production of food in peasant societies.

This was the signal for the cuter among the farming community to seize opportunities outside the farm gate and make an easier life for themselves away from the drudgery of hoking the earth for a living. Those left behind weren't able to buy the latest equipment to make life easier for themselves because they hadn't the money. People always wanted to better themselves and began to see education as an important step in their advancement. The opening of St Joseph's in the hospital grounds in Manorhamilton and afterwards the comprehensive school brought about this opportunity. Gradually, anyone with any grey matter at all upped and left. The few that remained couldn't get anyone to marry them so they faced a lonely existence for the remaining years of their lives. Of course, this was the same story all over rural Ireland.

Could it have been otherwise? I hardly think so. My eldest daughter, Miriam, when three years of age, asked the searching question: *Why do children have to grow up?* You could equally ask a similar question here: *Why do rural societies have to move on?* It has to be part of the evolutionary process which we are nearly all agreed upon now. Nothing is static. Even the earth beneath our feet is continually moving though we are not aware of it. There is undoubtedly an onward thrust which it will take billions of years to bring to its apex. And then, hopefully, we will all live happily ever afterwards. But in the meantime we have to accept what is. And that "*is*" embraces the reality that rural communities are no longer going to stay put on poor land in rural Ireland when the rest of the world are forging ahead and acquiring more of the material comforts of the planet.

Strangely enough, a programme on T na G called *Garraí Glas* is visiting people who have gone back to nature, using naturally-growing plants and organic cultivation because they are not happy with modern agriculture. To a growing minority, what some of us call "Progress" is anything but.

However, what I am attempting to do here is show how the people in Blackmountain and surrounding areas managed to cope with the circumstances in which they found themselves and with whatever knowledge they managed to pick up in the national school and from the elders among them. And all that on poor quality soil which only reluctantly yielded forth its fruits to their best efforts. One fact is certain – the priest and St Michael's Chapel played a big part.

Life in Ireland was very confined by the influence of the Catholic church and the authoritarian nature of society in general. Sexual matters were never discussed in the household. Indeed, people were so busy eking out a living (basically feeding themselves) that any talk of where people came from was very far from the minds of parents.

It wasn't easy for the young people to get to know each other. Even though they saw the animals copulating, they found it hard to visualise humans doing something similar. Many youngsters thought it was rectal with humans also! Consequently, there was an innocence abroad about sexual matters. It wasn't mentioned in school either.

Very often marriages were a very practical sort of an affair. Many were matches made when things were running a bit late for people and two were brought together who had known each other all their life, but were never romantically attached until the match was made. And indeed, they nearly always turned out successful; if they weren't in love before marriage, they were very soon afterwards when they had to knuckle down and make the best of things, frequently enough with their own mother and father, usually the husband's if the woman was "marrying in" to the husband's small farm.

Of course, those were the days of strict discipline and a severe moral code so it was unlikely that Johnny and Mary, if they had a crush on one another, got an opportunity to be together alone. Girls usually pretended that they had no interest in sex. They went dancing simply, they said, to hear the music. Boys had to be careful with their neighbours' daughters. They were almost like their sisters and you'd be very loath to do anything unseemly. This was a remarkable society. It's difficult to know how this strict moral code developed. It was certainly due to the acceptance of the authoritarian nature of the Catholic Church and its emphasis on hell and damnation if you infringed the strict moral code, which it preached ceaselessly.

How happy were the people is a question I'll pose at this stage. Very often we tend to picture a rather idyllic setting for country life – peace, quietude and self-sufficiency. All living close to one another and helping each other, the door always open and a big welcome for everybody. As an uncle of mine, Hughie Hughie Dinny (son of the original Hughie) put it: "Things weren't nearly as good as we thought they were." There was a sense in which each family had to put in their own effort to eke out an anyway comfortable existence. There were only certain houses you would ramble in. If you went to some houses you might make them uncomfortable because they mightn't have much. You'd try to avoid visiting at dinner time because they might not have much on the table. Few people had horses and implements to enable them to do their work in reasonable comfort.

It could be said that some people didn't put in much of an effort. This could well be because they were depressed, and who could blame them? Their best efforts couldn't do much to better themselves. If they could manage to grow enough pota- toes they'd at least have something to put on the table but many failed in this task. Some, of course, hadn't good cropland. They used to go down to John Larry's (McDermott) in the big bog and put in a few ridges.

It is difficult to know what sustained people. It must have been their faith in God. Without that they could have never survived. While there was always a helpfulness among the neighbours, there was always a sense in which you were on your own. While people were always in and out to each other's houses, you'd always announce your presence when approach- ing by whistling or coughing or some other such signal, so that they wouldn't be taken by surprise. Others would rattle the gate or latch on the door. Each one had great respect for the other. You never dared to look in a neighbour's byre because the cows might not be too well fed, and this would be embarrassing to the neighbour.

Even when out on local relief schemes you wouldn't look too closely at what your neighbour was eating, so the notion that people were living in each other's pocket was only partially true. Of course, true to form, people kept a sharp look out for one another and there were always the news carriers who kept the people informed about the goings-on in the locality. But in a sense, this was harmless stuff and there was rarely any malice in it. Some people were very sociable, went to fairs and gatherings, met strangers, had a chat, picked up a few items of news and were only too happy to pass it onto the world at large. After all, people didn't read newspapers and not everyone had the radio. You tried not to visit people at dinner time. They knew that they were poor and were sensitive about it. In a sense they were inclined to blame themselves for their poverty. Some people were referred to as no good or useless or good for nothing. Everyone tried to avoid these tags.

People inevitably got to know each other's routine. They might notice the first smoke in the morning. This would tell a tale about your work pattern. The early riser would catch the early worm. Successful people were up and out early in the morning. The time you reached the field was noted, the time you cut the first meadow, when you went to the bog. All these things were noted, and you got your reputation accordingly. Image was important then as now. The nature of the landscape was such that each house had a good view of four or five other houses. When the man or woman of the house rose and saw all the activity in the other houses, it was the signal to rouse their own by declaring that they would be shamed because all the neighbours were up and out for hours. The routine was much the same for everyone. Nobody could escape milking the cows, putting in the crop, cutting the turf and saving the hay and the weather had a huge influence on all these tasks. You were judged by how quickly and efficiently you carried them out. Some people always like to be first. The people have their own little heroics.

Chapter Eight

Telling stories

THE ONLY COMFORT THE PEOPLE HAD WAS to sit around an open hearth fire (if they had the turf) at night, as I already mentioned, and tell stories about fairies and ghosts. Some neighbour was almost sure to call in and add to the excitement. The children loved these visits from the neighbours. Everything was up for discussion. This and that fellow was described as having done an oegus day's work mowing with the scythe or cutting turf or carrying big loads. Some refreshments were passed around and everyone was happy. But the routine of hardship had to start again the next morning. Mind you, not every house favoured this sort of entertainment – they were too busy for it.

In the early part of the twentieth century not many people read newspapers and they hadn't the radio so their mode of communication was speech and oral tradition. Everything was handed down by word of mouth. There was time for storytelling around the open hearth in the winter. There was great interest in ancestry and lineage and co-operation at times of bereavement. Neighbours came in and did the chores like milking and foddering cattle in the winter, bringing turf from the bog, or whatever had to be done. When somebody died they were "waked" for two nights – that is, all the people crowded into the kitchen, chatted endlessly, smoked their clay pipes and drank their whiskies. The Irish wake is talked about the world over. It is a real celebration to send the person on his way. Indeed, the whole way of life is almost Neolithic living, comparable to the way of life on the Blasket islands where hunting rabbits and seals was the order of the day. Not alone were rabbits hunted in Leitrim, but hares also in the winter when they were tracked in the snow.

My father had a gun and as soon as the first snow arrived around Christmas he was out tracking hares all over Thor mountain and the heads of all the farms. Many's the night I listened to himself and John Joe Mc Morrow talking about shooting hares on the top of Maguire's land and on the top of Ned Rooney's land. They would describe the long trail, the unusual jumps off the main tracks and even retracing the steps on the original trail – all a trick on the part of the hare to throw the hunter off the scent before she would lie down. Then suddenly she would jump out behind you when you least expected it and make her escape without the chance of a shot. The dialogue and the drama of the telling was something we as children enjoyed very much.

"Do you remember the hare we shot at Ned Rooney's turf bank?" continued John Joe after gazing into the open fire for a few seconds. "We had followed her the whole way from your mountain meadow where she had evidently come down to graze. She even retraced her steps on several occasions to throw us off the scent. Then before she finally lay she took a couple differs backwards and forwards and before we knew she was out behind us. I saw her first and plugged the two barrels at her, but missed and you came up with the third. I noticed what I thought was a slight stagger, but that's all, as she rounded the bank. Lo and behold, wasn't she strumped when we got around to have a look? That was a mighty shot of yours, you had only a split-second from when you saw her and the blown snow was unbelievable."

"But you were very fast yourself, John Joe. They were the two fastest bangs I ever heard in rapid succession. It would be hard to beat you. Bernie Ned with his ciotóg couldn't match that the best day he ever had and mind you he was fast; nor, indeed, could Harry Carroll who spent many a day with him shooting in Corranmore."

All these dramatically told stories about their days spent shooting enthralled us as children as we listened by the fireside on cold wintry nights. It was an integral part of our lives; we couldn't do without it. If we didn't hear it around our own fire, we went to our neighbours. They were almost like the *scéalta fada gáisce* of times gone by.

Though we were living in Blackmountain, a townland up the Kilty road, we were aware of life in townlands all over the valley of Glenfarne. Word of mouth conveyed the news from all the outlying areas-the postmen were a great help. We would hear of births, deaths and marriages in Ballaghnabehy, Ardvarney, or the Barrs' line just as easily as in our own area. We had our newsmongers like every place else. They loved to be able to claim that they were the first to bring the news. People met each other at mass and got the latest news from their area. The priest read out the recent deaths and had prayers for their souls. When the people arrived home from mass, younger people with better hearing would be quizzed to clarify who was actually prayed for. (Sometimes the priest made little effort to make himself heard.)

People born around the end of the nineteenth century had lived through the 1916 Rebellion, the First World War, the Black and Tan War, the War of Independence, the Civil War, the Economic War for the non-payment of the annuities to Britain, and the Second World War. Though some people managed to do all of this in almost blissful ignorance if it didn't come within their own four walls, it still had the overall effect of creating a lot of uncertainties. Even if you were not directly involved, some of your neighbours could well be and this had some repercussions on you, and some nasty things inevitably happened which caused spleens and unrest – all that on top of the fact that there was not much of a market for any bit of produce you might have to spare after feeding yourself and your family. I often heard it said that there were good prices for cattle during the First World War: Young Cormac (Mc Dermott – he lived in Joe's) got eight pounds for two young calves during the war and this was considered a great price. He was described as fond of the drink. The story is told that he left Manorhamilton by way of Boley Hill and turned back in the new line. He later went to America. A son of his named Patrick came back from America and put up a headstone over his mother's grave in Kilmakerrill cemetery in the 'fifties.

These happenings would be much talked about around the fireside on long, cold, frosty nights in the winter. Some old people could trace kindred with great accuracy and it was very engaging listening to them. This was always done with great feeling and great respect which demonstrated how wonderful the solidarity between all people both past and present was. It wasn't just about relatives but covered all and sundry. Even if they didn't articulate it, it was obvious that they cherished each other and saw each other as important links in the chain of eternal society with a common destiny.

Whatever the troubles of my neighbours in Blackmountain and the Dubh area generally, there was always that resilience among the populace and there was never a dull moment. Everyone seemed interested in whatever news was circulating. Martin McSharry from Ballyboy was the postman and he kept everybody up to date with the latest news – no births, deaths or marriages were missed. Jimmy Walsh of Blackmountain was another great man for bringing the news, as they used to say, and there was a radio in our house and people came in to hear the news. My grandfather, Hughie Dinny Phaidí (my mother's father), came every night to hear the news, carrying his stable lamp. (I can still visualise him quenching it when he came in and relighting it before leaving.) The voice of Lord Haw-Haw, "Germany Calling", still rings in my ears. Those years 1939–1945 were difficult years. I remember the black seams in the bread from moist home-grown wheat. Tea was rationed. The rhyme was: "God bless De Valera and Seán McEntee / For the lousy brown loaf and the half ounce of tea." People didn't like the coffee. Red Indian meal became popular and we preferred it to oatmeal porridge.

I remember being in the bog and talking to John Donald McDermott, first cousin of Seán MacDiarmada's father. He had a turf bank beside ours and despite his disability he could cut turf all day long. He'd get somebody (probably one of the Eddie Pat Jimmies) to wheel them out to dry. His comment was that the bread with the seam in it would put a lodge in an ass. Despite being unable to sit because he would be unable to rise again, he managed to get in on the bank face and prop himself up, move himself along the floor and continue cutting all day long. When the sun was sinking, he had to head for home, inching his way forward, his legs crossed and the outer part of his feet to the front. The journey down to the house through heather and rough terrain, at least a half mile, was some ordeal. He never complained.

John Ambrose McDermott, the author's cousin

Paddy Frank Clancy from Móinín na gcaor, a neighbour of Johnny, Bizzie, Noel and Josie Cullen, often came to visit our house and tell yarns about the Barrs' people. If I happened to be going out to ramble I instantly changed my mind and stayed in to hear him. He was a great spinner of yarns, as they used to say. The Barrs' people had developed a most unusual mode of communication with one another. It was almost a coded language; they spoke mostly in whispers getting close to the ear and it was accompanied by all sorts of gesticulations. They were always poking fun at one another. Life seemed to be total comedy to them and it had to be because they hadn't much of the riches of this world. John Ketty (McDermott), a Barrs' man, was a paragon of this sort of behaviour; it was always followed by a little laugh. So also was John Farrell (also McDermott), a cousin of my father. His brother was married to an aunt of mine, Annie Hughie Dinny (McMorrow). They had spent some time in Scotland after marrying and had to come home when the Second World War started. They now lived in Michael Dermot's on the Line and Ambrose, as we called him, worked for the Leitrim County Council. They had eight of a family and they were very close with our family growing up.

Chapter Nine

Farming the land

WHILE UNCLE DENIS WAS HONING HIS talents and making a few shillings – and that's all it was because the people were poor, living on a couple cows' place with little income – my father, Wee John, was busy working the land.

The Mc Morrow horses: Dennis McMorrow (the yankee) and his brother Jack holding the horse, Frank McDermott in the background

My father reclaimed ten to fifteen acres of rough ground which had a root-matted top sod which was difficult to turn. He was the one and only ploughman in the Dubh area. When he started to use the plough, people were not too impressed with the sod it turned. It wasn't as neat a job as a tasty worker would do with the loy. Such a worker would join his sods impeccably, making the finish look wonderful to the eye. You'd see no grass sticking out. With the plough (especially in wet weather) you often had broken sods which looked very badly. Making ridges with the plough was a two-horse job and few people would have the team to do it. We usually teamed up with Francie Dermott (McDermott) or John Joe (McMorrow) or Uncle Jack (McMorrow) for the coping. The horses had to be well trained and work as a team. Sometimes there would be a lot of pulling and chucking, especially if they were getting it tight against the hill in tough, sinewy soil. Francie Dermott's horse was lazy and wouldn't pull his weight if he could help it.

Of course, much depended on the driver of the team. John Joe and Jack were the best drivers. They knew how to keep an even pull on the reins and make it easy for the ploughman. We usually put in an acre and this was a big day's work. My father always held the plough, either because he was regarded as the expert, or they were cute enough to know to keep well away from it, because it was very strenuous work as you were flung here and flung there when the team failed to pull in unison, which too frequently they did. Also, if the sod was tough and rooty, it had the habit of rolling back which was a complete nuisance. Uncle Denis invented a contraption on the mould-board to slit the sod and make it more pliable so that the sod would stay in place. One memorable occasion was when we had Nixon Moore working with us; he used to keep shouting, "It's coming," as the sod rolled from top to bottom. Michael Gilbride was a great man for belting the sod into position. I usually got the hated job of "walking the sod", as they called it, behind the mouldboard to make doubly sure that it wouldn't roll back.

Very often, this was in cold sleety weather that would skin a goat, but you had to continue once you started and you had several men there ready to help. A few of them would be dropping the seed. This was an important job. If you didn't get the seed dropped before you turned the sod, you couldn't put in two rows of seed up the middle and cover them during the setting. It was possible to cover 15 hundredweight of seed in one day. No matter what the state of the weather, you couldn't take shelter in the sheugh (drain) and leave the two horses standing there, so you powered on and made the best of it. If it was wet, it was a heavy job indeed with a lot of breakages on the sod so it was difficult to set. We usually got help to do the setting (filling up the middle) from the neighbours for whom we did coping. Paddy Frank Clancy always gave us a day setting furrows.

Working outdoors. From Left, Hubert McDermott, Patrick McDermott, Wee John McDermott, Sean McDermott

The setting of course was only the beginning of the hardship. After some weeks you had to remould them, that is dig up the furrows and put fresh soil on the ridges. We had a grubber for that which made it a bit easy. Uncle Denis made the grubber in the forge as he did all the other things. Those who hadn't a grubber had to dig the furrows with the spade or loy. Too frequently the land was shallow, so you met the daub immediately. This remoulding was considered as good as extra manure. Despite all the work, the weeds soon started to come, and the weeding was the lousiest job on the farm. Too frequently wet days were chosen for the job because it was easier to pull the weeds when they were wet and there was less likelihood of pulling off a hunk of sod. Redshanks were the most prevalent but there was good mixture of chicken and docks.

There was no regard for the human being; you were expected to knuckle down and put up with all the hardship. It was all in a good cause. After all, it was subsistence living. If you didn't have a good potato crop you went hungry. Most families ate potatoes a couple times a day. That was the way it was. Unpleasant work was expected of you. That's the way it was with everyone. Why should you be different? You had to keep the stalks green if possible and even the blossoms on them to have any chance of having a good crop. To keep them green and growing and to keep away the blight you had to spray them with a judicious blend of bluestone and washing soda. You could say that they were an expensive crop and after all the work the yield was often poor.

Potatoes and turf were of the utmost importance. There was little point in having the potatoes if you hadn't the turf to boil them. And it took good black turf to boil the three-legged pot with the equivalent of two buckets full in it. The next chore was saving the hay. As they used to say, "Weather that'll save hay won't save turf." And many's the year neither the hay nor the turf was got, the weather was so bad. Then you had the real hardship – hungry cows and hungry humans.

In bad years, the long days footing and re-footing turf on the bog only eventually to "lose" them was so much torment. All that time and effort, backbreaking work and nothing for it. Similarly, with the hay, turning, shaking, re-turning, re-shaking, grass cocking, turning them up on a middlin' day, only to see a shower coming in scairdeán (spout) from the sea at Bundoran to drench it all again and finally see it rot. Does anybody appreciate the torment of all this?

Left: scythe; right: drying turf

 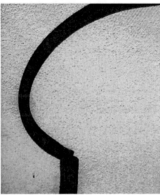

Left: Turf spade; right: reaping hook

This was just subsistence-type farming on poor soul with little depth in it. The experts call it "dauby" soil. After a few inches you meet the daub – an impervious layer of yellow cement-like stuff that nothing would penetrate. You could almost build a house on it without going further down for the foundation. There is little mineral-type soil in Leitrim. Glenboy and Bally-boy have some of it but that is about it. This shallow land won't let down the water, so it lies on top, creating an awful mess, especially if you attempt to drive a tractor over it. You can't use any kind of machinery on it. You can't mow except in very dry weather so you have to use the scythe or wait for better weather which might not come and you could lose your complete harvest. Indeed, in the days of the horse and cart you'd cut up land in wet weather. This is a big handicap. This is what they call marginal land. It shouldn't be used for food production at all. It is very suitable for afforestation. The experts claim it is among the best land in Europe for trees. Hard economic facts are all that they are interested in. And the powers that be would be quite happy to see it all planted. Now that we are all in the single payments regime with much less emphasis on food, it would suit everybody to have it all taken out of food production and covered in trees, except those natives who have a deep attachment to their ancestors' holdings.

Nature does not easily yield forth its fruits and even the best effort of man and modern invention cannot force it to do so. Every man, woman and child were out in the field from early morning till well after dusk struggling to get the work done with primitive weapons, rakes, pitchforks, turf spades (sleáin), crowbars, picks, shovels, loys and twisters for making hay ropes (sugáin) to tie down the cocks of hay. Relatively few had a horse or mowing machine, simply because a horse would eat the grass of two cows and a lot of people had not much more than that amount of grass.

In some ways size was not that much of importance. It all depends on how good you were at producing the food. Even a small farmer with a "two cows" place could produce plenty of potatoes, cabbage, turnips and other vegetables to feed the household, while a big farmer might fail to do so because his efforts might go in a different direction – tending to eight or ten cows and maybe sheep and pigs and not growing vegetables or much potatoes because of that. The big farmer would have more money because he would have livestock to sell but he could fail to get the turf, and this could cause a lot of hardship over the winter and create problems for the woman doing the cooking and keeping the house warm (nobody could afford to buy coal).

Having the animals off the land and housed early for winter meant you had more manure for topdressing and for the crops. The pasture never got anything simply because it wasn't there. Neither was any old pasture reseeded except for the potato patch which was used for corn the following year. A little grass seed was usually shaken on this patch, which in a lot of cases would barely be one eighth of an acre. Consequently, there was little new grass to be seen anywhere. Of course, if you had to put in the crop with the loy it would be some achievement to "cope" (that is, turn the sod on) even one eighth of an acre. You'd have a few blisters and a *tálach* (weakness of the wrist) to boot after swinging the loy all day, especially if there were roots in the soil.

Making a hay stack

It took the best efforts of the scythe men to keep the rushes at bay. The rushes love the rain and flourish where it is wet. The mowing of the meadows each year in July helped to keep the rushes off the hay fields but the pasture was another matter because they were not mowed and the rushes took over. People were loath to cut the pasture when the grass was growing and consequently there were always rushes on the grazing land.

The best and level fields were usually set aside for the hay to make it easy to use machinery. A single-horse mowing machine needed very level ground if there was to be any chance that the average horse would be able to pull it. It wasn't unusual to hear men shouting at the horse trying to force him to pull a machine in gear that he wasn't really able to pull. People could be very cruel to animals and even horses were asked to do more than they were able for on occasion. Of course, it wasn't just animals that were misused; it happened to humans also, and too frequently to children also. This was survival of the fittest for both humans and animals. They were both in it together. One relied on the other for their nourishment and, all too often, the best efforts of man and animal failed to accomplish that. You had to have nature on your side too. Look at what happened when the blight destroyed the potato crop during the famine in the eighteen-forties. People needed big acreage of hay because of the long seven-month winter.

As you move up the hill the land gets poorer; the top portion is called the tulaigh (from *tulach*, Irish for peak). When you leave the tulaigh and go out on the barr you are into poorer land still. Not alone have you cíob – a tough, unpalatable type of grass that animals would only eat in summer and then only reluctantly – but you also have heather, seisc (sedge) and ceann-nbhán (bog cotton). It would be said in a derisory manner of a farm: "What is it but heather and seisc?" Very often the horse was kept here though it was very poor-quality grazing. He was expected to do all this strenuous work but allocated the worst pasture. The best pasture was kept for the animal next to the human, the cow who kept the milk to the family and earned some money when the milk was sent to creamery, almost the only money seen around a lot of houses. The horse is a very bare grazer. Only the sheep gets down closer to the earth. If they get their way they won't leave a bit to the cow who can't eat so low. All animals, just like children, eat the sweet bits and won't touch anything else if they can help it.

The barr signalled the right to the open mountain where you could allow your stock, especially sheep, to "run" along with your neighbours. In the case of sheep each herd owner had his own mark which used to be made with pitch, but is now made by a marking fluid which washes out more easily. We had a "D" on the right hip, John Joe had "M" on the middle of the left side and so on. We also had an ear mark – a punched hole in each ear. This was very useful when the mark faded, as it invariably did with the passing of time. We had a shed on the top of the land which served a dual purpose of holding the turf and the sheep.

The application of lime was claimed to sweeten up this cíob-by-type grass. Cows were grazed on this type of land also, but the milk yield would be very poor – perhaps the full of a sweet can, that would be about it. As my mother used to say, "A heifer would never bull if left on it." But the milk tested very well. You got a bit more per gallon – about fourteen old pence per gallon in the 'forties.

Saving the hay. From left: Dennis McMorrow, Sean Mcdermott, Hubert McDermott, Wee John McDermott

I remember a Mr Doherty who was living in Bundoran was the "Plotman", as he was known locally. My father put in miles of drains and what a hard job it was. He first had to take off the top sod and then another foot at least before he took out what they called a spit (a narrow piece about eight inches deep leaving a ledge on either side upon which a slate was placed). The water ran in this spit and the slate or flag on top kept the clay from falling in when the clay was filled in. He also drained a three-acre field above the mountain byre which is still known as the drains' field to this day.

One of the great puzzles of the modern age is the huge popular-ity of such things as walks for charity, marathons, etc. Country people were killed walking. They had to walk to the bog for an ass load of turf. They had to walk to mass (and in places like Kerry this could be six miles). They had to walk to the well, to the shop, to bring in the cows for milking – in fact, everywhere; and now people are walking to raise money when they could be doing something useful like tidying up the countryside. This is absolutely incomprehensible to the farming community who used to describe themselves as "having their life pulled out of them", walking around to do all the chores to eke out a living. Old people would choose to stay in the field and have something to eat brought out to them rather than have to walk in and to have to walk out again to resume their work. That's why children are so useful for running errands. It saves precious energy for the adults. I suppose it's a sign of the times that the new generation are now only running for the fun of it. And I suppose we should accept the change with joy. Why live in the past with all the drudgery? Isn't it great to leave it all behind us?

In the earlier part of the twentieth century there was a mill in Manorhamilton where the Mart is now and you could take your oats in and have them ground. You got a "seal" (a period of time) when you would go in yourself and do the work. This meant you could have your own porridge and this could be eaten a couple times a day. Even though it is an established health food today, it was considered the food of the poor in the early part of the century. The joke was that a child in a certain family was heard calling his father in to his "stirabout" instead of his "dinner". The suspicion was that few families had a real dinner. Not everyone could manage to keep a pig and have their own bacon so all they could manage was bruise or porridge. John Pat Owen was said to have set the mill on fire once and his plea was that it was the only mill he ever burned.

A new era in the mowing was first heralded in by Ould Willie Evans when he was the first farmer in the Dubh area to buy a horse-mowing machine. Hughie Farrell (McDermott) was a close second and John Farrell (McDermott) was the third to buy one. And now Thomas Dermott was the first to buy a tractor. It was a great boost to one's self esteem to be seen to be the first to introduce new equipment. There is a hierarchical order in the rural life of the community, as there is everywhere else, and to be up there towards the apex gives a great feeling of well-being. So things were moving on. Mechanisation was coming into the Dubh area and the loy and the scythe were being slowly left aside. I remember Thomas was mowing for Paddy in Dinnies (Mc Morrow) in Blackmountain when it suddenly stopped. Uncle Denis was sent for and he soon got it going. This was in the early 'fifties. The arrival of the tractor was destined to transform the working patterns of the locality, though few people could afford to buy one. The big problem was the poor quality of the land. In bad weather you couldn't even bring the tractor in to the field.

It was of course, a gradual process as was the process or electrification. Old habits and routine didn't easily concede ground to new-fangled ideas even if they sped up things and made life easier for the general populace. Some people seemed never to have heard of evolution or the great onward thrust of society. They wanted life to remain the same for ever. They only changed after great hesitancy and much debate. Just like the plough, people didn't like the work the tractor did. It left many manes at the corners and it didn't cut as low as the horse machine. Old traditional workers were often heard to say, "Come over here and see the hoking that this fellow is doing with the tractor," but, eventually, prejudices were broken down and the new methods gradually took over. The job may not have been as neat but it removed the hardship of wielding the Leitrim loy and scythe; and life went on, with the odd diehard sticking to the old ways until he was called to grave.

All these activities were engaged in by everyone. There was no other way.

Chapter Ten

Keeping pigs

F EW PEOPLE KEPT SOWS AND NOT EVERYONE
could manage to keep a pig in a cró ("small house", i.e.
pigsty) to kill for the dinner, as they used to say. The bacon was
strictly for the dinner and rarely ever eaten at breakfast which
is now the common practice. It was generally fried because
it went further that way, as they used to say. If you boiled it
with the cabbage (one of the most popular dinners), large and
hungry families ate too much of it. Ideally, you'd need to kill
two pigs to keep the house for the year and not too many families had the wherewithal to manage that, so they had to make
do with one and go without for half the year. The killing of a
pig was a big occasion in the neighbourhood. Everyone knew
about it, even if only because you needed a meitheal (a working
party) to get the job done quickly and efficiently. Firstly, you
had to catch the pig; this might well be a difficult task, because
too frequently there was no standing room in the cró so every
ingenuity had to be used to lure the pig out and at the same
time you had to make sure that he didn't escape out into the
open. You might decide to send a couple cubs (young boys) into
the cró to urge it out while some adult held a bucket with a
little skim in it and as soon as the pig stuck his head in it two
strong men grabbed him by the two ears and another man by
the tail. A rope with a running knot was quickly put on the
right foot and he was led out to the street where some straw
was laid so that he would not be bruised when he was knocked
over. This was done amid great confusion with everyone
shouting instructions to the other... "Hold tight there... Good

cub... That's it... Keep a tight grip on the lugs... Mind yourself, I'm going to turn him over."

The rope on the foot was the important thing; without that you wouldn't manage at all. People might lose their grip on the lugs and the pig would run wild all over the country with half the country chasing him. This scenario had to be avoided at all costs. The screams of the pig could be heard for miles away. Only certain people "stuck" a pig, as they called it. Jack Hughie Dinny (Mc Morrow), my uncle, was the man in our locality. He had served some sort of apprenticeship under my grandfather (Big John) on my father's side who used to do the job before that. Jack used to dress (castrate) calves, pigs, horses and dogs. Indeed, the first castration he did was on a dog belonging to Biddie's Conn (Mcgovern). The dog used to ramble all over the country and he asked Jack to do a job on him. Himself and his brother Hughie completed the task and there was no stopping him after that. He also did dehorning and setting broken bones. There was no faith in the vet. Umpteen tales were told where Jack succeeded and the vet failed. Paddy John Mary (Cullen) in Glenfarne was another well-known pig sticker.

You always deferred to people who had the reputation of having special knowledge in certain areas. They were treated like gods. They got the whiskey the minute they arrived and choice food was prepared for them. Of course, you had to be very careful when castrating. You could easily lose an animal if it was not done properly. Things called clams made from the boortree were used on the testicle strings to stem the flow of blood. The inside of this tree is soft and this was removed and filled with some antiseptic cream. A small branch about four inches long was split down the middle, then cream put in the middle and the two pieces put on both sides of the string and tied at each end. They were removed after a few weeks. Of course, it's an implement called the squeezers that's used now.

The pig is hung up for a couple days before the great night of the salting arrives. It was always done at night. This made it a great community festive occasion. The day's work would be completed and everyone would be free to lend a hand at the salting, as it was called. The pig would have been well scraped with mad boiling water and spoons and knives on the day of the killing before it was hung up and now it would be cut down the middle with a hand saw (almost certainly borrowed from my handyman uncle Denis McDermott) and the two sides placed on two tables, first for the cutting up and then for the salting. Usually the pig sticker did the cutting because there was some expertise needed there and everyone else rubbed in the salt. You'd be admonished if you didn't do it properly. Quite obviously, they had experience of it not been done properly and the bacon "going bad", as they called it. This would be the ultimate catastrophe – the bacon not cured properly and rotting.

Everything was done amid laughter and the telling of yarns about everything under the sun. The "griscíní" (bits of fresh pork) fried on the pan were delicious and everyone ate them with relish.

All the close neighbours got some of the bones which were taken out of the bacon. The bones wouldn't take the salt; to leave them in would rot the bacon. If you didn't leave much meat on the bones you'd be considered mean. It would be said of the boner: "The louser left nothing on the bones." At any rate, every neighbour loved to get a taste of the bones and they made great soup if nothing else. This would also afford the boys and girls of the neighbourhood an opportunity to get to know one and other.

The sow is frequently brought into the kitchen to farrow. In Rose Ann Hughie's house (my grandmother's house) she is installed in behind the settle bed. It's pulled out from the wall and she is jammed behind it. She becomes almost house-trained and on the odd occasion when she does the unthinkable it's picked up immediately and brought out. We actually had the sow in the parlour for a few years. When we hadn't, my father had to sleep in the barn with her to keep her from lying on the suckers (bonhams). Sows were known to eat their own young. The story is told of the fellow who was left minding the sow when she was due to farrow. He hadn't any experience of the business, but he was told that when he'd see her gathering pieces of straw he could look out because this was a sign that she was about to begin. He soon saw her with the straw in her mouth and got at the ready to collect the piglets as they dropped out. She soon lay down and after stretching herself and giving a few pushes, out drops a piglet. The mother turns round immediately and gobbles it up and out comes another one and the same thing happens. The farmer arrives and asks him how things are progressing. "Jesus," he said, "I must catch that little fellow quick before he goes in again because he is after going in and out twice."

Sows can be cross, as they used to say, and we had a very cross one. You'd have to carry a piece of timber with you so that she'd grab it rather than you. She killed several hens when she met them running out the door of the barn after eating her leavings. She ate all the doors around the place. However, you could always sell a litter of bonhams. We used to try to have a litter for sale for the Eighth of May Fair in Manorhamilton. My mother claimed that they left the best profit if you could sell them at eight weeks. After that you had to start to feed them meal which was expensive. I remember £5 each was considered a good price in the late 'forties and early 'fifties. Only a few people kept sows because they were troublesome and hard to feed and mind. They tore everything down and raised the potato pit. For any comfort you'd want to have a well-fenced field if you let her out at all, otherwise she'd run the whole country. Ours often made her way to John Mc Gourty's brae garden and riddled his potato crop. My granny, John Joe Mc Morrow and ourselves (the Wee Johns) were the only ones to have sows in the Dubh area. Eddie Thompson of Cherry-field (a Protestant and gentleman farmer who always kept a few servant boys) also kept a few and a boar which was very handy when a sow was rambling and you had to bring her to the boar. Since a lot of people liked to keep a pig for the dinner, as they used to say, you had a good chance of selling them at eight weeks, otherwise you'd have to fatten them and this was a risky business because the factories gave you what they liked (as they do to this present day) and you had no option but to take it – the factories were in a monopoly situation and paid what they felt like.

Bringing away the sow (to the boar) was a big task, especially if you had to go a distance as my father had to on a number of occasions. I remember him travelling almost to Sligo town – getting the sow on the cart was a huge job; you needed a meitheal to catch her and lift her up and she might jump out immediately, as she did a few times, if the crate wasn't high enough. Anyhow, this particular morning a group of us managed to get her up about six o'clock and off my father started on the long journey to the boar in the teeming rain with a top coat and a reserve of several special manure bags to aid the coat. He didn't arrive back till midnight and it never stopped raining during the whole journey. The worst feature about it was that it might all be in vain if she didn't hold to the service and even if she did she might only have two pigs, which happened on a few occasions. Imagine all the hardship and frustration, sitting up for several nights and just two bonhams for the effort. It all depended at what stage in the heat she was served. People learned all these things the hard way.

Chapter Eleven

Sheep

SMALL NUMBERS OF SHEEP DIDN'T COME OFF the mountain at all and you'd hear their owners bragging about how good a condition they were in despite the fact that they never came down for a bit of green grass in the spring-time during lambing. They didn't usually lamb until well into April. An early March lamb would be considered a rarity. I recall Thomas Gallagher talking with great enthusiasm about an early lamb he had on the 6th March.

It was difficult to keep sheep on the mountain with the harsh elements up there, especially when the East wind blew. People were continually hunting them up towards the peak. Most people chased them up when they were going up to the bog for an ass load of turf. This worked quite well when people were cutting turf, but when they stopped there was no one to keep the sheep up and they kept coming down and even crossing from one side of the gleann (glen) to the other which never happened in the earlier days of the century. This made the keeping of sheep more difficult. They began taking over the lowland and eating the cow's grass, as they used to call it. This was something sheep were never meant to do. The cíob and the heather was supposed to be good enough for them.

We would see our ewes and lambs grazing among the turf banks and help to settle them in the rough herbage, knowing well that they missed the sweeter grass in the meadows where they were allowed to stay while they were lambing – they were only too ready to head back if they got half a chance. If it weren't for all the people going to the bog with their asses and creels and keeping them chased up, they wouldn't stay up at all. Indeed, we as children felt sorry for the little lambs bleating for their mothers with the reduced supply of milk.

And, worst of all, many of the lambs fell into cracks in the bog and were lost. In the nature of things, these lambs were light when they reached the two Summer Fairs in Manorhamilton in August and September and were sold as stores to buyers like McKeever from County Louth, Tom Ashe from County Meath and further afield. Myself and my brothers, Seán and Hubert, took a keen interest in the sheep and went to all the fairs.

Of course, the market for sheep was also changing. The white-faced ewe was being replaced by a speckled-faced or a brockey, as they used to call her. They were supposed to be easier to feed. They were a cross between a Scotch horney and a Wicklow cheviot. Also you were supposed to produce a better-quality lamb and this meant that the ewe had to get some grass if she was to have the milk to produce a better lamb.

The good thing was that you could always sell a sheep, even if the price was poor, but there were times when you couldn't give away a beast. The sheep men were very knowledgeable about the lie of the land and the landscape in general. They knew the mérin ditches (boundaries) of all the farms, who owned them and all that general information about the locality because sheep knew no boundaries and crossed from one farm to another with impunity until someone set a dog on them. People who didn't have sheep hated them. They even resented them feeding through their footings on the bog banks, claiming they knocked their footings. Sheep were continually hunted and many killed.

While the cow is next to the human being in the minds of all the people, any other animal is well down the order of merit. Still, there was always a market for sheep. You could always get a price for them even though it might not be very good and they did not cost too much. They ate more than their fair share of heather and cíob.

During those years sheep were not fed anything except what they could forage out for themselves. This meant that they were in dire straits in the winter when the fields were laid bare and there was hardly a bite to be found anywhere so they wandered all over the place searching for any bit of greenery; they raided the cabbage garden; they bored holes in the shiege of corn; they descended in to ravines in their search and, all too frequently, with little success. There was at least a mouth full of cíob or heather to be got on Thor mountain even though there wasn't much nourishment in it. But it kept them going.

We decided to teach the sheep to eat hay so we carried loads on our backs up to the shed on the mountain. Soon we had them eating it in the shed. This was considered a great success. All the neighbours, when they were up for turf, used to come to the shed to see the sheep eating the hay. It was thought that sheep wouldn't eat hay. To have them eating it when the blizzards and the heavy snow falls came in the winter gave great peace of mind. (There were big snow falls almost every winter in those years. The winters almost certainly seem to have got milder.)

The mountain has its back to the sun. Consequently, it doesn't get much of the early sun. All the farmers with grazing rights to the mountain had a bit of green land at the base and a turf bank on the barr. Of course, you needed to be active to have sheep. None of the dogs during the greater part of the twentieth century had much of the sense of the present-day sheep dog about them. None of them would keep out and round up. Indeed, they were usually put in the house in order not to scare the sheep away, especially when you were putting them in to dose or dip them. Anyhow, mountain sheep are by nature flighty and take off at the least provocation so that a dog could do more harm than good. The modern-day sheep dog will get in front of them and they will halt and look at him when he squats down behind them and slowly crawls towards them at the command of the handler. If they insist in running, the dog will keep getting out and eventually wear them out and you will be able to house them to do whatever you intend to do with them.

Indeed, sheep were only gathered up infrequently. They rarely got sore feet as lowland sheep did and not too many get fluke either, so there was only one big round-up and that was for the dipping which was compulsory. You were supposed to know by looking at their eye whether they had fluke or not. If the eye was pale with no blood vessels to be seen, it suggested the presence of fluke for which there was a capsule. The peat kept the feet healthy. Still, mortality was high, mainly due to falling into holes and being killed by dogs which were continually set upon them. There were a lot of cracks in the bog also and they got jammed in these, especially the lambs when they were young and inexperienced. You would be scolded if you did not examine a dead sheep to see who owned her as this would save a lot of time in searching.

Sunday was the principal day for the mountain. People regarded them as an extra income but the cow is the main earner so people reluctantly gave much time to the sheep, though very often they brought in good money when sold in August and September, mostly in Manorhamilton, though there were fairs in Lurganboy and Dowra also.

Sheep men met at mass on Sunday and exchanged information about the whereabouts of sheep on the mountain. After a while sheep tended to settle on certain sections of the mountain, e.g. Healy's askey, the binn, the barr's quarry or Mc Girrel's askey. When travelling the mountain you were expected to keep a look out for other people's sheep and then you could tell them where you had seen the sheep when you next met them. This co-operative effort made life easier for everybody and gave solidarity and a sense of confraternity to all the sheep men.

Few people would have more than thirty ewes. All they'd have to sell would be about ten wether lambs in August and September for about £2–£3 each. It would be considered a lob of money to get £20–£30 for sheep in the Autumn. It would be said that they didn't cost much eating, only heather and cíob on commonage.

As children, we were very interested in sheep. We let them out the mountain and spent a lot of time getting them settled outside our own land on Thor. Our parents gave us a few sheep to get us interested and it certainly worked. We spent every Sunday up on Thor as we called it and enjoyed it immensely. We sold them in Manorhamilton on the 12th August and the 12th September. I remember getting 38 shillings each for two ewe lambs and thinking it was a huge amount of money. These few shillings were very important. When Eugene McNulty, who came from the North, bought a farm beside Benny McGourty and began buying sheep, he gave a round £3 a head for wether lambs and we thought we were made up. In our innocence, we thought we could cover the mountain with sheep and become millionaires, but we soon discovered to our cost that the heather and seisc wasn't the best of nourishment and the mortality rate was high. So much for the enthusiasm of youth.

We, the Wee Johns, were the first to avail ourselves of the grant for wiring in the land. This was a Godsend for the sheep men. Prior to this it was impossible to keep sheep from wandering. The ordinary ditch, even with a row of barbwire on top, couldn't keep them within bounds. They thieved everywhere. Now they couldn't move with the three-foot net wire and the row of barb on top. But the sheep men were taught a very serious lesson, not to mention the sheep. Now that they were confined, they soon ran out of grass. As I mentioned elsewhere, Tim Pat Felie's sheep died when he wired in Healy's land. Sheep that were free-range up till now, eating a mouthful of grass here, there and everywhere, had to do with the one patch now and it wasn't sufficient to keep them alive. Farmers soon learned that they had to start feeding meal to them. And the worst feature about this was that they'd die before they'd eat it. So it took a long time to train them to eat it. That's the way it was for mountainy-type sheep like horneys and mixed cheviot types. Free-range grazing seemed their natural habitat.

As I already said, when Eugene McNulty came to Lisnagro-agh in the early 1950s he was giving around £3 for ram lambs. This was considered a better price than you'd get at fairs in Manorhamilton. The trouble was that the farmers hadn't many to sell.

Sheep were a nuisance for John Donald, always stealing down from the mountain and eating the grass he wanted for his cows. It was difficult to get the dog back and he sometimes killed the sheep. I caught him once sucking from the jugular vein in the neck of a sheep in the old bog as we called it. Once a dog got the taste of the blood, there was no stopping him. We were continually after dogs killing sheep. The trouble was that when the owner suspected that his dog was killing, he kept him in and it wasn't till he got free again that the killing started again. So all our nights sitting up were often in vain because the dog was tied. One memorable occasion was when a troop of us, including my good self, my father, Nixon Moore and John Joe McMorrow, set off in the middle of the night down by Tommy Curneen's and Bartley Sweeney's towards the Corranmore road to let out dogs we thought were the killers. I remember the cracking sticks in the planting around a house as we tried to make no noise and the dogs barking inside and Tommy Pat Willie putting his head out a gable window. Nothing came of our effort and anyhow we were at the wrong house as it tran-spired afterwards.

The sheep-dipping those years was compulsory to eradi-cate the scab which was a scourge in the sheep trade. John Joe McMorrow of Loughaphonta Barr had the pond for the dipping and it was a race between the shepherds of the Thor and Dubh mountains as to who would make it to the pond first to get the clean dip. We were all divided up to go to different areas of the mountain to ensure that we covered all areas and got all the sheep down. It used to take place in July and saving the hay might be in full swing so the job was often left to the young fellows like myself. It was an exhausting experience to search all the crevices where all the sheep were hanging out in search of any green leaf of grass which was scarce enough among the heather and cíob. (The older folk wanted to attend to the hay at all costs because the cow, the most important animal on the farm, had to be fed on it over a winter that could be seven months long.) Although the sheep brought in a bit of money in August and September, they begrudged giving any time to them. They were supposed to live on heather, cíob, seisc, ceannbhán and fresh mountain air. And they often did and were as fast and wild as the mountain hares among whom they lived along with the moorhens that could be heard cackling in the mist which often enveloped the mountain. When they saw you coming they took off like lightning and away from you to the top of Thor or some such place where they seemed to think they would be safe. The knack, which you learned after many failures, was to get around them before they saw you, and make sure that when they took off, that it was in the direction that you wanted them to go. Eventually, after much frustration, running and shouting (the dogs were mostly a hindrance because they weren't trained to get out in front), our combined effort succeeded in getting them all together in Balashantra bog and down to John Joe's land to the pond. John Joe would be his usual self, calm and welcoming: "Yise have done a great job and you seem to have all of them with you. Yise must be starved. Go up to the house and get a bit to eat."

Kate Dolan, his wife, as she was known, used to have oven-baked bread and delicious-tasting rhubarb jam which often won a prize at the cattle show in Manorhamilton and we gobbled it down greedily.

The dipping itself was a splashing affair with us all getting wet after throwing the sheep in and we had no protective clothing, so our tingling legs, which some of us still have, may be as a result of those roundups as we called them.

The people of Blackmountain had no regard for their own safety. You tackled into whatever had to be done with a determination which left no room for caution and we still see that in the farming community which suffers more deaths in the workplace than any other occupation. I remember an occasion on Thor mountain when at the hawk's nest, as we called it (where leabaidh is between the two Thors), I found a ewe down on a ledge unable to get up, having jumped down. I traipsed all the way home (about two mile) through heather and humps down to our house to tell my father. The two of us headed up again and he tied a rope around me and I slithered down to the ledge and we somehow managed to get the ewe up before she jumped or fell off the ledge – a most daring and dangerous exercise for a horney ewe that was worth only a few pounds. And to this day I don't know who owned the ewe, because she wasn't ours. It shows how the people respected their animals – they were more anxious about their animals sometimes than about their family. The passing of an old person might be less grieved than the death of a cow. Cows were their livelihood, the death of an old person simply a natural event. I heard of a man who lost his last cow saying that "Neither God, man nor the devil" could take another cow from him. And a lot of people had only one cow.

The author with his sheep at different periods

Chapter Twelve

Setting potatoes

SETTING THE POTATOES WAS THE FIRST BIG job facing my father as he emerged from the winter with all the tedious work of foddering the cattle that were housed indoors. First of all, he had to choose a suitable field. He always chose a field he had reclaimed. It would be about an acre in area. The next problem would be to get the farmyard manure to the field. If it was at the byre at the house it would have to be carted up a big hill to the crop field. The manure had to be spread and lined up. The day of the coping was the exciting day. We had to have a meitheal that day. You had to have a team of horses, a driver and, of course, the ploughman which was always my father. Then, you had to have people to drop the seed and a good strong young fellow to walk the sod which turned out to be myself mostly. It wasn't easy to turn the sod on this rough sinewy soil and too frequently the sods kept rolling back. That's why I had to walk the sod – to keep it down. About 15 hundredweight of seed was sown on the day. This was a considerable amount. The neighbours set no more than a couple hundredweight of seed and this had to be done with the loy, huge heavy work. The only thing worse was mowing with the scythe. Many of the neighbours had only the most rudimentary weaponry. The loy had got shorter and shorter with the years and ended up with a bit of a blade. The cow dung had to be brought out to the field in the *pordóga*. This was slavish work. Because we had a horse and cart we avoided all this. However, Wee John had it rough. He had to cope for

Uncle Jack, John Joe, Francie Dermott and maybe Maurice McPartland and Pat Gilgunn.

The digging of the early potatoes was a time for great rejoicing and people who had a good yield shared some of the early potatoes with the neighbours. Eddie Pat Jimmie (McDermott) was a "great warrant", as they described it, to have the early potatoes. He'd put them in before St Patrick's Day and his wife Kate often brought down a few early potatoes to give us a taste of the early spud. There was, of course, an element of bragging in this whole exercise. The husband who put in the early potatoes was regarded as industrious and thrifty and much talked about and praised. A yield of four or five times the seed put in would be considered a great yield. The only manure available was cow manure and often times that would be in short supply. They sometimes cut rushes and mixed them with cow dung to make it plentiful. It rotted in and blended in with the cow dung. The process even continued after you turned the sod on it. Gradually, people began to get the odd bag of sulphate of ammonia down the North, as it was called, and you could see a freshness on the stalks shortly after you put it on – a little fistful at the base of each stalk. We are talking about organic farming now, but sure, wasn't all farming organic then and were the people any healthier? Doubtful…

Very often the yield was not too good. Frequently you'd go fifteen yards for a good bucket of potatoes when digging out the ridge. The ridge in Leitrim was the way of "setting the potatoes". You just set a line, put the manure along it and turned in a sod on each side and filled up the middle. The filling up the middle was referred to as setting also. One seldom saw any drill, which was the usual way of planting potatoes in the better land in other counties. There wasn't enough depth of soil for them and the land was too wet.

As soon as the potatoes were in, people headed for the bog. Francie Flynn was often up there at the end of February or the beginning of March. The earlier you had the turf out the better. If the good weather came early then they benefited, and you just got your turf saved early. The late cutters didn't get theirs at all if July and August turned out bad. So, the early bird got the worm – you got the turf.

The Economic War was in full swing in the early '30s and Britain wouldn't take our produce. Calves had to be slaughtered. As in the Great Famine, the people once again became reliant on the humble potato. I often saw old people putting potatoes in the hot cinders at night and roasting them. They were delicious with homemade butter and a mug of milk. Rambling around the neighbours was the big pastime, especially in the winter months. This was a time for catching up with the gossip circulating in the locality. We, as children, loved these nights by the fireside. We heard stories about haunted houses, ghosts and fairies, about people getting lost at night in fields because the fairies cast a spell on them and remedies to get the better of the fairies by turning your coat inside out, for example. On May day if you pulled your spancel across your neighbour's fields and said, "All that's here come to me," you'd take all the butter from their churn. Since this was the era of carrying big loads we heard great stories about exceptionally strong men. Oweney Walsh, known as Oweney Power, carried two huge flags from the Barr's quarry down to his house, which we now know as Keoghans. (It is now planted.) There were especially strong men for carrying in the hay in the Autumn to the haggard to be stacked and very often these men were bare footed. It would be said of a man that he did an eogeos day's work

Some people ate potatoes three times a day if they were lucky enough to have them and had nothing else. They eat kilogrammes of them. Of course, they were good food, especially if you had an egg and butter to go with them. Sometimes the potatoes were mashed and milk put on them to make a dish called bruise. Other times they grated the potatoes, squeezed the water out of them and mixed them with flour and made a palatable food called boxty. The Gallaghers from Leitrim make boxty in Templebar in Dublin. Another use for the potato was slim cake. So it is a versatile commodity.

Chapter Thirteen

Making extra money

WHILE THERE WAS STAGNATION IN THE Irish economy up to 1958, the year the Whitaker Report saw the light of day, the people who didn't emigrate had to make do with whatever was available to them. They milked their few cows and sent the milk to Mullán creamery where they got their 12–15 old pence per gallon and if the calves lived, which they didn't always because many died with hooze (the cough), they might get a few pounds for them. And there was the egg money which was helpful also. Apart from this, there were few ways of making money. The really adventurous kept a sow which tore down everything about the house – hoked your potatoes and your neighbours as well.

This was just living from hand to mouth. Generally speaking, you could sell nothing. If you had an orchard, which few people had, and you collected a few bags of apples, you weren't likely to get any shop to buy them from you. If you had a few hens you could sell, a similar situation prevailed. Even if you had extra produce there was little chance of selling it because those who might be in a position to buy had their few friends from whom they bought. The know-alls of today are continually telling the farmers that farming is a business like any other business and should be approached with that mentality, but this is patently not true. How could it be a business with all the restrictions on it like quotas, retention periods during which you cannot trade, and many others? How would a hotelier like to be told that he could only take x amount of people when he has the capacity for many more, or a shopkeeper that he could not sell more than x amount of products?

It was difficult to turn anything into money. The barter system was still in vogue. People exchanged produce. Nobody liked to part with what little money they had. This might be needed in situations of life or death when you had to pay the doctor or bury a loved one. Shoes and clothes had to be bought also – especially shoes, though nearly all children went barefooted from April to November. These were a considerable expense. It was always a problem to get money together before winter to buy several pairs of shoes in large families. There were no tarred roads then. Children had to walk on rough stones on the way to school and they all looked forward to their new shoes. They are proud of themselves with their new shoes. Walking in bare feet was no joke. But it didn't seem to do anyone any harm. They all grew up to be fine healthy young people who faced the world as best they could with nothing but primary education. And it almost invariably meant going to England in the heel of the hunt.

There were fairs in Manorhamilton every month and this is where they brought their animals to sell. There were also fairs in Kiltyclogher, Glenfarne and Blacklion and later in Dowra. The average farmer had little to sell – a calf now and again and a few sheep if he kept any. That was all. Perhaps an old cow once and a while.

There sometimes was a fellow about called the hen man. Cathal Kelly was such a fellow for a while. You'd hear people asking, "Did you see the hen man around?" And you might hear the answer: "He was up in Kate's last week. I heard her talking about having a few nonlayers that she wanted to get rid of; she said that they were only eating on the layers."

A few crumbs would be shaken on the ground and some active young fellow would pick them up. The hens, despite their hunger, soon spotted the lifter and they got more cautious. They were then chased with a sally rod and knocked off their feet which gave a bit of time to pick them up. There would be great telling about the fun chasing the hens for the hen man. Young fellows were in great demand the day the hen man came around.

Even then there were hygiene regulations. You had to have an egg house, as they called it. My granny Rose Ann had one. I often helped my mother to wash the eggs. There could be a big bucket of them. For a while there seemed to be a few bob out of them, but as always in agriculture this fizzled out and it just didn't pay to produce the eggs anymore. We even built a special henhouse with electric light on at night to fool the hens into believing it was still day so that they would lay more eggs. We also installed a hot slab for the sow to keep the bonhams warm. This became another white elephant. You had to be what they called a progressive farmer to be doing these sorts of things. In reality, of course, you were being led astray by agricultural advisers who knew the vagaries of the marketplace and of governments and must surely have suspected a rise in price would not last. (Just recall James Dillon's policy of encouraging the building of glass houses to grow tomatoes. Very soon they were just handy places for drying clothes.)

The home market in Ireland couldn't absorb much produce and bad and all as the price for exports was, especially as we were almost completely dependent on England with its cheap food policy, we couldn't afford not to export it because we had to have some few shillings to buy things like shoes and clothes without which you couldn't move out among your neighbours at all.

There was what we called Relief Works on lanes and bog roads during the winter. The lane into our house got a grant every few years as did the bog road to Balashatra bog and Blackmountain bog. The money from this was often the only few bob some people got for the whole year and proved very useful for the few essentials like tea, sugar and flour.

Michael Ambrose (McDermott) and Francie Boylan were working on Leitrim County Council in the Second World War years and after for many years. They were the road makers under the ganger Frank Gilgunn from Ballyboy. Things were primitive then. Tarred roads were unheard of. Stones were broken in Brennan's quarry on the moor by men sitting on a birtín of hay, no matter how cold the weather, and carted out on the roads by somebody like Joe Dermott of Lisnagroagh who used to cope a couple of ridges of potatoes before he went on "the road" (council) in the morning. He was one of the lucky ones. He had a job and a weekly wage as well as the "bit of the land" when diehard farmers like my father Wee John and uncle Jack Hughie Dinny had to make do with the creamery cheque and the few bob when they sold the ram lambs in August and September in Manorhamilton. Joe's job was attributed to his support of the Fianna Fáil party and his friendship with Frank Gilgunn of Ballyboy. Fianna Fáil supporters got any jobs that were going. The other party, Fine Gael, never seemed to be able to deliver on the job front. It was said you'd die of hunger if you didn't know anyone of influence, and isn't it much to the same today, despite all the talks of meritocracy and the points system of the leaving cert. (certificate) which Noel Dempsey[*] seems hell-bent to get rid of? This points system is a huge stumbling block to the well-off like doctors and dentists, pharmacists and vets who traditionally got to University with a pass on the leaving cert., but now can't get their own children to follow in their footsteps because they can't get the points. If Dempsey were to get his way then all students aspiring to those jobs will have to do a science degree first and then some selection system will be put in place to choose people for those professions. Just imagine how that will be done. You'll see the people with influence right back again.

The poor old farmers were literally fleeced by jobbers and tanglers who gave them what they liked for their animals. Often times they'd meet you out the road, round about dentist Keaney's, if you were coming from the Glenfarne side, and bid you what appeared a good price, knowing you were unlikely to take it because you wanted to try the fair and then buying for far less in the cold of the evening when they spread the rumour

[*] Irish Minister of Education when this chapter was written.

that the market was collapsing. They were up to all sorts of tricks and usually worked together to bring down the price.

The reality has to be faced, farming was never a viable business like shop keeping or being a publican or a blacksmith or owning an eating house, which of necessity the farmer had to visit of a fair day if he wasn't to collapse with the hunger. Since he was the primary producer and didn't know anything about where his produce was going or who the final consumer would be, he was at the mercy of the person who did. That was the reality in the 'thirties and 'forties and the position hasn't changed much since we joined the EU. The factory agents are the new tanglers. You should be able to go to the factory directly yourself but you can't trust them, so you sell in the mart to the agent who will take your stock there. He knows where he stands. He gets his commission irrespective of what price he pays in the mart and if he buys them cheaply he gets that too. Just as I write, the factories are paying 330 cent per kg for lamb, 117p per lb in the old money, but you'd give that for the bones in the butcher's shop. All food makes good money after the farmer parts with it but the consumer doesn't benefit. That's the position and the farmer accepts it lying down. Despite all the talk about the power of the farming organisations, they seem to be unable to improve the farmer's lot.

One has to wonder how it was that the farmers failed to capitalise on the reality that they were the ones who produced the food and should have been able to get a good price for it. And to this day this is still the great wonder despite all the farming organisations and their efforts to improve the quality of life of the farming community. Were it not for the subsidies from the EU many farmers would be making nothing now. Indeed, many farmers are eating into their money from Europe. Of course, it is the policy of all governments the world over to have cheap food for their people. After all, food and shelter are the basic requirements of all human beings. Morally, you are entitled to steal if you are in dire need of food. And that makes complete sense despite the organised nature of modern society where great store is placed on private ownership. That wasn't always so, as we know that early man was free to have anything he could find on the earth. So there is a price to be paid for this evolutionary movement which has brought us to this point in the onward thrust of mankind so convincingly described by Teilhard de Chardin in his book *The Future of Man*. Now the emphasis is on the individual and his right to private property.

It seemed almost an anachronism that people would still be living on poor land in a backward place like Blackmountain in 2016 one hundred years after the 1916 Rising, which promised so much in its Proclamation but which our politicians failed to deliver on. There has now been a summer school on Seán Mac Diarmada in Kiltyclocher for the past seven or eight years. This year* Ruth Dudley Edwards will be one of the speakers. Her take on 1916 will be interesting. Who'd ever imagine that you'd see a summer school in Kilty?

As is the case now, agricultural prices were often depressed – that is, everyone else made a margin of profit except the farmer, the primary producer. However, the people, powerless to help themselves, struggled on from day to day, finding it hard to even feed themselves. Indeed, it wasn't till sons and daughters went to England or America and sent money back that the bills were paid off in Hughie Dinny's shop. Some were never paid.

We often hear about the self-employed boss but in the case of farming one wonders. Most other self-employed people have a regular flow of money but not the farmer who sees months go by without a penny coming in, and to make matters worse his scale of production is small because of his low acreage and the labour-intensive nature of peasant farming. On top of all this is the poor market for his produce if he has anything to spare after he has fed himself and his family. Our being linked to Britain means being caught up in a cheap food policy. Not only have we suffered from our economic war with Britain when we had to slaughter our young calves but even after succeeding in brokering the Anglo-Irish agreement we are still getting poor

* This part of the book was written in 2016.

prices for our exports. And now that we are in the EU, we've discovered that there are too many farmers and a considerable number have to be got rid of. Hardly the stuff of future dreams of prosperity for Irish farmers.

In the nineteen-thirties and forties, you had the Economic War and the Second World War. The economic war with England over the annuities meant that calves had to be slaughtered and there was rationing during the war – little tea and sugar, and the worst of wheat which left a black seam in the bread. There was compulsory tillage, but this didn't affect too many people in Leitrim because the land was so poor. People who went to England during the war had to work in the coalmines which brought many to an early death and they were frequently ill-prepared for the totally different life in England.

Just as I write I learn that there is a mark-up of 214% at the retail stage on milk even in the cheapest stores. This means that the primary producer, the farmer, who works all those long hours in all kinds of weather milking and tending to cows, gets a pittance no matter how efficient and cost-effective he is. And for all the talk of the power of the farmers' unions, they don't seem to be able to do much about it. The cíob and the heather is considered very healthy herbage for the cows. It was believed they wouldn't get TB on it and the milk tested very well, as they called it. This is probably due to the peat which is cold and not the ideal home for many of those disease-carrying paddocks close to the house which harbour all sorts of deleterious germs and viruses like hooze and fluke in cattle and the pip in young birds. As they used to say, there wasn't much "proof" in the cíob but it was ideal for slips of stirks in the summertime, even if they'd be slow to bull on it.

It was a hand-to-mouth existence. Children would be sent to the shop for the messages. It was less embarrassing that way. Who'd send off a poor innocent child without the few necessaries to sustain life, knowing that the family hadn't a bit in the house? This was almost inconceivable and it certainly wouldn't happen to my grandmother Rose Ann who had a heart of gold.

Very often the children would be badly dressed, just a few rags on them, barefooted, running noses, oighear (inflammation) on their legs and stone bruises on their big toes or heels. Hopefully, they wouldn't have all these at the one time, but as my mother used to say, "They had all the signs of hardship on them." There were several other shops around the area also. You had one in Felie Clancys, in ould Willie Evans's, in Nan Walshes, in Robbie Melia's and later in Mickey McMorrows (now John Joe's). They all did their own little trade. As they used to say, a lot of people from Killea went to Mickie James's.

Maggie Boylan from the Line had even a travelling shop. She went around the houses with a basket on her arm and went the whole way over to Paddy Frank Clancy's – some distance to carry stuff on your arm from the Line. So you'll have to admit there were entrepreneurs even then. So even then the saying, "Get a customer, not a job", would have been well understood among the enterprising rural dwellers, even though it was not articulated in that way.

The country shop was the mainstay of the area. Without it people would have died of hunger.

The shopkeepers always did well relative to the rural counterparts living on the land and were able to send away their children to boarding schools like St Pats in Cavan or Summer in Sligo or even further afield.

The people in the towns and villages seemed to be able to get a few bob wherever they get it, but the people in the country had nowhere to turn except they were lucky enough to have emigrant remittances. Without this they would literally die of hunger – so much for the subsistence economy when nature turns against them.

Chapter Fourteen

The Church

AUTHORITARIANISM WAS RIFE IN STATE AND Church, in families and in organisations – in any area you'd like to mention; almost anyone but yourself knew what was best for you. Of course, this made life easy for the governors. If people did what they were told, life went along smoothly for everybody and you had practically no criminality.

But who governed the governors? It was grand when they were right, but what about when they were wrong? In a way the best form of government is to have a benevolent despot ruling. But even he can be wrong from time to time.

The amazing thing about the Christian religion is that everyone is forgiven if they repent so we take sin in our stride knowing that we will be forgiven someday if we have any "luck" at all – or so it appears. However, many people have become disillusioned with religion. They have begun to think that all the fire and brimstone preaching of the past was done to control the people and keep them in tow. It's difficult to get the right balance between the temporal and the spiritual. A lot of people, and especially politicians, don't seem to have much trouble in reconciling the two. Indeed, like Macbeth, some of them appear to be prepared to jump the life to come.

So where does all that leave us? One has always to be optimistic. There is no point in anything else. The final solution to the human predicament will almost certainly be perfect. It's difficult to visualise anything else. We may not make much sense of our everyday shenanigans, but we somehow feel that the final solution, when it comes, will be fair and equitable. And maybe that's what keeps us going.

There must have been something which kept districts like Dubh, Killea, Corranmore, Ballyboy, Ballaghnahbehy, and Barrs going over the centuries. Was it religion, I ask myself? It could well have been. Corranmore and Killea people went to mass in Kilty while the Dubh, Barrs and Ballaghnabehy people went to St Michaels in Upper Glenfarne. There were missions held every few years. Hell and fire were the order of the day in the sermons. The missionaries, mostly Redemptorists and Passionists, put the fear of God into the people. The high point was the sermon on company-keeping. You couldn't date a girl unless you were going to marry her. It was well known that some girls suffered nervous breakdowns after the missions.

St Michael's Church

Eternal salvation was the only thing that mattered: "What doth it profit a man to gain the whole world and suffer the loss of his own soul?" This was to be the guiding principle. We were to be in this world but not of this world. It would appear that this material world was all a mistake. That we might need some material comforts to survive was hardly mentioned. It's difficult to know what the people made of all this preaching. Some of them just made it to the back of the church in St Michael's Chapel in Upper Glenfarne. However, one did hear talk about fulfilling one's religious duties, whatever they were supposed to be. It all appeared to be about following a set of rules, mainly making sure you got to mass on Sundays. Ridiculously, you were told it was a mortal sin to miss mass on Sunday. If you didn't go to confession between Ash Wednesday and Trinity Sunday you committed another mortal sin. And there were reserved sins that only the bishop could forgive. One has to wonder what the average priest thought of all this. One thing is certain, they didn't mix too much with the common people. What we now know as clericalism (using the collar for prestige) was rampant. Their opinions were what counted. You went against them at your peril. Famous priests were Fr John Brady who was around during the Civil War and helped to sort out problems between the government of the day and the irregulars, and Fr Maguire whose reading of the office was said to be effective. I heard of one case where he was reputed to have said after reading his office that he could have cured a person but she might not be fully right mentally afterwards. The people were in awe of the power they thought the priest had. I heard of another case where the priest was alleged to have said to a man that he could have stopped the churning machine from functioning. (The man he was speaking to had a system of churning that was turned by a horse.) The priest's hands were sacred. To strike a priest wasn't just a sacrilege, it was enough to earn you a place in hell. They were God's ministers on earth – anything they did had God's full approval.

How things have changed. At one time it used be said that outside the Catholic Church there was no redemption – that is, you couldn't get to heaven without being a member of the Catholic Church. We felt sorry for Protestants because we thought they were going to hell. You couldn't go into the Protestant church when there was a funeral. Of course, it does appear that Christ did want one shepherd and one flock and He prayed that we be one.

Now we are becoming more secular by the day. The big question as I write is: should we repeal the eighth amendment which doesn't allow abortion, even in cases where there is some foetal abnormality which is thought not to be able to survive outside the womb? The whole climate of opinion about moral issues has changed. Not too long ago, pregnancy outside marriage spelled doom for the unfortunate girl who happened to find herself bearing a child. She could find herself in one of the infamous Magdalene laundries about which we heard so much in the television programmes. The family would be ostracised; her sisters would be shunned at dances and their prospects of finding someone to marry them would be greatly diminished. This was a real problem when I was growing up though fortunately rare enough in our locality. It wasn't easy on young people. There were few secrets in the countryside. The neighbours kept an eye on you as well as your parents.

I often wonder what life would be like in the country were there no sex. There was a great friendliness among the people and a great welcome when you visited their houses. Card-playing was very popular in many houses and feats of strength could be seen at the crossroads among the menfolk. Many widows who didn't remarry finished off their lives happily without any further relationships, which leads me to believe that sex is only a cause of division. And now with contraception and the consequent freedom to have sex at any hour of the day or night without the fear of conception, we have a free-for-all which has to be detrimental to the whole notion of intimacy. Sex outside marriage must leave one or other of the parties anxious and worried about the future of the relationship. It is a well-established principle that girls consent to sex to get love while men may well give love to get sex. Good friendships are far superior to sex any day of the week and many people in our locality had great friendships. (Of course, there were feuds also, but we'll leave that for another day.)

The average family was so caught up with all the chores of subsistence farming and only basic tools to get enough out of the soil to feed themselves that sex was far from the minds of most of them. Indeed, many of those who stayed at home never managed to get a wife and this failure was often contributed to by selfish parents who were happy enough to have them around the house doing the work for them. That they should get married was never mentioned until it was too late.

First Communion. From left: Frankie McDermott, Hubert McDermott, Delia Boylan and Winnie O'Hara

Most of the priests were from Cavan. Local priests were Fathers Hunt, Brennan, Travers, Cullen, Flynn and McManus. Not much was heard about these except when they came home on holidays. The servers at mass usually got a few bob when these priests said mass in St Michaels. Of course, we knew little or nothing about the daily lives of priests then. We wondered, perhaps, what they did after they said mass in the morning. They all had a housekeeper called the priest's girl who was usually very knowledgeable about the affairs of the Church and was very loyal and protected the priest from contrary members of the parish. There was a great mystique around the priest-hood. The great suspicion was that he had exceptional powers: hadn't he to be close to almighty God? Hadn't God called him? Wasn't he the mediator between God and man? He could do no wrong. Not many recalled the story of Judas.

Anyhow, there is a certain innocence about peasants when it comes to religious matters. Although they are no fools, they can be brainwashed when it comes to matters of life and

death and what are called the last things. As Woody Allen is
alleged to have said, it's a good insurance policy to believe in a
hereafter because if there is something out there you'll get the
benefit from it, whereas the nonbeliever may not.

Many authors claim that it suited the clergy to keep the
populace ignorant. It made them more malleable in their
hands. It's nice to have a captive audience who are poor and
unsure of themselves, always anxious to be well thought of, and
accepting of almost anything from authority, be it clerical or
lay. You could say that this type of society lasted up until the
early 'sixties. And then, o then, what a change came about –
the shackles of dependency were quickly cast aside. Henceforth,
people felt free to do almost anything. Maybe it was the arrival
of the contraceptive pill which brought about the sudden
change. If science could enable women to control their fertility
and thereby the avenue to greater intimacy, what other great
possibilities might lie out there? This realisation was intox-
icating. Some just blundered along from now on. Whether
this was a good or a bad thing – well, the jury are still out on
that one. The era of the soaps had arrived. Even old women
could be seen glued to the television watching programmes like
the *Thornbirds* and worse. Is this just a question of evolution
or is there something more sinister about it? Perhaps it's just
that biology is coming into its own. After all, what are we but
biological creatures just like the animals? We are described as
rational and the animals as irrational. But who's to say that
heaven isn't there for them too?

Theologians and other thinkers are slowly coming to the
conclusion that we may be *all* saved. But this has to be reconciled with a just God. How could you visualise a Hitler sitting
up there in heaven beside Pope John Paul II? That wouldn't
appear to be justice. But then again, we have to take into
account God's mercy. So the mystery as to how we can all be
saved is still there.

It used to be said that the priesthood ran in certain families. The Flynns were related to the McManuses of East Barrs
where Francie Felie Éilis had two brothers priests and a son

133

Michael also. On the other hand it is sometimes said that some families are fated (if not worse) to never have a priest in the family. *Pisreoga an ea?* (Is this superstition?)

Anyhow, this was a society almost wholly dependent on oral tradition and deeply ingrained in the psyche was a belief that out there was a force directing their lives. If you led a good Catholic life, received the sacraments, avoided the occasion of sin and didn't steal from your neighbour, you expected that God would look favourably on you and your family. If this didn't always happen, you were consoled by somebody telling you that God's ways are not our ways and if everything didn't go right for you there was a very good reason for it.

The Catholic life is the way of the cross. Didn't Jesus die on the cross? Those who suffer are close to God. We had our own example of Matt Talbot. All the saints saw suffering as a path to intimacy with Jesus. Didn't Padro Pio have to bear the stigmata? Hasn't Sister Bríd (author of *Miracles Do Happen*) to spend several hours of daily adoration before the Blessed Sacrament in obedience to Jesus?

The Catholic religion is a demanding religion. It means renunciation of many of the pleasures of life and the people of Blackmountain and surrounding area were aware of all this and tried to live up to it as best they could. So the rhythm of life and the seasons with all its ups and downs continued on and had to be tolerated by this rural population. Every family did their best with whatever resources they could muster to meet the good and not so good days. And life continued apace.

Chapter Fifteen

Dances & raffles

T HERE WAS A SET OF CHINA IN OUR HOUSE
for years which my father won at a raffle in John
Keoghan's just after he got married in 1933. Some of the lads
at the raffle had eaten a lot of bread before the tea was served.
Francie McSharry, who had eaten a share of it, was alleged to
have said when he was proffered more bread – "No thank you,
I'm more dry than hungry."

Dances and raffles were common then – a bit of both. They
were one of the few opportunities for socialising. The raffle
was the means of earning a few bob and, mind you, those occasions were few and far between.

But to get back to the raffle: it would usually be for a goose or
a turkey; a card game of twenty-five was the game they played.
Sometimes the turkey was gone when the winner went out to
collect his prize. One notable occasion of the missing turkey
was when the Dubh lads cooked their spoil in McGoldricks,
a vacant house between Eddie's and John Joe's. This was the
kind of mischief the lads used to get up to. It was usually a shilling a head to play. People got tea, bread and jam and if there
was a dance all the local girls would come. The music would
be provided by John Joe or Joe Clancy or Michael O'Hara, or
maybe by all three of them.

When people came home on holidays there was usually
a *spraoi* (Irish for fun) in the house – that is, the neighbours
came in and there was dancing in the kitchen to the music of
musicians like John Joe McMorrow, Joe Clancy and Michael
O' Hara. These were enjoyable nights and they went on until

135

the early hours of the morning. In the early years of the twentieth century if these nights occurred in the summer months the men would have to go out to the meadow with the scythe to cut the meadow when they got home from the *spraoi*. The early morning was the preferable time for mowing with the scythe because the sun hadn't risen and it was cooler. Many of the old people were not too happy about the sons going to these *spraíonna* (sprees) because they wouldn't be able to get going the next day. However, in the early part of the twentieth century that was the only outlet they had to meet the opposite sex and, if luck had it, their future wife. There was no talk of partners then. My mother always lamented when she heard that some girl had married into a small holding: "God help the poor lassy facing in to all that hardship for the rest of her life."

Besides these occasions, the opportunities for young people to find a partner were few and far between. When dances and raffles died out, there were no places to go and I knew girls, especially girls, who didn't go to any dances for years. You could say that they were caught in a transition. The country house dances were a thing of the past and the hops, as they called them, hadn't started. Phildie's (Keaney's) were the first to start running hops near the black rock on the way to Glenfarne. They appeared to accept their position without much complaint. Very often a match was made. It was often said, mostly about a girl, that she was easily pleased in the end when she married someone that she wouldn't have looked at when she was younger. Practicality and common sense won out in the end.

At this stage the country house dance and raffle were coming to an end, Phildie's hall had opened and the Ballroom of Romance in Glenfarne was in full swing. Matchmaking was on the wane. Young girls were no longer prepared to settle for old bachelors who had no prospect of giving them a comfortable living. Up to now it could be said that several of the Dubh marriages were matches. Girls who didn't emigrate – or got a taste of it, didn't like it and came home – often married fellows they had known all their life but never dreamed of marrying.

As a local wag used to say: "Anything in a pinch." Or it might be said that a girl was very conceited in her day but easy pleased in the end. Don't fool yourself, everyone wanted to get married. The biological urge was strong in most people. They saw their purpose in life was to leave progeny after them.

Some parents wouldn't allow their daughters out as they called it "gallivanting" along the roads. As in every society, there were always the odd few girls who managed to get that freedom and often brought their families into disrepute. Life was all about respectability. If you came from a "respectable" family you had some standing in society.

The Ballroom of Romance

Chapter Sixteen

Education

TAWNYINSHINAGH NATIONAL SCHOOL, MY old prima mater, a byre for Patrick Mc Gourty now, is still standing, a monument to the people of Dubh and surrounding area and in particular to Master Hunt, Séamus O Boyle and Miss Kilkenny who taught for years there.

The buildings of Tawnyinshinagh National School

My early school years were in the second war years which began in 1939. My companions included Johnny Kilkenny, Josie Cullen, Kevin in Eddie's (Mc Dermott), Bridget in Joes, Rose Mary John Joe (Mc Morrow), Laurence Boylan, John Ambrose (Mc Dermott), my first cousin who had to come back from Scotland where his parents were working during the war years. My uncle Stephen who was just two years older than me was also with me. Joe in Biddie's and his sister Margret were home from America and staying with their grandmother Biddy. They attended school in Tawnyinshinagh also. Down the road further you had the McGourty family: Aggie, Bridy and Benny. And the Lees – Packy, Willie, Rosleen and Tom, of course. Also Bridget and Ellen Kelly and Tony and Pauric Murphy. And after Mullaun national school closed where master McGourty, brother of Peter John Molly, taught for many years, we had Larry Joe and his sister Mary Kate (McDermott) and Rose and Eugene O'Hara from the Barr's line. All these and more were my contemporaries in Twanyinshinagh school and by and large, despite all the hardship, we were mostly a happy lot.

The standard wasn't too high. Too many students were kept at home to work. (Every little help was necessary to eke out a living). Many found it hard to learn to read and write. They envied those who had left and were only waiting to join them and the world of work, even though there was no work except the emigrant ship.

At the end of the nineteenth century, Master Hunt was the Principal teacher in Tawnyinshinagh National School. There are many stories told about him. They were using slates at that time and he is reputed to have often broke one on a fellow's head. There were many imitations of him during his teaching. He seems to have been there for many years; so also was Ms Kilkenny. I also heard talk about a monitor called McGourty, a relative of Brian McGourty. There is a school photograph with my father and his brother Denis in it, taken during the early years of the twentieth century.

Few people continued beyond the age of eleven. The odd person didn't go to school at all. Most people would have read little. Exceptions would be people like Hughie Keaney of Lisnagroagh, a neighbour of Francie Flynn, who was reputed to have never gone to school, but read everything he could get his hands on. He was very good on quizzes and marvellous at question time.

Pupils from the school: the early 1900s (top); 1930 (middle); 1949 (bottom)

Everyone wanted to leave school early. They saw no point in continuing on. You would have to knuckle down and work eventually, so why not get going as quickly as possible? The whole emphasis was on work. It took the whole family to put bread on the table. No one person could possibly attend to the endless chores of subsistence farming with primitive tools for cultivation and harvesting. But very soon economic necessity would force the paterfamilias to let the older members of the family unit emigrate, mostly to England but also to America and further afield. Despite all these handicaps, most people succeeded in learning the "three Rs" very well and could quote many poems from memory and they fared very well in their adoptive countries, sending home money to help the rest of the family to survive more comfortably. There was a saying that poets and politicians die in the workhouse. Some parents even burned the odd book if someone in the family spent too much time reading.

The nearest secondary schools were miles away in Cavan or in Sligo so there was no chance of a secondary education. They hadn't the money anyhow. Eventually, a technical school opened up in Manorhamilton and later in Kiltyclogher and this gave an opportunity to people to learn skills. However, many people just went for a year or so and then emigrated because there was no prospect of a job, even if you had picked up some sort of a skill.

Though the evidence of poverty could be seen in the faces and ragged clothing of the children on their way to school, barefooted and picking their way through the stones, often walking on the grass margin to try and avoid stone bruises, little was done to improve their condition. This, like everything else, was just accepted as the reality of rural living on poor land in backward areas. Anyhow, shouldn't they be happy to have their little bit of land and the independence that went with it? And they now even owned it and could sell it for the first time in their life. I remember a great athlete named Jamsie Rooney who came late one morning to school and when confronted by the Principal, Séamus O Boyle, said, "Please Sir, the stones were sore."

And the Principal replied, "Didn't your neighbour Rose Mary (Mc Morrow) make it in time over the same stones?"

And Jamsie replied: "Please Sir, but she had shoes."

If you got wet on your way to school, you remained all day wet. Pupils brought ass loads of turf to school to keep the one fire going. It was a cold miserable place and to boot the children were afraid of the teacher, in contrast to now when they torment the teacher.

It would be noticed in school that there were children who would have no lunch, and indeed, very little might be done about it. If the teacher asked, it would draw attention to the child. In fact, very often another child proffered a bit of their lunch. Indeed, the most any child would have would be a couple of slices of bread and butter and, if they were lucky, a sauce bottle of milk. If the parents had hens laying, they would be trying to sell as many eggs as possible to have a bit of change about the house, so the children would be unlikely to have egg sandwiches or indeed bacon sandwiches, because the bacon was for the dinner. People had to be economical with the little they could generate on the poor soil. Strangely, many children survived reasonably well on the less than nourishing diet. Eddie Thompson from Cherrybrook collected the eggs from the country shops.

Little effort was made to help past pupils of any National School in the area to further education or any job other than manual labour. Few, if any, made it into the Guards or into preparatory colleges. Other counties prepared students for the civil service – Tipperary was noted for getting a lot of girls in as Clarke typists. Leitrim students seemed to be only destined for the *bád bán*, even after the comprehensive school came into being and they had a leaving cert. Of course, we never had a minister for a department in any government. Consequently, we never had any political clout in any area which might produce jobs. In many ways Leitrim was a neglected county and probably remains so to the present day.

As often happens in poor societies, much of the rearing of children was done in a rough and ready way – and necessarily so – because everybody had to chip in to make sure that everyone had a bit to eat.

Sometimes boys got out of control a bit (we read about this in an Irish book called *Bullaí Mháirtín* by Máiréad Ní Chéilleachair where Máirtín tears around the place) and were inclined to show off their physical strength by engaging in fights at dances, frequently enough about girlfriends. Girls were usually a little more sophisticated than the boys and were not prepared to go out with the rougher types, and this often caused fights. The very nature of the work, struggling to dig the soil and look after the animals in hail, rain and snow, meant that their clothes were often wet and dirty. They had no bathrooms or toilets and couldn't wash themselves properly, so they often presented in a very dishevelled manner, with the sleeves of their tags (jackets) torn up to the elbows and beyond. And in the nature of things they accepted it as their lot to take whatever the worst of nature threw at them.

Some managed to get shod with hobnail boots for the winter if they could earn the price of them with a few bob here and there. When they did, they paraded themselves around the houses showing them off. They kept the uppers in good flexible shape with a piece of bacon heated at the fire and the oil rubbed into them. With a pair of putties usually made from a bag and straddling the butt of the trousers and the top of the hobnails, you had an outfit nearly as good and as waterproof as, and more comfortable than, a pair of Wellington boots. The man in the harpers was usually hired out and that's what enabled him to manage to buy the shoes in the first place. He was probably getting the princely sum of £30 per year as a servant boy, as they called those hired out. But very soon the man with the hobnail boots was gone overseas and probably handed on his shoes to another member of the family who had a chance to play out the same heroics for a few years before he followed in the footsteps of his elder brother. And so this chain of emigration continued for decades.

We have been hearing a lot about the family farm down the years but little government action to ensure there was a family wage. I'm afraid we too often underrate the intelligence of children. Many of those children realised when quite young the futility of farming in this mountainy region and even though they wanted to be loyal to their parents who had to keep up the image of the progressive farmer among the neighbours, they, nevertheless, saw no future in it and had to take the emigrant ship at the first opportunity. And how right they were is borne out daily when we see the difference between what the farmer gets for his produce and what the consumer pays for the pleasure of eating it. But nobody seems to care. People eventually learn that you have to look after yourself and if you don't, or are unable because of some deficiency, you pay the price and are forgotten about by your neighbours, friends and the government.

Cuteness is perhaps the quality that is most important and you neglect it at your peril. This means that you have to seek out the best connections for advancement. You'll get nothing in this country if you do not know someone who has influence to smooth the way for you. The predominant party in this country since the foundation of the state is, as we all know, the Fianna Fáil party. So if you want to make doubly sure of succeeding you have to join that party and that is what the majority of people have done. As the saying goes, "If you can't beat them, join them." They always look after their own irrespective of what your ability is. Qualifications or ability are of secondary importance. It's who you know, not what, that counts. This is not cynicism: it's the reality. You overlook it to your cost. Anyone with any knowledge of the sociological make-up of the country can demonstrate that to you. Just look at the breakdown of the better jobs and who holds them and you'll soon see. All rate collectors, almost to a man, are members of Fianna Fáil; the higher ranks in the Gardaí, pension Officers, school principals in the V.E.C., County Council gangers – you name it, you'll find if there is any importance attached to the job, the Fianna Fáil members have the monopoly. Of course, if you allude to this in conversation you'll be watched and you and your family are likely to be discriminated against if further vacancies are to be filled. This is why a lot of people keep their head down and hope not to be singled out for exclusion for the best jobs around.

Even the clergy are not averse to giving teaching jobs to favourite people in the parish. This made people suspicious about the sincerity of preaching, especially when they heard such readings as "God has no favourites". Then, of course, you were told that human nature was frail and that otherwise good people failed to live up to the ideal – a handy and convenient explanation but hardly convincing. There were just too many people including clergy, politicians, teachers, guards, and many others high up on the hierarchical ladder who were failing to be fair and equitable in their dealings with people. And all this left a bad taste in people's mouths, but there was little they could do about it. Their cuteness ensured that you could not organise them to do anything about the unfairness. They just kept their heads down and waited patiently for the next time when they hoped to have more "luck". That's the kind of society you had then in Ireland and still have; and, as Gene Kerrigan says, it will remain that way.

The chances to have a second-level education were also increasing in the area. Paddy Coyle, a County Councillor and prominent businessman who had a bakery and a button factory in Manorhamilton, played a big part in getting St Joseph's, a secondary school, going at the old hospital site. This was a great success. Olive Gallagher from Kiltyclogher, one of the first students, was called to training as a national teacher and many others to An Garda Síochána and the civil service.

Despite the lack of jobs and despite the emigration, there was still great affection for the land. Few people wanted to close the door and depart; fewer still wanted to sell to a neighbour – that would be the ultimate shame, to be seen by the neighbours not to be able to make a living out of it. And yet as the economy improved and jobs became available, the obvious thing was to get a job, reduce your activities on the land, and have more money and an easier lifestyle. Those who did so, of course, became gradually removed from the mindset of the full-time farmer who became isolated and was left to struggle with poor prices and the rising cost of inputs.

Once upon a time it was the small farmer who supported the clergy. The cottier with his patch of an acre or so had nothing to give the clergy. Now that had all changed. The cottier had a chance of getting a job. It could be on the County Council or with some skilled tradesman. He now had money whereas the small farmer he had left behind him hadn't. There was pride involved also. It was a big let-down for the farmer to have to go out to a job, so he was reluctant to do so. Sometimes the priest had to be sought to plead with, say, the Council to give a job to a farmer who had a large family but couldn't make ends meet. Politics was important here. If you were a member of the Fianna Fáil party you had a better chance of getting a job.

The one memorable thing about all those school years is how innocent we were. It was almost a closed community. We knew little about what was happening in the outside world. Not many houses had a radio and few read newspapers. Most of us would have wanted life to continue as it was. Few of us sensed that we would be the last generation of children from the last generation of parents (1930s) who stayed put to bring us into the world. Though parenthood had been declining since the beginning of the twentieth century in the Dubh area, the tumble now was catastrophic. As I write I can only think of one school going child from above the Kilty cross.

Of course, there is no obligation on us humans to inhabit all the wildernesses on the earth – and above the Kilty cross is certainly a bit of a wilderness, all the way to Kiltyclogher and beyond. We always felt that we were home when we reached Felie's stile and looked over at James Walsh's (McCormack's) and Dinnie's big meadow below the house and even Paddy Frank's Barr. Incidentally, Felie's land mérined (bordered) the school and Felie had a busy time with the scholars who frequently trespassed on his land. Willie Lee used to take a sally rod in his hand each day at the lunch break in the school and chase scholars all over the countryside. When the bell went for the end of the lunch break you could be a half-mile from the school with your tongue out and Willie in hot pursuit. Innocent pastimes. As I write, Kilty is trying to lure new inhabitants with children so that they can keep the school open and they are having some notable successes. So not everybody is afraid of wildernesses. It's not unusual to see mansions in America in a wilderness. Didn't Jesus spend forty days praying in the wilderness?

Chapter Seventeen

Emigration

MANY FELLOWS ON SMALL HOLDINGS KNEW that they couldn't support a wife. And, indeed the girls were reluctant to marry into poverty as it was often called. Even parents who managed to rear families themselves on these same holdings didn't want their children to follow after them. I often heard mothers declare that their son was too good for the hills. Those members of the family who had that little bit more intellectually were the first to leave the nest – they were that bit better at school. They learned to read and write, while many of the others didn't, or did so poorly.

Of course, no one emigrated too happily. Many of us, when young, thought that we could carry on the tradition. We saw our parents reclaim land and we knew that they had a great love for it, despite the hardship. Not everyone was so lucky to have land. It was an heirloom to be passed on within the family. Widows could never hope to inherit when their husbands died. It frequently reverted back to the family.

Despite the emigration, most houses had an inhabitant who remained to take care of the holding, usually the youngest. This meant that the main activities of the year were carried out on all the farms in the mid-'thirties and early 'forties. Of course the Second World War was in full swing and you had to be prepared to go into the mines if you went to England. When the war was over, emigration increased, especially to England. This surge increased year by year and in the depressed 'fifties became a steady stream.

Though there was a history of emigration going back a long time, most of the houses were inhabited in the 1920s – that is, somebody stayed at home to keep the home fire burning for the others to return if needs be. The average size of the holding was somewhere between 15 to 25 acres and four or five cows would eat the grass of the biggest farm. Only the more adventurous would keep sows or sheep. The sows were hard to handle and the sheep would eat the cows' grass that produced the valuable milk without which no household could survive. Those with access to commonage on Thor mountain could manage to keep some sheep. While you might have to bring them down to lamb you could always put them back to the mountain in mid-May.

As opportunities opened up abroad, especially in England after the war, emigration increased. Sonnie in Eddie's (Mc Dermott) emigrated to England and worked in the mines. So did Frank Mc Gourty for a while. Sonnie stayed in the mines. Nobody stayed at home because you made no money. It was heartbreaking to see them leave. These were the people who created a bit of fun around the area. They congregated around Hughie Dinny's shop in the evenings, bought their ten Woodbine and used do cycling gymnastics up and down the road to Biddie's bridge, played pitch and toss and generally discussed their futures. Perhaps someone was home from England and told about the great money they were making on the building sites. We, as children, loved to watch their escapades. Now that they were gone the place seemed empty. And their poor parents who suffered hardship rearing them and were now having a little comfort with their help setting the spuds with the loy (that implement of torture), cutting the turf with the sleán and mowing with the scythe would have to suffer on without them – back to where they were before they brought them into the world. This, inevitably, had to lead to some sort of depression. They had to ask themselves the question: was this their only purpose in life to simply bring children into the world for the foreign market? I'll never forget the departure of

Paddy Clancy, our next-door neighbour, on the sixth of March 1948 to America. The house was down within a year or two.

The trouble was that the farm could only sustain one member of the family (if even that) with the possibility of getting married, having a family and continuing the tradition. All the others had to emigrate, so in a sense the rural areas of Ireland were simply breeding grounds for the emigrant ship. On an interesting programme on T na G called *Bibeanna*, about women going to America from a Gaeltacht area in Kerry, I heard a woman telling about bringing a pig's head with her to America.

The area was just a breeding ground for foreign lands. Despite this, few left easily. The wrench from leaving home was often heart-breaking. It was called the American wake. Much of our literature deals with it. All these emigrants knew what scarce resources were. These people got few letters from home. Of course, some thought they weren't good at writing and if they did write it would give an opportunity to other people to judge them. So when you left you were soon forgotten about. This was in the 'forties and, of course, the war was on for the first half of it. As I mentioned already, most of the houses were occupied, but the best of the population were gone or going. Those who remained had little chance of marrying. All the young girls were gone. The men were destined to remain as bachelors with the houses falling down around them. There was a certain humour about all this. They were asked to weddings and efforts were made to match them up with suitable partners. And where this succeeded the marriages worked out well.

During the 'thirties, 'forties and early 'fifties, people didn't see prospects at home and had to emigrate. While the whole family chucked in and did their bit around the farm, all the responsibility was left to the father; he was the last to leave the hayfield, straightening the haycocks and collecting the weapons. The young people ran to the house looking for something to eat, glad to be free from gathering in the rucks. Parents had a full-time job keeping the children engaged. It was as if they had some premonition that their future lay elsewhere. And they were right. Four out of every five children born in the Republic of Ireland between 1931 and 1941 emigrated in the 1950s. And in the 1980s emigration was rampant again despite the fact that in the seven years after the Whitaker Report, industrial exports rose by one hundred and fifty five per cent. In 1989 alone as many as fifty thousand young had left the Republic of Ireland which had only a population of three and a half million.

But you could misread the statistics too: you could watch unemployment rise above twenty per cent; you could be told that the entire revenue from personal income tax went to pay interest on the national debt; you could look at the emigration figures; but some people lived well in Ireland. Since the end of the eighteenth century a new Catholic class had emerged in Ireland – people had opened shops, educated their children to enter the professions, slowly increased the size of their farms and gained control of the business life of the towns. This class remained extremely conservative and cautious. They were happier to put their money in the bank rather than take any risks. This was, and is in general, the class from which the Catholic clergy come in Ireland.

Many of our neighbours who emigrated got the scenes of life in their adopted countries. It was tough on the building sites in England. I spent a spell working in London in the late 'fifties. I thought that I was well tuned into hard work till I arrived on the building sites in England. I had been working hard, as I thought, setting potatoes, cutting turf and saving hay, and even the odd bit of building and plastering, but this was something else on the building sites. To begin with, I couldn't manage the short shovel. It had my back broken because I had to stoop down and you couldn't use your knee as we did back at home with the long shovel. You were expected to dig solid concrete with it. This also entailed the use of the jackhammer which was a real instrument of torture. The vibration shook the guts out of you. And your worst employers were your own fellow Irishmen who became subcontractors and exploited the fears and uncertainties of their newly-arrived countrymen. It was a pleasure to work for an English ganger in comparison. You'd think that we who were colonised for centuries and knew what landlordism and tyranny was would be more sympathetic to our fellow exiles when we got up a bit in the world. But no, we exploited each other at every given opportunity.

And things haven't changed much as I write this in 2017. It seems that we humans can't help taking advantage of one and other. It is all part of the human condition. Was it G B Shaw who said that we Irish are the fairest nation in the world because we never have a good word to say about one and other? Though we all realise the importance of good relationships and the command to love our neighbour as ourselves, we see everywhere around us the reign of selfishness and self-interest. It isn't until relatively recently that we have become aware of the global nature of our existence. Henceforth, as never before, we must accept that the sphere on which we rotate belongs equally to all of us, even if some of us are destined to accumulate more material wealth along the way. And here it should be observed that this same wealth is often acquired by the exploitation of our fellow men. In fact, it is hard to see how this wealth could have been accumulated in the first instance if the rules of justice had been adhered to. But then we look at the animal kingdom where no fairness prevails either. Are we to be different simply because we are rational and the animals are irrational?

Some people who got a taste of places like America were glad to come to those fields and start again. It used to be said of people who came back from America to a smallholding that they must have seen a ghost in America. It is important to remember that living at subsistence level can be a fulfilling exercise if you have a certain philosophy of life which doesn't place much reliance on material things. Enough is enough. What more does anyone want?

In the latter part of the nineteenth century (from about 1870 on), many Irish men joined the IRC. Memories of the famine would have been fading somewhat and the land acts would have been appeasing the Irish, giving them ownership of their land for the first time. Three men from Blackmountain joined the occupier's police force. They were three McDermotts: Farrell and Cormac McDermott (two brothers) and Thomas McDermott. Several others were in the force, including Michael James Regan and Sergeant Travers in the area. Of course, this is not unusual. It happens in all colonised countries. (If you can't beat them, join them.) Diehard republicans, relatively speaking, are few in number. The average person wants peace at all costs.

These men were envied as they had pensions. Farrell, my grand-uncle, was alleged to be getting sixteen pounds a month in the 'thirties and the saying was that he couldn't possibly be able to spend that amount of money. Of course, the reality was that he was a bit of an alcoholic and went on drinking binges every so often. He had a Model T Ford and people availed of it for lifts here and there. It was known as Farrell's car. Denis, my uncle, was the usual driver. Farrell held the rank of Sergeant. There would be some significance attached to being in the IRC. It might denote some acceptance of the imperial regime. Staunch republicans wouldn't approve of any Irish man being a member of the IRC, though I wasn't aware of any great antagonism against any of them.

Paddy Keown, Willie Evens and Michael in Eddie's (McDermott) were the first to get cars in the Dubh area. This gave them some status. People looked up to people with cars. They were hired by the neighbours to take them here and there – to weddings, christenings and funerals when their loved ones died. The days of driving sheep to the fairs were coming to a close; they were now carried on trailers pulled by cars or Jeeps. From now on you had a good chance of getting a lift from one of the neighbours if you were walking on the road. Eventually, life was getting easier for the people in the Dubh area. But this did not mean that the average person could think of settling down on a small farm, get married and raise a family. This was totally out of the question. Your first priority was to get a job, or failing that emigrate. There was no other option.

Chapter Eighteen

Blackmountain now

IT IS SAD TO SEE THAT OF ALL THE CHILDREN
raised in Blackmountain (close to fifty) in the first half of the
twentieth century, only the three Kilkennys – Johnny, Owney
and Annie – are still alive, Rosleen in Eddies (McDermott),
myself and my sister Annie.

The author's house

From above our house, and especially from the barr, you have
a good view of everything from Owen Keaveny's the whole
way across the Dubh braes to Andy Keown's. All the houses
are down except for Gilbride's where Eugene lives and a couple

in Jimmie Oweney's and James Evans and his wife who came home from Dublin. And his brother Norman next door with his wife and family.

There were at least 18 houses in Blackmountain at the beginning of the twentieth century. Except for Oweney Kilkenny who is living on his own now,* there are just three houses inhabited: Jimmy Walsh's, John Keoghan's, and Eddie Pat Jimmie's (McDermott). And these are all blow-ins, mostly from Dublin. Starting at Eddie's and working down the empty houses are John Donald's (ancestral home of Seán MacDiarmada's family), Moore's, Clancy's, John Farrell's (McDermott), Burns's, Kilkenny's, Keoghan's, Johnny Dermott's (a relative of Seán MacDiarmada's), Pat's Tommy (Kilkenny), Peter Walsh's, James Walsh's, Dinny's (McMorrow), Honor's (McMorrow), Joe Clancys.

Then if you move to the farside of the glen and start at Brennan's quarry on the line you have Owen Keaveny's, Molly Keaveny's, John Frank's (McGourty's), Wee Roger's (Reagan), Healy's, Terry Rooney's, Michael Dermott's (where the Ambroses (McDermott) lived for some years), Boylan's, Hughie Keaneys Flynn's, Joes, Margarets, McSharry's, Gilbride's, Pat Larry's, Oweney James's (McMorrow), Johnny Farrell's (McDermott), McLoughlin's, Even's (still occupied by James Evens), Francie Dermott's, John Joe McMorrow's, McGillin's (last two planted). It had to be a severe wrench to people like John Joe McMorrow to see his land being planted, even though he had no son. He had five daughters but they all emigrated except for two: Rose Mary, who married Denis McGuire and eventually lived in Killcoo in County Fermanagh; and Vera, who didn't marry. Late in life Pat Ferguson reconstructed his house and he had a hay shed built. As many others he must have thought there would be continuity. Other people got rid of the thatch only to see the house closed in quick time.

I suppose it had to come to this.

---

* This chapter of the book was written in 2016.

There is a great sadness about all this. Of course, time does bring changes and, perhaps, places like this should never have been inhabited.

There is a part of me which deeply laments the depopulation of my native area. All those hedges, ditches, nearcuts, mountain paths will continue to be part of my thoughts and the people who traversed them until my dying day. In moments of reverie I can still see Paddy Frank (Clancy) heading up almost daily with his ass to the top of the land for a load of turf, or Jimmy Moore for his three creels of turf when they had them, always carried on his back. Was this heavenly or just plain drudgery? All I can think of is to quote Pádraig Pearse: "Where mountainy man hath sown and soon would reap near to the gates of heaven."

It was Franz Kafka, considered one of the great writers of the 20th century, who said that we live and die in the hedges and ditches in which we are born. The savage loves his native shore. There is nothing I like better than stand at Brennan's quarry on the moor just above Molly Keaveny's and look towards Thor mountain with all those farms running up towards it and think of all those years I spent chasing sheep up there. (I can even imagine I can see Annie McManus helping her daddy foot turf at the end of the Barr's road and the upturned cart and mare standing by.) The view is equally exhilarating if I look towards Glenfarne valley or Glenboy. To think that one day this will just be one huge blanket of afforestation with none of the houses I once knew visible is a depressing thought. The least we should do is mark and name those houses before it is too late. A whole history will be obliterated. These people were children of the earth and children of God as we are. They deserve to be remembered just as much as the people of the Blasket islands in Kerry which were abandoned in the early 'fifties. The recent book *Glenfarne – A History* is a step in the right direction.

This is one of the great dilemmas of the human condition – do we just forge ahead and conveniently forget our brethren of the past, or do we cherish their memory in every way possible? We are now hearing about the decline of the rural community and some people are saying that we can't afford one. Everything tends to be seen through the lens of economic development. More and more people are crowding into our cities and content to lead a congested life in some building or other where they don't even know their immediate neighbour. We have to ask ourselves: is this a healthy thing? At the same time, we are demanding our right to travel through the lands of the few remaining diehards who have chosen to remain in the countryside (roughly 120,000 farmers now compared to 350,000 in 1950) without much consideration for the fact that they are not getting their fair share of the retail price of the food that we eat and we might well be disturbing their livestock into the bargain.

Were it not for this effort in tracing some of the history of Blackmountain, none of this would be known. The poor souls who were forced to take the *bád bán* to England, America, Australia, New Zealand or Canada, often solely because they did not know someone at home with influence to get them a job here, frequently suffered from loneliness and real hardship, as did the men who had to go into the coalmines during the war. This is the sad reality of our history – of a country unable to look after its people in a fair and equitable manner.

Dennis and Annie McMorrow

Mary and Hughie McMorrow

Large family gathering. Front (from left): Rose Mary Ambrose McDermott, her mother Annie, Mary Dolan, Mary Keown and Brigid Kilbride. Further back (from left): Paddy Keown, Maurice McPartland, Michael Ambrose McDermott, Philomena McDermott, Agnes McMorrow and Maggie McPartland

Front, left to right: Aunt Lissy, Author himself, Francis MacGourty.
Back, left to right: Frankie and Seamus McDermott

Front row, left to right: Blathnaid McDermott, Kevin MacMorrow,
Padraig McDermott, Deirdre McDermott. Second row, left to right: Miriam
McDermott, John McDermott, Bernadette O'Connor. Back row: Author with
Donncha McDermott in his arms

Chapter Nineteen

The new Ireland

O F COURSE, THERE WAS A LOT OF UPHEAVAL during the first half of the twentieth century. It took some resilience to survive all this. The Fianna Fáil party were in power from 1932 onwards, except for a short period between 1948 and 1951 when you had a coalition government. They saw to their members very well, giving whatever jobs there were to their loyal supporters. England was good during the re-building immediately after the war so emigration accelerated. The economy was very sluggish at home until Ken Whitaker produced his report, the first programme for economic development, in 1958. This began to encourage some badly needed development. Up until now Ireland was following a protectionist policy which was what De Valera wanted. As my father used to quote him: "One more sow, one more cow and one more acre under the plough." And comely maidens dancing at the crossroads.

People living in the countryside in places like Leitrim who remained in the holdings of their ancestors were gradually left behind in the brave new world of the new Ireland. With slow beginnings after the Whitaker report and a quickening in pace of change in the 'sixties, which continued (with the odd dip) until the arrival of the Celtic Tiger, the position was soon reached where the slowcoaches were left behind in rural Ireland. Gradually, anybody who wanted to get a job off the farm could do so, and this meant that they could take the farming more leisurely as there was a weekly wage coming into the house. It also meant that they were not putting too much pressure on the farming organisations to improve the lot of the farmers. Things began to slip. Those depending solely on the land began to feel the pinch, and now they are about to be wiped out altogether. Of course, there is a core of diehards who will continue on regardless and stupidly subsidise their farming from good but hard-earned money from working on the buildings, or the wife's wages from teaching or nursing, or even from old age pensions – just imagine it, grandparents who scrimped and scraped all their lives now keeping their grandchildren in bread and butter because they don't like to see the holding abandoned. That it should come to this. That the huge effort of countless generations should fade away in relatively few years is most disconcerting, to say the least. But that seems to be the way that evolution is going. There is little that any of us can do about it but go with it and try and be happy about it. We cannot be slaves to the past. We have to accept what life brings and play our part in shaping it.

Afforestation began to be seen as a good use for marginal land in counties like Leitrim. Tim Pat Felie (Mac Manus) had got Healy's land after the death of John Healy. Prior to Healy's owning it, it belonged to a family called McGolderick. A great story circulated about the Dubh lads stealing a turkey after a raffle and cooking it in the McGolderick house. This was the sort of prank the Dubh lads used to play on their neighbours, though it wasn't very nice for the winner of the raffle or, indeed, for the owner of the turkey. If it was now you'd see legal action taken. Tim wired in the land which was adjacent to Eddie Pat Jimmie's land and put forty ewes on it. Most of them died during the winter. He sold it to the forestry department in the 'forties. Thus began afforestation in the Dubh area, though it was resented. Sold for five pound an acre, nobody could muster up the price of it. Now Oweney Kilkenny has sold his own farm, Keoghan's and Johnny Dermott's. How long more will the few remaining farmers in Blackmountain resist the lure of afforestation which will now give them over 250 euro an acre and tax-free income for 15 years? As I write, the IFA are objecting to the continued planting of Leitrim, but will it succeed? There is no way farming can compete with afforestation. We are told that we are the least-planted country in the EU. The land is also supposed to very suitable for the growing of trees. Many people want the old traditional way of living to continue and are totally against planting the land which permanently removes it from cattle rearing and tillage crops which are the life-supports of the people. The memory of the famine is still there – you can't eat trees. It took centuries to clear the scrubs of the country to enable the production of food to take place. Why return it to a scrub again? That there might be an evolution offering a new and improved lifestyle to the people never entered their minds. It was nice seeing their neighbours moving about through their farms each day rather than looking at a mass of trees overshadowing their farms and keeping the sunshine out.

The trouble was that while prior to this people were satisfied to have enough to eat and a few shillings to clothe themselves, they now had to have some money to help them keep a car on the road and there was no way you could make this on livestock. But you could, if you planted your land, get a tax-free income which might be small enough, but it would at least leave you more free to pursue some other pursuit like a part-time job, as once the forest took root you didn't have that much expense, or need to work it. The keeping of livestock was an expensive burden, especially in winter.

Leitrim's population fell from near 60,000 to 26,000 and now it is beginning to rise again. It's even becoming popular as a place to buy old derelict houses and do them up. It's happening in my townland, Blackmountain: John Keoghan's, otherwise known as Oweney Powers (Walsh) beside Oweney Kilkenny, has been bought and the old house that Jack Hughie Dinny (my uncle) fed cattle in for years has been turned into a mansion all surrounded by trees. So also has Eddie Pat Jimmie's (McDermott) been bought and made into a mansion also. What a turnaround. None of the neighbours would dream of ever buying either of them, because they would have been associated with poverty. Indeed, they wouldn't live in them even if they got them for nothing. One wonders what the new owners are going to do with them. The land is planted around them. The sun will never manage to shine on them; whether it is shines on the new owners is another matter.

The truth is that farming as a way of life is on the way out and very soon there will be fifteen to twenty thousand farmers left in the country. Sad but true, and it's unlikely to change. Food can be produced more cheaply in almost any other country in the world, so whatever we decide to do with our land it cannot be the continuation of our present system of farming. Of course, we're not hearing this too clearly at the moment, because there are too many vested interests still doing well out of the agri-sector. You have first and foremost a huge army of civil servants caught up in a complicated bureaucratic exercise of enforcing rules and regulations, checking forms and imposing penalties and generally keeping the whole thing up and running – one wonders if they had anything to do before we joined the EU. A cursory glance at the telephone directory will amaze you when you see all the jobs that are out there. Then you have Teagasc and the veterinary service, the latter doing very well out of the whole thing, while the farmer can't cover the costs of production. What a scenario! The irony is that everybody makes plenty of money once the produce leaves the farmers' gate but the consumer doesn't benefit from the pittance the primary producer gets. So the lesson: don't get involved in primary production; let some other fool do that. There are still plenty of them around – indeed, well over a hundred thousand of them who despite free education continue to give away their produce for a pittance well below the cost of production. Of course, not too many are "full-time" farmers; they'll tell that they own a bit of land and they are running a few cattle and sheep on it. Indeed, how many guards are full-time guards or other full-time servants of the state?

Farmers are notoriously slow to sell up, realise their assets and move on to something more profitable. A farm is an heir-loom and must be held on to at all costs. There might still be a new famine and they would be the lucky ones who would, at least, be able to feed themselves. However, that famine is a long time coming and the whole-time farmer remains just above the famine line while the rest of the country forges ahead, driven by the Celtic Tiger. One is tempted to suggest that farming is but a social service to feed the population, and this seems to be borne out by the way farming is faring out in the EU. It is becoming more obvious by the day that the land surface of the globe belongs to all the people and that those legally owning it are expected to keep it in good shape for the various nations and their teeming populations.

While all this is being thrashed out in the media, the people in the valley of Glenfarne, and elsewhere, are struggling to do two jobs – hold on to their farms and go out to a job also, if they are lucky enough to find one. We don't hear too much about this in the newspapers. Indeed, our two principal papers, the *Irish Independent* and *Irish Times*, have very little to say about agriculture; it's no longer of much interest to the average individual, and especially to the young. Why bother about reporting it? The fact that we export about 13 billion of agricultural produce doesn't create any euphoria among the general populace. Of course, it's not the farmer, the primary producer, that benefits from all these exports. All the money is made after it leaves the farmers' gate. This is the unpalatable truth of the situation.

Life in Ireland is no longer about subsistence farming. We have had our Celtic Tiger era and now we are emerging from our recession during which we had to pay 60 billion to keep our banks afloat. And yet Vincent Browne, our esteemed journalist, claims that we are still one of the richest countries in the world. That is certainly some achievement.

Now, as I write, almost everybody succeeds in getting a job in Leitrim. What a change this is. The Health Board and the Old People's home, together with a few factories in Manorhamilton, are a great help in procuring employment. Many people have arrived back from England to take up jobs there.

This has succeeded in putting new life into the area and proves that people don't want to leave the area if they can help it. The hare returns to her form in the same field even after been chased by dogs:

> And, as an hare whom hounds and horns pursue,
> Pants to the place from whence at first she flew...
>
> I still had hopes, my latest hours to crown,
> Amidst these humble bowers to lay me down;*

Oliver Goldsmith knew his country life. Though we are all born with a curiosity to see the world, there is still a sense in which we have a right to live in our own country if we choose to do so. There is nothing sadder than to see families scattered all over the world because of economic necessity.

Nobody knows what the future will bring. More and more people will be living in cities. That's the way the trend is going despite all the lip service that's paid to the beauty of the countryside and peace and quietude to be found there. Governments are starving the rural community of good infrastructure and are reluctant to establish industry there. The country people are gradually being left to their own devices.

We have global conferences discussing the land usages of the world. Of course, the average farmer isn't even aware that these conferences are being held. The great thinkers, as it were, are in their ivory towers, thinking up clever solutions for the future of the food industry, while the average farmer is collecting his so-called dairy herd in the rainy wind-swept fields of rural Ireland with but the faintest notion of what is happening out there. He is so busy doing the ordinary chores of every day farming, often working up to a hundred hours a week, that he is too exhausted to do any serious reading at night. Their conferences' thinking is European, global and universal, whereas his is about feeding his wife and family. His effort is destined to

* From Oliver Goldsmith's poem *The Deserted Village.*

be soon forgotten, while they hope to make it into the pages of history and be remembered as the pioneers of change which revolutionised the production of food in the world.

The question has to be asked: can it be different? There is no easy answer; of course, at one time we were all farmers. We had to be to be able to survive. But that day is long past. The Malthusian theory that the world's population would outgrow the means of subsistence is long forgotten about. There is more than enough for everyone now if it could be got to them. It's mostly a problem of distribution if we could sort out the economics of the situation. It's about ownership of the land of the world now. Though we fought hard for the "Three Fs" (fixity of tenure, fair rent and free sale), it is transpiring gradually that the farmers of today are not going to be trusted with the possession of the land. Bit by bit their right to farm and rear their families is being eroded by the failure of successive governments to guarantee an income which can sustain a household. All the schemes like REPS (the Rural Environmental Protection Scheme) and the single payments are but carrots to lure the farmer away from production of food which should be his main occupation, but which is no longer sustainable in a world where just a few countries could produce enough for the whole world if we gave them the expertise to do it. That's the sad reality. Our farmers here in Ireland will just have the task of keeping things tidy (and mind you, that is no easy task as everyone who was ever in charge of the kitchen for a day knows) and if they pay for it, they'll soon learn that the basic payments won't cover the costs.

Chapter Twenty

The modern view of religion

I HAVE SPOKEN ABOUT THIS ELSEWHERE, BUT IT is important that I should return to the religious theme, especially in the context of the revolutionary change in attitude to the whole business of religion in the twenty-first century. What the priest says in St Michael's Church in Upper Glenfarne is no longer infallible. The people are now listening to voices elsewhere.

Life in twentieth-century Ireland, despite all the drawbacks, had one thing of importance going for it – few people expected too much from life and they had a firm belief in the hereafter. The continuation of birth and decay is, without doubt, the overriding certainty – that's the way it's going to be, whether we are on the moon or on mars.

Of all the changes we have seen, those to the Catholic Church must rank high among them. Who would have foretold that sexual morality would have reached the stage that Mary Harney says eleven-year olds should get the morning-after pill? Couples are living together and not bothering to get married. The idea that marriage is a sacrament, or that we should pray, is old hat.

We have now repealed the 8th amendment which gave equal right to life to the mother and the baby in the womb as far as practical. This was interpreted by some as endangering the life of the mother though some experienced obstetricians said they never had a problem over many years with saving the life of the mother where both could not be saved. Now for all intents and purposes, we have abortion on demand for any reason up to 12 weeks.

On the other hand, we are circumscribed more tightly day by day by more laws – you can hardly move at all without infringing some rule or regulation. There is hardly a place anywhere to park your car – you could accumulate enough points for traffic offences in one day to put you off the road. You can't open a bank account without a plethora of identification papers, and very soon you'll have to carry an ID card telling everybody what you had for breakfast, dinner and supper. As a fellow said to me recently: "We were far freer even in the worst days of communism than we are today." Is this progress, or is this the price of progress? Just because of a few criminals among us we all suffer.

The latest form of terrorism is, of course, the suicide bomber who offers his life to Allah in return for making love to many virgins in the next world. The Muslim religion is like ours in many respects, but like a lot of religions there is an extreme element in it with a fundamentalist approach to things which makes them believe God wants them to do silly things, like killing off Americans whom they regard as infidels.

Writers and thinkers of all kinds are at their wits' end trying to figure out why the Catholic Church is at such a low ebb. All sorts of reasons are attributed to its decline – from the recent scandals to the obligatory rule of celibacy – but are these the real reasons? Though possibly a contributory factor, I hardly think so. It runs much deeper than that.

Most people today are mature enough to realise that priests, despite their sacred calling, are just as human as the rest of us who are prone to sin. So, in a sense, they are capable of anything that we are capable of – even the most heinous deeds like paedophilia and murder. Of course, this raises a huge question for God. Perhaps that's not the right way to put it. But we were always told that God called them. How often have we heard talk about "the call to the priesthood"? Recently I was at a wedding and I gave the priest who married the couple a lift home the following morning when he was still under the influence. He was berating the father of the bride because he was separated from the mother of the bride and boasting about his being called to the priesthood. But in no time at all he was gone from the priesthood himself and had taken unto himself a bride. So much for the "call". Of course, we'll be told about Judas – that he was called and that he is one of the most likely to be in hell because he despaired and hanged himself. What of this priest? Is he a likely candidate for hell?

I think that we have to go back to the basics. We don't know why what is is, how we came to be part of it, or where we are going to. That puts us at a great disadvantage. Despite all the visions and revelations, there is no hint of an answer from these sources. In fact, the visionaries in Medjagoria make it all appear rather simple: "Say the full rosary every day, read the bible every day, go to mass every day, fast once a week and go to confession once a month."

It appears that we are not to ask any of the ultimate questions about life, but just get on with doing the things that the Church tells to do. We are told to be in the world but not to be of it. And in this is the great crux of the whole Christian position. We need material things to live, but we are constantly reminded of the birds of the air and the lilies of the field that "labour not" but still are not forgotten about by God, as if we should do little in the material sense because God will look after us. All this is very confusing. For most of the time we don't know whether we are coming or going. In other words, we don't know how to blend the temporal and the spiritual together, though there are loads of advice from several quarters.

In Ireland we observed the "externals" (as some writers described them) of the Catholic Church. We went to mass and devotions, told our sins and abstained from meat on Fridays and had our children baptised. This last was described as the gateway to all the other sacraments. If some people thought all these exercises trivial enough and, indeed, easy enough to do, they never said so. It was a time when comments like that would not be appreciated and people learned to keep their mouths closed. Indeed, making it to mass meant little more than getting inside the front door before the first gospel and oftentimes that was little further than the porch. But surely there is more to the Catholic religion than all this movement. What about your state of mind? This has to be important also. This was sometimes referred to but people generally seemed to get on with the actions and leave the thoughts to somebody else. And so it went on for hundreds of years without as much as a whimper of complaint from anybody.

In the meantime people had to work their backsides off, especially in rural areas on small farms, to make a living – feed themselves. They knew that the priest could be got when someone was dying. The idea of going into eternity without the helping hand of the priest was frightening in the extreme. They had heard about the difference between Perfect and Imperfect Contrition at school. The ultimate insult was to refer to someone who had died without the priest. But those days are long gone and now it appears that no one is afraid of eternal damnation.

And, of course, this is the ultimate test. If some people don't go hell, why worry about it?

Whether the Pope is infallible is a debatable question for a lot of people. Indeed, whether Jesus actually founded a Church is also a debatable question.

So where does all this get us? Not very far, I'm afraid. How many people out there have automatically excommunicated themselves? It would appear a huge number.

So what's the problem? To the average person born into a Catholic family with little instruction in his religion, it all appears a bit vague. He has undoubtedly heard about Jesus and he is aware of the principal church feasts like Christmas and Easter, but is he able to relate them to his daily life and the life of his friends? I think not.

On the contrary, he is probably hearing more about Richard Dawkins and his book about *The God Delusion* than about Jesus. That's the kind of society in which young people are being brought up now. In this new scientific age people don't need a God as they did in the past, or at least that's what they think.

To be a good Catholic you have to be utterly convinced that Jesus did come on earth, that he was both God and man at the same time, that he redeemed us and that you can only be saved through him. And on top of all this, you must recognise the present Church as the institution he left behind him when he was taken up to heaven after the resurrection.

A lot of the criticism at the moment is that the Church has gone astray, as it were, in its power structure and in things like its insistence on celibacy. Maybe it has, despite its claim of infallibility and that God will be with it until the end of time. But this prompts the question: why is the permissive will of God allowing this to happen? Is it that the Church has free will like we are told that the individual has and that God allows it to wander here and there as it were but that it will never lose the essentials and everything will turn out all right in the end? Perhaps this is all theological nonsense. But which theologians are right and which are wrong? Perhaps the Church should exercise the prerogative of infallibility more often.

If we were to follow through the logic of priests like Fr Darcy CP and Fr Tony Flannery CSSr we would let the Church die on its feet. They are saying that the Orders and Congregations shouldn't take in any more novices. Of course there are many writers out there who think that the Catholic Church is just a phase in the evolutionary process and that it has served its purpose and that something else will take its place very soon. If other beings were to be found out here in space, would they have to be redeemed also? They claim that the biological process will bring us to heights undreamed of in the billions of years ahead of us before final unity is attained.

In an atmosphere such as this it's not going to be easy to motivate young people to follow the rituals of the Catholic Church – the strange clothes and (to them) the strange ceremonies. Some priests have made heroic efforts to motivate the young to take part in the sacramental life of the Church but without much success.

The worst thing that could happen is that the Catholic Church would water down its doctrine to attract new members or to keep members who are wavering. I don't think there is any danger of this happening. Jesus was clear in his message. He wanted one shepherd and one flock. Everyone is called – politicians and leaders as well as ordinary people. There is only one morality. The notion of a pluralist society doesn't fit into this, or that there should be a separation of the Church and State. The collective body of the State is as much called as every individual in it. Jesus came to save everyone and only through him can anyone be saved.

However, the conviction that this is so seems to be weakening. When we look at the turmoil in the world we cannot help wondering how some people will, as it were, manage to be saved. Of course, if everyone is saved that puts a different complexion on things and makes a lot of our effort redundant.

Much is being written purporting to explain the present and the future for us; but in the nature of things it can only be pure speculation. *Where to from here? The Christian Vision of Death*, by Brian Grogan SJ, attempts to explain what lies ahead of us. So does a book entitled *All You Ever Wanted to Know about Heaven.* But here again it's all speculation, though sometimes very convincing. It would be too much to suggest that the Dubh people went into things that assiduously. The drudgery of subsistence farming saw to that; life had to be practical if you were to feed yourself comfortably. There was no other way. No doubt many families managed to say the rosary most evenings, at least for periods, until some circumstance or other interfered with the routine.

Few are the houses now where the rosary is said in the evening. The private lives of the priests themselves are being scrutinised as never before. Nothing is taken at face value; everything has to be investigated. Our national seminary, Maynooth, is considered unsuitable for training priests by Archbishop Martin and he is sending his candidates for the priesthood to Rome.

THE MODERN VIEW OF RELIGION

Even the Catholic Church today is afraid of freeing up the system. It knows only too well that once you let go your grasp, anything goes. An odd error in truth is bad, but it is as nothing compared to the chaos that follows when everyone goes his or her way. So here we have a real dilemma which is as old as mankind and will remain with us to the end of time – when to intervene and when not to. The Catholic Church claims to be infallible when teaching on faith and morals so we can be bound under pain of excommunication to believe defined dogmas such as the dogma of infallibility itself. This is a great irritant to many people, including many Catholics, but the Church sticks to its guns and maintains that when Christ promised to remain with His Church forever and that the gates of hell will not prevail against it, he was conferring infallibility on it. That, of course, is a huge claim. One can rightly wonder why it is used so sparingly when they are so sure they have it. It has to be a marvellous thing to know that you are right even if only in the limited area of faith and morals – but isn't this the only area that counts in the long run? No other Church makes such "outlandish" claims, as some people describe it. If it is true, it is the equivalent of a hotline to heaven. What a privilege! We are also told that sacred scripture is "inspired", which used to be taken as meaning that God guided the hands of the writers – which, presumably, implies that they didn't err in what they wrote.

These are all big claims and they are either true or untrue. No intermediate position is possible; you either accept them or you don't. There is no scientific test which can clarify the position. Now, there is great respect for the people who make these claims, especially for our late Pope, St John Paul II, who had such great faith and did such wonderful work during his time on earth. But the doubt remains – are they claiming too much? One thing is certain: God does not force people to be good or to believe any particular truth. Neither does He tell the ordinary citizen whether the Church is right in her claims nor, indeed, has He told any visionaries such things. We know from history that even great churchmen can lead less than edifying lives and are often wrong in many things. So the dilemma remains – to believe or not to believe? There is no certainty this side of the grave. All we can do is hope.

We may not have certainty about anything, but we know that it would be wonderful if we could manage to tolerate our inadequacies and live in harmony. If we could do that it would be a great beginning. We could always add to it as we go along. But, unfortunately, the prospect of this happening at the moment is somewhat distant. Change in our attitude, not to talk of in our deeds, is always slow in coming. Let us try and hurry it up.

Reading the Dalai Lama in his call for a revolution of compassion, one is inclined to see the futility of conflict and many writers are now telling us that, despite the many wars raging in the world, there is clear evidence that our world is beginning to learn that whatever the provocation, the way of peace is the way to follow. And so may it continue. The prayer of Christ "that we may be one" could well be on its way to fulfilment. Hope is the virtue that we must now cultivate.

The encyclical *Laudato Si* of Pope Francis, considered to be the most important encyclical in the last hundred and twenty years – though there is no mention of deregulating the hierarchical order, or ordaining women, or doing away with celibacy – has a lot to say about the interrelatedness of everything in the universe. It warns us about the destruction we are doing to our home the earth and the obligation that is on all of us to change our attitude before it is too late. We, in Blackmountain, had no such worry about the continuance of the earth. Except for the dunghill at the back of the byre, you wouldn't see a bit of rubbish, or an empty can or even a shrub or flower about many houses. The ozone layer was in no danger of being punctured by the activities in Blackmountain on John Donald's farm.

Of course, the biggest problem we have as a global society is how to be fair to everybody in the way we rule ourselves and to make sure that the wealth we create is shared fairly among all people. The great obstacle here is that we are not all equally endowed – some of us think we have exceptional talents, that we contribute more to the well-being of the human race than others and should therefore get better compensated for our efforts.

To people who feel like that it's difficult to demonstrate that there is more happiness in giving than in getting. Since our capacity for great enjoyment like good sex and good food is severely limited, we soon turn our attention to extravagant ways of living, like buying huge houses, expensive cars and all sorts of material goods which we can't possibly enjoy because we have too many of them. But for many people the psychological enjoyment must be there, otherwise they would stop accumulating at some stage.

Image is very important. We want to be seen to be successful. Even in a small rural community we want our neighbours to think that we are great. We all have an ego which craves recognition; we frequently can't see beyond our own needs.

This raises the question of importance of the individual in society. Is life a collective thing or mostly an individual thing? If we could get this right, we'd have solved a lot of our problems. Ultimately, this is a religious question: are we going to be saved individually or collectively? That's the crunch. It would seem to suit a lot of us if it was collectively. But then we would have to do away with the particular judgement immediately after death.

Just as in the animal kingdom, I'm afraid, power and might have reigned from the beginning. If you could you did and if you couldn't you didn't. It's as simple as that. If you fought against the odds the danger was you'd lose your life. And this seems to be the way that evolution is continuing. Despite all the laws curbing individual power and greed, many people are still so powerful they seem to get more than their fair share from society despite all the checks and balances. The odd few are caught out, but, in general, the powerful or well-in continue to prosper.

At some stage in civilisation it was the people with land who were the most powerful. They could feed themselves – the others couldn't. But very soon this began to change. Tradesman came on the scene and soon made themselves felt. Their skills might protect you from the elements and for this you relieved them from the tedium of having to produce their own food. This you could say was the beginning of specialisation which has continued apace to the present day. Society has daily become more complex and now we have reached the position where food producers are taken for granted and their average earnings are less than half the average industrial wages and things are getting worse. The World Trade Organisation is seeing to it that we can't guarantee a living wage to our farmers here in Ireland because it would disturb world trends for agricultural products which are being produced much more cheaply elsewhere. There are few farmers out there who can make the minimum wage no matter how hard the work. Not too long ago we had 350,000 farmers; now we're falling rapidly towards the 100,000 mark, and very soon, according to the bright sparks, we'll be down to 40,000, if not 20,000. What a slide! And it's all accepted without a whimper – just as if it was the most natural thing in the world. No place for sentimentality here.

Chapter Twenty-One

Ireland and the EU

THE FIRST OF JANUARY 2005 WAS A HISTORIC day for Irish farmers. All subsidies were done away with and, hopefully, all of the restrictions, like quotas and retention periods will also disappear (we'll have to wait and see) and farming will have a chance of becoming a real business like the making of cement blocks or any other product for which there is a market, provided you are able to compete. The sting is in the last word "compete". It's difficult to see how we in Ireland will be able to compete because our production costs are too high and markets are limited. South America, Brazil or Australia could supply all of Europe with food more cheaply than any country in Europe with the exception of Poland, perhaps, which some people claim could become the granary of Europe – and its abattoir, dairy and vegetable garden also. The average wage in Poland is €550 per month, while here in Ireland you'd earn that in a week.

Poland is only at the stage of development we had reached in the 'fifties. That means there is huge potential for the Polish economy that she is now in the EU. She will be our greatest competitor in the agricultural field for years to come. Despite all the talk about how good the EU has been for agriculture, which eats up more than 40% of its budget, the sector was being totally exploited in the Celtic Tiger era with all the big money being made after the produce leaves the farmer's gate. The average wage of our farmers is now closer to the Polish average than it is to the Irish, but our consumers are not bene-fiting from the pittance that our farmers get. At the present moment the cheapest milk in the supermarkets is 214% higher than what the farmer gets after all his trouble and costs maintaining a good milk herd.

With the Celtic Tiger in the industrial sector roaring ahead, we were leaving rural Ireland struggling to maintain any vestige of a rural farming community who could live solely on their earnings from the land. Perhaps this is part of the evolutionary process. Though food is necessary for life and eating is an enjoyable activity, man is moving on to greater and more exciting pursuits and the diehard cohort of people who are clinging to the land are being left behind. There is little respect for them, though if they had the will they could starve us all into accepting the vital role they play and make us pay handsomely for it. But, apparently, they haven't this determination and will, though we hear a lot about how powerful the farming organisations are. This is all very interesting and shows the kind of people we are: we acquiesce very easily despite our reputation for complaining. But we do nothing about it.

And things have even got worse in the new millennium, despite all the outcry about subsidies and decoupling, but no one wants to see it. We're hearing about over 40% of the EU Budget being spent on Agriculture as if it was a terrible calamity, though life cannot be sustained without food – we could do without doctors who are held in high esteem and paid hundreds of thousands annually, but we couldn't without the farmer. Of course, food can be produced more cheaply in other countries where there are still peasants (that pejorative term) hoking the earth with primitive weapons and in richer countries where there are huge tracts of land and food can be produced extensively and the easy way – what lives, lives and what dies, dies. But has this to mean that we just forget about our own farmers here in Ireland. Of course, we'll be told that they are not forgotten about, that they are being well looked after, that they now have decoupled payments, REPS, afforestation grants etc., but it is quietly forgotten that the cumulative effect of all these "handouts" can't bring them up to half the average industrial wage and they are still living in poverty if they cannot find a job.

We're not able to compete on the world market in terms of price and quality anymore. So what are we to do with our land? The decoupled option has been conjured up as a carrot to get Irish farmers to drop production for a payment which doesn't oblige you to produce food. Of course there are a lot of snags, the full effects of which have not been felt yet but they soon will. Farmers are now obliged to keep the countryside neat and tidy and this will be no easy task. It will eat up all of the payments and more if you have to pay to get it done. They are not index-linked and Tony Blair was trying to get rid of them when in power.

As I write, England has voted to leave the EU.* Many regard this as a backward step and so it may well turn out to be. Didn't the founding fathers visualise all the European countries coming together and living in harmony ever afterwards – no more wars, trading together, having freedom of movement for all its people; in truth, a veritable utopia? Far from it. We humans are unpredictable. Nobody can foresee what we may do. It cannot be denied that we in Ireland have benefited. Look at the great roads it has helped us to build and all the subsidies that has helped our farmers to stay in business. (I can still remember the euphoria when farmers discovered that they were getting paid for just keeping animals, even if they never sold them.) But, alas! the subsidies now fail to keep them in business because the market prices cannot defray the costs of production and they are in a loss-making situation. Few people fully understand the path on which the EU is travelling. Farmers are tied up in paperwork to draw down the subsidies. Satellites can pinpoint every rock, rush, fern and scrub throughout the country on which you will not get paid. Tagging animals has become a real nuisance and there is considerable doubt as to whether it is in anyway effective – can the sirloin steak you are eating in the Shellbourne Hotel really be traced back to the

---

* This part of the book was written in 2016.

animal and the farm? No wonder England had second thoughts about their membership and voted themselves out. The suspicion is that other countries are thinking likewise. Unions are all very well but what often happens is that an elite takes over and the ordinary individual has no say in anything. This is what is happening in the EU. Farmers have now to pay people to fill their forms because they cannot do it themselves – anyhow, they think that say a *teagasc* man will get more leeway with the department. It's the same way with the factories – the farmer feels safer with an agent, rather than bringing in his animals directly himself. There is no trust. Consequently, a whole battalion of middlemen has been created who can manipulate the system. Even our Minister for Agriculture can be changed at a whim and a new man appointed who isn't acquainted with the intricacies of the industry at all. So much for the importance of agriculture. Imagine how all this affects my neighbours in the Blackmountain. Once upon a time they were in charge of their little enterprise – subsistence farming. They could sell a beast anytime they wanted and they could grow whatever crops they wanted, but that was all changed. Now, effectively, you have to get a licence to farm and still there is no living in it. The producers of food are just being used to feed the teeming millions for a pittance.

Though none of us are too far removed from the soil and *clábar* (muck), we soon forget about the hardship associated with farming – out in all kinds of weather and poor prices for products – when we leave it behind us for better jobs. It is a source of annoyance to the mandarins in the EU that the agricultural budget is one of the biggest they have. They seem to regard it as an expense: *look what we could do with the money if we hadn't this expense*, they appear to be arguing; *what a relief it would be if we could pop a pill and get on with the important things.*

We are being told now that farming is just a business like any other business, but this can't be true. When we had the quotas for the dairy farmers, it was like telling a hotelier that he could only take so many guests each night though he could take double that. The truth is that the production of food is just a social service to feed the population and if the farmers didn't do it, it would have to be done by another agency like the civil service and then we'd see the astronomical cost for the taxpayer. In the EU a small percentage increase or decrease in the amount of food produced creates a glut or a deficit. So it is very difficult to get it right. We had mountains of butter on occasions and ships at sea storing it. Few of our entrepreneurs become primary producers of food except when they have a monopoly; but they are quite happy to take over the retailing of it. That way you won't get caught with a surplus. When all the new technologies arrived, they created whole new areas of endeavour and opportunities for employment which were far more interesting than the perceived drudgery of peasant farming. Hence the exodus from the land. The poets might laud the beauty of the countryside, but it wasn't enough to keep the peasants there. They abandoned their farms in their thousands and very soon we'll have no rural communities. All my nostalgia will not bring it back. Anyhow, I left myself. Why should I expect my relatives to stay in their holdings? Just to be there to welcome me back and allow me to reminisce about my earlier years there, which were no great shouts anyhow?

This has to be part of the evolutionary process. There is no other explanation. This must be what God ordained. At least, this is the Christian belief. We are being swept along; whether happily or not, that is the big question. Maybe this earth is its own explanation: what we see is what we get.

Things do change, of course. Now, as I write, there is a real danger that the whole suckler cow industry will collapse because it is not profitable. If it takes eight hundred euro to feed a cow for the year, how could it be profitable if the majority of farmers cannot manage anything like that for her weanling calf? Of course, there are so many mixing their money from earnings in the construction industry or elsewhere that they have no notion what they are making. That's the stupidity of the average farmer for you. They have the land; they have to put it to some use. Wasn't it handed down to most of them? It would be a crime to sell it, or even let it. Anyhow, if you had a few bob, what could you do with it?

Historically, if you go back far enough we were all farmers. First of all, of course, we were just foragers picking up anything edible we could find on our planet. The good God, or whoever it was, did see after our early ancestors when they came down from the trees – they had something to pick up on the ground to whet their appetite. Some authors claim it was a bad day for them when they discovered how to farm. Henceforth, they had to settle down in one place and go through the back-breaking task of cultivating the soil which brought on all sorts of pains and aches, as those of us who ever wielded the loy or the scythe know only too well. (It was much more fun picking berries and killing the odd wild animal.)

Of course, everything changed when we joined the EEC (as it was then) in 1973. From now on you got a subsidy on your ram lambs whether you sold them or not. And you also got a subsidy on your hogget ewes. The farmers couldn't believe their good fortune. But time brings change and the years ahead will be very challenging for the farming community. The mandarins in the EU are intent on reducing the budget for agriculture which amounts to more than 40% of total expenditure.

The world was changing and so was rural living. Real poverty was becoming a thing of the past. Almost everybody could now feed and clothe themselves and provide some sort of a shelter. Jobs outside the farm were becoming more plentiful. Our joining the EEC in 1973 meant that we now had a Common Agricultural Policy (CAP). This revolutionised agricultural production. Henceforth there would be grants for farmers to produce food. However, despite all the grants, it is now becoming obvious that there is no way you can make a living from farming. This year is a very wet year* and there is an acute shortage of fodder and an awful lot of farmers will not manage to survive it. Animals are dying in their hundreds.

* This part of the book was written in 2018.

No doubt the government will make some effort to appease the farmers – that's always the way it is – but it won't be enough.

On today's *Farmers' Journal*, 21 July 2018 – for the first time ever and most belatedly, I suggest, because this sort of analysis has been crying out for years – we have an editorial by the editor Justin Mc Carthy under the heading "Sucklers – should they stay or should they go?" He mentions three possibilities which I won't go into, but says that support payments on suckler farms in Ireland have declined by 177 euro per cow in the last decade and ends by saying: "Sitting back as the sector grinds to a slow death serves no one's interest." The neighbours in Blackmountain who are still keeping sucklers are living in a fool's paradise supported by their working wives. John Donald's four cows might not have been doing much damage to the ozone back in the 1950s but would they now? – That is the question. There is a suspicion that the government thinks they would.

An otherwise great letter from Stephen Crampton, Co Offaly, also in the *Journal*, correctly pointing out that there is no point telling farmers to bargain with a cartel, is spoiled by saying he has a good job and will survive. Of course, it does take a good job to keep a farm going. Don't Mairéad Mc Guinness, Darragh Mc Cullough and Martin Dempsey know all about that? The question must be asked: why should people in good jobs be keeping farming going? Of course, they may have big basic payments and doing the minimum to draw them down. There was a time when you wouldn't get any if your wife was working. Now the greatest bureaucracy on earth is necessary to run the show, which is the Department of Agriculture. Great would be the genius who could unravel the turns and twists in all the schemes since we joined the EU as it is now. And in retrospect, all they seemed to do was to appease the farmer and fool him into thinking that he was getting money for nothing. The latest figures published a couple days ago show that the average sum of money got from Europe is about 5000 euro per farmer, a mere pittance, seeing that the marketplace returns a loss. There are now only 3,384 farmers in Leitrim getting the payments and these are kept going on money earned outside farming. "Farming not Fracking", how are you?

The World Trade Organisation is the dominant factor now. Its policy is to keep food cheap for the human masses. There are many poor countries out there that could produce food much more cheaply than Ireland if they were given the chance. Our inputs are too high to be competitive. It appears that we'll just acquiesce and accept what's coming. Rural life as we knew it will disappear for ever. No longer will we see fields full of cattle or sheep because they can't be produced at the prevailing prices. And we mustn't forget that it was these same animals that distinguished rural living from urban living; without them you may have a rural landscape, perhaps largely dominated by trees (poor us, we had too little of them till now), but you won't have rural living without the activities that went with the care of these animals. Rural living was about creaturehood. The old red polly might have driven you mad when she wouldn't go through a gap, but she also gave you that spark of interest which gave you a bit of vitality to keep the mind healthy. Of course, there may be a new breed of human beings out there who will walk themselves into the ground for the pure of fun of it, but it will not be rural living. That will be gone forever.

Chapter Twenty-Two

The future of farming in Ireland

THE GLOBAL VILLAGE CONCEPT IS GATHER-ing momentum and the World Trade Organisation will see to it that there will be no protectionism or subsidies. If the poorer countries were allowed to sell food to the West, they'd be able to feed themselves and also be able to supply us with cheap food. While much of the world goes hungry, countries like Ireland cannot sell food so that it leaves a margin of profit to the primary producer, the farmer, without whom there would be no food. There is a very real danger that there will be whole tracts of land in Ireland just lying fallow, except that the farmer will have to comply with stringent rules in order to keep the countryside neat and tidy if he is to draw down his single payments.

The question must be asked: How did things come to this?

Traditionally, there used to be great respect for the producer of food, the farmer. What happened to put an end to this? When tools were basic, everybody had of necessity to play some role in the production of food if there was to be enough to go around. It took a lot of manual labour to put food on the table. People instinctively knew this and they co-operated to make sure there was enough to go round. But this has all changed. Modern machinery can now produce high quantities of food with relative ease and more and more people are entering the service industry and the professions and expecting to get cheap food from the slow coaches they left behind.

A strong argument could be made for saying that the production of food is just a social service to the community. If there wasn't a captive farming community already there (a mere remnant of what used to be there but still a real entity), governments would have to get a special force to feed their people. If they had to do that they'd pay through the nose for their food and nobody would complain, or if they did it wouldn't matter. It would be like complaining about the civil service – the complaints would fizzle out and the bill would keep increasing. As it is, they are getting it on the cheap, even including subsidies which have now been done away with and replaced with the single farm payments. This so-called single farm payment is a sop to appease the farmers and to ease them out of the production of food which relative to world markets is too dear in Ireland and cannot be sustained, especially in the context of what the WTO is about – namely freeing up in the global context.

Food is just like petrol/diesel for machinery; it keeps the human equivalent going. If it could be done without completely, it would be a Godsend for the human race. There are many more exciting things out there if we could do away with the need for food, or if we could just pop a few pills instead of the huge bulk which we are forced to consume to keep our engines running.

According to the Bible, we lost our original innocence when our first parents ate of the forbidden fruit and henceforth we were condemned to earn our food by the sweat of our brows. One might reasonably conclude that in the age of the Celtic Tiger we'd only be too happy to shed all this drudgery of having to feed ourselves and leave it all quietly and sensibly behind us and move on and do something more exciting and creative than tending to animals and crops that made slaves of us all. Patrick Kavanagh tells about the anxiety of his mother who tells him to "see about the cattle". All of this may well arouse some nostalgia in those of us with rural roots, but shouldn't it be left at that? Places like Brazil and Argentina are much more easily able to produce beef and mutton than we are and at a third of the price. Wouldn't it be sensible to leave it to them and not to be codding our own farmers into believing that there is a future for them when the dogs in the street know that there isn't?

These are all very interesting questions. There will always be the diehards who will want to stick with it – old habits and routines die slowly. Why not leave it to them? If they are foolish enough to continue to work for nothing, let them at it.

Despite all the great thinkers among us, no one seems to be able to predict the future with any great degree of certainty – we might say that man will one day be living on the moon or on Mars and this may well happen, but whether he will have to eat as he does now is something few people want to spec-ulate about. There is one certainty of course – we will tend to be vying with each other for millennia to come and whatever there is, there won't be enough to go around – hence conflict will be of the essence of mankind for untold years to come until we reach Teilhard de Chardin's point of unity when the travail of the earth will have ceased. But since there is no sign of this unity about which we pray so much, we have to do with what we have and make the most of it.

Of course, this is the Christian, Catholic approach to life. It evidently is not to every one's taste. It's based on Faith – believ-ing beyond human evidence – which has become more difficult in an age of science and technology where all reality is assumed to be measurable. It is also more challenging in an age where the urgency is on the search for life and personal fulfilment here and now. Why wait? And all this reasoning surely makes sense. After all, and despite all the obstacles, this earth does offer great possibilities if you succeed in grasping them. We see examples of it every day. But religion, especially our Catholic religion, throws a spanner in the works. Though we are in this world, we are told not to be of it, meaning we should not be interested in material things – not even in success. And worst of all, we are being told that this planet will not last for ever. Stephen Hawking, who unfortunately is no longer with us, was telling us that we must be preparing to inhabit another planet because this planet will not be able to sustain us forever.

So what does this tell us about the people of the Glenfarne valley generally and, in particular, about Blackmountain and the Dubh area? Not an awful lot, really. It just adds to the mystery of our being here at all and especially to our finding ourselves in such wretched circumstances on poor land in a backward area of the globe.

I have just watched a programme on T na G about Inis Caorach, an island about two miles off the Donegal coast, and close enough to Árann Mór where they used to go to mass. There were twelve families living there until 1955 when they evacuated the island. They had a school but no doctor or nurse. The menfolk had to go to Scotland and the women did all the farming which supplied most of their needs. It was very sad to watch them viewing the ruins of their former homes and the places where they played as children. Just like Blackmountain, they said they were continually running in and out to each other's houses. There is a sense in which this is an idyllic way of living but it does not fit too well into the evolutionary process which forces us to move forward with the changing times. The question arises: are we to stay put like our ancient ancestors, leaving our talents for new things idle, or are we to forge ahead making new discoveries which may improve the quality of our lives? However, we answer this question, there is no doubt but something is lost when we move from the simple life. My happiest memories are seeing my grandfather, Hughie Dinny Mc Morrow, over across the Corr na bhfeannóg river at the old house (reputedly a school at one time) setting potatoes with the loy and putting a cabbage plant between the sods which grew simultaneously with the stalks so you would have greens before you ever dug the potatoes. And, of course, the sun was always shining! Or the day we made forty rucks of hay, cocking all below Donald's house and the first field on Farrell's mountain. That was some achievement for the Wee Johns.

Now only Oweney Kilkenny, the last of the true native stock with a family history in the townland of Blackmountain, remains: "the last historian of the pensive plain", as Goldsmith described a similar scene in *The Deserted Village*. In Lisnagroagh, the, adjacent townland across the Corr na bhfeannóg river, still live John Joe in Jack's, his wife Tess, his three children Declan, Keith and Treacy, mostly gone from the homestead. Just across the county road, as it used to be referred to, lives Hubert in Jack's (all Mc Morrows and cousins of Seán Mac Diarmada). Further up the field lives Mary Theresa in Joe's (Mc Dermott) and to the right my nephew John Francis, his wife Carmel, his daughter Sarah and his mother Margaret and brother Kevin. That concludes the inhabitants of Lisnagroagh – a sorry tale of desolation for the townland.

Though all these families are relatively well off – they are the lucky descendants of parents like Jack Hughie Dinny and Wee John and further back, Hughie Farrell who saw some hardship in their day – what the future holds for their children remains to be seen. But one thing is certain: they won't be cropping, cutting turf or milking cows ever again unless some catastrophe or other befalls them. And shouldn't we all be glad that they have left behind them the backbreaking drudgery associated with all those peasant tasks? A very interesting programme on TV recently showed a woman from Cork from a big dairy farm spending a fortnight with a primitive tribe still doing the chores like carrying water long distances, milking emaciated cows and killing goats as we killed pigs in the early part of the last century. They even punctured arteries in the cows to draw blood and drink it, something we no doubt did during the famine. A very interesting part of the experience saw them driving animals all night to fairs as we did and all the haggling associated with the selling. Our modern, twenty-first-century, sophisticated way of living has no appeal to them. They seem perfectly happy as they are. And in some ways we should envy them. What has this modern technological age given us but grief? Look what it has done to our children with all the cyberbullying, often ending up in suicide, watching porn, giving them an unhealthy attitude to intimacy and creating expectations which cannot be realised? As an old lady said to me recently: " The young people don't know what they want but they want it immediately."

Of course, all this has to be balanced against what appears to be the onward thrust of the world around us. There is no stopping it and it is leading us somewhere and that can't be total perdition. As Teilhard de Chardin tells us, we must jump on the waggon and speed ahead. There is no other way. Otherwise, we stay stuck in the muck, as it were. Hence the dilemma I'm in. I'd like to find some solid evidence to prove that life as we had it in Blackmountain could have continued forever, but alas this is not the destiny laid out for us. Some people thought the same about the Blasket island so beautifully written about by Robin Flower in *The Western Island*. He spent his honeymoon there he loved it so much.

We humans are taking control of our earthly lives as never before and strangely enough I'm just after learning that we almost certainly would not be here at all were it not that an asteroid hit the earth 66 million years ago and killed off the dinosaurs. Were they around when we arrived, they would have eaten us up on the spot. So the mystery of our being here grows deeper by the day. And finding ourselves in Blackmountain eking out a living on poor soil makes no sense at all.

This sense of no sense was reinforced over the weekend of the 8th and 9th of June 2018 when I was present at the "Seán Mac Diarmada Summer School" in Kiltyclogher. This Summer School has been in existence now for over ten years and was highly organised that year with an elaborate brochure and wide advertisement reach. (I saw it advertised in Bundoran as I was coming.) Besides local speakers like Susan Cartan who was born in Dublin and moved to Kilty in 2004, Jim Connolly of Rural Resettlement Ireland, Declan Sweeney, Cofounder of the Start-up CampusConnect (and a native of Kilty) and Rob Doyle from Wexford who moved to Leitrim 17 years ago, you had George O' Malley, an honours graduate in pure mathematics and the sciences with an interest in afforestation, Eamon O'Cuív, Caoimhghín O'Caolain and Mairéad Mc Guinness, all politicans of repute. You couldn't wish for a better set-up in for a great day: something that would augur well for Kilty and all of North Leitrim. But ALAS! It was all a damp squib.

Firstly, the attendance was most disappointing – mostly ageing women out for the day and, except for a few squalls, it was a good weekend. A decent farmer was nowhere in sight, though signs saying "Farming not Fracking" were everywhere to be seen. It must have been very disappointing for Regina Fahy whose Trojan work as Chairperson of the event to awaken the WEST brought such a poor response. And in the June 13th 2018 issue of the *Leitrim Observer* it was most disappointing not to see any mention of George O' Malley's presentation "Saving the West – What Time is Left?", arguably the most important contribution. Incidentally, he didn't seem to think that there was much time left. Nor was there any mention of Eamon O'Cuív's or Caoimhghín O'Caolain's contribution. What we get is a photo of Mairéad McGuinness under the bland heading "Rural Leitrim needs to plan for the future". No mention that she said farmers should marry teachers or nurses to give them a chance of surviving. John Heney in his piece in the *Farming Independent* (Tuesday 12th June) must have had telepathic hearing when he said that it is the women with the off-farm jobs who are keeping the beef show on the road. What good is planning when the primary producer isn't paid for his effort?

No wonder that somebody has suggested that Leitrim should become some kind of preserve (after they are done with the planting) or some sort of a museum to remind people of how people used to live.

Let us not kid ourselves: the bureaucrats in Europe have no interest in a backward area such as Leitrim with poor quality land mostly unsuitable for any food-producing enterprise. Indeed, they are not unduly worried about the production of food at all beyond feeding the teeming masses for whom food is but the fuel to power them to get on with more exciting enterprises. And it does not matter what the likes of Mairéad McGuinness thinks; she's but a lonely voice crying out in the wilderness. Nor, indeed, for that matter Phil Hogan. (Mairéad has just profited from the resignation of Phil and taken his place.) The EU are only too ready to trade off agriculture like the supermarkets do bags of potatoes here for industrial opportunities outside the Union. A shame for some of us but the sensible reality for more of us.

And that's why the flight from the land will continue. They have already sensed that there is no future for them. And this applies to the diehards in the milk game who despite the volatility manage to make a living – but for how long? The perceived wisdom of uncontrolled expansion may end in grief. And all this despite a *Farmers' Journal* writer in 2018 telling them that if they worked harder they could make a few more hundred euro per cow. Keep the fools at the absolute slavery which is the milking of cows.

There has to be some valuable lessons to be learned from what we see around us in the world today. Not to see them could be disastrous for many of us in a personal way. There is no point in being nostalgic about the past. Our parents did their best for us in the circumstances in which they found themselves, but those circumstances have changed; they have passed on into eternity and we are left to carry on. It's up to us in a different set of circumstances to continue on the road of life availing ourselves of the many new technologies that were not there for them. Of course, we could choose to live like the man reported in the paper today to be living a Robinson Crusoe-style existence in an island all on his own for the last thirty years, simply to get away from the noise.

Bit by bit, we humans are discovering more and more about ourselves, about the past and, indeed, about what we may expect in the future. This may not be of interest to everybody but the human race is forging ahead to unimaginable discoveries, though our final destiny may well remain a mystery for millennia to come. But my purpose here is to tell you about myself and my neighbours in the Blackmountain and in the Glenfarne valley generally and what they accomplished during their lifetime.

As I have said already, some put in a huge effort. Others not so much so. But then who is to say what the correct philosophy of life is. There is an Irish seanfhocal which says: *"Ní lia duine ná tuairim"* ("A person is no more than an opinion"). And this seems to sum it up neatly enough.

One thing is certain: there was never much to forage in the heathery, cíoby hills of Leitrim. So there should not be any sorrow for the so-called good old days then. It wasn't until the cow came along and butter was churned that a little comfort was possible for the peasant. I used to hear about ferkins of butter being found in the bog. And there was a mountain trail for selling it at certain destinations. This enabled the people to make a little money.

Strangely, there is no evidence of people dying of hunger during the Famine in the Blackmountain and Dubh area generally. There was a workhouse in Manorhamilton, but this, in itself, is not evidence that they were actually dying of hunger. John Donald Mc Dermott, who died in 1955 and was still living in the ancestral home of the Seán Mac Diarmada clan, used to tell about a man in Famine times coming into the house during Ould Donald's (that is, his father's) time and getting oatmeal and a turnip to eat and heading up Thor mountain, never to be heard of again. He was probably on his way to Derry to get the boat to emigrate. My granduncle Cormac Mc Dermott who was born in 1857 and died in 1946 said that no one actually died of hunger. He said that the blight was not as severe in the area and was later in coming. And they were fortunate enough to have a corn mill in Manorhamilton where the mart is now. It would appear that they had a "seal" (period) as they used to call it locally to do the grinding of the corn if they were lucky enough to grow some during the Famine. This would have helped to keep them from starvation during the Famine. (See the story in Chapter 9 about John Pat Owen who set the place on fire.)

One of the things that strikes me forcefully about my time in the Blackmountain is the huge effort that the women put into the running of the farms. In many cases they were the real managers and their husbands tended to be rootabouts, creating a lot of unnecessary hardship. And were it not that God in His mercy called them to their eternal reward a bit early they would have killed off their wives with all the drudgery. I can think of half a dozen such women who, when their husbands passed on, managed to live into their nineties, long enough to see the so-called good times and a "roughness of money" as my mother used to call it.

I have just watched a programme about country life as they like to depict it. This is in Muckross Park. The whole setting is perfect – a beautifully thatched house, a large open hearth with a glowing fire, nicely dressed women doing all the chores like baking, washing and spinning – how it annoyed me. I know it is for the tourists, but how different real country living was, as I hope I have demonstrated. There were two million mud cabins in Ireland around the Famine.

Chapter Twenty-Three

Covid 19 and Blackmountain

WHEN WE ALL THOUGHT THAT WE IN Ireland had left the recession behind us, when it cost the tax payer 60 billion to bail out the banks, here comes this pandemic Covid 19. It has literally brought us to our knees. Just as in the case of the Black Death and the Spanish flu, no one can explain how a good and merciful God, as we are assured He really is, should permit such a scourge to hit the human race. This remains the huge mystery of human existence. Some writers suggest that creation is the fall of God as it were – that if He had not bothered with it, so much suffering, pain and unhappiness would have been avoided. Pure speculation, of course. How something can come from nothing is a puzzle that will remain with us for millennia to come.

The story of the development of life on earth has been for the most part one of slow, steady change. Every creature has spent its entire life being tested by its environment. But to make matters worse, this gradual change has been violently interrupted at certain points by such calamities as Covid 19. And, even worse, every hundred million years or so, after all the evolution so painstakingly brought about, something cata-strophic happens – a mass extinction. Let us hope this Covid 19 is not part of it. Such mass extinctions have happened five times in life's four billion-year history.

We, in the Blackmountain, were not aware of this. We just got on with it – the endless chores of subsistence farming. Whatever good there was in the world around us – and there was plenty of it; look at all the big houses and estates that the landlords had – we were at the tail end of things. We were certainly being tested by our environment and there was little we could do about it except become a revolutionary like Seán MacDiarmada who sacrificed his life to try and improve the material comforts as well as the spiritual lives of his fellow Irish men. It appears that perpetual conflict is of the essence of all creaturehood. Look at the way the animals treat one another. Are we to be different simply because of our rationality? The answer to all these questions is far away in the future. As it is, power and might seem to be the dominant factor in our lives, though there are signs that it may be changing.

TS Eliot's line about having the experience but missing the meaning should be a spur to us not to let the Covid 19 experience pass us by in vain. What is it saying to us? In what direction is it pointing us? Should it bring a new alertness to the earth, our common home? The virus has certainly brought the environment agenda to the fore. Pope Francis' line in *Laudato Si*, whose fifth anniversary occurs this year, certainly rings through: everything is connected. Human frailty and the woundedness of our planet have revealed a great poverty that calls for humility, care and co-operation. Linked with this is a new global consciousness. None of us – individuals, states, churches – can resolve issues on our own. We need to work together. We have learned that technology is a "must". We didn't have it in the Blackmountain of my time. How useful it would have been if we had. When I was over at the Barrs' quarry looking for my sheep, it would have been marvellous to be able to ring my brother over in the Corranmore braes, Seán MacDiarmada country, to say that I had found them. What time it would have saved. Now, luckily, though we have to remain separated, we have our mobile phones and our streaming which makes it possible for all of us to come together in virtual form and for a lot of people this is almost all they want – that is, they like to avoid people as much as possible. Søren Kierkegaard, the eminent philosopher and existentialist, said that hell was other people. He'd be completely at home with our new technology which brings us together without being together, as it were.

Solidarity and subsidiarity have become central in our thinking on how to handle this pandemic – qualities that were very evident in our daily lives in the Blackmountain of my early years in the first half of the twentieth century. The European Commission President Ursula von der Leyen has said that Europe has become "the world's beating heart of solidarity that will likely redefine our politics, our geopolitics and possibly globalisation itself." And long may this continue so.

I think this is a fitting chapter to end this history of my ancestral townland and home as well as Seán Mac Diarmada's. I just pray that all those souls gone before me may face the rising sun as John McGahern, our greatest novelist, and a Leitrim man, wished for his characters in that great novel of his: "That they may face the rising sun."

Afterword:
Further reminiscences

Note: the four texts in this section, included here for the sake of completeness, were originally written as free-standing pieces, separate both from each other and from the book as a whole. As a result, there will be some overlap in subject matter with parts of the main book.

WEE JOHN AND HIS BROTHER DENIS

Now that we are in the 21st century and moving quickly forward with our many celebrities getting more than their fair share of attention, it is opportune to look back on the last century and examine some of the great people who lived then and are now forgotten.

In the 19th and 20th century we, in Ireland, were largely a rural population eking out a bare existence, often on poor land such as we have in many parts of Leitrim. I'm thinking of the men and women who worked the land to provide for their children and only too frequently had to take the emigrant ship when they reached the age of sixteen or seventeen because there were no jobs for them outside agriculture, and the family farm could only sustain one, if even that.

Two such people were wee John and his brother Denis McDermott who were born towards the end of the 19th century to big John McDermott and his wife Nora in the town-land of Blackmountain, ancestral townland of Seán MacDiarmada's family.

Wee John was an expert handler of the loy and the scythe, but being the man he was, he soon laid them aside and bought

198

a mowing machine and plough. He was one of the first in the area to do so. Many of the neighbours never managed to buy either. They hadn't the resources to do so or the grass to feed the horse that would pull the single-horse mowing machine. Indeed, some people were not happy with the way that the machine cut the grass or the sod that the plough turned. They felt that they could do a neater job with the scythe and the loy. Old ways change slowly, but wee John persisted. Very soon a pole was put in the mowing machine by his brother Denis and it now became a two-horse mowing machine which made the job much easier. You could down several acres of meadow with the two horses whereas the single horse was always struggling. Similarly, you could cover an acre of seed with a team of horses in one day.

Wee John was the only ploughman and the only man with a double-horse mowing machine in the whole Dubh area. This showed his pioneering spirit and his great courage and tenacity – a man certainly before his time. It was possible to cover an acre of seed in one day with the plough. This could be 15 cwt of seed whereas with the loy you'd be hard put to cover a few stone.

Holding the plough was no easy task and wee John was the man who had the skill to do it. Nobody else appeared too anxious to learn the skill. They knew only too well you'd be thrown here and there with the horses finding it hard to pull evenly in the tough sinewy Blackmountain shallow soil with the daub near the surface. The driver was important and Jack Hughie Dinny was the best driver. Wee John ploughed for people like John Joe McMorrow, Francie Dermott, Maurice McPartland and Pat Gilgunn.

Wee John also reclaimed about 12 acres of land which Francie McSharry said God had failed to do. The plotman, as he was called, who lived in Bundoran was a man called Mr Doherty and he oversaw the drainage. The department paid the princely sum of one shilling and sixpence per perch. And believe you me, it was hard work. You first had to take off over one foot of top soil which almost surely contained some daub in the shallow Blackmountain land with the Leitrim loy and then you took out what they called a spit about eight inches deep and the same width leaving about four inches of a ledge on each side upon which you placed a flag, or failing that a cíbby sod with the cíb turned downwards and the then you filled it in. The water would run in this and help to dry the field. It did work. You could see the difference. These fields were ploughed for potatoes the first year and for corn the following year. A meitheal was needed for the setting of the potatoes each year. You had to have people to drop the seed and someone to walk the sod after the plough to keep it from rolling back. I was the sod walker each year and you certainly had to be fit for it. These sinewy, rooted sods kept rolling back until Denis, John's brother, the handy man put a contraption on the mould board which scored the rooted sod and kept it in position over the seed.

Denis, for his part, was the handy man in the area. He was multi-talented. He could turn his hand to anything. This was a real boon to the area. They came from far and near to his workshop. He roofed houses, wired them for electricity when the scheme came to the area, repaired watches and clocks, made spinning wheels for the Vocational Educational Committees and even harnessed the Corr na bhfeannóg river and had his own electricity before the ESB came along. He also made a threshing machine which was used in the area. There was no limit to his inventiveness.

It was the combination of these two brothers which made life easier for many people in the neighbourhood and beyond, many of whom were struggling to eke out a hand to mouth existence on the poor, dauby soil which wouldn't let down the water.

Only those of us who lived through the greater part of the twentieth century which had two world wars, the war to gain independence, the civil war and the economic war can appreciate the difference two men of the calibre, of wee John and Denis can make to the welfare of a community that had little going for them in the material sense, especially in the last century when there were no jobs outside scraping a living from a reluctant soil which only responded to the best conditions that nature could provide – there were no artificial manures to boost the crops. What a boon it was to have men who pioneered new ways of doing things which brought that little more comfort to suffering humanity. Wee John never got paid for his mowing or ploughing and Denis got very little for his work also. For instance, he got a mere one shilling for charging a wet battery. The best money he ever got was for the spinning wheels he made.

Since the rural Ireland that we the older citizens knew is on the way out, we will not hear about men like wee John and his brother Denis again. I don't hear any one talking about scythe stones any more, setting potatoes, cutting turf or keeping hens or turkeys, or milking cows through the fields. These jobs are relegated to the waste bins of modern living and shouldn't we be glad. They made slaves of the people. Imagine the hardship of chasing cows through wet fields morning and evening for a few porringers of milk from each of them, or turning up grass cocks on a middling day only to see a shower coming in scardán. It has to be experienced to be understood.

The sad part is that the houses, except for a few, are all in ruins. The one native occupant in the townland of Blackmountain, ancestral home of Seán MacDiarmada's family, is Oweney Kilkenny, "the sad historian of the pensive plain", as Oliver Goldsmith described a similar scene in *The Deserted Village*.

Not alone should people like wee John and Denis be remembered. All the peoples' houses which are now in ruins should be marked with all the names of the last inhabitants. They deserve this little compliment just like the people on the Blasket islands off the Kerry coast whose houses can still be seen. In the townland of Blackmountain you have the Eddies house, Donalds (ancestral home of Seán MacDiarmada's clan), Moores, Clancys, Wee Johns, Burns, Kilkennys, Keoghans, Johnny Dermotts (cousin of Seán), three Walsh families (Tommy, James and Peter), Joe Clancys, Dinnies, another Kilkenny family (Pat Kilkenny) and a Mac Morrow family. They should all be remembered fondly. They lived in hard times but they faced life with a resilience that has to be seen to be appreciated. And I saw it. And wee John McDermott was my father and Denis my Uncle.

MOUNTAIN BYRES

I don't know if mountain byres are special to Leitrim. I suspect that they are not. But there is no doubt there were several of them in the townland of Blackmountain, ancestral townland and home of Seán MacDiarmada's people. John Donald McDermott, cousin of Seán MacDiarmada and last resident in the ancestral home, had one; so also had the three Moores, his next-door neighbours. Paddy Clancy next to the Moores also had a mountain byre and he had to move the hens up to it when the crops were growing down at the dwelling house because they would scrape them apart. We, the wee John Farrells (McDermott), had one. Indeed, we could almost claim to have two because on the first hill above the house we had another byre besides the one at the house. Tommy Kilkenny had one and also Joe Clancy.

There is no doubt that these byres served the purpose of housing the cows near the rough grazing of cíb and heather which could be very useful if the hay ran out in the early spring. There was always a bite to be got there, even though it was not very nourishing, when the better pasture further down was skint.

We also discovered that the cows were very content there because there were no disturbing sounds which were usual around the house like buckets rattling which created the expectation of something to eat. However, the one great disadvantage was that it created a lot of drudgery in having to carry up hay up to them if there wasn't enough saved in the mountain meadows.

We kept sheep on the mountain and were continually passing our mountain byre. It was a halfway resting place between our house and the mountain. Sometimes you'd be exhausted after travelling the mountain looking for the sheep and delighted to reach the warmth of the byre with the heat of the cows radiating through it. You might even lie down at a cow's head for a while. There was even the idea that if the cow licked your hair you'd get curls. If there was a blizzard blowing it was a tremendous feeling to reach the sanctuary of the byre.

The trail to Thor mountain from our house passed these two byres and they were welcome shelters from passing showers as we made our way up to gather the sheep. They also provided dung for the potato crop each year – a great relief, because if we hadn't it up there, we'd have had to cart it up a steep hill from the byre at the house, putting pressure on the mare in the process.

In the 1950s ours was the only byre in operation. We kept six cows in it in the winter and many's the morning we found a calf in the sink, the poor cow having calved without any help during the night. This often necessitated the heavy job of carrying the calf down to the house. But these were the years when real hardship accompanied peasant farming. There was no way you could avoid it. The weaponry was primitive. All these byres had to be thatched with rushes which were cut with the scythe, that instrument of torture, and carried on your back and fastened into scraws with scollops to keep the wind from stripping the roof.

How they managed to get stones to build these mountain byres remains a mystery as, indeed, the stones to build the houses because there are none readily available in the vicinity. Dragging them from the Barr's quarry remains a possibility. A man named Oweney Power (Walsh), an exceptionally strong man, who lived in a house now known as Keoghans, was reputed to have carried two large stones for the brace in the house from the Barr's quarry high up on Thor mountain, when the man with him failed to carry his. He is also reputed to have got in between the shafts of a cart in Blacklion when the man he had borrowed the horse from fell out with him and took the horse from him and pulled it the whole way to the

Blackmountain. After the Keoghans vacated the house it was used as a byre by my Uncle Jack Hughie Dinny (McMorrow) for several years before it came into the possession of Oweney Kilkenny. The house is now a mansion owned by somebody in Dublin. The once poverty-stricken County Leitrim is now becoming a haven for people who want to get away from it all, even in houses buried in afforestation as this house is.

There's no telling what you'll see if you live long enough. Houses such as Keoghans would have been associated with poverty. As it is, none of the locals would live in it.

Not alone will mountain byres not be needed in the future, the slatted shed will disappear too, as will the suckler herd as it is no longer sustainable in the present market conditions. Just imagine it – a countryside without cattle.

Thor mountain from Blacklion

THE TRINITY

There they were, the three brothers, living happily on the banks of a tributary of the Corr na bhfeannóg river which rises in Healy's askey at the foot of Thor mountain and winds its way down by Eddies turf bank on the one side and Healy's on the other side. It swings around cnocán bhan, under which lies black slate which was once used for brick-making when Glenfarne factory first opened and was later used for road making when the timber was been taken out of Healy's forestry. Then it has to pass Healy's alt and its first waterfall where I often shot a woodcock. After that you have the sweat house where many an early inhabitant sweated the bad from his bones in the hope of curing some ailment or other, past Eddie Pat Jimmy's house and down to Poll an Easa which mérined the land of the three brothers.

There is no spectacular scenery in this area of the Blackmountain. You can, no doubt see Munakill lake between you and Scardán and the tips of the Glencar mountain peaks and you have a direct view of Dubh mountain and Brennan's quarry where Michael Ambrose and Tommy the Butt spent many a long winter's day sitting on a beirtín of hay breaking stones for the County Council. But that is about it. The land is rough, heathery and cíbby with but little nourishment in it except for the wandering sheep foraging for the odd bite along its banks. It might manage to feed a few stirks for a couple months in the summer, but as my mother Mary Hughie Dinny was wont to say they'd be very slow to bull. Some times milk cows grazed it for a month or so also to give the lowlands a chance to recover from over-grazing in the early spring. It was very "proofy", as they used to describe it – you got a great test for your milk in Mullán creamery, gaining an extra penny on the gallon, but this was offset by the lower quantity of milk. The cíob and heather was reputed to be very healthy for the cattle and warded off the TB which affected cattle as well as humans. This is possibly because of the nature of the soil, peat, which doesn't harbour any germs or other deleterious matter.

All the people have land running up the mountain, have a right to grazing there and have turbury rights also. You can see all the the paths to the bog as they call the place where they cut their turf.

To get to the residence of the three brothers you follow the Kilty road leaving Manorhamilton behind you, turning left at Ambroses, up past the black hollow, past Felies, Towny-inshinagh school, Biddie's bridge and in to the right through Jack Hughie Dinny's gate. A bridge constructed by wee John Farrell takes you across the Corr na bhfeannóg river and up the cutting, through the windy gap and in by the great palms to the house which is set snugly beside a big laurel bush and an alt and waterfall a little further up towards the mountain.

There they are ensconced in this once comfortable holding when the original family was much bigger and the mother was alive and kept them all working the land. When the mother died, the other members of the family emigrated, leaving just the three brothers.

To all outward appearances they pass the days happily enough. They are always referred to as Bob, Nixon and Jimmy, in that order, though Jimmy is the eldest and should properly be given the seniority. Bob, "the youngest", is the one who faces the public and does the messages. He buys the groceries in Hughie's shop, takes the milk to Mullán creamery with the mare and cart and goes to Manorhamilton occasionally where he has a meat-tea in Daisy Nixon's and tells jokes about Daisy when he comes home. She's about the only female company he ever has, with the exception of Rose Ann in Hughie's shop who is very nice to him and gives him the messages on tick till his brother Nixon sells the sheep. Nixon's only outing is to the two sheep fairs in Manorhamilton each year – the 12th of August and the 12th of September. He is a wonderful salesman and always succeeds in knocking that bit extra from the cute dealers which surpasses the best that the neighbours can manage for their wether lambs and old ewes who have seen better days.

Nixon always buys a rig-out for these great annual outings. They are usually spectacular colours like blue or green and a good belt. (I dont think he ventured out to do the shopping himself; it was almost certainly Bob who did the buying for him.) Except for the two fairs, I never saw Nixon out anywhere. As my mother puts it: "he attends neither mass, meeting or service." Of course, it's not unusual for bachelor boys to withdraw a bit from society and, in a sense, what's wrong with it? What's out there for you if you haven't a partner and family? However, whatever reticence Nixon has about meeting the public disappears when he takes to the road with the sheep and he is completely in command when he stands behind the súgán – tied sheep pushed tightly together up against Campbell's wall to make them look bigger and heavier than they actually are.

Days on end are spent scouring every nook and cranny on Thor mountain to gather up the sheep for the fairs. It is the only chance that the sheepmen have to get a few bob to buy clothing and shoes, especially shoes, for the bare-footed children for the coming winter. Though there are other fairs around – in Lurganboy and Dowra in particular – Manorhamilton attracts the most jobbers and there is a better chance of a sale, except for the odd year when you can sell nothing. The sheep are out on the mountain and can stray anywhere, though it is possible to settle them on certain sections of the mountain like Healy's askey, Mc Girrill's askey, between the two Thors, the head of Mc Guire's or Paddy Frank's land, the bin or the quarry

Mortality is high. Many lambs fall into cracks in the bog and ewes get stuck in sloughs. The community effort among the sheepmen helps people to puzzle out where their losses might occur. Each flock owner has a special mark – we have a "D" on the right hip; the three brothers have an "x" on the left shoulder and John Joe has a "M" on the middle of the left side and so on. Indeed, some people have an ear mark also – we have a punched hole in each ear. So anything found dead could point to the owner and save much searching.

After the great round – up all the sheep are put on our big hill the night before for an easy get – away in the early morning as the field mérins the main road. There is usually after – grass there and it is hoped that the sweet taste of this will keep them quiet during the night so that they wont escape back to their friends on the mountain. The three brothers, John Joe Mc Morrow and other neighbours put their sheep there along with ours.

We, the young cubs in the locality, are expected to be on full alert for these annual sheep fairs. Not only have we to do the running on the mountain, but we have to do the running on the fair morning also. The expectation and the excitement is so great that we are unable to sleep much the night before though we know that we will have an early rise. We'd have to be moving before six o' clock. The first problem is getting the sheep counted in the half light. The odd one is bound to escape, but the aftergrass is sweet compared to the heather and cíob, so even a wild one separated from her friends is reluctant to leave it.

The two Huberts (Hubert McDermott and Hubert Keown)
and Seán McDermott

We do the best we can. John Joe usually arrives first on his bicycle and rounds them up on the top of the hill. Nixon, the salesman for the three brothers, arrives in his new colour-ful regalia. We eventually get them out on the road and the running starts. All the cubs are expected to be to the forefront in the chase. This normally includes the two Huberts (Hubert in Jacks and my brother), John Joe in Jacks and my good self. The purpose of the run is not to give them the time to cross the ditch or turn up the Blackmountain road and escape to the mountain. The trouble is the weak one that lags behind and often lies down when the going gets too much. Sometimes this one has to be carried, creating an almost unsurmountable problem, or worse has to be abandoned altogether. John Joe Mc Morrow has the advantage of having the bike, but we have to do the running on shank's mare. Poor Nixon can't keep up at all and is out of breath. He decides to take the near cut across by Bob Nixons and hopes to rejoin us when he comes out at the Protestant school. John Joe offers him the bicycle, but he can't ride a bike so he has to suffer on the whole way to Manor-hamilton.

When we reach Willie Mc Morrows, we have to be careful not to mix with the sheep from Ballaghnabehy which could be trying to beat us to the best position for showing off our sheep in the fair. We are anxious to have tied – up against Campbell's wall which is considered the best position in the fair: "*muna mbíonn ach gabhar agat, bí i lár an aonaigh leis*" (even if you only a goat be in the middle of the fair with it).

Sometimes the dealers meet you out the road and bid you. This is just a ploy. They know that you are unlikely to accept it. They often bid you more than you expect, but this just leads you to believe that the trade is good and you hold out. Very often you don't get anything like that at the fair. The dealers hold back, form a ring and wear the sellers out, often spreading rumours that the market has collapsed; the jittery sellers get nervous and sell and it is only a matter of time till the others follow suit. Poor people haven't much choice; if they don't sell at these two fairs, they probably wont sell at all that year. What a predicament they are in: they haven't a notion what happens further on down the food chain. This is a well-kept secret known only to the jobbers; this is a case of knowledge being power. Jimmy Walsh, a local, describes the situation very dramatically. "He brought the sheep to the 12th August in Manorhamilton and was getting £3 a head for his wether lambs; he didn't take it; he brought them out again on the 12th September and couldn't get anything like that and he traipsed out again to Dowra, stood all day on the fair green soaked to the skin and never got a bid. And when the stars were in the sky and the frost bitting the air he had to accept £2 a head for them. That's the way it was for the primary producer; he was totally in the dark and at the mercy of the jobbers."

Nixon always holds out: "God damn it; you're not giving half enough; what do you think I am – a fool to give away my stock for a pittance like that?"

The dealer walks away disgusted: "You do not want to sell them."

"Come back, you're getting them," somebody shouts.

The dealer pretends not to hear and keeps going. Somebody catches hold of him and drags him back as he struggles to release himself. Nixon shouts: "You'll have to bid me right."

As the struggling jobber is hauled back he shouts, "I told you that you mustn't want to sell them," and he breaks free and makes a run for it again. But Nixon shows no sign of yielding even though the three of them need the money badly. Nixon's firmness usually pays off and he manages to get the extra few bob.

Bob and Jimmy wait patiently at home for Nixon and are delighted to get the news of the fair when he arrives home. When we cubs arrive home, we can't wait to get up to their house to partake in the drama recounting the activities of the fair and the verbal exchanges of the sellers and dealers. "Ai, God Ai it was a bully fair: the lad got a top price: McKeever from Louth was there again this year; a top buyer he is too; he never noticed the rumbusted one they were so close together." The farmers are trying to shift less than perfect sheep and they want to sell them all in the one bunch. If any are culled you get very little for them and it brings down the overall average, so it is important to sell them all together if possible. They're also very reluctant to sell to a neighbour because other neighbours might be saying he got them cheap. Jimmie is a great storyteller and does it with great drama, landing a big spit in the heart of the open fire with great effect to clinch the telling, though he hasn't been seen out in public for over forty years. Then he turns to great characters of earlier times. He loves telling about the rouser McGrath and Francie George who were great fighters and took over the fairs in their haydays. He enjoys himself, sitting there on his creepy, having no sense of time because they have no clock; and when you rise to go at 2 am, perhaps, he claims it is only early in the night and is very disappointed

When they have turf, which is seldom, Jimmy makes three journeys to the head of the land for three creels of turf each day and keeps shouting at an imaginary dog: "Come up... Hep... Come back behind." I occasionally meet him in the mist on the mountain and he immediately goes down on one knee on the wet ground and we have a lively conversation about Jimmy's great heroes of the past. I have great trouble in getting away from him. He never wears a coat, frequently gets drenched and never changes his clothes, but is always in the best of humour.

The Protestant minister calls occasionally and leaves the sacred bread in a bowl on the dresser for Jimmy who always manages to be absent when he comes. After the fairs are over, Jimmy and Nixon rely on Bob for any bit of news that is going.

Nixon has one neighbourly act he has to do every Friday. John Donal McDermott has to collect his pension in Manorhamilton, but he is badly crippled and unable to get up on the cart; in fact, his two legs are completely crossed on one and another; as he puts it himself, he has to turn the backside of his trousers away from him in order to get them on. Nixon does him the good turn of helping him up on the cart where he has to kneel behind the box with the rains in his hands and drive the wildest mare imaginable through seven gates to the county road, managing to open them and close them using a loop on the end of a stick. John Donal is known far and wide because of his disability which is most unusual. Once in the upright position with his two sticks firmly in his hands, and despite his crossed legs with the outside of his feet to the fore, he is able to edge himself forward and make his way to the bog more than a half mile away, get in on the bank and cut turf all day log and he can't sit down because he would'nt be able to get up unaided; he similarly saves the hay while standing all day long.

When he safely makes it to the county road, as it is called, he gives a lift to anyone going his way. He careers up and down the town, gets his pension brought out and several whiskeys plus the flat loaf – the box-loaf, as he describes them – and heads for home again in the evening, giving a lift to anyone who wants it. Once again Nixon is on hand to get him off the cart, the mare untackled, and put him safely in the corner where Bizzie, his sister, sees to his needs.

As the three brothers grow older they have great difficulty getting the chores done. The house isn't thatched; the byres fall down; the hay isn't saved; Jimmy no longer goes for three creels of turf; nor can he be heard shouting at the imaginary dog around the alt; the great annual fares in Manorhamilton no longer bother Nixon, nor the yearly outfit. Bob, the young-est (the lad, as they refer to him), does his best to keep things going, but gradually everything disintegrates. The family who loved visits, for whom time meant little, are now being destroyed by time. The folk heroes are in serious decline; their likes will never again be seen.

Around this time an uncle of mine, Denis Hughie Dinny, comes home from America who remembers the three brothers from his youth and has a sense of their uniqueness. He was a heavy whiskey drinker. Sometimes his brothers and sisters would have to sit up all night with him to accompany him in his bouts of drinking. Everything and anything would be open for discussion. My mother, his sister, didn't like his wayward ways. One night she was explaining to Denis that there were three divine persons in one God which she described as the great mystery of the Trinity. Denis – the Yanky, as he was better known – was not impressed. The retort was quick and sharp. "Ah! The three Moores – Bob, Nixon, and Jimmy."

OBITUARY OF AGNES KEOGHAN

Death of Agnes Keoghan, Glenkeel, Kiltyclogher, County Leitrim

Tuesday 5th November 2019 sadly saw the demise of the last of the Hughie Dinny Phaidí dynasty of thirteen children, namely the death of Agnes Keoghan (née Mc Morrow) of Glenkeel, Kiltyclogher, Co Leitrim.

Agnes (otherwise known as Baby) was the second youngest of thirteen children born to Rose Ann Johnny Farrell (Mc Dermott) of Lisnagroagh, Manorhamilton and Hughie Dinny Phaidí (Mc Morrow) of Cornmore, Kiltyclogher.

Hughie (her father) and Seán Mac Diarmada were first cousins.

Rose Ann (Baby's mother) was reared by her uncle, Hughie Farrell (Mc Dermott) whose house was built on the banks of the Corr na bhfeannóg river which rises in Healy's askey at the foot of Thor mountain and eventually flows into Lough Mac Nean in Glenfarne village. Her father, Johnny Farrell, was married twice, first to Kate Mc Loughlin of Townylust Barr and secondly to Sarah Mc Morrow of Blackmountain. Rose Ann belonged to the first family and moved to her uncle as he had no family and heir when her father married the second time. Her brother, known as John Johnny, married a sister of his father's wife called Cecily. This was the unusual case of father and son marrying two sisters. (Joe Dermott and Michael Dermott, as they were popularly known, were products of the second coupling.) The man known locally as Francie Dermott, married to Maggie Mc Caffrey, was a son of John Johnny's and Kate Dermott was a daughter. Kate married twice. Her first husband was John Biddy Mc Dermott who died during the great flu of 1918. They had one daughter, Molly, known for her beauty, who married John Roughneen who taught for a while in Tawnyinsinagh national school before moving to Kiltimagh. She then married Eddie Mc Dermott with whom she had eleven children of whom only Roslleen (England) is still with us, Michael having died recently.

Baby, as she is more popularly known, was married to Paddy Keoghan (predeceased) in Glenkeel, who was the first to have a car in the area after the demise of Farrell McDermott's which was around in the early 1920s and took people to dances and weddings.

Hughie Dinny Phaidí and Rose Ann Johnny Farrell (Baby's parents) married in 1900. Hughie was known as a *cliamhain isteach* – that is, he married into Hughie Farrell's place which Hughie had given to Rose Ann because he had no family himself.

Soon after marrying they started a shop which was destined to serve the area (known as the Dubh area) well into the 'fifties. This became a famous meeting place for all the Dubh lads. They congregated there in the cart shed when they came to buy their ten woodbines in the evenings when they had foddered

The eldest in the McMorrow family Mary (my mother) married Wee John Farrell (McDermott), her next door neighbour who lived on the hill across the Corr na bhfeannóg river; Maggie married Maurice McPartland; Brigid married Willie Keaney; Lizzie Frank McGourty; Baby Paddy Keoghan; Jack Brigid Gilbride; Hughie (Sonny) Nora O Sullivan, a Kerry woman; Annie Michael Ambrose (McDermott). Denis and Stephen did not marry. They were a formidable crew who worked very hard and helped out in the shop also. There was great poverty in the area but Rose Ann (the mother) was a very kind woman who saw nobody needy. But like all great dynasties the family found it difficult to emulate the success of their parents. Eventually country shops were superseded by the travelling shops.

Interestingly, Hughie's original family – the Dinny Phaidí's of Cornmore from whom Mary, Seán MacDiarmada's mother, came – had a shop also at the bridge which served the people of Cornmore and surrounding area for many years

Paddy Keoghan and Baby had a large family: Hubert, Seán, Pat, Andrew (who died as a baby), Desmond, Francis (who predeceased Baby), Denis, Mary, Eileen and Martina. I offer them my sincere sympathy in parting with a mother who was there for them all in keeping a home to which they were all welcome to return and they, on their part, rang her daily.

Rose Ann with Francis and Elizabeth

She was a bridge between the old and the new. She saw the days of little money and the hardship of saving hay and turf with primitive weaponry like the scythe, the loy and the sleán, but she was also destined in her long life to see the Celtic Tiger which threw money around in all directions.

She often described how she had to bake four large brown cakes in the oven on the open-hearth fire (often with bad turf) to put bread on the table for her large family.

Baby, like Máire Mhac an Tsaoi, could claim to be almost the same age as the State. Thankfully, she missed the civil war, but lived through the rigours of the economic war and the Second World War when she spent some time in England and trained as a nurse before returning to marry Paddy Keoghan in Glenkeel. Herself and Maggie McLoughlin were frequent visitors to my mother Mary Hughie Dinny (McMorrow) in the Blackmountain after the death of my father in 1970. This was much appreciated.

Baby has left 36 grandchilren, 16 great grandchildren and over 40 first cousins among many more relatives after her. She is the last of two great dynasties: the Hughie Dinny's of Dubh and the Dinny Phaidíe's of Cornmore, all second cousins of Seán Mac Diarmada. *Ní bheidh a leithéid ann arís. In iothlainn Dé go gcastar sinn. Ba Aintín iontach dom í. D'fhán mé léi go minic nuair a bhínn thíos i gCondae Liatroma. Mothóidh mé uaim go géar í.*

A large congregation thronged the church in Kiltyclogher on Friday morning last. The mass was celebrated by her grand-nephew, Father Gerard O Connor CSsR, assisted by Fathers Maurice Mc Morrow (cousin), Quinn, Sexton and Farrelly. Afterwards she was laid to rest in the cemetery in Kiltyclogher. *Ar dheis Dé go raibh a h-ainm dílis.*

The community centre provided food after the burial.

The local choir, under the direction of Olive Gallagher (retired NT), sang some lovely hymns and the soloist, Mícheál Shanley, sang inspiringly. At the graveside in the cemetery, he played the last salute to gently send Aunty Baby on her way. *Solas síoraí di ar lámh dheis Dé.*

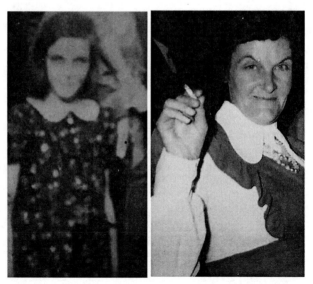

Agnes "Baby" Keoghan: in 1934 (left); and in later times (right).

Glossary of Irish and other unusual Words

Pardóga	Panniers
Spraoi	spree
Mérin	boundary between farms
Sheugh	drain
Meitheal	working group
Loy	spade
Sleán	turf spade
Spancel	rope for tying cow
Barr	top/highground
Hoose	cough in cattle
Clábar	muck
Eouges day's work	big day's work
Bád ban	emigrant ship
Seisc	sedge
Cíob	rough wine-coloured grass
Ceannabhán	bog cotton
Spadar	sodden turf. Turf lying on the bog bank from the year before
Galar	disease
In iothlainn Dé go gcastar sinn	may we meet in God's haggard
Ní bheidh a léithéidí arís ann	their likes will not be there again

Suaimhneas síoraí da n-anamacha	eternal rest to their souls
Cnoc na ráithní	the hill of the fern
Cnoc na cearta	the hill of the forge
Snig	to pull along the ground. "Snigging cocks of hay".
Seal	period
Tangler	a jobber /bargain-seeker at a fair. Suggestion of unfairness, if not worse.
Brash	helping at churning-moving the dash to shake the milk to bring the butter on.
Slounging	cosied up in bed when you should be working
Bibeanna	bibs
T na G	Teilifís na Gaeilge (television in the Irish language), Irish TV channel, known as TG4 since 1999.
IRC	Irish Royal Constabulary; more properly known as RIC (Royal Irish Constabulary)
Teagasc	an organisation dealing with agriculture
Bonham	young pigl
Strumped	dead
Scéalta fada gáisce	long stories of bravery
Slow coat	slow coach
Bootree	local name for flowering tree with soft inside
Naggin	small whiskey bottle
Sruthán	stream

Setting potatoes	planting them
V. E. C.	vocational education committee
Kilty	short for the village of Kiltyclogher where Seán Mac Diarmada's memorial is.
Cutting	reducing a steep hill by cutting through it
Haggard	A specially-prepared place for securing the harvest
Iothlainn De	God'd harvest of the blessed in Heaven
Crosscut	a long-handled blade with a handle at both ends worked with two people to cut timber.
Stirk	a year-old heifer or bullock. (Heifer as used in book.)
Garraí glas	green garden
Near cut	short cut to a place
Matt Talbot	A Dublin man – reformed alcoholic who led an ascetic life.
Patrick Kavanagh	Irish poet and novelist of distinction
Padro Pio	A priest who had the stigmata
Harpers	a type of shoe worn outdoors
Ar dheis Dé go raibh a anam.	'May his soul be at the right hand of God.' – Said of a dead persion
Poll an easa	waterfall
Pissmires	flying ants
Lodge	blockage in the gut

Appendix 1: Inhabitants of the Dubh area

(This name Dubh covers several townlands whose names gradually went out of use. It's not exhaustive.)

Starting on the road known as the Line, above where Margaret McDermott now lives, we have:

1. Owen Keaveny, wife and family (beside Brennan's quarry).

2. Molly Keaveny and Tom Keaveny – sister and brother.

3. John Frank McGourty, his wife and children – Brian, John Patrick and Mary Ellen.

4. Roger Reagan (wee Roger).

5. John and Mary Ann Healy and Hugh.

6. Terry Rooney.

7. Michael McDermott.

8. Francie Boylan, wife Mary Ellen. Family: Laurence, John, Sonny, Paddy, Mary and Delia.

9. Hughie Keaney and his wife.

10. Pat Flynn and wife Rosie. Family: Mary, Maggie, Biddy, Rosie, Lizzie, Agnes, Paddy, John James, Francie, Peter (priest) and Michael.

11. Francie McSharry and wife, Agnes. Family: Peter, Frank, Liam and Mary.

12. Joseph McDermott and wife Julia. Family: Mary, Bridget, John, Patrick, Annie and Celia. Mary Theresa marries John and now have Family: Patrick, Carol, Marie.

13. Margaret McDermott and son Keven and her daughter Caroline who is married elsewhere.

14. John Francis McDermott, wife Carmel and daughter Sarah.

15. Michael Gilbride and wife Bridget. Family: Ann Marie, Elizabeth, Eugene, Johnny, Patricia. (Michael's father and mother, Owenie and Bessie had nine children: Johnny, Jimmy, Eddie, Terry, Michael, Owney, Mary Alice, and Ann.)

16. Pat McDermott (Pat Larry's).

17. James McMorrow and his wife Ann (née McGowan). Family: Rose Catherine, Molly, Patrick Joseph, Jimmy, Charlie, Vincent.

18. John McLoughlin and his wife. Family: Mary Ann, Kate, Maggie, Bridget, Hughie, Eugene and Michael

19. James Edward Evens and wife Lavinia. Family: Willie and Marian. (Willie married Kathleen from Kerry. Family: Norman, Raymond, James, Eileen. James now lives there with his wife from Dublin.)

20. Norman Evens and his wife and children.

21. Francie McDermott and his wife Maggie. Family: John Patrick, Owen, Dessie, Mary Margaret, Celia Elena and Rose.

22. Paddy Keown and his wife Agnes (Baby). Family: Hubert, Mary, Seán, Pat, Dinny, Dessie, Francis, Martina, Eileen

23. John Joe McMorrow and his wife Kate. Family: Mai, Josie, Nancy, Vera and Rose Mary.

24. Tommy Curneen and his wife Maggie – no family.

25. Johnny Cullen and his wife Bizzie. Family: Josie and Noel.

26. Patrick McGourty and his wife Maura. Family: Séamus, Éilis, Pauric and Mícheál

27. John McGourty and his wife Lizzie. Family: John Francis, Patrick, Mary Theresa.

28. Michael Ambrose McDermott and his wife Annie. Family: Anna, John, Delia, Frankie, Séamus, Rose Mary, Philomena, Therese.

29. Séamus McDermott and his wife Bridie. Family: J.J., Paul, David, Denise.

30. Jack McMorrow and his wife Bridget. Family: Hubert, Mary Theresa, Elizabeth, Imelda, Patricia, Denis, Eugene, John Joe.

31. John Dolan and his wife. Family: Mary.

32. John and James Brennan.

33. Felie and Ellen (brother and sister who had a shop).

34. Hubert McMorrow and his wife Mai. Family: Majella and Mary.

35. Eugene Gilbride (single).

36. Rose Mary and Brigid McGourty, sisters.

37. Three Kilkenny families.

Appendix 2: Blackmountain

Surname	Forename	Age	Sex	Birthplace	Occupation	Religion
Mac Diarmada	Patrick	71	M	County Leitrim	Farmer	Roman Catholic
Mac Diarmada	Edward	17	M	Leitrim	Farmer's Son	Roman Catholic
Mac Diarmada	Bridgid	68	F	Leitrim		Roman Catholic
Mac Diarmada	Patrick	22	M	Leitrim	Farmer's Son	Roman Catholic
Mc Dermott	Daniel	71	M	Leitrim	Farmer	R Catholic
Mc Dermott	Thomas	43	M	Leitrim	Farmers Son	R Catholic
Mc Dermott	John	39	M	Leitrim	Farmers Son	R Catholic
Mc Dermott	Beesie	33	F	Leitrim	Farmers Daughter	R Catholic
Moore	Margaret	58	F	Co Leitrim	Farming	Church Ireland
Moore	James	22	M	Co Leitrim	Farming	Church Ireland
Moore	Nixon	19	M	Co Leitrim	Farming	Church Ireland
Moore	Bob	17	M	Co Leitrim	Farming	Church Ireland
Moore	Katie	16	F	Co Leitrim	Scholar	Church Ireland
Moore	Susan	14	F	Co Leitrim	Scholar	Church Ireland
Moore	Dora	11	F	Co Leitrim	Scholar	Church Ireland
Mc Dermott	John	50	M	Co Leitrim	Farmer	Roman Catholic
Mc Dermott	Ellen	58	F	Co Leitrim		Roman Catholic
Mc Dermott	Denis	17	M	Co Leitrim	Employed on Farm	Roman Catholic

in the 1911 Census

Literacy	Irish Language	Relation to Head of Household	Marital Status	Specified Illnesses	Years Married	Children Born	Children Living
Cannot read		Head of Family	Married		31	8	
Read and write		Son	Single				
Read and write		Wife	Married		31	8	7
Read and write		Son	Single				
Read only	Irish and English	Head of Family	Widower				
Read and write		Son	Single				
Read and write		Son	Single				
Read and write		Daughter	Single				
Can read and write		Head of Family	Widow		35	12	10
Can read and write		Son	Son				
Can read and write		Son	Son				
Can read and write		Son	Son				
Can read and write		Daughter	Daughter				
Can read and write		Daughter	Daughter				
Can read and write		Daughter	Daughter				
Read and write		Head of Family	Married		20	3	2
Read and write	Irish and English	Wife	Married		20		
Read and write		Son					

Surname	Forename	Age	Sex	Birthplace	Occupation	Religion
Mc Dermott	John	15	M	Co Leitrim	Employed on Farm	Roman Catholic
Kilkenny	John	42	M	Co Leitrim		Cathlick
Kilkenny	Anne	44	F	Co Leitrim		Cathloick
Kilkenny	Owen	68	M	Co Leitrim	Farmer	Catholic
Kilkenny	Sarah	60	F	Co Leitrim		Catholic
Kilkenny	John	22	M	Co Leitrim		Catholic
Kilkenny	Thomas	15	M	Co Leitrim		Catholic
Kilkenny	Busy	14	F	Co Leitrim		Catholic
Kilkenny	Anne	10	F	Co Leitrim		Catholic
Walsh	Owen	72	M	County Leitrim	Farmer	Roman Catholic
Walsh	Catherine	69	F	County Leitrim		Roman Catholic
Walsh	John	40	M	County Leitrim	Farmers Son	Roman Catholic
Dermott	Michael	76	M	Leitrim	Farmer	Roman Catholic
Dermott	John	42	M	Leitrim	Farmer	Roman Catholic
Dermott	Rose Ellen	22	F	Leitrim		Roman Catholic
Mc Morrow	John	43	M	Co Leitrim	Farmer	Roman Catholic
Mc Morrow	Bridget	35	F	Co Leitrim		Roman Catholic
Mc Morrow	Michael Joseph	11	M	Co Leitrim	Scholar	Roman Catholic
Mc Morrow	Thomas Hugh	9	M	Co Leitrim	Scholar	Roman Catholic
Mc Morrow	Charles	7	M	Co Leitrim	Scholar	Roman Catholic

Literacy	Irish Language	Relation to Head of Household	Marital Status	Specified Illnesses	Years Married	Children Born	Children Living
Read and write	Irish and English	Son					
Read and write	English	Head of Family	Single				
Read and write	English	Sister	Single				
Read only		Head of Family	Married		24		
Read and write		Wife	Married		24	5	4
Read and write		Son	Single				
Read and write		Son	Single				
Read and write		Daughter	Single				
Read and write		Daughter	Single				
Read and write	Irish and English	Head of Family	Married				
Read and write		Wife	Married		21		
Read and write		Son	Single				
Cannot read write	Irish and English	Head of Family	Widower				
Read and write	English	Son	Married		0		
Read and write	English	Daughter in Law	Married		0		
Read and write		Head of Family	Married				
Read and write		Wife	Married		12	7	7
Read and write	Irish and English	Son					
Read and write	Irish and English	Son					
Read	Irish and English	Son					

Surname	Forename	Age	Sex	Birthplace	Occupation	Religion
Mc Morrow	Patrick	6	M	Co Leitrim		Roman Catholic
Mc Morrow	Mary	4	F	Co Leitrim		Roman Catholic
Mc Morrow	John	3	M	Co Leitrim		Roman Catholic
Mc Morrow	Martin	0	M	Co Leitrim		Roman Catholic
Mc Morrow	Denis	35	M	Co Leitrim	Farmer	Roman Catholic
Mc Morrow	Anne	25	F	Leitrim		Roman Catholic
Mc Morrow	Owen	2	M	Leitrim		Roman Catholic
Mc Morrow	Margaret	1	F	Leitrim		Roman Catholic
Walsh	Peter	69	M	Leitrim	Labourer	Roman Catholic
Walsh	Bessie	71	F	Co Leitrim		Roman Catholic
Walsh	James	30	M	Co Leitrim		Roman Catholic
Walsh	Mary	32	F	Co Leitrim		Roman Catholic
Kilkenny	Patrick	56	M	Co Leitrim	Farmer	Roman Catholic
Kilkenny	Mary	60	F	Co Leitrim		Roman Catholic
Kilkenny	Thomas	15	M	Co Leitrim		Roman Catholic
Walsh	Thomas	70	M	Co Leitrim	Farmer	Roman Catholic
Walsh	Thomas	32	M	Co Leitrim	Farmer	Roman Catholic
Walsh	Peter	30	M	Co Leitrim	Carpenter	Roman Catholic
Walsh	Michael	25	M	Co Leitrim		Roman Catholic

Literacy	Irish Language	Relation to Head of Household	Marital Status	Specified Illnesses	Years Married	Children Born	Children Living
Cannot read		Son					
Cannot read		Daughter					
Cannot read		Son					
Cannot read		Son					
Read and write	English	Head of Family	Married		3	3	2
Read and write	English	Wife	Married		3	3	2
		Son	Single				
		Daughter	Single				
Read and write	Irish and English	Head of Family	Single				
Read only		Head of Family	Widow		48		
Read and write		Son	Single				
Read and write		Daughter	Single				
Cannot read		Head of Family	Married		20	2	2
Read and write		Wife					
Read		Son					
Read and write	English	Head of Family	Widower			7	6
Read and write	English	Son	Single				
Read and write	English	Son	Single				
		Son	Single				

Appendix 3: Family tree of Seán Mac Diarmada

Jimmy McMorrow
Born: 1789
Died: 1800s

Patrick McMorrow
Born: 1813
Spouse: Anne Wrynn
Died: 12 Apr 1904

Denis McMorrow
Born: 1843
Married: 1870
Spouse: Anne Gilgun
Died: 1930s

Mary McMorrow
Born: 1845
Spouse: Donal McDermott
Died: Aug 1892

Hugh McMorrow
Born: 1875
Married: 1900
Spouse: Rose Ann McDermott
Died: 1950

Seán Mac Diarmada
Born: 28 Feb 1883
Died: 12 May 1916

Mary McMorrow
Born: 9 Aug 1903
Married: Jan 1933
Spouse: John McDermott
Died: 28 Aug 1993

Patrick McDermott
Spouse: Kathleen O'Donovan

ABOUT THE AUTHOR

The author, Patrick McDermott, is a third cousin of Seán MacDiarmada, the 1916 Easter Rising leader who was one of the signatories to the Proclamation of Irish Independence. Patrick was born in the townland of Blackmountain, which is the ancestral townland and home of Seán MacDiarmada's people. He grew up doing the same farming tasks as Seán MacDiarmada's relatives, namely, John and Bizzie McDermott, who remained in the ancestral home, when other members of the family moved to Corranmore, nearer Kiltyclogher. This is where Seán MacDiarmada was born.

Gordon Thomas grew up in Palestine. After graduating in
honours Scripture in E. . . . .
foreign correspondent
afforded him a rare op
background of the Bib
twenty-six books, incl
(with Max Morgan-W

THE TRIAL
'A SUSPENSEFUL I
SOLILOQUY . . . TAKES ON A DIMENSION FEW LAY
READERS HAVE EVER ENJOYED. THE PACE IS QUICK
AND COMPELLING. THE JESUS PRESENTED BY
THOMAS IS REAL, PAINSTAKINGLY REAL. AS A
RESULT, THE MAGNANIMITY OF HIS SACRIFICE – IN
THE VIEW OF ANYONE'S FAITH – IS
OVERWHELMING. THE AUTHOR DOES NOT DISPUTE
JESUS' DIVINITY IN PORTRAYING HIS HUMANITY'
DAVID JENSEN, THE WASHINGTON TIMES

'*The Trial* is perfect for all those people, and they are legion, who
for one reason or another feel guilty about knowing little about
the New Testament . . . A sometimes strange, often over-
powerful story, capable of reminding almost any reader why
Jesus' short life shook the world'
Douglas Todd, Vancouver Sun

'THERE ARE MANY BOOKS ABOUT THE LIFE AND
DEATH OF JESUS, BUT THERE IS NONE OTHER QUITE
LIKE THIS ONE . . . PERFECT AND ACCURATE, IT IS
AN INVITATION TO GO ON TRUSTING IN THE
GREATEST STORY TOLD BY ANY WRITER . . .
OFFERING A NEW ASSESSMENT OF THE MOST
IMPORTANT EVENT IN HISTORY . . . WILL HAVE A
PROFOUND EFFECT ON ANY READER'
REV JOHN WADDINGTON, CHURCH NEWS

THE TRIAL

The Life and Inevitable Crucifixion of Jesus

Gordon Thomas

CORGI BOOKS

THE TRIAL
A CORGI BOOK   0552 13006 0

Originally published in Great Britain
by Bantam Press, a division of Transworld Publishers Ltd.

PRINTING HISTORY

Bantam Press edition published 1987
Corgi edition published 1988

Quotations from the Bible are from the Authorised (King James) Version
for which it is claimed: 'translated out of the original tongues and with
the former translations diligently compared.'

This book is set in 10/11 Plantin

Corgi Books are published by Transworld Publishers Ltd.,
61-63 Uxbridge Road, Ealing, London W5 5SA, in Australia by
Transworld Publishers (Australia) Pty. Ltd., 15-23 Helles Avenue,
Moorebank, NSW 2170, and in New Zealand by Transworld Publishers
(N.Z.) Ltd., Cnr. Moselle and Waipareira Avenues, Henderson,
Auckland.

Printed and bound in Great Britain by
Cox & Wyman Ltd., Reading, Berks.

To Joachim Kraner
A friend who became a father-in-law yet remained a friend

Many years ago we spoke, among other things, of books. In your forthright way you said none could equal the Bible. In some embarrassment I admitted to having hardly looked at a copy since my school days. You urged me to correct the situation, adding that one of the unspoken tragedies of our times is that Bible-reading is largely a pleasure of the past. Next day I purchased a Bible.

Though you are physically no longer with us, that Bible remains a reminder of you as well as being a continuous reading experience. Itself unsurpassed literature, my Bible has led me into many Scriptural byways – which finally brought me to tell the story in these pages. It deals with the most momentous event in history, one which you also said is the greatest challenge any writer can face: to understand the form of His life insomuch as it shows us all how to live, not for a few years, but for ever.

In recounting it faithfully and reverently, I have the support of the one person you surely would have approved of as a collaborator – your daughter, Edith. Like you, she has a questing mind coupled to the faith of true belief but is concerned with neither clever explanations for the inexplicable nor attempting to interpret what defies interpretation.

The Trial of Jesus is the most interesting isolated problem which historical jurisprudence can present.
A. T. Innes, *The Trial of Jesus Christ: A Legal Monograph*

You may object that it is not a trial at all; you are quite right, for it is only a trial if I recognise it as such.
Franz Kafka, *The Trial*, 11, 'First Interrogation'

The historical question about the responsibility for Jesus' death is still wide open. There is in any case very wide agreement that there existed a religious issue between Jesus and His own people which went far deeper than an attack on the collaborating priestly aristocracy; that He brought a theological challenge of the most fundamental kind, making claims for Himself, whether directly or indirectly, which were either true or false, and if false demanded His condemnation and death.
J. P. M. Sweet, *Jesus and the Politics of His Day*
(edited by Ernest Mabbek and C. F. D. Moule)

CONTENTS

The Principal Players

Our playwright may show in some
Fifth Act what this wild drama means.

Alfred Lord Tennyson *(The Play)*

The Immediate Family

JESUS

(of Nazareth). Yeshu. His given Jewish name etymologically means 'Jehovah is the Saviour'. Exact birth date unknown, but definitely not 25 December. Newest scholarly presumption points to late summer, 12 BC, around the time Gospel 'star in the east', later called Halley's Comet, seen in sky over Bethlehem. Makes Christ close to forty when His ministry began and approaching middle-age when crucified. Spoke four languages but left no written personal record. Mesmeric public orator in spite of broad Nazarene dialect mocked by sophisticated Jerusalemites. Confined His ministry largely to countryside. Immediate followers numbered no more than seventy, including twelve He designated Apostles. All deserted Him in Garden of Gethsemane.

MARY

His mother. Only child of Anna and Joachim. Born to them during early part of reign of Herod the Great after long barren marriage. Her father one-time servant to Jerusalem Temple priests; mother member of well-established Bethlehem artisan family. Given name of Egyptian origin, Miriam, but raised in strict Hebrew tradition, ensuring word perfection in Holy Scripture. Law pronounced a girl could only marry when physically ready, usually at age of twelve and a half. May have waited a few more months before betrothal, but bore her Son when still under the age of fourteen. Typical regional physiognomy would give her remarkably dark eyes and hair, olive skin. Died some time between death of

Emperor Caligula (AD 41) and before Saint Matthew wrote his Gospel (AD 50). Fifteen hundred years later, having been designated Mother of God (AD 431), and pronounced without sin, officially proclaimed as having ascended into Heaven body and soul (AD 1950). Only her Son has the same status.

JOSEPH

His putative father. Son of Jacob, carpenter. Mother unknown. Settled in Nazareth some time between end of turbulent rule of Jewish Queen Salome Alexandra and Pompey occupying Jerusalem. Took over family business around the time Caesar assassinated on Ides of March. Onset of reign of Herod the Great and crowning of Emperor Augustus almost certainly had little effect on his lifestyle. Knew Mary's parents through common artisan background and regular synagogue worship. Details of courtship circumstantial, but married late in life, defying rabbinical warning about such age-gap unions — in this case perhaps as much as fifty years. Died during period of ruthless oppression of Jews around time Pontius Pilate appointed procurator. Although not converted to Christianity subsequently sanctified by Catholic sainthood and currently patron of thirty-five religious orders.

JOSES, JUDA and SIMON

All younger blood brothers of Jesus whose biographies have so far escaped history, along with His two sisters, whose names remain uncertain. Their existence shows that after the Annunciation — that one event which was to make their mother blessed among women and unique of all her sex — the Virgin Mary enjoyed a full married life with her husband.

Their Relations and Friends

ELIZABETH

First cousin and close confidante of Mary, the mother of Jesus. Well beyond child-bearing years. Married to equally aged Zachary, village priest. Zachary reportedly struck dumb by angel when given news Elizabeth would bear a son. After the birth Zachary immediately recovered speech and called infant Yochanan, 'Wished by God'. Later known as John the Baptist.

JOHN

(the Baptist). Born a few months before Jesus. Physical distance kept them apart in childhood. John confined his ministry to the banks of Jordan. Discarded conventional dress of short-sleeved *kolbur,* vest, and *subrikin,* trousers, for shift of camel hair girdled at loins. Lived on locusts, wild honey and river water. Garment and diet fitted style of ascetic prophets from days of the Exodus. Strong elements of Essene radical influence in John's doomsday preaching. Core of his teaching was repentance only possible through baptism after full confession of sins. His use of water in liturgy not new: centuries prior to John, Indian Brahmanism taught immersion in the holy river Ganges exorcised evil. John largely responsible for spear-heading the rebirth of prophecy that 'Kingdom of God' finally at hand. At same time singled out Herod Antipas, tetrarch of Galilee, for sustained attack. Finally imprisoned by his tormentor after John railed against Herod Antipas' seduction of sister-in-law, Herodias. Her daughter, Salome, asked for the Baptist's head on platter as reward for dancing at her stepfather's banquet.

MARY
MAGDALENE

Born at Magdala, tiny fishing village on Sea of Galilee, famed for preparation of muries, salt-cured fish exported as far as Rome. Worked for a time as hair-dresser; versed in use of dyes, especially fashionable auburn and black tints. Controversy over why, but drifted into life of prostitution while still young. Abandoned immoral life after rescue by Jesus when she anointed His feet during dinner with Simon the Pharisee. Died before Nero became Emperor (AD 54). Details of her relationship with Jesus raised subsequent speculation of whether she had grounds to hope they would marry.

MARY

(of Bethany). Born and raised in village fifteen strades, or just under two miles, from Jerusalem. Parents died shortly after birth; raised by elder sister, Martha, and brother Lazarus — immortalised as the man brought back from the dead by Jesus. His exact relationship with Mary also a matter of conjecture.

The Apostles

SIMON

(called Peter). Born *Shi'mon*. First and eldest of Disciples to answer call 'Come, follow Me'. Early on Jesus changed his name to *Kephus*, Aramaic for 'stone'; through translation into Greek and Latin became 'rock' and thus Peter — from which Catholicism and papacy trace their origin. Like his Master, Peter wore full beard as symbol of resistance to clean-shaven Roman occupiers. Gave Jesus a home at outset of His ministry around Capernaum on Sea of Galilee. Died a martyr in Nero's Colosseum. Left unresolved tantalising question whether Peter was married and if his wife suffered a mysterious fate.

BARTHOLOMEW Name means 'Son of Tolmai'. Family tree possibly traceable back to revolt of the Maccabees (200 BC). By all accounts devoted and caring. Went to Turkey with Philip, ministered at southern end of Caspian Sea. Finally fell into hands of heathen brigands who skinned him alive.

THOMAS Also known by the Greek, Didymus, meaning 'twin'. No record of his having identical brother or sister. A fisherman born and raised on banks of Sea of Galilee. Moody, suspicious, despondent and a questioner, earning him accolade: 'Thomas doubted that we might have no doubts.' After long eventful life as a missionary died in Mylapore, now suburb of Madras in India.

MATTHEW Born *Matthai*, itself shortened version of *Mattaniah*. Roman-appointed tax collector, scorned by fellow Jews until he became eighth Disciple. Fluent in Greek and Latin but wrote his Gospel in Hebrew after a long life of ministry in Ethiopia, Persia and Macedonia. Died peacefully and buried in Cathedral in Salerno, Italy.

JAMES Born *Ya'kob*, but known among the Disciples as 'The Less', because of small body. Genealogically the most fascinating of all the Apostles. Blood brother of Jesus and second eldest of Mary's children, only sibling to believe without question in Him. Became one of the most authoritative figures in the Christian community in Jerusalem, the city's first bishop and author of the hotly disputed Protevangelion of Birth of Jesus. Finally martyred by procurator Caspius Farus (AD 44−7), hurled from cliff-top and remains buried on Mount of Olives. Continuing controversy over James equalled only by one other Disciple − Judas Iscariot.

ANDREW

Name of Greek origin. Younger brother of Simon-Peter and second Apostle recruited. Crucified in Patros, Greece. Survived three days on cross. His last words: 'Accept me, O Christ Jesus, whom I saw, whom I love and in whom I am.'

JAMES

Eldest son of Zebedee, patriarch of devout Jewish family. James middle-aged and a widower when he joined Jesus. Executed by Herod Agrippa in AD 44.

JOHN

Younger brother of James. Subsequently credited with authorship of Gospel that is not only most mystical and dogmatic of all Apostolic accounts, but one apologists insist holds priority over Matthew, Luke and Mark. Almost two thousand years later controversy still rages among Scripturalists who devote entire careers, and reputations, to debating how untutored Palestinian fisherman acquired deep knowledge of Greek philosophy and theological reflections that give John a primal vision of Christ. This learned image in marked contrast to other Gospels which suggest John was quarrelsome, indolent and a self-seeker eager to usurp Peter's position as closest Apostle to Jesus. John executed alongside his brother.

PHILIP

Greek-named, meaning 'lover of horses'. Barely out of teens when answering call of Jesus. Remained a constant companion up to the Last Supper. Subsequently went to Asia Minor, preaching in Turkish city of Hierapolis. Married after death of Jesus and fathered three daughters. Passed closing years in Ephesus, where early Fathers of the Church were subsequently to elevate Mary to status of Mother of Jesus. Finally crucified on order of local Roman proconsul whose wife became Christian.

JUDE THADDAEUS   Often called *Trionius* — the man with three names: his own, Matthew's *Lebbaeus* and Luke's *Judas-ben-Ya'kob*, meaning 'son of a man named James'. Grandson of Zebedee, followed his widowed father James and uncle John into ranks of Disciples. Was missionary in Syria and northern Persia where he died and was buried at Karg Kalesia. Disinterred almost five hundred years later and bone fragments brought to Vatican where they are mingled with those of Apostle Peter and remain under papal edict in tomb sealed until Day of Judgement.

SIMON   (the Zealot). Also called *the Canaanite* or *Canaanean*. Former member of Zealots, Galilean-based, outlawed patriots who continually resisted Roman occupiers. After Jesus' death preached throughout North Africa before crossing Alps into France and sailing Channel to reach England in AD 60, onset of Boadicean war. Evangelised Britons and castigated Romans. Arrested and crucified at Caistor, Lincolnshire, on 10 May, AD 61.

JUDAS ISCARIOT   The last to be called. Only Apostle not from Galilee. Born in region of the Ghor, geological trench close to whose brink stood the accursed cities of Sodom and Gomorrah. Appointed treasurer because of his expressed business acumen. Undoubtedly originally loved Jesus but somewhere along the way, perhaps as late as during that last journey into Jerusalem, became dangerously mentally confused, convinced time had come to force Jesus into confrontation with both Roman and Jewish priestly aristocracy, thus hastening the coming of the Kingdom of God. His infamous act of betrayal swiftly followed by suicide. Was treachery or misguided belief the motivation?

The Establishment

JOSEPH
CAIAPHAS

High Priest of the Temple and president of
the Great Sanhedrin, the supreme court of
the Jews in Jerusalem. Physically pùny but
with remarkable skills in political chicanery.
Placated Romans and Jewish civil
administration through fawning and
manipulation. Almost twenty thousand
priests, acolytes and soldiers under his
command. As soon as Jesus emerged as
public figure, assigned spies and *agents
provocateurs* in attempts to entrap Him into
Scriptural breaches. But initially did not
regard Him as serious threat. Only when
Lazarus raised from dead was full danger to
established religious life recognised, and
Jesus elevated to status of prime threat to
public order, paving way for most notorious
show-trial ever held. Died about ten years
afterwards.

PONTIUS PILATE

Roman procurator for Judaea. Debated with
Jesus during legal proceedings. Cultured,
introverted, self-taught expert on Judaism.
Initially found Sanhedrin charges failed to
meet requirements of Roman law, yet fatally
flawed personality resulted in crowning
blunder that blighted hitherto promising
career. Was he already a secret Christian
when he condemned Jesus? Six years later
banished to Gaul. Committed suicide.
Became saint of Coptic Church.

HEROD ANTIPAS

Tetrarch, ruling prince of Galilee and
Peraea. Fifth son of Herod the Great.
Inherited paternal traits for violence,
wanton impulses and behaviour verging at
times on insane. Since murdering John the
Baptist obsessed with idea of being
constantly plotted against. Disliked and

feared Caiaphas. After Jesus publicly insulted him became convinced He must die. After death of Jesus banished; died in exile.

The Other Women

CLAUDIA PROCULA

Imperious grand-daughter of Emperor Augustus. Married Pilate ten years before they came to Judaea. An increasingly empty childless union which would have avoided historical record but for one momentous event. She dreamt about Jesus on the night before His death and sent her husband a message that could have changed history. The desperate intervention of a woman who loved Christ secretly — or a calculating response to use her husband to promote her social ambitions? Promulgated saint by Greek Orthodox Church.

JOANNA

Wife of Chuza, chief steward of Herod Antipas. Middle-aged convert to His teachings. Constantly risked her life to provide Jesus with information about the tetrarch's growing fury. Fate unknown.

MARY

Aged widow of Zebedee and mother of Apostles James and John. Devoted camp follower, ready to endure severe hardship on His account. Fate unknown.

In Search of Christ

I am the pause between two notes
that fall,
Into a real accordance scarce at all:
For Death's note tends to dominate –
Both, though, are reconciled in the
dark interval tremblingly.
And·the son remains immaculate.

— R. M. Rilke
The Book of Hours, 1

ONE

Towards Understanding

What is truth? said
jesting Pilate; and would
not stay for an answer.
— Francis Bacon
Of Truth

Everyone has a Jesus of Nazareth.

There is a Catholic Jesus, a Protestant Jesus and a Jewish Jesus, as well as a Jesus of the Celts, Latins, Greeks, Nordics, Russians and Chinese. There is a Muslim Jesus, a prophet born indeed of a virgin and second only to Mohammed, and the Jesus of Africa, Asia and Latin America – symbols of imperial power that conquered in the name of religion. Colonialism is dead but the memory of what those Jesus figures brought lives on; they are still linked to a mailed hand carrying the Cross. They were Jesus figures for whom millions faced violent death, because they either believed, or did not believe, in Him. For those crucified figures seas were crossed, continents conquered and empires founded. Today His name is evoked to justify outrage in such bedevilled places as Northern Ireland, the Lebanon and South Africa; much evil is done in the name of Jesus by those who claim to preach His word and live by His Commandments.

Every new church since the Reformation has created its

23

own Jesus. So have the atheists and agnostics, the charismatics, the ecumenicists and the Jesus People of all persuasions. Yet, increasingly, believers – and, for that matter, non-believers – grapple with what they *can* accept about Jesus of Nazareth. They face a confusing and often contradictory task. It is a sobering statistic that more has been written about Jesus in the past twenty years than in the previous two thousand. The subject continues to attract prominent theologians of all Christian denominations as well as Jewish scholars and, more recently, feminists and cultists of all kinds. The current wave of Christological interest coincided with a social upheaval in Latin America which led to liberation theology. The emergence of that creed is striking proof that, while the study of Jesus must be rooted in the past, it has become divorced from the traditional approach to historical and theological investigation. Those who lead a quest for Christ can be properly described as modern men and women who have clearly before them the need of a modern and troubled world – the redefinition of the essential Christian message for people who will be alive at the end of this century.

The search for new answers to old questions has inevitably accelerated with the approach of the third millennium of the Christian Church. The year 2000 has become an emotive beacon for both Protestant and Catholic theologians and exegetes. For the first time they have openly united with non-Christian scholars, especially Jews, over such crucial questions as to whether Jesus thought He was divine, whether He actually made any of the messianic claims which the Gospels proclaim. By the late 1980s – today – the historical data have been reinterpreted to suggest that Jesus may actually have died on the Cross without any intention of ever founding a new religion.

Hans Kung, the distinguished theologian, has written that this is no longer a matter of dispute between the denominations. Not all agree, especially the Church of Rome. Kung's view ensures he will remain out of favour with the Vatican. But he is secure with his professorship at

the University of Tübingen and master of his own ecumenical institute in a medieval town of heavily timbered
houses north-west of the Black Forest. Barely a century
ago, the so-called Tübingen School of biblical criticism was
founded on the premiss that, while the New Testament
does contain nuggets of probable fact, each one has to be
dug out from a quagmire of religious mythology. People
once came to bodily harm for daring to promote such
thinking. Kung merely lost one of his titles: he was forbidden in 1979 by the Vatican to call himself a Catholic
theologian. He has remained outwardly untroubled by
Rome's punishment: when he does discuss it he manages to
convey scorn which is devoid of malediction.

Kung's Christology has been honed to a belief that those
care-worn figures – the 'Jesus of history' and the 'Christ
of faith' – can only have any real historical validity if they
are removed from what he sees as the opaque strata of
time-bound interpretation. Kung's views have provided
further impetus for those concerned to get to the very root
of Christianity: the seeming discrepancy between how
Jesus saw Himself while on earth and how the Church
came to perceive Him after His death. In the debate which
continues in seminaries, cloisters and indeed where two or
more Christian thinkers meet, the claim is defended, and
increasingly challenged, that it is neither sensible nor
required for Christianity to attach any importance to
Jesus' perception of Himself while still alive: all that matters is to accept Simon Peter's assessment of Christ. If
nothing else, this has added to the lack of consensus which
still exists among Christians over what is the real message
of Jesus and how it can be applied. In spite of the credal
affirmations of the mainstream Christian faiths, there is
even less agreement among worshippers as to the actual
identity of Jesus.

Yet, totally convinced that He loves them, and they Him,
hundreds of millions of ordinary people still manage their
daily lives in His name. They ask no more than that, just as
He gave them hope through His own death, they in turn can

25

await their own earthly ending with a certainty no other figure has ever come remotely close to instilling. For them it is enough that the story of Jesus begins and ends with what the four Apostles – Matthew, Mark, Luke and John – say happened once upon a time and long ago.

But at the core of a deepening theological crisis is a challenge to the veracity of the canonical Gospels. A combination of archaeology, philology, linguistics and semiotics has been brought to bear on more traditional kinds of Scriptural examination: source criticism, redaction criticism, form criticism and literary criticism. Those who have developed these techniques argue they are able to show that the Gospels may well be the work of any number of individual chroniclers – which those critics insist accounts for the ambiguity, inconsistency and at times the sheer improbability of New Testament accounts.

Until recently this revolution in biblical exegesis had been dominated by the Protestant scholars. But, led by the indomitable Kung, a growing number of Catholic scholars have entered the arena, as undaunted as their Protestant colleagues that the raw material they seek often requires an act of faith on their part that it exists. Nor is their task made easier by the permanent jury of their peers ready to challenge and often reject every line of a new claim. Yet men like Edward Schillibeekx, a doughty Dominican theologian, work on in the belief there is a need to give old concepts of faith a new starting point – including a dramatic reassessment of the Gospels.

Their closely argued and often dense arguments, protected by thickets of caveats and frequently amplified by some of the lengthiest footnotes in scholarship, often peter out when trying to reassess the Gospel accounts of His life which, according to the faith of all believers, began its earthly form in a manger, continued as Jesus grew through childhood into a working man and ended on a cross after the most infamous trial ever held.

Most people know, if not all the details, that Jesus was condemned and crucified and that through His death came

26

a religion that is now not only the faith of a very large part of mankind but has influenced the entire culture of the world – including, and not least, horrific results for the Jewish people: they are still accused of having a collective responsibility in the murder of Christ. In stressing the religious significance of His death, the four canonical Gospels not only reinforce the Christian belief of Jesus being the availing sacrifice, the Son of God dying to save all mankind, but also emphasise the guilt *the Jews* must bear. That is both the greatest historical distortion and the most cruel calumny upon the Jewish people. Inevitably, His trial has become a playground where jurists indulge in legalistic rough-and-tumble and dazzling sleight-of-hand.

Nevertheless, establishing the truth does not depend on specialist forensic knowledge and experience. Attempts by eminent lawyers to dissect the trial of Jesus have frequently failed through a misunderstanding that the canonical Gospels provide inter-related accounts of His trial and that the evidence is essentially beyond dispute apart from small differences. The Gospels are stark accounts, none of them objective, of a man who lived and died in a world quite different from modern daily experience; Jesus simply cannot be judged by present-day standards.

People continue to look only at the New Testament as their guide in trying to understand the life and death of Jesus. Few may have considered the importance of knowing upon what real authority the New Testament rests; that as well as the canonically accepted Gospels there are other, equally important Scriptural writings. These were once accepted when the Church was young, but were subsequently rejected in the formation of doctrine that often grew from personal jealousy, intolerance, persecution and bigotry.

Much of the revision took place during and between the great councils of Nicaea and Chalcedon in the third and fourth centuries. Those gatherings codified religious doctrine and Jesus was proclaimed as true God and true man, while the canonical Gospels were secured as the basis of all orthodox Christian faith. They have remained so. Many of the other Gospels cast aside include stories about the Holy Family, the boyhood of Jesus and far more intriguing and detailed explanations why a handful of Jewish notables – among them the High Priest of the Temple, Caiaphas, and the Jewish puppet ruler, Herod Antipas – wanted Jesus killed. Those sources form an important part in understanding the total truth about Jesus. That is not to deny the authenticity of so-called accepted Scripture; if anything, that discarded mass of evidence buttresses the often only hinted-at truth of the New Testament.

While the New Testament can still be read without an understanding of the prevailing political, social and economic portents, a simple and inescapable truth does remain: there must, inevitably, be a limit on how thoroughly the language of Scripture can be fully accepted without a clear grasp of the world in which the Word was written.

It is particularly important in understanding Jesus, the man and His mission, to see Him in the context of His time; to try to understand how He and those around Him lived – His immediate family; Mary and Martha and their brother, Lazarus, in Bethany; the priests in the Temple; Pontius Pilate and his wife, Claudia Procula; the Jewish aristocracy; the Romans in their citadels. That understanding requires knowing their life-styles, their dress and eating habits, their legal systems; it requires re-creating, in all fidelity, the world in which the Gospel was first preached – and both to see and understand its effect on those who heard it first-hand.

Equally, it is perfectly true that faith does not stand, or fall, on the details of history. God, inspiring men, allowed them to write within the framework of their own time, mind and culture. What they created was not – as some churches insist – simply a series of unchallengeable and eternal truths; to promulgate that is to reduce Scripture to little more than theological principles, virtually devoid of the true revelations of God. Instead, Scripture conveys its own

28

unique truth – in the case of the New Testament it can properly be called Gospel truth – by mingling parables, anecdotes, deeds, formal statements, laws, miracles, poetry and hymns. The richness of it all is part history, part hagiography, part biography and something else: the message of God's revelation, while indeed founded on fact, does not depend on each precise detail of fact.

That explains why, for example, the Garden Tomb in Jerusalem is not the Tomb of Jesus; the pavement in the basement of the convent of the Sisters of Zion in the Old City is not the site, mentioned in John 19:13, where Pilate judged Jesus; nor was the *Ecce Homo* arch spanning the Via Dolorosa built when Christ was presented to the High Priest of the Jews and his cohorts with the procurator's cry: '*Ecce homo – behold the man!*' Or was it '*Behold: The Man*'?

Yet, at least since the Crusades, pilgrims have journeyed to these sites, filled with a deep longing to be close to where Jesus spent His last days. Religious pilgrimage has bestowed a sanctity which does indeed show that faith does not depend on purely historical fact.

In writing about Jesus it is essential for the reader to know what lies behind another attempt to try to explain.

For as long as I can remember I have always wanted to believe. My interest in His life and death began when I was taken as a child to the Holy Land. The map of what was then Palestine became the first I drew and coloured: the straight line of the coast, the central mountain range and beyond the River Jordan, all given their hues, from copper to purple, colours which are unforgettable to those who have lived there. As a young man I began seriously to study the life of Christ; my Scripture graduation prize is the only one I kept from schooldays. Through a career first as a journalist and then as a full-time author I became deeply interested in the Protestant exegetes who emerged in the fifties. Men like Günter Bornkamm, Hans Conzelsmann, Ernst Käsemann and Ernst Fuchs offered differing and challenging new theological concepts about how and why the four evangelists came to include certain material and leave out other data. Those German critics, Protestant to a man, were at the centre of high wrangling which frequently brought religion on to the front page of the newspaper I worked for. I played a part in promoting the debate – and I am certain I did not escape its influence. I was quite ready to accept that the Gospel form in which His life and death had been set down was assailable; I was the willing victim of other, more persuasive minds: Huxley's claim that 'miracles did not happen' and Matthew Arnold insisting there could be such a state as a 'non-miraculous Christianity'. Yet when it came to the person of Jesus I retained a deep and properly respectful regard that my mother implanted on those first trips through the Holy Land. Much later, when I had experienced war, pestilence and famine, the workload of any foreign correspondent, I still felt a sense of shock and anger at the misuse of His name. It was naïve – and I only mention it now as part of an honest attempt to try to explain how and why I came to write this book.

Nor is this the first attempt to put on paper my account of His life and inevitable crucifixion. Some twenty years ago, when I was going through a difficult crisis, I wrote a play based upon His trial. It was never performed – but writing it did provide peace of mind.

Writing books on religious matters brought me into contact with scholars who encouraged and deepened my interest in the trial and execution of Jesus. One was S. G. F. Brandon, Professor of Comparative Religion at the University of Manchester. Shortly before his death, which would leave unfilled a large gap in Scriptural interpretation, I shared a sense of mounting excitement with his students as Brandon lectured that so many accounts of the trial of Jesus assume a manifest improbability because they attempt to disguise the real nature of what lay behind the proceedings. Brandon's Jesus was a political threat to the Jewish establishment. Only a handful of them finally acted against Him;

yet because of what they did the Jewish people would be forever condemned.

It was the starting point for this book. Over several subsequent years, having acquired along the way the collective wisdom of many eminent men, both Protestant and Catholic, I realised that no matter how long I remained on the trail I could never hope to reach its end unless I discussed the matter with Jewish scholars.

I returned to Jerusalem where, almost two thousand years earlier, the drama had unfolded against a background of chicanery and psychological stress. I read on the flight the words of a man, Frank Morrison, who, almost sixty years earlier, had set off on a quest not dissimilar to mine. He produced a book in 1930, *Who Moved the Stone?*, which was devoid of a single source note. Nor did he encumber himself with a line-by-line defence of or attack on the Gospel Passion narrative. In the end he produced a book which was his personal testament and yet had a considerable universal appeal to common sense. He had concentrated on the Resurrection. But Morrison's approach struck me as a worthy model for tackling in many ways the more difficult task of making sense of Jesus' trial.

In Jerusalem I received a number of challenging reinterpretations of that trial from Jewish scholars. Haim H. Cohn, a ranking authority on Jewish legal history and a judge of the supreme court of Israel, guided me through ramifications of His trial that I had hitherto not suspected. Haim's complex argument can be distilled into a belief that almost certainly Christianity would have begun and developed very differently if that trial had been conducted in a way other than it was – and, equally important, if it had been reported more fully and accurately in the canonical Gospels. Ze'ev W. Falk, Professor of Family Law at the Hebrew University in Jerusalem, was among those who offered a lengthy catalogue of what Falk called the historical carelessness of those Gospels. I became convinced, as a Christian, that the Jewish interpretation of His trial must be given full credence.

31

I began to make other judgements. They were based on my own quite extensive reading. Those who wish to follow my trail can do so in the Bibliography. What that list cannot, of course, explain is the judgemental criteria I used. But, then, what use would it be for anyone if I indicated that, for example, I favoured Kung's interpretation of a point at the expense of a claim by Bultmann – or vice versa? My judgement is not anyone else's. How could it be? The verdict of others, especially over such a profoundly important historical figure as Jesus, often does not coincide with mine. Much of the scholarship of the past few decades, brilliant though it has often been, has, in the end, so it seems to me, concentrated far too much upon demythologising – and at times debunking. Some of the most unkind judgements have been left to the footnotes.

In preparing this book I decided, knowing the risk of attack was great, that I would not burden, or bore, reader with foot or source notes. What function, after all, would they really serve? My sources are the Gospels – and not just the canonical ones, but those discarded in the wake of the councils of Nicaea and Chalcedon. My research also includes a respectable body of Jewish and non-Christian literature, such as the tractates of the Mishnah, the Tosophta, the Talmud, the Midrashim and the Tarqamin. A list can be found at the end of this book. But they still do not go all the way to unravelling the tangled skeins of prejudice, passion and political intrigue which govern the life and death of Jesus. That, ultimately, must be a matter of interpretation. In this case, and I say so with all humility, it is mine.

From beginning to conclusion – if I only take as a starting point that meeting with Brandon – this book has taken me twelve years of constant thought, intermittent research and several drafts. In between I wrote other books before returning to this one story which I felt compelled to write. With each draft the interpretation I placed upon the facts differed. In some indefinable way my perspective was changed by facts that could not be altered. Jesus had lived

His brief life during a period in which Judaism was gripped by traumatic developments on the political and social fronts. For me to fail to take account of that would be to try to understand Dante without grasping conditions in medieval Florence.

Whether or not Jesus was actually born in Bethlehem is, in the end, of small consequence. Whether as Mark says (6:3) He had brothers – James, Judas, Simon and Joses – about which we know almost nothing – is of no real import. Whether it really was in AD 28 or 29 – or, according to Jewish reckoning, in the year 3788 since the creation of the world – that Jesus was baptised is not ultimately significant. Yet such issues are portrayed as providing the ultimate key to Jesus. Scholars of many disciplines begin and end their careers trying to prove, or disprove, among other matters how many times Jesus visited Jerusalem and what route He travelled; who were the Disciples closest to Him and in what order were the Gospels set down; did Mark's version precede Matthew's, Luke's come before John's? Increasingly clinical procedures are brought to bear to try to discover His height, weight, the colour of His eyes and hair – as if any of this will make Jesus more understandable. When Jesus asked His Disciples that most important question, 'Who do you say I am?', He surely could not have wished the debate to have developed the way it has. Wilfred Sheed's remark, 'another damned theologian comes grunting out of the Black Forest', has never been more apt. There is a growing, determined and, at times, disturbing move to demythologise, to replace faith with scepticism and even disbelief. Somewhere along the way the Jesus of ordinary people has been lost. Those who have tried to expropriate Jesus, His words and involvement with mankind have left Him further removed from the real understanding of Christianity. All that finally matters is that a deeply sensitive religious Jew was convinced He had been born first to reform Israel and then to launch the Kingdom of God.

It is *that* Jesus that these pages are concerned with; the man as well as the God-man.

33

In every thought and deed Jesus showed that His life and death remain the greatest story ever to be told – and that the only way to tell it is to present Him, in the true sense of the words, as a *real man*, as well as the only perfect one. He would surely have asked for no more. I have tried for no less.

28 Anno Christi: The Continuing Preparation

O Jerusalem, Jerusalem,
thou that killest the
prophets, and stonest them
which are sent unto thee,
how often would I have
gathered thy children
together, even as a hen gathereth
her chickens under her wings,
and ye would not!

— Jesus, contemplating
Jerusalem from the
Mount of Olives

Matthew 23:37

TWO

Jesus

*Whosoever will come after me, let him
deny himself, and take up his cross,
and follow me.*
— Mark 8:34

The hour of ritual sacrifice and celebration was once more close. As evening approached the entire community began to gather around the twin plots. The fields were roughly equal in size, each separated and encased by low walls of rock. At the centre of one was a hewn boulder upon which the rabbi would stand, as priests had done for centuries, to offer prayers when the time came.

Though it had less than a thousand inhabitants, Shechem was classified by the Romans as a medium-sized city and one of strategic importance: it was on the main road from troublesome Galilee to Jerusalem; and revolutionaries in northern Judaea intent on marching on the capital would have to pass this way. In less than a day troops from the imperial coastal citadel at Caesarea could be deployed between the two hills in whose lee Shechem lay, cutting the trail at the first sign of further civil insurrection. In the ninety years since Pompey had first led his legions southwards between the hills into Jerusalem, Roman forces had regularly been rushed here. When the soldiers returned

37

to barracks, the village elders resumed their talk about the nation being rescued from foreign tyranny. In recent years people in Shechem had spoken again of a Jewish king who would one day come and free them. Increasingly, they used the old biblical name for such a deliverer – *the Messiah*.

This longing for liberation was further reflected in the game Shechem boys played: Zealots and Romans, patriots and tyrants. That part of the game which depended on the capture of Mount Gerizim always ended in defeat for those luckless enough to be cast as Romans. Legend said Noah had erected the first altar after the Flood on top of Gerizim. Those playing Zealots invariably managed to drive their attackers away from the mountain shrine towards the nearby slopes of Mount Ebal. Joshua had placed a curse upon its summit a thousand years earlier; since then evil spirits were still reputed to haunt its peak. Shechem's other claim to fame was the well, as Holy Scripture related, which Jacob had dug, going down seventy-five feet to reach one of the sweet-water springs.

There was tremendous competition among the children to be on the Zealot side and particularly to play the roles of the two most recent heroes of Israel: Judas of Gamala, called simply The Galilean, and Sadduck the Pharisee. Twenty-two years before, in AD 6, they had led their followers against the Romans when another of the hated Imperial head-counts had been ordered. The Jews detested a census designed to suck more taxes from them. While Rome's gubernatorial appetite for enrichment was common throughout the empire, the population of Judaea was not only more financially impoverished than other occupied lands, but was also the victim of the capricious methods employed by Rome. Pontius Pilate, the latest Roman procurator, had made it clear he intended to extract the last possible shekel of tax – and that defaulters would be sued or imprisoned, their lands seized, their families driven out of their homes and, if need be, sold into bondage to pay off debts. He had also ensured that the once powerful Zealot movement, while maintaining public sympathy, had been greatly reduced numerically by ruthless Roman search-and-destroy operations. Now there were only a few hundred Zealots left, partisans operating for the most part in Galilee and Samaria. They attacked the enemy at night, cutting Roman sentry throats with their short daggers, the *sicarii*, and then slipping silently through a legion encampment, butchering as they went. Their exploits continuously excited the passions and hopes of the Jewish people.

During one of their mock battles near Mount Ebal the Shechem boys saw a group coming down the track from Thebez to the north. Their first instinct, a well-developed one, was to turn and run. Romans were not above snatching a handful of Jewish youths and using them for spear practice. But the boys quickly realised these strangers were not soldiers. Except for their leader, who was dressed in a cassock-like garment with wide sleeves reaching to the ground, the men wore the traditional *haluk*, a long woollen garment, girdled with a thong at the waist; over it was a cloak woven either from goat or camel hair. Behind them, at a distance, trudged a group of women, each robed in a voluminous *istomukhuium* and girdled either with a plain black *pinzomata* or a coloured *zonarim*, waist sashes.

For months now the people of Shechem had heard stories that far beyond where they would ever dare venture was a man who performed astonishing feats around the shores of the Sea of Galilee. Was this leader the man? He was becoming as celebrated as that other extraordinary preacher, a physical giant who spent his time ministering on the banks of the Jordan, and who was known throughout the land as John the Baptist.

Watching the approaching group each boy could have recounted how the thrilling story of John once more graphically illustrated the truth of the Scriptural texts they were taught as they squatted round the rabbi behind the Shechem synagogue. As well as memorising all the ceremonies connected with the Sabbath and the various festivals, especially Passover, each child also learned that Yahweh

39

was capable of anything. The entire story of John, from his birth to his emergence as a prophet, confirmed this omnipotence.

★ ★ ★

It was known to them that John's father was a country priest in a village so small that its only claim to recognition was being on the dirt track which eventually led to that historic spot where David slew Goliath. John's mother was called Elizabeth, respected within the tiny community for three reasons: her great age, the lineage she claimed with the Royal House of David, her long and happy marriage to Zachary. Their union had entered its fiftieth year and the couple had long come to accept they would end their days alone, without the joy of their own child to disturb the dignity of their home beside the synagogue where Zachary continued to marry, circumcise, and bury the dead.

Each year they made the pilgrimage to the Temple in Jerusalem for Passover. There they would meet Elizabeth's cousin Joachim and his wife, Anna, who travelled south on foot from Nazareth. When she was born, they brought with them their only child, Mary. Elizabeth and Zachary had wistfully watched her grow from an infant in swaddling to a pretty olive-skinned and dark-eyed girl. While Zachary and Joachim, like men everywhere in the Passover crowds, spoke feelingly about the Roman oppression, Elizabeth, Anna and Mary explored the latest delights of the city. Jerusalem was a three-day walk from Nazareth – and the wonders of the metropolis were far removed from those of the isolated mountain village.

On each visit there seemed to be new stalls selling even finer silks from all over the Orient: the Street of the Perfume Makers in the Lower City grew longer and more aromatic. At the end of the celebrations, the two families would go their separate ways, exchanging kisses and promising to meet in twelve months.

As the years passed, Elizabeth and Anna both agreed

Mary was approaching the time when she would take a husband. The news stirred an old longing in Elizabeth for a child of her own.

One year, Anna had sent word to Elizabeth that they would not be coming to Passover; Joachim was still recovering from a long winter illness. She also had one other piece of news. Mary had been promised in marriage to one of Nazareth's carpenters, Joseph, son of Jacob. Though Anna admitted there was a considerable difference in their ages, something the rabbi of Nazareth was unhappy over, Joseph was a fine and honourable man, abstemious and devout. All in all, she and Joachim had decided he would be a good husband for their daughter.

The news of the betrothal must have been a talking point between Elizabeth and Zachary as they made their slow way to Jerusalem for another festival, but as for a child of their own whom they could give in marriage, God had decided otherwise – and Yahweh's will was not to be questioned.

Elizabeth had, as usual, stopped in the Court of the Women, beyond which any female was forbidden to go within the Temple. Her husband, reputedly stiff-legged from rheumatism, had slowly climbed the steps which allowed him, as a priest, to enter the inner courts. In one of them he had put on ceremonial robes, ready to join all the other rabbis in leading the religious ceremonies. Seventy and more years Zachary may have been, but he had never lost his reverence for the rubric of the sacrifice, the utterance of the ancient prayers, the swinging of his censer that held the burning, pungent spice whose smoke cast its own spell over the worshippers. Dressed and ready to perform his functions as an anointed servant of the living Lord, Zachary had waited his turn to approach the great altar where the High Priest, the legendary Annas, ruled supreme.

What happened then had produced a spate of stories. In one, Zachary had suddenly turned and stumbled back into a robing room. In another, he had gone to the vault where the solid gold candlesticks for the high altar were stored. A

41

third report had said he disappeared into the kitchens under the Temple where votive cakes made of wheat and barley were baked along with the twelve loaves of holy shewbread. Wherever he had gone, Zachary had emerged, divested of his raiment and censer, a dazed look on his face, and had fled past the altar, one hand pointing to his open mouth from which came no sound. He had found Elizabeth and clung to her speechlessly. She had taken the stricken husband home. There, Zachary had motioned for a wax tablet and *stilus*, writing implements. Squatting on the floor, he had carefully formed the characters which would ensure them both a place in history.

'*An angel spoke to me at the Temple.*'

Then, watched by his wife, the old rabbi's *stilus* had bitten at speed into the wax, forming further astounding words. These, too, would become legendary, to be quoted and paraphrased as veritable proof of the truth of the Scripture that angels did speak with humans. His winged messenger had made a prediction.

'*Fear not, Zacharias: for thy prayer is heard; and thy wife Elizabeth shall bear thee a son, and thou shalt call his name John. And thou shalt have joy and gladness; and many shall rejoice at his birth. For he shall be great in the sight of the Lord, and shall drink neither wine nor strong drink; and he shall be filled with the Holy Ghost.*'

Elizabeth's reaction would be variously recounted. She had laughed in hysterical disbelief. She had wept. Finally she had asked whether the angel had given his name. Zachary had scratched the word: *Gabriel*. Husband and wife were overcome by the enormity of the revelation. Gabriel was one of the four archangels of the heavenly host; he had been the divine messenger who was sent to reassure the greatest of all the prophets, Daniel. Zachary resumed writing, explaining that Gabriel had struck him dumb as verification that he was indeed God's principal herald and that he would not be able to speak again until his son was born.

Zachary's congregation had been stunned; what had happened was beyond their comprehension. Then, in the sixth month of Elizabeth's pregnancy, a young and attractive girl arrived alone in the village. She was covered in dust and her feet were swollen – and the sharp-eyed village women noticed that she was also with child. She walked towards the house of Elizabeth and Zachary, and the older woman had waddled forth to greet her young cousin from Nazareth.

'*Hail Mary!*' Elizabeth had cried, her face alive with pleasure. '*Blessed art thou among women, and blessed is the fruit of thy womb!*' Then she had delivered a further unforgettable outburst. '*Whence is this to me that the mother of my Lord should come to me? For, lo, as soon as the voice of thy salvation sounded in mine ears, the babe leaped in my womb for joy.*'

Then, sensing the open-mouthed stares of her neighbours, Elizabeth had taken Mary by the elbow and led her into the small house: a construction of stone, covered with white plaster.

Inside the dwelling Mary had revealed her momentous decision. She too had been visited by the archangel Gabriel, who had told her she would conceive, and already she felt as if she was a new person, someone filled with glory and humility; she felt strong and wonderfully protected.

Staring at Elizabeth she had spoken. '*My soul doth magnify the Lord! And my spirit hath rejoiced in God my Saviour. For he hath regarded the low estate of his handmaiden: for, behold, from henceforth all generations shall call me blessed. For he that is mighty hath done me great things; and holy is his name. And his mercy is on them that fear him from generation to generation.*'

When she had finished, tears rolled down her travel-weary face. How, she asked Elizabeth brokenly, could she still expect Joseph to believe that she had not been with another man? How could she hope he would marry her now? Then Elizabeth had quietly told her how she had conceived. Sobbing in relief, Mary had clung to the old woman. Later, she had left the house, walking proudly out of the village, never once looking back.

Elizabeth's pregnancy had been normal, and on the predicted day she was delivered of a baby – a lusty, screaming son. Zachary helped to bathe his son, then rubbed his body in salt to harden the skin, and wrapped the child in swaddling clothes. On the eighth day he circumcised the boy, and upon writing upon his tablet that his son's name was John his speech returned.

All this had begun to be recounted when John started his ministry, dipping converts into the River Jordan and assuring them that the Messiah was finally on earth. The news had been passed on with muted voices. Spies were everywhere. It was dangerous to repeat anything which could be construed as a political or religious threat to the Romans, the Temple authorities or the tetrarch. But the word had spread: The Expected One was here.

* * *

To the youths of Shechem, their game forgotten, eyes on the approaching strangers, their assumption was that these were more converts making their way to where John performed his baptisms. They had heard how he would stand in the water, raising his massive bronzed arms heavenward, and uttering through his tangled beard words which had become a chant for Jews throughout the land. *'The Kingdom of Heaven is at hand. I indeed baptise you with the water unto repentance, but he that cometh after me is mightier than I, whose shoes I am not worthy to bear; He shall baptise you with the Holy Ghost, and with fire.'*

John had uttered them a year ago when his cousin had walked from Nazareth to the spot on the banks of the Jordan where the Baptist ministered. Many had been present at their encounter. The story of what happened had been endlessly repeated around the camp fire of the caravan routes and in the squares and souks of Jerusalem and a hundred other cities and towns. To the youngsters of Shechem, already steeped in the local folklore of Noah, Jacob and Joshua, the meeting had taken on an unforgettable aura.

* * *

They had finally stood face to face: John, knee-deep in the water, his hair a damp tangle from his exertions, his voice hoarse from hours of shouting about the need for repentance; Jesus, slimmer, features tranquil and free of any exhaustion in spite of the long trek from Nazareth, had walked into the river until the water reached His thighs.

The crowd had suddenly fallen silent, as if they, too, recognised the historic importance of the meeting. Those closest to the two men strained to hear every word. There was a quiet certainty about the request from Jesus to be baptised by John, whose response was a simple, unequivocal statement: it was he who should be immersed by his Cousin. Jesus' answer was filled with implication. '*Suffer it to be so now, for thus it becometh us to fulfil all righteousness.*' Then John had baptised Jesus.

The brief ceremony over, the silent, watchful gathering were convinced they saw a snow-white dove suddenly descend and hover for a moment. Folding its wings, the bird perched on the shoulder of the new convert. Then it flew away, finally only a speck that vanished from view. The stunned crowd would later swear that at that moment an unseen voice had cried out from the cloudless sky: '*This is my beloved Son in whom I am well pleased.*'

John had led Jesus from the river and brought Him to the cave where he, the hermit prophet, lived. The spectators crowded close to the entrance, straining to catch the quiet exchange between the two men, hoping for an explanation of the celestial events they had witnessed. Among them were the brothers Andrew and Simon, soon to be called Peter; James and John, the sons of Zebedee; as well as the youthful Philip. They were all from Capernaum and knew each other well.

Inside, almost lost in the gloom, John and Jesus squatted

opposite each other, the Baptist hunched forward, intent on what his Cousin was saying. Jesus was describing the circumstances of His birth. After leaving Elizabeth, Mary had walked back to Nazareth, a trek of nearly a hundred miles through some of the most dangerous terrain in Judaea, a route along which Roman patrols had been known regularly to take women for their pleasure. But, filled with the reassurance that she would be protected, she had safely reached home. Her parents, who assumed her lengthy absence had been to help Elizabeth through her confinement, had only too clearly observed the condition of their daughter. Their stricken looks had turned to wonder when she told them what had happened.

Jesus had continued to take His cousin through the sequence of events. Joseph, too, had been dismayed at her condition and had even thought of breaking off the betrothal until the night he experienced a dream so vivid that it seemed to be actually happening as he lay tormented in his bed. Jesus described how, in that dream, '*the angel of the Lord*' had gently spoken to Joseph and told him not to be ashamed to take Mary as his wife, for the child she was carrying was not from any other man, but had been placed there by the Holy Spirit, God Himself, and that she would bear His Son so that He could come into the world and redeem its people from sin. John had uttered a prophecy which had sustained generations since the prophet Isaiah first spoke them: '*Therefore the Lord himself shall give you a sign. Behold a virgin shall conceive and bear a son.*'

The cousins had come out of the cave and the crowd had drawn back in respectful silence. Jesus had looked at the faces of the men from Capernaum, searching each in turn, before telling them to wait on the bank of the Jordan near where John baptised until He returned for them. Jesus had then walked south, away from the river delta into the greatest of all Judaean deserts – the one simply called the Wilderness.

★ ★ ★

Jesus led the Disciples, Mary Magdalene and the other women into Shechem to where the activity around the two plots had gathered pace. In front of the rabbi's boulder-platform was a trench about four feet wide and nine feet long, lined with scorched-black unhewn stones. This was the sacrificial pit, where since noon a fire had burned. Resting on wooden poles across the top were several cauldrons of steaming water. In the adjoining plot was a circular pit about ten feet deep. It, too, was lined with stones, glowing from the intense heat.

The first stages were completed for a sacred ritual which went all the way back to God's Covenant with Abraham. What was about to happen was part of the endless process of spiritual development of the Chosen People: it was as important as their pledges of righteous behaviour, brotherly love, moral worth and justice. It had a deep mystical meaning of holy purification. Abraham had called it '*the mark of the flesh*' – the circumcision of every new-born Jewish male child, a requirement so binding that the operation could be performed upon the Sabbath.

Originally Abraham had circumcised his firstborn and the rite had remained for centuries the responsibility of the father. Then, when Joshua had descended the Hill of the Foreskins – named after its phallus-like shape – and led his people into the Promised Land, circumcision had been elevated to a profession. Each town had a *mohel*, a practitioner trained to perform the delicate operation. Working only with a flint knife, an experienced *mohel* was a revered figure, allowed to partake in the special offerings that the family of the new-born made to the priest. All of Shechem was jostling around the plots when the boys arrived with Jesus and His party. They may have been in time to see the *mohel* follow the precise sequence demanded in the tractate: '*The making of the cut, the tearing of the skin, the sucking of the wound and the placing of a plaster of oil, wine and cummin upon the wound.*'

The strangers were promptly invited to join in the forth-coming feast. There was nothing unusual in this: Jews were traditionally generous with their hospitality, and indeed Abraham had invited God Himself to sup with him at Mamarea.

The host, the father of the circumcised child, received each of them with the kiss of peace and ordered water to be brought for their feet to be washed. Separate pails were provided so that each right hand, the one used for eating, could be carefully cleansed. Then, to show the importance of the feast – a circumcision celebration ranked with a wedding banquet as a cause for rejoicing – scented oil was sprinkled on the heads of the men and the head-dresses of the women. Those who performed the ritual reacted as they did towards all strangers – looking into their faces, taking their measure; and among the strangers this day was Jesus.

The stories of what Jesus had done had grown to a point where no one could be absolutely certain which event followed the other. There had been so many miraculous happenings. But it was generally agreed that the first one had been at Cana. What occurred there had been witnessed by many. Caravan traders carried the news to Jerusalem and the ears of the High Priest, Joseph Caiaphas, and the tetrarch, Herod Antipas. Shortly afterwards there had passed through Shechem rabbis from the Temple and agents of the tetrarch hurrying to Cana to probe further the extraordinary event which had finally plucked Jesus out of obscurity. It would once more be the sheer detail that would defy rejection; if it had not happened as recorded, how else could it have occurred?

* * *

Jesus had spent the time in the Wilderness walking through that desolate area where David had cut off a strip of Saul's coat; where Samson had reputedly slain ten thousand men with the jawbone of an ass; where Abraham had had his unhappy encounter with Abimelech; where Jacob had stolen Esau's blessing: a distance perhaps of two score zig-zagging miles, trudging through an enervating landscape of deep ravines, beds of treacherous shale, and acres of blistering sand, seemingly empty of life except for prowling leopards and wild pigs. At night when the sun set, it was icily cold. Jesus had remained here for forty days, facing and overcoming temptations He would never speak about – but which others would ascribe to Him. Here, they said, He had encountered Satan and rejected his blandishments. Satisfied at what He had achieved, Jesus made His way past the eerie mists of the Dead Sea and the Herodian fortress atop Masada, on up along the left bank of the Jordan and finally back into Galilee and Nazareth.

His family was now sadly depleted. His father, Joseph, had died a few years after Zachary succumbed. His aunt Elizabeth was also dead. His brothers and sisters were grown-up; before he died Joseph had arranged marriage contracts for several of them. They were settled in Nazareth or the other towns in the fertile plain of Gennesaret bordering the Sea of Galilee. Over the years the gap between Jesus and His family had widened, with two exceptions. He still had a close and loving relationship with His mother and the eldest of His brothers, James, who openly adored Him. But from now on the familial ties would further loosen under the sheer pressure of what He had to do and the time He had left in which to accomplish it all.

If Jesus' mother was shocked at her son's appearance after His lengthy stay in the Wilderness she gave no sign to those men He had brought home, the first five of His recruited Apostles: Peter, Andrew, James, John and Philip. Returning from the desert Jesus had met them on the route to Galilee and issued for the first time the command: '*Come follow me.*' His brother was the sixth to respond; to avoid confusion, he was known as James the Less.

Mary had made them all welcome. Now, into middle-age, and her figure that much fuller after years of child-bearing, her life had become no different from that of any other Nazarene widow: an endless round of housework, shopping, and Sabbath candles to be lit; her spare time spent gossiping with neighbours about the focus of her life –

49

her growing number of grandchildren. If she felt it, she had hidden any sadness that her eldest Son had not produced any babies for her to nurse and spoil. She realised that few still understood Him – especially why He had felt it necessary to spend almost six weeks in that desolate region far to the south. She was one of the few who knew that as well as conquering temptation He had spent time contemplating the events which had made His life so different from that moment she had first felt Him moving in her womb. When, ran the story, He had been old enough to understand she had told Him how, on the eve of His birth, she had been forced to ride on a donkey, one of those stubborn Galilean asses, down to Bethlehem to comply with the latest Roman edict. The governor of Syria, who then had jurisdiction over neighbouring Judaea, had announced that its population was to be counted, tribe by tribe, for tax purposes. Those who failed to register would be severely punished. Joseph had known he would have no alternative but to expose his young wife to the lengthy journey as she came to termination. His own lineage went back to King David, Bethlehem's most exalted son; therefore Joseph had to register himself and Mary in that ancient seat of the tribe of David. In a cave, on the outskirts of Bethlehem, she had finally been delivered. Afterwards, Joseph had settled them both on the back of the donkey and led his wife and baby Son far beyond the Dead Sea and into the Sinai Desert, where their ancestors had wandered for forty years after Moses had told a Pharaoh to let God's people go. Joseph had brought his family back into Egypt to avoid another tyrant, King Herod. In the city of Alexandria, where Cleopatra had fallen in love with Julius Caesar, his parents had waited until Herod the Great was dead. They had then returned to Jerusalem only to find themselves amidst the tyrannical rule of his son, Herod Antipas. So the Gospels would retell.

Much else had happened to them both since Mary watched Him grow into maturity. But she never questioned her Son's actions or motives – nor had she done so when He returned home with those five men who, He calmly told her, would carry on His work. Instead, she had invited them all to the wedding of a distant cousin at Cana.

They had left Nazareth in the early afternoon to give ample time to arrive for the marriage feast on a fine autumn evening. The harvest had been gathered, the vines stripped, and the grapes were fermenting; it was a time when everyone was content and it was pleasant to sit up late and enjoy oneself.

Jesus, His mother and the Apostles arrived as the bridegroom's procession went to fetch the bride from her home. Scrubbed and dressed in his finest clothes, the groom wore a crown as Solomon had done at his nuptials. The bride, veiled and her hair freshly hennaed, was carried on a litter through the streets lined with people singing songs which went back to King David's days. When the procession reached the bridegroom's house, the rabbi offered traditional Scriptural blessings, each invocation intoned in turn by the crowd. After the religious service the celebrations began. There was dancing in the street; as dusk fell the bridal couple sat under a canopy, the *huppah*, surrounded by the usual ten bridesmaids. The guests squatted around low tables stacked with platters of boiled meats and vegetables either raw or cooked in oil. Nathanael the caterer and his staff moved with practised ease, refilling pitchers of red and white wines and jugs of water for the children. Jesus and His mother were seated at the table of the bride's father. Like John the Baptist He had no desire for alcohol. But around Him the atmosphere was becoming increasingly rumbustious under the heady influence of the wine.

Suddenly the caterer was at the host's elbow, whispering urgently. The wine was about to run out. To bring more from Nathanael's cellars would take time. No doubt crimson with embarrassment the host murmured to Mary what had happened. At several tables she saw guests draining their goblets and beginning to pound the table for more drink.

John would recount that Mary turned to Jesus and '*saith unto Him, They have no wine*'.

51

Jesus had answered: '*Woman, what have I to do with thee? Mine hour is not yet come.*'

The singing and laughter had begun to be matched by growing demands for the caterer and his staff to refill the pitchers. A look of determination on her face, Mary rose to her feet and motioned for Jesus to join her near where the waiters were draining the last of the vats. What passed between mother and Son in their brief conversation would be a moment of significance for the future of all history. Here, in the tiny square of a town, virtually unknown beyond Galilee, an event was about to happen which would forever remain beyond human comprehension. Mary turned to Nathanael's men. Once more John would remember her words. Pointing to her Son, she ordered: '*Whatever he saith unto you, do it.*'

Jesus asked the waiters to fill the wine vats to the brim with water. They did as bid. He then invited the caterer to dip a ladle into one of them. Nathanael, perhaps shaking his head at such time-wasting futility, did so. He withdrew the spoon. The water had changed to a rich red colour. He lifted the ladle to his lips and sipped. It was the finest wine he had ever tasted.

Even before the caterer had delivered his verdict, the story had spread, as Jesus knew it would. He also knew, and accepted, there could be no turning back.

Following Cana, Jesus preached in the open air, in synagogues and the courtyards of private homes. His message was simple and compelling. The Kingdom of Heaven was drawing ever closer; people must repent and believe the good news. Every sermon was designed to encourage His listeners to achieve a greater awareness of the *immediate* presence of God – not as a distant divinity but as a life-force among them. He attracted a growing and varied following, including the Twelve finally chosen as His closest confidants. Among His devotees were a number of women – whom Jesus treated with a respect and seriousness which was exceptional for the times. He often motioned for them to come from the edge of the crowd and sit at His feet. They looked up at Him in astonishment and delight when He attacked the dual morality which often allowed a man to be forgiven his transgressions and yet branded a woman for life who had succumbed to the smallest of temptations. When He led them in prayer He invariably called God '*Father*', an old Jewish concept, but one to which He gave a new intimacy. Everywhere Jesus went He reaffirmed that the dark inner forces which ravaged the souls of every man and woman could be exorcised by faith. '*If by the power of God I drive out the demons, then be sure the Kingdom of God has come upon you.*' To enter it, all they had to do was to accept that the old order was being swept away.

Jesus spoke a great deal about love, illustrating its meaning with stirring stories and parables: the Prodigal Son; the Good Samaritan who rescued a victim of highway robbery. In a score of different ways He stressed that love meant being tolerant, patient and always seeking to help others without thought of self-reward. He was laying out an ethical commitment, a direction, a standard of behaviour that was radically different from previous concepts.

His listeners were exhilarated. But among the crowds were mischief-makers trying to entrap Him. He had first challenged them over the Sabbath. Jesus made it clear He did not oppose the concept that it was a day of rest, not only for those in authority but for those whom they exploited; that it was a pause for everyone to pray and remember that God was the Creator of all things. What He objected to was that the Sabbath had been demeaned by being surrounded with rabbinical restrictions. He steadfastly attacked these as pointless dogma. Where was the sense, He asked, in a law that said it was permissible for a person to travel twelve miles but not a yard further on the Sabbath? Where was the logic that allowed someone to write one but not two letters on that day? What religious basis could there be in a regulation that allowed a housewife to fasten a rope to a bucket but not draw water from a well during the hours of the Sabbath? How was it justifiable for a musician to tie the ends of a broken lute string but not replace it; for food to be eaten but not prepared; for vinegar to be used to relieve headache but not spat out? How could these everyday actions offend God on His day of rest? He had demanded where was any of this rooted in Holy Scripture? Jesus had summed up His attitude in one memorable sentence. *'The Sabbath is made for man, not man for the Sabbath.'* Sensing His opponents ready to attack, He silenced them on that occasion with a resounding challenge: let them show where He was wrong. There had been no response. But Jesus knew they would return.

Soon everyone around the fifteen-mile length of the Sea of Galilee had their favourite story of His determination to alleviate suffering and sorrow. The miracles which He began to perform were an integral part of His ministry.

There had been that unnerving moment in the township of Gergesa, on the west bank of the Sea of Galilee, when a raving lunatic had rushed to Jesus, teeth bared, howling he would kill Him. Jesus had extended His hands and gently asked the man to kneel. After a tense wait while the man remained half-crouching, as if he was about to spring, snarling like a werewolf, Jesus had quietly asked him his name, and the demented reply had driven some of His Disciples to move forward protectively. Jesus had motioned them back and again addressed the man. *'What is thy name? And he said, Legion: because many devils were entered into him. And they besought him that he would not command them to go out into the deep.'*

The wretch had flung himself on the ground rolling and sobbing uncontrollably. Jesus had knelt beside him, one hand on the man's head, who was suddenly still, asleep. After a while Jesus rose and stepped back, commanding the man to rise. When he did so, and opened his eyes, the madness in them was no longer present.

Then who could forget – certainly not Peter – what had happened when he asked Jesus to help his dying mother-in-law? The doctor in Capernaum, held to be the cleverest physician around the Sea of Galilee, had prescribed every known remedy for her sickness: swallowing the brain of an owl, pounded and strained, to alleviate her crippling bouts of stomach cramps; chewing toads' legs boiled in vinegar to end her blinding headaches; massaging the urine of unweaned calves into her legs to reduce the swelling. Nothing had worked. One by one her bodily functions were failing.

Jesus had gone to her bedside and held her hand. For a moment, just like the madman at Gergesa, the old woman had stared with hostility at Him. Then her face had cleared and she had smiled. Her sickness had gone. Within an hour she was out of bed and cooking supper for her family – something she had been unable to do for years.

In all he continued to say and do Jesus made it clear that He perfectly understood the correct interpenetration and intermingling of the human and the divine. Never far from His mind was the realisation that His methods must one day provoke a final clash with the ruling religious authorities in Jerusalem. That was inevitable: what He had come to do was to demonstrate the power and the pity of God experienced solely through love. No High Priest or tetrarch, let alone a Roman procurator, could do that. Yet it had been difficult at times for Jesus to convince even his immediate followers that they must see what He was doing not merely as a passing phenomenon but as part of a new eternal truth which was both supernatural and human.

* * *

Those Jesus had brought to Shechem knew how intensely human He was. There was the balding Peter, called Simon until Jesus had changed his name, and his brother Andrew. Both still had the rolling gait of fishermen. They would come down through history depicted as standing shoulder to shoulder with Jesus, intensely proud they were the first He had called. James and John might well have been the siblings of folklore: James short and portly, the belt around his waist barely meeting, older than his forty years, sometimes a sadness in the eyes that was ascribed to his wife having died shortly after the birth of their son, Thaddaeus;

55

John tall and spare-framed, his slimness accentuated by the breeches and close-fitting vest he invariably wore.

The Twelve were comprised of other differing personalities. Philip, whose beard was reportedly the blondest of them all, supposedly born a year after the last Zealot uprising, and still fired with the impetuosity of youth. Legend would insist he had been drawn to the older Matthew, the former tax-collector, depicted as a patient and thoughtful man, who spent the time on the road teaching Philip the rudiments of Greek and Latin. Bartholomew was muscular, with a warrior's stride and a face made to appear more pale by his thick jet-black beard; James the Less, a small figure whose robe was frayed at the hem and trailing in the dust; Thaddaeus, given his father's stout figure. Matthew, for a reason no one understood, called him Lebbaeus. Then there was Thomas, whom Matthew had nicknamed Didymus, the twin. A popular view would survive that Thomas's belligerence was never far from the surface. True or not, the nickname stuck, just as Thomas remained, perhaps by choice, a man alone.

Simon the Canaanite was reputedly taller and broader than even Peter or Andrew. Closer to seven feet than to six, winter and summer Simon wore a woven cloth wrapped tightly around the loins and reaching to the knees, with one end flung over his shoulder. Even in his bare feet he must have looked every inch as imperious as an emperor. Simon had been a Zealot and still saw himself as the group's natural protector with his knowledge of Roman tactics and those of the soldiers of Herod Antipas. No doubt he knew the safest routes through the countryside infested with hostile patrols.

Judas Iscariot would survive in mythology as a slight, dark-skinned man, dressed in a short-sleeved *kilbur*, the linen garment which was the usual garb in that village he had been born in on the edge of the Ghor. He would be given darting eyes that never failed to return to the large money-purse the treasurer clutched to his person. It contained the shekels which paid for the group's needs – a new

56

pair of sandals, a girdle, the barest necessities of their lives. Tradition would have Judas a tireless bargain-hunter, his enthusiasm for driving a deal matched only by sustained praise for the ministry of Jesus. Why not?

After a year some friendships were closer than others; harmony was frequently broken by outbursts of anger, pettiness and jealousy. Peter and Matthew made no secret of their dislike of Judas; John often bickered with Thomas. The others squabbled over who should sit next to Jesus at meals, walk beside Him on the road, sleep near Him under the starlight. The Gospels would hint at no less. When it became too irksome Jesus chided them for their childish behaviour. He must also have understood that, being simple country men, they had no previous experience of the wiles of the Temple agents from Jerusalem and their cunning questions, or the spies of Herod Antipas, who pretended they were eager to overthrow the Romans and urged Jesus to give one, just one, encouraging sign. He had ignored these marplots – just as He had side-stepped those Jews who had taken the Roman coin and stood on the edge of the crowd hurling questions designed to provoke treasonable responses they could report to Pilate.

Facing crowds – increasingly larger groups of mostly impoverished men, women and children come to hear Him preach, bringing with them their sick, lame and infirm for him to cure – Jesus had shown the Twelve more than ever that He would need their sustained and selfless support if He was to succeed. People came from everywhere: running the gamut of the Roman patrols on the coastal plains and avoiding the troops of Herod Antipas inland to make their way to the Sea of Galilee; from the northern Phoenician ports of Tyre and Sidon; from the west, far beyond the Jordan; from as far south as the Valley of Salt in the Wilderness of Idumaea, reaching Galilee after a walk of a week or more. What was happening was both awesome and sobering.

Jesus decided He must escape momentarily from the incessant demands for healing and ministering, and had brought the Disciples away from the port towns and villages around the Galilee lake. Shechem was only a stopping point on the way to the secluded place where He wanted to take them and finally explain what He expected them to do.

Shortly before sunset the crowd parted to allow shepherds through, each leading a tethered unblemished white-fleeced sheep to the enclosure. The rabbi rapidly checked the animals; this was part of the precise rules governing sacrifices: a brown mark on an animal's head rendered it unfit to be an offering. After passing inspection the sheep were led close to the pit with its steaming cauldrons of water. The priest resumed his position and began to chant further prayers. The crowd joined in the responses. Before the rock were the parents of the circumcised child, the *mohel* to one side.

The rabbi beckoned into the crowd. Youths vaulted over the wall to stand behind the shepherds, two to each man. When they were all positioned the priest nodded. The trio assigned to each animal moved swiftly, throwing the sheep to the ground; one youth pinned it down, the second held fast its legs and the shepherd pressed back the head to expose the throat. The rabbi produced a knife from under his robes. He stood beside the first animal and with one swift deadly slash, a back and forth movement of the blade, severed the head from the body. The shepherd turned the carcass on its side allowing the blood to drain into the earth. The priest moved to the next prostrate sheep and repeated his action.

While the slaughter went on, the singing resumed, prayers were offered and blessings evoked upon the infant who had just been admitted into the community.

When the last animal lay inert the shepherds carried the carcasses to the edge of the pit, lifted down the cauldrons and poured boiling water over them. Then they began to pluck away the wool, tossing it into the pit, sending a stenchy smoke spiralling into the cool air. As the process continued the infant's father brought pieces of unleavened

58

bread to the priest and *mohel*. When they pronounced it to their satisfaction servers went among the crowd distributing the offering. Among the first to be served was Jesus and His group, a sign of respect after the cure of Peter's mother-in-law.

*　*　*

Jesus had gone on to complete His first tour of the lake towns, healing as He went; preaching, as was His right, in every synagogue around Galilee. He was only too aware of the agents from Jerusalem still dogging His footsteps. Yet they had been unable to find a single fault in what He said, claimed or did. His preaching was rooted in impeccable doctrine; not a word of heresy passed His lips.

The more deadly the verbal traps, the greater His skill in avoiding them. Increasingly, though, He began to speak in apocalyptic imagery of the coming new age. Before it dawned, he said, there would be disasters, war, the emergence of false prophets, pestilence and the persecution of those who believed in Him; there would be tribulations at every turn. But for those who remained true to the faith which He had given them their reward would be salvation. The choice was starkly clear: there was no middle road. Jesus was describing an eschatological vision that even the shrewdest of Temple agents could not easily challenge; there was nothing in their holy books from which they could mount one.

When the spies became too irksome Jesus avoided them by slipping away under cover of darkness, walking with the Apostles through the moonlit Galilean landscape, reappearing next morning at some new venue. He had done this several times on the tour of the lake. On one occasion He had back-tracked, following the banks of the Jordan. As dawn had broken over the river Jesus had asked the Disciples what people were saying about Him. They had scuffed their feet in the dust, each anxious not to be the first to speak. Finally, Thomas had blurted out that many were convinced He was the reincarnation of Elijah. Thaddaeus reported that in Magdala some firmly believed He could be Moses. Andrew said that in Capernaum the talk was that He was really Jacob. One by one the Apostles had made their reports. Finally, Jesus had turned to Peter: *'Who sayeth thou am I?'* His first follower had not hesitated: *'The Messiah.'* Jesus had quietly praised Peter for his perception. It was the first time He had admitted His claim to divinity. He had firmly cautioned them to keep the knowledge secret: the time had not yet come for the world to be told such a shattering truth. Jesus added a sombre warning: those willing still to follow Him must be prepared to shoulder the cross. They all knew that crucifixion was the ultimate Roman punishment, the cruellest of all forms of death, and His words almost certainly were received with foreboding. Without waiting for their decision, Jesus turned and headed towards Capernaum. He may indeed have only walked a few yards before they caught up with Him. The details, as such, would be unimportant. What would not be in dispute is that, as so often in the past, after facing them with reality, Jesus had commanded their loyalty.

He had once more led them into Capernaum where He had a room in the home of Peter's mother-in-law. One claim was that the Apostle's wife had died in child-birth, her first baby still-born. Another report said she had drowned in the Sea of Galilee. A third postulated that she had run off with one of the caravan traders who regularly passed through the town. Her exact fate would be lost to history.

Outside the town they found a now familiar gathering waiting patiently. At every stopping point around the shores of Galilee people had entreated Jesus to stay. The crowd, spotting His approach, began to surge forward. The Apostles, themselves very possibly tired after another long day, bundled Him into a nearby inn and bolted the door. Too late they must have realised their mistake: several of their tormentors from Jerusalem were lodging there. They began to ask more questions. With the crowds outside

60

clamouring for Jesus to preach there was no way to leave. The agents grew more confident as they challenged Him about the basis for His teachings. Where did Scripture say this or that? The deadly probing was interrupted by an overhead disturbance. The occupants of the crowded room were startled to see the ceiling steadily torn away, and in the ever-widening hole appeared expectant faces. A woman pleaded to be excused such behaviour, explaining it was the only way to bring her paralysed father to Jesus. The throng outside had made it impossible to reach the door. With the help of friends the daughter had brought her father's pallet up a rear staircase that led to the flat roof. Jesus ordered the hole to be widened and the pallet lowered down by ropes. John would record how Jesus knelt beside the old man, laying His hands on his brow. Bending closer and speaking in a clear distinct voice Jesus said the man's sins were forgiven.

Sudden exultant cries came from the Temple agents. After months of fruitlessly stalking their quarry, they finally had something. Only God could forgive sins. Jesus, they shouted, had committed a blatant blasphemy. Matthew would note how Jesus turned and faced the agents and asked: *'Wherefore think ye evil in your hearts?'* Before they could answer, He fired further questions. What was easier to say: that sins were forgiven? or: arise and walk? Without waiting for a reply Jesus turned back to the cripple, His voice gentle: *'Ye may know that the Son of man hath power on earth to forgive sins. Arise! Take up thy bed and go unto thine house!'*

The man's body began to stir, almost indiscernible movements at first which rapidly grew stronger. Slowly, then with growing confidence, he raised himself on one elbow. From that position he delivered his first words: *'Glory be to God.'*

The man eased himself off the pallet and stood on the floor, also looking dazedly upwards at the rapturous cries coming from his daughter and her friends. When his gaze turned to Jesus, tears ran down his face. Then, doing as he

61

had been commanded, the cured man lifted the bed and, waiting until one of the Apostles unbolted the door, left the house.

Jesus and the Disciples followed, leaving behind the stunned agents. When they finally began to speak, they asked one question. What had He meant by '*The Son of man*'? The oldest and cleverest of them, a scholar respected even by the High Priest, remembered. Daniel the Prophet had used the words to encourage the belief that one day the Messiah would come: '*I saw in the night visions, and, behold, one like the Son of man came with the clouds of heaven.*' The import of what Jesus had said was only too clear. It was heresy. It *had* to be. But, even so, the words by themselves were not enough; He could always claim He was merely quoting Daniel. But by the time the spies had forced their way through the joyous crowd, Jesus and the Disciples had once more vanished. They had taken the road south, finally to reach Shechem.

★ ★ ★

The last sheep was plucked, fastened to a short pole and carried on the shoulders of two boys to the adjoining enclosure where the village butchers were cutting off the right fore-leg of each animal, drawing the sinews from the hind legs and disembowelling the carcass. Care was taken to ensure not a piece of flesh fell to the ground. The shepherds zealously collected the entrails and placed them on the wooden poles where the cauldrons had stood. The innards sizzled and shrivelled before dropping into the pit. The severed legs and the edible offal were placed in pots of fresh cold water; these would be taken home later by the rabbi and *mohel* as their reward.

The butchering completed, a pole about fifteen feet long was inserted lengthways through each carcass. Its skin was then cut in a series of gashes on either side of the rib-cage and salt rubbed into the openings. A final check that each animal was securely fastened, then, at the command of the rabbi, the stakes were lowered into the pit – kept clear of the growing ash-bed by inserting the pole tips in gaps between the hot stone walls. A large wooden grid was positioned on top. Grass was spread over this and finally panniers of mud layered over the greenery until the opening was airtight.

Among the select number of women who had accompanied Jesus was one who followed Him everywhere. In spite of all she had done, recklessly and deliberately, lore would ensure there was an innocence and purity about her, a chasteness which men who had once used and abused her no doubt would have found clearly bewildering. She had once been a spoilt, bejewelled and painted wanton; a whore to whom they had always returned, making her the richest harlot in the town of Magdala. More than its fortress and its fleet of fisherboats, she had spread the port's fame throughout the province. Clients brought her silks from Arabia, jewellery from Egypt and spices from India. Her reddish hair had been braided with pearls; her arms once weighted with bracelets and her fingers glittered with rings. She had been wealthy enough to afford slaves and brazen enough, rumour had it, to have doubled her normal fee to share the bed of any Roman. For a price she had even slept with the odious Simon the Pharisee, one of the wealthiest men in Galilee. Mary Magdalene had agreed to do so again on that night her life changed irrevocably.

* * *

When Jesus received Simon's invitation to dinner, the Apostles had been of one voice: this was another trap. Simon was a lawyer versed in all the subtleties of biblical precepts; an advocate who knew which arguments to cite, depending on whether he was appearing for the plaintiff or for the defendant. Once, calling upon a precedent dating back to Solomon, he successfully argued that a Capernaum landowner who had killed a thief who entered his home at night should be acquitted. Conviction for murder was only possible if the offence had taken place in daylight when the robber might have been taken alive; in the darkness there would have been no way of knowing if he was armed or alone.

Apart from his thriving criminal practice, Simon was an expert on other serious crimes – the lengthy catalogue of offences against religious law which had always demanded the severest punishment. These included idolatry, necromancy and the performance of sorcery. Each, upon conviction, automatically carried the death penalty. So did blasphemy, which included not only the smallest infringement of the Sabbath, but also misusing the Holy Name. The Apostles had warned Jesus again: to eat at this man's table was to run the very real peril of being ensnared by legal tractates. Jesus had assured them that He feared nothing – and there was no need for them to be afraid.

Simon's house overlooked Capernaum and the road to Magdala. It was a place of inner courtyards and rooms furnished without accounting for cost. He had arranged for Mary Magdalene to arrive before Jesus. The servants knew her as an habituée, and the prostitute was escorted to the long panelled gallery overlooking the dining area. Leading down from the balcony was an enclosed staircase; when he was bored with his guests Simon used it to slip away to his bedroom – and Mary.

From her vantage point she saw Jesus led in by a servant. Simon motioned Him to be seated, making no attempt to offer the traditional kiss of welcome. She immediately sensed tension. The lawyer further broke with normal social mores by having no other guests present – a studied insult to Jesus. The meal offered was frugal: boiled rice and vegetables served with wine from a pitcher she had once noticed the servants use. The lawyer's conversation was immediately taunting. Did Jesus see Himself as some sort of unqualified doctor who had to treat the outcasts of society? Jesus answered equably: '*They that are whole have no need of the physician, but they that are sick.*'

The guest was an equal match for His host. Simon persisted. What did Jesus mean by those words? The reply might well have sent a shiver of excitement through the listening woman. '*I came not to call the righteous, but sinners to repentance.*'

The lawyer pounced. Jesus sounded like a Disciple of John the Baptist with no original thoughts of His own. Was that what He was? A blind follower of a man most people thought was mad?

Jesus would not be drawn.

'*Why*,' demanded Simon, '*do the followers of John fast often . . . but thine eat and drink?*'

Jesus' reply had likely brought a smile to Mary Magdalene's lips. '*Can you make the children of the bridechamber fast while the bridegroom is with them?*'

The image of the lawyer slumped back on his divan, annoyed and nonplussed, survives with his next questions. Was Jesus trying to diminish the Baptist's importance? Were His words a clever polemic?

Jesus answered with a reply that He had used before, and would do so again, when faced with such a challenge. '*Verily I say unto you, Among them that are born of women there hath not risen a greater than John the Baptist: notwithstanding he that is least in the Kingdom of Heaven is greater than he.*'

Simon pressed. Jesus was still just using words, clever phrases that might well impress an ignorant proletariat, but ones that the lawyer could see through. Was not the truth that Jesus perceived Himself as greater than John? Was He not guilty of self-aggrandisement? Or did He really believe He was only one step away from God?

Where such questions might have led remained unresolved. Simon's interrogation was interrupted by the arrival of Mary Magdalene. In her hands she held an alabaster box. Her eyes, fixed on the penniless mendicant Jesus, began to fill with tears. Simon remained too stunned to move; his mouth worked but no words came.

Weeping copiously, Mary knelt at the feet of Jesus and, using a finger-bowl from the table, washed in turn His

65

calloused soles, drying them with her long red hair. Then, after tenderly kissing the insteps, she massaged cream into the skin before she resumed kissing it.

The lawyer finally managed to speak. Visibly out of control, forgetting the reason why she was in his house, Simon screamed at Jesus. Did He not know who this woman was? That she was a whore more infamous than any found even in Babylon? Anywhere in the Roman empire!

Jesus stared steadily at His angry host. Then He asked Simon to ponder a parable: A money-lender had two debtors. One owed a thousand shekels, the other one hundred shekels. Neither could repay their debt, but the money-lender forgave them both. The question, Jesus concluded, was which of the two freed debtors was the more grateful? Simon had replied that it must have been the one who had owed the most; anybody could have deduced that.

For the first time Jesus moved to the attack. *'I entered into thine house, thou gavest me no water for my feet.'* He pointed at Mary Magdalene. *'But she hath washed my feet with tears, and wiped them with the hairs of her head. Thou gavest me no kiss: but this woman since the time I came in hath not ceased to kiss my feet. My head with oil thou didst not anoint: but this woman hath anointed My feet with ointment. Wherefore I say unto thee, Her sins, which are many, are forgiven; for she loved much.'* Then, ignoring Simon, Jesus helped Mary Magdalene to her feet and closed the alabaster box. He addressed her directly for the first time. *'Thy faith hath saved thee.'*

The next certainty is they both left Simon's house, and she became His bond-slave, selling off her home and possessions and distributing the proceeds among the poor, offering herself as a living example of the positive value of His love, which had been strong enough to overcome the evil of her former life. Never once had she flaunted her new-found purity and modesty, but time and again had shown an infinite capacity for comforting those who grieved, encouraging those who felt disheartened, guiding those who appeared lost. She always gave without demanding, and recognised the weaknesses in others without judging. In that way she was as close to Jesus as any Apostle.

* * *

The pit was uncovered and the lambs removed. They were cooked to perfection, and laid on prepared beds of dried grass. Once more the butchers fell to work, carving and slicing. Pitchers of wine were distributed. Then the meat was hastily devoured, a rite that spanned the gulf of ages, linking the past of the Jewish people with the present.

Next morning, after bidding Mary Magdalene and the other women to await their return, Jesus led the Apostles out of Shechem to lay the final foundations for a new chapter in that story.

Jesus took them on their longest journey so far. For a while they travelled east into the desert land of Decapolis, where even Herod Antipas' troops rarely patrolled. Then they headed north, keeping well clear of the Roman-built road to Damascus and its camel caravans and imperial checkpoints. In the distance was the permanently snow-capped Mount Hebron, blessed among all mountains: from its topmost peak Gabriel had banished Satan and later the she-devil, Lilith; on its slopes God had spelled out the Covenant to Abraham. The ancient book of Zerubbabel promised that, when the time came for the redemption of the Israelites, heralded by the advent of the Messiah, the Temple would be miraculously transported from Jerusalem and divided between Hebron and the four other holiest of mountains – Lebanon, Moriah, Tobor and Carmel. Fording the Jordan, Jesus led them back into northern Galilee to their final destination, the altogether more modest Mount Hattin, a mere fifteen hundred feet above the Sea of Galilee and so far with no religious significance. Jesus had chosen Hattin for one speech to the Apostles which would crystallise all His teachings, ensuring for ever a complete and indisputable explanation of His message.

At some isolated point, Jesus found a place on the mountain relatively sheltered from the wind – one of the many ledges which act as stepping stones to the top. The Disciples squatted in a ring around Him.

He began to speak.

From the outset, Jesus made it clear that this was not a sermon but a succession of unchallengeable and inviolate maxims, each given its explanatory illustration. His listeners could hardly have needed reminding that not since the days of Moses had anyone promised to be so explicit. But the commands of the ancient patriarch had mostly been a catalogue of prohibitions: about not coveting, stealing and killing. Jesus' prescription for the future – not only for the Apostles but for the whole world – was a very different kind of divine revelation: a carefully ordained philosophical system and a practical charter for all future human behaviour. He promised them at the outset that when He had finished, they would know all that was required to fit God into daily life, to understand that beyond today lay a far more rewarding tomorrow – by accepting His vision of the future.

Just as there would be an endless search to identify His physical features and voice – was it high or low pitched, broad and heavily accented or mellifluous and compelling? – so in time to come passionate argument would try to prove, or disprove, what Jesus said on Mount Hattin was far from original; that His mantle of a lawgiver had been sewn together from passages in the Psalms and Proverbs of the Old Testament. All these future exegetics in the end would only provide a very unexpected denouement – that Jesus was not an iconoclastic revolutionary, nor did He look with contempt upon the people of His day. Neither had He come to destroy. The Law and the prophets remained valid for Him as the ultimate expression of God's will. What set Him apart on Mount Hattin was challenging not the law, but its interpretation. He had come to offer a penetrating new insight into God's will. His secret, the power of His magnetism, was His unique ability to take familiar expressions of faith and redefine them with a compelling certainty. Most important of all, He made it clear that everything He would promise was on the verge of realisation: the Kingdom of Heaven would begin here, on this mountain. Yet when He began to speak – the wind tugging at their robes – He did not cozen the Apostles with illusory hope of a new national prosperity for their nation, a fresh political resurgence; He would not discuss whether the Romans could be driven from the land, along with the Herodian dynasty. Instead He concentrated upon personal justice and human happiness. There was nothing demagogic in His approach – though His strictures against the rich and powerful would subsequently be seen as such. Instead, to the dozen men clustered around Him, Jesus expressed Himself in the only way He knew – from the background of His own impoverished upbringing, in which there were no luxuries for His brothers and sisters, let alone for His mother and putative father. Mary, very possibly, had sown the seeds of the argument for a brave new idyllic world, where the brotherhood of man could live in perfect harmony if certain basic rules were followed. Jesus began to unfold an uncompromising manifesto.

'Blessed are the poor in spirit: for theirs is the Kingdom of Heaven. Blessed are they that mourn: for they shall be comforted. Blessed are the meek: for they shall inherit the earth. Blessed are they which do hunger and thirst after righteousness: for they shall be filled. Blessed are the merciful: for they shall obtain mercy. Blessed are the pure in heart: for they shall see God. Blessed are the peacemakers: for they shall be called the children of God. Blessed are they which are persecuted for righteousness' sake: for theirs is the Kingdom of Heaven. Blessed are ye, when men shall revile you and persecute you, and shall say all manner of evil against you falsely, for My sake.'

In summarising all He represented so succinctly Jesus was clearly aware the Apostles still vied with one another to impress Him of their worthiness. Such behaviour, He said, must stop. The rules He was laying down allowed for no further conflict among them. Equally, He could offer them no immunity from the threats and railing of the world that still existed beyond the mountain ledge. They would need all their belief to combat the pressures.

Matthew recorded how, having outlined the broad concept, Jesus developed it, expanding it into a stunning new interpretation of the law, choosing as His first example the Mosaic commandment: *thou shalt not kill.*

'But I say unto you: that whoever is angry with his brother without cause shall be in danger of the judgement.'

Even *thinking* harm about another required an act of reconciliation with that person – and asking forgiveness from God. Jesus warned that the same stricture applied to lust: an adulterous thought was as bad as the act of unfaithfulness itself; a potential libertine should pluck out an eye before being led into temptation. The continuous demand to resist all temptations was embedded in the reward of infinite succour.

There followed rules which opposed everything the men around Him had been taught from birth. From now on they were not to answer force with force; above all they must ignore one of the most revered teachings of the Bible about demanding an eye for an eye or a tooth for a tooth. This was a hallowed principle of revenge, one which a community could evoke or a family claim or a single injured person demand. For centuries it had been enshrined as the ultimate vengeance of God, a counter-balancing of divine punishment. The Disciples were given a radically different instruction.

'Whoever shall smite thee on the right cheek, turn to him the other also.'

Once more Jesus stressed this was the state of mind essential for even being *considered* worthy to enter the Kingdom of Heaven. But there was more; an end to praying as hypocrites did, striking exaggerated poses, making sure everyone around was aware of their piety. It was better to pray alone. God would hear: that was all that mattered. No more complaining about obligatory fasting: it should be regarded with eager anticipation, a further chance to sacrifice a part of daily living to Him.

Through all these commandments ran a consistent theme: *agape* – love. That was the core of the life He was proclaiming: the outer mould for a new kind of inner living, a pattern of personal conduct. Rather than judge, people must love; rather than condemn, people must love; rather than criticise, people must love. Yet – and He made the distinction clear – this love must not be the possessive, clinging kind. It must strive to come as close as humanly possible to God's love. Jesus was asking no one to feel blind affection for an enemy; rather, that a foe be prayed for, his crime forgiven, and his punishment left to God. That was what He meant by love.

Jesus reminded them they must concentrate on ending their criticism of others and try to improve their own defects. He told them the story of the two brothers: one only saw the mote in the other's eye, totally failing to see the beam in his own. He reminded them never to squander the treasure of spirituality – illustrating this with the futility of casting pearls before swine. He cautioned them again always to be on the lookout for false prophets. They would soon come to know them – just as easily as they would recognise a wolf covered in a sheep skin. He told them they must always assume full responsibility for every word and thought. All this formed part of the only basis for the kind of living He envisaged, where everyone served God and no one else. In future there could be no place for the tiniest division of loyalty: no one could serve two masters.

But even then there was no absolute promise: a person could appear to live by all these precepts, and yet in the end be refused admission into Heaven because God would know it had all been a sham; the Disciples must learn to discern. '*By their fruits ye shall know them.*' For miscreants genuine repentance was never too late. That was their only hope of salvation.

Always seeking an example they could readily grasp, Jesus recounted the foresight of the man who built his

71

house on a rock. It survived storm and flood while his neighbours who erected theirs on sand saw them swept away. For Matthew the message was again clear: to those who believed in Him, their faith – like that house – would survive. Others would be consigned to spiritual oblivion.

Jesus cautioned that this new lifestyle would not be easy; it was not meant to be. But in return for making every effort to follow it, Jesus made them promises which He guaranteed would be honoured: '*Ask and it shall be given you. Seek and you will find. Knock and it shall be opened unto you.*' Then He asked them to rise, bow their heads and repeat after Him the prayer He wanted them to use from then on – and encourage everyone else to use. It was the *Our Father*.

So ended the Sermon on the Mount – and Christianity was born on a hill overlooking a land occupied by pagans, possessors of the greatest empire the world had yet known. Within a year its Emperor, Tiberius, a living divinity, would make a pilgrimage to another summit, close to the very centre of imperial power, to beseech his gods. Not for a moment would he suspect there was nothing they could do to preserve him and all he ruled over from fate.

29 Anno Christi: The World of Rome

*This Agglomeration which
was called and still calls
itself the Holy Roman Empire,
was neither holy, nor Roman,
nor an empire in any way.*

— Voltaire

THREE

The Emperor

___

*Depart from me, ye cursed, into
everlasting fire, prepared for the
Devil and his angels.*
— Matthew 25:41

The first light of a new day revealed the procession climbing Palatine Hill. Its approaches were guarded by the arch erected in memory of the Emperor Augustus, step-father of the short, bull-necked figure sprawled in the litter. The recorders of such detail would be no less sparing elsewhere.

Since that day in AD 14 when the consuls had sworn their loyalty to him after Augustus' death and Tiberius had taken the sacred emperor's oath of office, he had regularly been carried to the hilltop. There were those in the Senate who said that upon his accession Tiberius continued to act out a role he had perfected early in life: that of dissembling hypocrite. Others claimed the emperor was obsessed with the thought that the gods made a mistake in allowing him to be elected.

He had never found it easy to reconcile the various factions within the Senate and, from the outset of his reign, was over-awed by the sheer size and responsibility of the empire. He had tried to cope in the only way he knew: vacillating between placating and threatening, provoking

75

servile smiles from his aides. Everyone in Rome knew that behind the Emperor's outward arrogance lurked a deeply insecure man; that while he had ample blood on his hands, that which flowed through his veins was tainted with venereal disease after a lifetime of sexual indulgence. Finally, tired of being dominated by his mother, the Empress Julia Augusta, and inconsolable since the death of his favourite son, Drusus, Tiberius had, three years earlier, in AD 26, virtually relinquished imperial responsibility and retired to Capri. The funeral of his mother had brought him briefly back to the capital.

The emperor had been effusively welcomed by the man he had entrusted with the daily affairs of state, Aelius Sejanus, the prefect of the Pretorian Guard. Sejanus had organised the procession with the same relentless efficiency with which he managed everything. But he was more than a ruthless administrator. In a city of natural plotters the prefect was the arch-manipulator: controlling by continuous persecution, treacherous friendships and the ruin of the innocent. It was widely whispered that, to bring him even closer to Tiberius, Sejanus had first seduced Drusus' wife, Livilla, before persuading her to poison her husband, whom Tiberius had hoped would succeed him. The prefect had then coolly asked Tiberius if he could marry the widow. The emperor was still considering whether the gods favoured the idea. Sejanus had hesitated over enlisting the imperial astrologers to manipulate Tiberius. This time they might refuse – unlike a previous occasion when they had collaborated in sending Pontius Pilate to Judaea, removing another threat against Sejanus' burning ambition to sit on the imperial throne.

At that time Pilate had been back in Rome awaiting a new posting after service in Germania, where he had met his wife, Claudia Procula, the grand-daughter of the Emperor Augustus. She had introduced her husband to imperial society as part of her campaign to obtain for him an important post in the capital. Pilate had been flattered to be treated as an equal by Sejanus. The prefect had eventually

76

enquired whether, with Tiberius already into his dotage, Pilate had any interest in the highest office in the land; with his wife's connections he would have a good chance of being considered by the Senate. Pilate had finally admitted that the prospect of one day wearing an emperor's toga was certainly attractive. Shortly afterwards, he had been summoned before Tiberius and told he was being appointed procurator of Judaea, one of the remotest and most insignificant of imperial postings. To refuse would have ended Pilate's career. Sejanus had been placatory – Pilate should see it as an interlude – and suggested he consulted the court astrologers to see what portents the move indicated. The sooth-sayers were reassuring. Not only should Pilate go to Judaea – but he must take his wife with him. The astrologers had merely faithfully repeated what Sejanus had ordered them to say. With Claudia Procula out of the way, her husband had lost a Roman power-base to run for emperor; her formidable connections would be dissipated by distance.

To make absolutely certain Pilate's chances of being a contender for imperial succession were forever destroyed, Sejanus had set out to ruin the procurator's credibility. He had instructed Pilate to submit regular and detailed accounts of events in Judaea: nothing should be too insignificant to go unrecorded. From Caesarea had come a stream of scrolls dealing with every aspect of social, religious and political events impinging upon the Roman occupancy. Tittle-tattle mingled with affairs of state. Pilate's pedantic mind missed nothing. They were the boring outpourings of an isolated bureaucrat who increasingly felt the world revolved around his pettifogging accounts of warring Jewish sects and the scheming of the tetrarch, Herod Antipas, who in any event sent his own confidential reports to Tiberius. These were in turn intercepted by Sejanus; many were critical of the procurator. Increasingly, Pilate's own assessments had a complaining tone: the Jews were always trying to stir up trouble; their High Priest was a charlatan; their rites were revolting. Nevertheless, the prefect was careful: proof of consistent and sustained stupidity on Pilate's part could see him being recalled to Rome where, with the help of his wife, he could set about redeeming himself. Sejanus ensured just enough material came before the emperor to make Tiberius shake his head.

The procurator may or may not have mentioned John the Baptist or Jesus in his reports. To the prefect the pair would in any event have sounded about as threatening as the ants scurrying across his path on Palatine Hill. Soon the gods would once more awake and begin manipulating the all-important seven planets which bore their names: the Sun, Saturn, Jupiter, Mars, Venus, Mercury and the Moon. It was a Roman article of faith that each heavenly body had some lordly or terrifying influence on all earthly lives. Sejanus knew that the emperor shared his view that no Roman should take Jews seriously; in no way could their religious claims ever threaten Rome's invincible gods.

To bring Tiberius to the summit of the Palatine Hill required several hundred men. Ahead of the main procession marched a cohort of sixty infantry, led by the signifier carrying their legion standard, its symbol drawn from paganism. There followed a squadron of cavalry, wrapped, like foot soldiers, in the long red cloaks of the Imperial Army. Immediately behind rode a legate, commander of the procession, and three tribunes, younger men, high-born citizens of Rome who had chosen military life. Distanced from them, mounted on his Arabian stallion, rode Sejanus. He was unusually tall for a Roman, swarthy and thin-lipped, dressed in his *toga praetexia* bestowed by the Senate as a mark of distinction. Over the heavy woollen wrap he wore the embroidered cloak of his high office. His feet were encased in a pair of hand-tooled riding boots.

Next came two cohorts of the Pretorian Guard, one hundred and twenty of the finest fighting men in the empire. Each had sworn a personal oath of allegiance to Tiberius when he gave them their shields, embossed with ancient protective symbols and curved to deflect spears and slingshot. They wore short capes fastened around their shoulders with silver chains. Scabbards sheathed short-bladed swords, designed for close-in fighting; these men were always the last line of defence between the emperor and any threat on his life. To further emphasise their status they marched with two standards, the personal emblem of Tiberius and their own, far older, banner, dating from the time when the praetor, a Roman magistrate, commanded them. Tiberius formed them into the Guard in AD 23 when he detected the first plot against his life. They marched on either side of his litter. Twenty-four slaves supported the huge ornate sedan upon their shoulders.

At the rear in a smaller sedan rode Livilla, hidden from view behind heavy lace curtains. Once more Sejanus had called upon her to further his ambitions. She had always seen Claudia Procula as a rival to her position as Rome's leading hostess and needed no encouragement to damage her rival. Livilla had mentioned to Tiberius she had heard a story that Claudia Procula was becoming captivated with some wild prophet in Judaea. She knew, instinctively, there was no need to press the matter. The poison had been planted. The emperor's mind would do the rest: nurturing the titbit, trying to fit it into all the other pieces which nowadays never quite seemed to come together in his brain.

The procession was completed by the emperor's astrologers, a dozen men in cloaks covered with a variety of mystical symbols. They had decided Palatine Hill was the most favoured by the gods for Tiberius.

The group moved at a pace which ensured the emperor reached the summit before Jupiter, the greatest of all the gods, ordered the sun to appear. It was a cherished belief of the astrologers that, if Tiberius basked in the first glow of sunrise, the omnipotent ones would continue to look upon him benignly, thus ensuring the emperor remained the ultimate authority in nearly all of the known inhabited world.

Only China was a comparable power. From within its remote borders came the silks for the high-born women of Rome, brought by a series of camel caravans over alps, through jungles and deserts, a journey that took almost a year. From Asia came spices and grain, jewels and precious stones, conveyed across the Indian Ocean in Arabian dhows and up the Red Sea to the great Roman warehouses in Syria, at Antioch, Damascus, Palmyra and Petra. From there they were shipped to Rome. Every nation, occupied or free, supplied the needs of the emperor and his subjects – and was glad to do so. Yet there were those in the Senate and the Forum who had begun to urge Tiberius to abandon his frontier policy of non-aggression and once more to extend the boundaries of empire in all directions. Why should Romans have to pay exorbitant prices for elephant ivory, hides and slaves from the depths of Africa when they could be there for the taking once the land was conquered? Why not send Rome's famed war galleys to capture and hold in the name of the emperor the Persian Gulf? Why not go even further – into India, and perhaps, ultimately, China itself? Rome, insisted those senators, had the military resources; the risk would be high, but the rewards greater.

Tiberius had rejected the arguments. Rome's twenty-seven legions were fully occupied with containing existing frontiers. Even then, there was continuous skirmishing along the Rhine and the Danube. In North Africa Roman-held territory was regularly attacked by savage nomadic tribesmen. Gaul was still restless in spite of the crushing of a rebellion in AD 21; the country's fanatical Druids could rise again at any moment.

On the climb up the Palatine slope the emperor lay inside the litter, his massive round head reclining on pillows stuffed with soft plumage plucked from under the wings of partridges, and his flabby body motionless upon blankets dyed purple and embroidered with gold. Over fifty years of age when elected, Tiberius had steadily developed an old man's fears of plotters stalking the corridors of power. Only the gods could protect him.

The procession reached the hill-top. The soldiers and cavalry formed a protective circle around the litter. The legate ordered it lowered on to its stubby legs. That done, the slaves remained motionless: to move without further command would mean being sentenced to savaging by lions in the arena. Sejanus dismounted before the emperor. Tiberius' protruding red-rimmed eyes were those of a man in the depths of his winter who appeared an even more vulnerable figure under the brightening sky. The once jet-black hair, kept short and combed forward from the crown to the forehead, Roman style, was wispy and grey. The formality of his *toga picta*, with its distinguishing purple hem and golden embroidery, contrasted with the *udo*, a pair of homely felt slippers.

Yet, from that summit, Tiberius knew that when he looked north he ruled in an unbroken line of over twelve hundred miles, across the River Po, over the Italian Alps and on into northern Europe. From there came iron and timber for his warships, along with pigs and sheep for his banquets. A shuffling turn to the west and he could picture the six-day sea journey to the north-west coast of Spain and the longer voyage to Cadiz, at the very tip of Iberia, where a large, unnamed rock guarded the exit to the unknown wastes of the Atlantic. From this region came the olives he preferred to the Italian ones, as well as stonemasons to chisel idols and whores to stock the brothels of the capital. Peering south, Tiberius, on a clear day, could glimpse the trading ships, sails fully rigged, plying between Rome and Carthage, a four-day sea journey, taking legionnaires back to their North African posts and bringing home salt and dates. A half-turn would bring him in line with the long sea route from Rome to Alexandria, a twenty-day voyage that could be twice as long if the wind veered. From the Egyptian port came perfume, papyrus, linen, exotic fruits, granite, marble, grain and asphalt. Another full turn would bring him north-east, to face out across the great overland trading route that began in the centre of Rome and ended sixteen hundred miles away in Byzantium; it was the busiest and most diverse of all the trading routes within the empire's borders. Finally, facing fully east, Tiberius could look towards the furthest extremity of his empire – the frontier that incorporated Syria and Judaea.

He had never understood why his predecessors had clung with such stubbornness to Judaea, the second-smallest of all the Roman provinces, probably the poorest and certainly the most troublesome. A succession of procurators had done nothing to quell the rebellious nature of its people. Nothing seemed to work – tact, an iron hand, appeasement, mass execution; there was always trouble. Part of the problem was that Judaea was not fully integrated into the empire. Its foreign and military affairs remained in the hands of the locally appointed representative of Rome, Herod Antipas. The emperor was represented by Pilate. In theory the procurator had the last word; in practice the tetrarch and, even more so, the High Priest wielded considerable responsibility over their people in all matters which did not impinge upon direct Roman concern; two indigenous legal and religious systems existed side-by-side. When he appointed Pilate, Tiberius had delivered a standard reminder: the Jews enjoyed autonomy in legal affairs except for political offences; Roman policy also totally distanced itself from all local crimes of a religious nature. Julius Caesar had granted these freedoms; from time to time the Jews had fought for more concessions. There had been bloodshed. Tiberius had often considered withdrawing all privileges, but had been counselled against this by Sejanus – to do so would provoke further unrest. Roman blood would be spilt quelling it and there would be more angry debates in the Senate. The cantankerous emperor reluctantly decided to let matters stand. He could only have hoped that Pontius Pilate would absorb some of the native cunning Herod Antipas displayed.

From when he had first come to Rome, a dark-skinned slip of a boy, the Herodian prince had impressed Tiberius. He bore the mark of a scion of Herod the Great: the same coal-black eyes, thick lips and short-cropped crinkly hair. He had demonstrated what he had learned at his father's knee on that day when they had sat together in Tiberius'

82

box overlooking the Roman arena. Invited by his host to choose whether a group of Jewish gladiators who had shown particular bravery should live another day, young Herod Antipas had given the thumbs-down sign. The fighters had been disarmed and then devoured by lions. Tiberius had decided here was a Jew who knew his place and accepted Roman mores – and history would have another footnote.

Isolated on Capri, tired from a long life of wasted opportunities, an object of mockery in the streets of Rome, Tiberius had increasingly turned to mysticism to sustain his last years. The predictions of his astrologers were of paramount importance. Through them he sensed matters that his faded political acumen no longer divined. They had alerted him that something unusual was about to happen. Whatever it was, his astrologers must have assured him it would have nothing to do with Pilate's reports about those Jewish preachers. No one had the power to overcome the gods of Rome.

Suddenly, the astrologers dramatically extended their hands towards the horizon. Gaining size by the second came the fiery planet that Jupiter had once more commanded to rise. The sun's rays reached out and touched the emperor, the power of its light forcing him to close his eyes, its warmth removing the chill from his body. The veneration over, the procession descended towards the city, itself now a burnished glow of terracotta roofs, marble colonnades and stone arches.

While Romans continued to speculate how long the gods wished to provide their emperor with his reassuring sunrise, few wondered what lay behind Tiberius' increasing preoccupation with other portents. He had ordered his seers to study the miraculous powers of Pythagoras, dead for six hundred years, to discover if he really had foretold the future by geometric symbols. Imperial sooth-sayers had travelled to Alexandria, home of the greatest library in the East, to pore over the words of the most celebrated of all the Persian *magi*, author of two million verses in which magic merged with philosophical speculation. Had he also been able genuinely to forecast happenings? Closer to home, in the records of the Roman Senate, astronomers continued to search for signs of a forthcoming comet similar to the one which had plunged across the sky after Caesar's murder. Still other investigators sought evidence for another unscheduled eclipse – as timely as the one which had once quelled a mutiny by one of his own legions on occupation duty in Germania. The suddenly darkened sun had convinced the soldiers the gods were angry at their behaviour.

Everything Tiberius did nowadays was based upon fallacious associations which linked to the gods all human doings, as well as the physical properties of the earth. He found a satisfying neatness, completeness and total indisputability about the method. His astrologers had recently interpreted the way the entrails had emerged from a slaughtered hen to mean the time was right to deport some four thousand Jews from the comforts of Rome to the inhospitable rock of Sardinia. His other advisers had observed that since then the emperor had become still further obsessed about the movements of the sun, moon and stars and the way they affected the life and death of all mankind. For him they were the controllers of the human race; they determined its future – and his.

Even in gossipy Rome – where sharing a sworn secret was a sacred duty – few realised that Tiberius was driven by a real and growing panic that the gods would one day soon casually take away what they had bestowed: his supreme power over every man, woman and child in an awesome empire, conquered and established in little over a hundred years. A fear of impending death had become another fixation. He tried to rationalise to himself and others his feelings but this often created a terror that left him a gibbering ruin of a man. But nowadays it was not only death which frightened him: somewhere within his great fief was a threat which had no shape or form. Yet it was there. This certain knowledge had come to him in a dream. He had first experienced it thirty years before when Augustus had exiled him to a lengthy period of lonely duty on Rhodes. There Tiberius had consulted the legendary Thrasyllus of Alexandria, an astrologer who was an outstanding Platonist and the author of a standard text on numerology. Thrasyllus had not only predicted that Tiberius would become emperor but had also interpreted the vision as meaning that during his reign '*a great challenge would arise in the East*'.

Recently the dream had returned. Yet, in spite of all their skills in creating elaborate patterns indicating what the disposition of the heavenly bodies meant at any given time, his astrologers had not been able to identify the form this challenge would take. He had urged them to search harder for signs that would reassure him he had not offended the gods. He could never forget they had demonstrated their power to take terrible revenge upon Julius Caesar, who until then had been their most favoured son on earth.

In 45 BC, three years before Tiberius was born, Caesar had met and seduced Cleopatra in Egypt. She was a nubile twenty-two-year-old; he well into middle-age, virile and battle-scarred, until then more at ease around chariot steeds than in a boudoir. Romans had smiled understandingly when Caesar confirmed his mistress as Queen of Egypt; a hero was entitled to his peccadilloes.

Many, however, felt he had gone too far in tampering with the calendar. They waited uneasily to see how the gods would respond. Rome had calculated the year by a lunar method which lagged behind solar reckoning. In 45 BC, Caesar saw the Roman year was shorter by sixty-seven days than the solar one. Displaying his renowned impetuosity, he decreed that every ensuing imperial year would contain 365 days. This still made the Roman calendar different from the one used by the Jews. Their rabbis had told Caesar's astrologers that in the Jewish holy *Book of Jubilees*, God had ordained that '*man must observe a year of 364 days and those that do not bring upon themselves misfortunes*'. Caesar learned that another essential of their religion was believing that one day their God would visit earth and walk

85

among them as a man. To a Roman this was pure nonsense. Why should a god ever want to assume the shape of a mortal? Caesar had not been given long to ponder such a question. Three months after changing the calendar he was murdered on the Ides of March in 44 BC by Brutus, Cassius and others upon whom he had bestowed favour and pardon.

Anarchy had subsequently befallen Rome and the empire. Hundreds of Senators were executed for conspiring in the death of Caesar. Cleopatra committed suicide. For three years the world trembled as factions in Rome fought for control. From the carnage emerged Augustus. Many now said his achievements were greater than even Caesar's. Augustus had streamlined the cumbersome Roman administration and ruled through careful delegation. But on the advice of his astrologers he did not reinstitute the old lunar calendar. When he became emperor Tiberius was counselled that the gods had forgiven the great Caesar and were content that the solar calendar should remain on the statute books.

Perhaps it was the return of Tiberius' dream, once more with its hint that the threat lay in the East, which had aroused the emperor's interest in the way the Jews calculated their year. They regularly added an extra month, *Vaeder*, inserted between the spring months called *Adar* and *Nisan*. An important date was the spring equinox called *Tisni*, celebrated by Jews throughout the empire. The emperor had learned that during the last *Tishnin* Jews started again to refer openly to the most mysterious of all figures in their religion, the one they called in Aramaic the *Messiah* – the Expected One.

For the past five centuries – dating around the time the code of the Twelve Tables had been given to Rome by the gods so that its citizens would know how to order their lives – there had been almost no mention of when this *Messiah* would come. Instead, throughout the empire – from the mountains of Armenia overlooking the Caspian Sea to the wastes of Pannonia and on to the verdant coast of Gaul – Jews had chanted their mournful lament. '*There are no prophets left now, none can tell us how long we must endure.'*

But in the carefully screened news Sejanus forwarded to Capri, the emperor's consuls, procurators and tribunes reported that within the empire tantalising whisperings had continued to seep from within their closed communities. The *Messiah* was coming.

On previous occasions when they had been angered, the Roman gods had exacted tribute in the form of massacres upon this people who worshipped a single God without an image. In the past forty years there had been no fewer than fifteen pogroms against Jews. Never far from the surface was a virulent anti-Semitism which Tiberius resolutely believed the Jews brought upon themselves with their clever schemes to avoid paying taxes, and their refusal not only to enter a Roman home, but even to touch, by as much as a handshake, anyone but their own people. They rejected pork on the grounds that their holy books called it unclean – a further affront to Romans, who regarded suckling pig as essential for any feast. They included in their religion the degrading ritual – performed in the name of their God – where the foreskin of each male child was removed. Tiberius had nevertheless been astonished to learn that, in spite of massacres and exile, there remained within his empire an estimated seven million Jews; one out of every ten he ruled over professed a faith and adhered to customs he regarded as repugnant and profane. Unlike all other races – Greeks, Gauls, Cyrenaicans, Africans, Britons, Germans and Iberians – the Jews steadfastly clung together in a remarkable way. Even in Rome they remained in close-knit ghettos living by their own strict regulations. They gathered together every week on their holy days to pray and sing psalms. They called this place the *kinneseth*. Tiberius preferred the Greek, *sunagoge*. Whenever they could, if only once in their lifetime, Jews returned to Judaea to partake in great feasts and pray at the Temple. Then, imbued with fervour, many would spread their religious propaganda, patiently explaining the virtue of a weekly day of rest, their festivals, their custom of lighting lamps and rules about food. This proselytising, when it stretched the forbearance of the gods too far, led to renewed bloodshed. Yet, in spite of this, attempts to Romanise them had failed. The greater the pressure, the more determined the resistance.

The humblest Jew displayed a mysterious pride suggesting that he or she not only belonged to a people far superior to the Romans, but was also a member of the greatest race to walk the earth. Even in the literal jaws of death facing the lions in the arena, Tiberius had watched, both baffled and impressed, how Jewish gladiators accepted their fate unflinchingly. Sometimes they had even fallen to their knees and cried a last prayer to their God, assuring Him they were glad to be a part of His greatness. The emperor had once ordered a thousand Jews in succession into the hippodrome sands to see if one of them would show fear. None had. He could not understand such reaction. Neither could he grasp why so many Jews, having claimed they had been given a piece of land by God, should leave it. This incessant movement was their Diaspora.

Like much else associated with Jewish history, Tiberius discovered their restless dispersion had its origins long before Rome laid down a history. Having come out of Egypt, the *Exodus*, they soon returned there. Caesar had brought back to Rome evidence that the equivalent of a legion of Jews had borne arms for a Pharaoh in the sixth century and had captured and held a vast tract of desert around the oasis of Aswan. They were given honorary Egyptian citizenship – but steadfastly clung to their own religion. Later, tens of thousands of Jewish warriors enlisted in Alexander's army to capture Mesopotamia. They had been similarly rewarded, taking from Greek culture what they saw as worthwhile, like its language, but never its religion. The Romans had themselves found their fiercest opponents often were Jewish fighters. As a token of respect some had been spared upon capture and offered the chance of settling in some new and inhospitable part of the empire. The opportunity had been accepted, the areas had prospered.

Gradually the Diaspora took on a new meaning: the wandering pedlar Jew became absorbed as a successful businessman into every town and village under Roman domination. Within the past fifty years Rome had joined Alexandria as one of the two main centres of the Diaspora. The Egyptian metropolis contained as many Jews as lived in Judaea; three-fifths of the city's population worshipped the God of Abraham. In Egypt there were over a million who did so.

Caesar had encouraged them to settle in Rome, allowing them to build their underground cemeteries and openly worship before the seven-branched candlestick of their faith. Many, through favour or purchase, had acquired Roman citizenship – though Tiberius still resisted the idea of Jews holding any imperial appointments. Denied any official authority, Judaism continued to wield an influence that clearly strengthened the mood of those of its people who remained in their tiny homeland. Scattered to all corners of the empire, the Jews, unlike any other of Rome's subjects, had a well-established communications network which kept them in touch with each other and events in Jerusalem. Again, at the core of that bond was their religion. Jews could never forget that, no matter how well they did living among the heathen, the Diaspora was still their *galut*, the Exile: a curse God put upon them for the sins of their forefathers. No Roman, least of all an emperor, could understand how foolhardy they could be.

Upon the death of Herod the Great, Jews had launched an uprising against the Roman forces. In spite of an early success in all but overwhelming the small garrison, the revolt was doomed. Within a week's march were two legions in Syria; from Cyprus and Egypt, scores of Roman war-galleys were swiftly sent with further forces. Yet the insurrection had gone ahead. The quick-thinking Jerusalem garrison tribune had ordered the Temple to be put to the torch. Thousands of Jews perished, including a large number of priests. The population then surrendered. For the next three months the predominant sound in Jerusalem

89

was the hammering of crosses to hang some two thousand men and women judged to have been involved in the rebellion. To reduce the risk of further revolt the country was divided between three of Herod's sons: Archelaus, Philip and Herod Antipas. The brothers had fought and plotted against each other. There had been uprisings. Jew had killed Jew. High Priests had been replaced. There had been further fighting. The final victor in the family battle for power had been Herod Antipas. In the face of his political manoeuvring some procurators had lasted only months. The emperor had not intervened in the matter: if a Roman was not skilled enough to withstand the machinations of a Jew he had no place in Judaea. If nothing else, Pontius Pilate had learned that much.

30 Anno Christi: The Unholy Triumvirate

*How would you be if He, which
is the top of judgement,
should but judge you as you are?*

— Shakespeare
(Measure for Measure)

FOUR

The Procurator

Thou art not far from the
Kingdom of God.
    — Mark 12:34

What would endure of his biography, as well as in the
memory of those who knew him, however slightly, would
be that punctuality remained one of the many inflexible
rules of Pontius Pilate. He had awoken when the level of
liquid, released a drop at a time, had reached the fifth
marked division on the side of his bedroom *clepsydra*, the
most elaborate of all the water-clocks in Judaea. This was
one of the few hours he enjoyed in Jerusalem, when the
infinity of shades were at their most captivating, the tints
moving from black to mauve to the first hint of yellow.

During the night he had slept fitfully as he often did when
Claudia Procula was not there; he blamed his insomnia on
the bed, even though it was identical to the one in his palace
in Caesarea, his wife having arranged for a pair of these
elaborate beds to come with them from Rome. Whenever
Pilate travelled on duty to Jerusalem he brought one with
him. Like the *clepsydra*, it was far superior to anything
available in this god-forsaken land. The frame was carved
from the best wood, the mattress and pillows were stuffed

with wool, the coverlet came from Corinth and was the handiwork of the finest seamstresses in the empire. Yet perhaps alone, away from her, he did indeed brood that in Rome his future had been finally settled: that he was destined to end his days as a forgotten cipher of imperialism.

Claudia Procula would upbraid him for such defeatism; reiterating that while they were both victims of Sejanus' machinations he must never forget her imperial pedigree. She would fight for him; all he had to do was listen to her. Her connections in Rome assuredly had sent word that in the past year Sejanus had begun to over-reach himself, becoming embroiled on too many hostile fronts; that a ground-swell was developing against the prefect's intrigues; that the emperor no longer blindly trusted him. A wise woman, she might well counsel that this was not the time for her husband to go to Rome and confront Sejanus. Let others do that. Far better to bide his time.

Their marriage, for all its outward signs of harmony, was, in its tenth year, an empty barren union, sustained only by her determination to see him elected to the highest possible office.

Despite her coldness and indifference, his wife was the only person to whom he could speak freely. On this trip she had promised to join him in Jerusalem, showing no reluctance to do so, as she had in the past. Nor had she expressed detestation of Jews since she had begun to read his reports on Jesus and John the Baptist. He had never asked her to explain her interest in them. She could certainly be imperious and secretive when she chose. Those were the times he felt most keenly the gulf between them.

Overnight more drovers with their sheep, cattle and caged birds – all to be sacrificed – had camped out on the hills around the city. Mingling with them were thousands of new pilgrims. Their presence gave credence to the ancient Hebrew expression '*next year in Jerusalem*', the one promise which had brought Jews here down the centuries. Huddled around the camp fires they waited for the city gates to open. Then they, too, would converge upon this capital standing in the centre of the Judaean land, amongst hills which not only presented a formidable physical barrier, but also in the eyes of every Jew held a special significance. For them, those mounds, when finally seen, were a reminder that their journey was almost over; that behind the slopes and escarpments lay the holy courts of Jerusalem, whose glories they had chanted about while on their journey. The closer they came to Jerusalem, the louder grew their Hebrew psalms of ascent, as they picked their way upwards to the high plateau almost three thousand feet above sea level where the city stood. No matter which way they approached – over the top of the Mount of Olives, along the Valley of the Cheesemakers, across the rocky slopes of the Gereb, through the bleak Kidron ravine or traversing the Mount of Scandal where Solomon had allowed altars to be raised to the gods of his heathen wives – they still had to climb. Pilate understood why their Scriptures constantly called it the '*city of the high place*'.

He could have recited word-perfect the passages about Jerusalem not being '*rebuilt in its entirety until all the children of Israel will be gathered from exile*'; that the city was '*The tent God will spread forth in all directions*'; that '*in the end of time Jerusalem will become the metropolis for all lands*'. No doubt it was about as realistic to Pilate as the claim that '*one day*' this invisible Jewish God would surround the city with seven walls: including one of silver, another of gold, a third of precious stones, finally an outer wall of fire to ensure that the existence of Jerusalem '*will radiate to the four corners of the world*'. Even Saturn would not have dared to make such a promise. Yet those people out there on the hillsides and within the city wall believed it all implicitly. Pilate had never understood how they could seriously think for a moment that this city would ever replace Rome as the centre of global influence; it was another example of their arrogance.

No doubt, too, they would be astonished at how much he

95

knew about their holy writings and the rituals controlling their daily lives; of customs peculiar to Jerusalem such as displaying a flag at the door of a house where a feast was being held; of doubly fining a caterer who produced a bad banquet for the disgrace he had caused the host and the upset to guests; of city ordinances which included a ban on renting out private homes to pilgrims and forbade an oven because the smoke would blacken the Temple: all baking was done in the Tower of Ovens, a huge edifice in the Lower City. He was above all aware of the special significance Jews attached to one particular gate in the Temple walls, built by King Solomon to await the day when the *Messiah* would enter.

To Pilate this was as foolish as the popular Jewish belief that deep inside the Temple was a stone which miraculously hovered in the air and would only fall to earth when the *Messiah* came. Pompey had thoroughly searched the Temple and never mentioned such a phenomenon. The procurator understood the need for such legends: the Jews, for all their innate violence, were a weak people. He knew they saw him as inflexible and stubbornly relentless, ready, if the occasion demanded, to act with pitiless savagery. While he never hesitated to do so, they totally failed to understand that his response – like that of any Roman – was a natural reaction to their attitudes. All things Rome held sacred Jews regarded as profane: every Roman was the living incarnation of idolatry and debauchery, sensuality and materialism, power and tyranny. While in the rest of the empire Jews were content to remain aloof from their neighbour, here, in Judaea, they displayed an open revulsion that no self-respecting Roman could tolerate – let alone the appointed representative of the emperor. It was all there in his accounting to Tiberius.

Well into his forties, Pontius Pilate, after a career representing the empire in various provinces, was used to total respect – not to being ostracised, or treated with barely disguised contempt and hatred. What made it particularly galling was that these reactions were not the natural responses of the conquered to the victors: the Jewish attitude seemed to be rooted in an ancient superiority complex that was an essential part of their religion.

Pilate possessed a highly developed mind and was a voracious reader. In his four years in Judaea he had mastered Hebrew and among Jewish works he had read was the *Sybilline Oracles*, written around the time Rome had really begun to expand its empire. The procurator discovered within its pages a prayer which could only have infuriated him. '*A holy king will come and reign over all the world – and then his wrath will fall on the people of Latium and Rome will be destroyed to the ground. O God, send a stream of fire from heaven, and let the Romans perish, each in his own home. O poor and desolate me! When will the day come, the judgement day of the eternal land of the great king?*'

That awesome entreaty historically reaffirmed Pilate's strong sense of mission. Not only was he the ultimate representative of the emperor; he was also an emissary of the gods. For all of Sejanus' trickery he also believed he had been sent to this forsaken land to continue to make its people bow, to break their will further, to reinforce the authority of Rome upon them with a rigour and severity in a way no previous procurator had done. But he had not made the mistake of his predecessors and acted impulsively. Every step he had taken had been calculated: reporting to Rome the renewed talk of a coming *Messiah*, the emergence of preachers in Jerusalem and Galilee; strengthening his surveillance on Herod Antipas and around the Temple. From whatever quarter trouble might erupt, Pontius Pilate believed he was ready to overcome it.

This time he had been in Jerusalem a week; as usual it already seemed like a year. To him it was a dirty, smelly city, not to be spoken of in the same breath as Rome. Yet Jews continuously used the syllables of its name in their prayer life. Every year at Passover pilgrims from the farthest reaches of the empire travelled to what they called the Lord's Home – the massive Temple edifice adjoining his quarters. Some had actually wept at the onset of their journey here to celebrate the greatest of all their feasts. It drew vast throngs from all parts of the Diaspora: Jews from Babylon with black robes trailing in the dust; Jews from the steppes of Anatolia in their goat-hair cloaks; Jews from Phoenicia dressed in tunics and striped trousers; Jews from Rome in togas; Jews from Gaul in leather skins; Jews from Spain with sheep pelts around their shoulders; Jews from Persia in their silks, brocades and adorned with gold and silver. Battening on them were the pedlars of sacrificial animals and the money-changers, scandalously over-charging, just as in Rome the purveyors of votive offerings to gods doubled their prices at certain times.

Pilate hated coming here not only for Passover, but also for the Feast of Weeks, the Day of Atonement and the Feast of Tabernacles. At these times the air was particularly filled with the sickening smell of burning animal and bird flesh from the sacrificial altars, and the cloying aroma of incense. Each festival was a highly dangerous time, when popular sentiment could overflow and the air fill with talk of insurrection and revolt. These were the occasions when the Jews felt most keenly the yoke of foreign rule and their patriotic motivation was closest to the surface. Pilate was certain there would be the usual rabble-rousers, whispering that any Roman presence in the city – especially at this hallowed time – was the ultimate and never-to-be-forgiven insult.

Yet informers had reported that the indignation of Jesus continued to be directed at what happened in and around the Temple. He had increasingly challenged what went on within its hallowed courts and rooms, where the rabbi-scholars taught amidst the shrieks of the sellers of sacrificial birds and animals and the din of the money-changers offering pilgrims coins which had been ritually cleansed in exchange for their pagan currency.

The difficulty in trying to assess the response to Jesus, like all else reported to Pilate about Him, was the system the procurator had inherited. Paid on the importance of their information, he found the network of spies notoriously prone to exaggeration. They often brought tales to his headquarters at Caesarea which bore the hallmark of lengthy sojourns in village taverns, where Hebraic mythology was rife. In one, shortly after He was born, the parents of Jesus had come to the Temple to partake in the ritual observances which accompanied the birth of every Hebrew baby. A Jewish woman was considered ritually unclean for forty days following the delivery of a son and eighty in the case of a daughter. To purify herself she made a sacrificial offering of two doves to a Temple priest. He cut one bird's throat, allowing the blood to flow down the side of the altar, removed the crop and feathers, broke the wings and threw all the remains into a fire. The blood of the second dove was sprinkled over the altar. The ritual was completed when the rabbi pronounced the woman cleansed, and the husband handed him five shekels – the prescribed payment for the sacrifice. This commonplace occurrence had, according to one informer, in the case of the baby Jesus, an unusual twist. Leaving the Temple, cradled in His mother's arms, they had been confronted by an old man – *'just and devout'* – named Simeon. He had peered at the infant and at once hailed Him as the Expected One. A few minutes later an old woman named Anna, who lived on the charity of the faithful, spending her days in the Court of Women, had repeated the prediction. Both Simeon and Anna were long dead. There had been no way for Pilate to have that particular report verified. For his soldiers to question the mother of Jesus would almost certainly have proven fruitless. She would no doubt have denied any such happening.

There had been another incident.

At the age of thirteen Jesus had come to the Temple for the custom of *bar-mitzvah*. For a Jewish boy this meant being embraced as a son of the law – forever responsible for observing all religious and civic duties; from now on an adult who acknowledged sacred commitments. Once more an informer had offered an account which made Jesus exceptional, describing how the boy had come with His

99

parents who had once more paid for a sacrifice to mark the occasion. When the ceremony was completed, Jesus had disappeared. After spending three fruitless days searching for Him they had finally returned to the Temple to offer prayers for His safety and found Him debating with the priests over their interpretation of faith. The story ran that He had challenged and corrected them on numerous points – and they had been astounded and fearful of this prodigy. When Jesus' angry mother had chastised Him for such behaviour the boy had reportedly given a puzzling reply: *'How is it that ye sought me? Wist ye not that I must be about my Father's business?'* Pilate had concluded at best it was no more than a determination by Jesus to give an early sign he intended to devote Himself to a religious life. To try to give it any deeper meaning was nonsensical.

The reports about Jesus which had reached Pilate after the wedding feast at Cana could neither have alarmed nor seemed exceptional to him. The poetry of Homer and Virgil was filled with similar fantasies. Besides, many of the accounts of His miraculous powers had taken on a suspicious similarity; His curing of a possessed madman was very close to a subsequent account of His healing an epileptic boy.

The procurator had come to recognise that his spies were rich in metaphors and imagery but short on case histories which would warrant the slightest accusation that Jesus had set out to show He was in any way equal to the empire's gods: they could inflict plagues, deflect the arrows of an entire army, make men fall in love or go mad, change one person into an animal and another into a rock. Compared to them, Jesus was no more than the object of harmless adoration mostly still confined to Galilee.

While he had continued forwarding details of the less farcical stories about His work to Rome, Pontius Pilate regarded Jesus, three years after He had first come to the procurator's attention, as still a curiosity rather than a threat. However, it did not explain to Pilate the attitude of both the current High Priest, Joseph Caiaphas, and Herod

Antipas towards Jesus. They had still made no move to silence His sustained attacks against the Jewish establishment.

The relationship between Pilate, Herod Antipas and Caiaphas had never been smooth. The procurator had expanded the infamous system of tax-gathering through private contractors. These men – reviled as *publicans* and *sinners* by Jesus – often had their own armed men to enforce their demands; they could also call upon the imperial army for support. While many were Roman citizens, imported for the task, a growing number were Jewish. These collaborators were treated by other Jews as outcasts, denied any place in Jewish society and disqualified from giving evidence in any Jewish court. Their families were equally ostracised. Herod Antipas and Caiaphas had appealed to Pilate to stop using Jews to collect taxes. He had refused. The tetrarch had asked the emperor to intervene. The response from Capri was that in this instance matters must remain as they were. On learning of Herod Antipas' intervention Pilate ended all pretence of treating him on anything resembling equal terms. To the procurator the prince was no more than a Jew aping his betters, and he regarded Caiaphas with similar contempt.

Pilate now only met the High Priest when the official came to collect his vestments. The expensive stole and other regalia were kept in a stone-lined chamber in the base of the Antonia Fortress which the procurator used as his headquarters in Jerusalem. The door of the chamber was triple-sealed, one affixed by the High Priest, the other by the chief of the Temple guard – an official named Jonathan – and the third by Pilate himself. The seals had been broken a few days ago in preparation for Passover. Keeping the apparel of the High Priest under Roman custody and handing it over only for high festivals, reclaiming it immediately a feast ended, was a deliberate measure to curb Caiaphas' authority and protect Rome against any surprise move he might attempt in his capacity as the most senior

101

Jewish dignitary in the land. Under certain circumstances, Caiaphas would need his full religious regalia to enforce his authority – such as presiding over a session of the Great Sanhedrin, the supreme court of the Jews.

The procurator knew the restrictions over vestments not only rankled Caiaphas' own highly developed sense of personal pride but painfully reminded him he could not exercise his power without the permission of Rome's representative. To salt the High Priest's wound – and to increase his own wealth – Pilate had continued the custom of his predecessors by demanding from Caiaphas a substantial annual payment to remain in office. This further soured daily contact between the two administrations.

From his bedroom high above the Sheep Gate, Pilate had an unsurpassed view of one of those stretches of water Jews regarded as holy; this one was called the Pool of Bethesda. Winding between the Mount of Olives and Mount Gereb were the roads to Jericho, Bethlehem, Shechem and Caesarea.

A hundred feet below where he stood came the measured tread of sentries patrolling the stairways and the entrances to the secret passages which led from the fortress under the Temple and into the heart of the city. In one of these the quick-thinking tribune's men had broken out a hole and started the fire which quelled the revolt of AD 6.

Pilate could be certain that any rebellion would now be even more swiftly crushed. All Jerusalem's gates had been further fortified under his order. At each entrance the massive wall had been deepened to three times its depth and heavy iron gates replaced wooden ones. Above each was a platform from which defenders could rain down spears and sling-shot upon attackers. The Golden Gate had five hundred lances permanently racked in its guardhouse. The Fountain Gate had the natural defence of the Kidron Valley before it; few Jews would want to wage war by crossing their hallowed cemetery of Jehoshaphat, where the prophet Joel had predicted all souls would gather on the Day of

Judgement. In the west of the city were the Gate of Ephraim and the Corner Gate, already strong defensive positions, but now permanently manned by two cohorts of Roman soldiers. Another cohort protected the Dung Gate, leading to the foul-smelling Valley of Hinnom where child sacrifices had been made to the Phoenician god, Moloch, and the Temple courts had been filled with prostitutes. Hinnom was also a place to be avoided. Finally, there was the Fish Gate, where the roads from the coastal villages converged. These tracks were constantly patrolled by cavalry who ran spot checks on Jews; anybody carrying an unauthorised weapon was invariably executed. In the event of trouble in Jerusalem's narrow streets and alleys, the horsemen could ride to Caesarea to summon more troops. Force-marching they could reach the city in under sixty hours.

Caesarea was a Roman port. Within its walls Jews were barely tolerated and Romans could walk streets which were filled with statues to their gods and emperors. Here in Jerusalem such totems were forbidden under what the procurator complained was yet another sop to the Jewish faith. In Caesarea coins were struck bearing the portrait of Tiberius. But they could only be used within the city limits – and never displayed in Jerusalem because their image offended Jewish susceptibilities.

The longer he lived amongst them, the more intolerable Pilate found the Jews; they were full of incomprehensible prejudices and exponents of intrigue. At every opportunity they sought to make Judaea almost ungovernable. Pilate had six thousand troops to deal with any insurrection. Five hundred of them formed the Jerusalem garrison. The remainder were in Caesarea. Like the procurator, they hated duty in Jerusalem, which at times like Passover contained more potential trouble-makers than would be found in all Rome.

At this hour of the morning within the city wall – ringing it for three unbroken miles – all was virtually silent. The only sign that people lived here was the stench of excrement, decaying refuse, cooking grease and, from the

103

west, the reek of diseased animal carcasses thrown on the city's rubbish dump. The smoke from its perpetual fire reminded Pilate of the place to which the gods of Rome regularly consigned those who had displeased them. The stench reinforced his distaste for this country, its people and its leaders. Pilate had learned they could be as ruthless towards their own kind as Sejanus. The fate of John the Baptist proved that.

* * *

It had been in the month the Jews called Iyar when news reached Pilate of what had happened at Machaerus. In his squat and menacing fortress, Herod Antipas had kept John the Baptist imprisoned for over a year. Yet, brought from his dungeon, the prophet had continued to reproach the tetrarch over his relationship with Herodias, the wife of Herod Antipas' brother. Several times the tetrarch had made the uncomfortable journey from Jerusalem to his hill-top keep far beyond the Dead Sea to try to persuade the prophet to cease his attacks. Groomed and scented, dressed in all his finery, he had sat with John, clad in his shirt of camel-skin, hair matted and tangled, beard flowing and unkempt. Alternately cajoling and pleading, then threatening and screaming in fury, Herod Antipas had tried to persuade John to accept his relationship with Herodias. The more the tetrarch talked the greater John's intransigence. God, he insisted, told him he could not remain silent. Herod Antipas should be an example to his people, instead his behaviour had aroused Divine anger. Deeply troubled, the tetrarch had discussed the situation with Herodias. She consulted the High Priest.

To celebrate his forty-ninth birthday Herod Antipas moved his entire court to Machaerus. Invited, too, were Jerusalem's most important businessmen and traders. Pilate had ordered no Roman could attend. But he had his informers in place. The birthday festivities lasted a week, culminating in a sumptuous banquet which kindled memories of the day the tetrarch's father had been crowned: then a thousand lambs had been roasted and a hundred of the loveliest dancing girls had performed. His son also had a similar number of lambs slaughtered as well as importing delicacies from all around the Mediterranean. At the height of the revelry, a shocked murmur had swept through the women seated at the far end of the huge banqueting hall. Herod Antipas had urged his step-daughter, Salome, barely fourteen years of age, to dance before the drunken men at the tetrarch's table. The women were stunned into silence when Salome rose to her feet.

Pirouetting slowly at first, then gaining speed, she swirled bare-footed before her step-father. Skilfully she removed one silken veil after another, tossing each one to the clamouring men. Finally, she stood almost naked before them. Herod Antipas promised Salome any reward she cared to name for her erotic performance, even, he added, half of his kingdom.

She, perhaps a child seeking guidance, or possibly acting out a role rehearsed with her mother, hesitated. Her step-father repeated that she could have anything. Salome walked across to the table where Herodias sat with the other women. After her mother had whispered in her ear, she walked back to stand before Herod Antipas. He paled at her request, and appeared to hesitate, to be on the verge of refusal, when she repeated the words more firmly. He had promised, she reminded him in her little-girl voice, now he must not disappoint her. Two guards were despatched to the dungeons. There, below the marbled floors where Salome waited, silent like everyone present in the hall, one guard had held John the Baptist's head over a block, while the other severed the neck from the body with a sword. The two men returned with the head on a brass tray. Salome reportedly screamed. Herodias had smiled and raised her glass towards Caiaphas who was seated with a select number of his priests at a table adjoining that of the tetrarch.

Even in death – so his spies had told Pilate – John the Baptist's face possessed an expression that chilled their hearts. Herod Antipas had offered to bring the head to Caesarea so that the procurator might try to have his astrologers interpret its meaning. Pilate had coldly refused. The tetrarch had then thrown the skull to his mastiffs.

* * *

Arriving in Jerusalem, Pilate's agents had brought news of a growing rumour that Jesus intended to confront Caiaphas during Passover concerning the death of His cousin. If that was the case it would remain a matter for the Temple authorities. Caiaphas had his own efficient force policing the Temple; he could also call upon the tetrarch's troops. That sort of superiority should be enough to deal quickly with Jesus and His followers should they create trouble. But to apprehend Jesus in the name of Rome when there was no evidence to show He had committed a crime under imperial law could provoke the wild backlash the procurator was here to prevent.

Pontius Pilate recognised only too clearly that if the Temple authorities moved against Jesus or indeed any other preacher in the super-heated emotionalism of Passover without the greatest skill and stealth, coupled with the strongest of legal reasons – instead of the personal vindictiveness which had led to John the Baptist's death – the whole country could again be plunged into bloody revolution. The chances at the best of times of avoiding this were not improved by the position of Caiaphas. On the one hand he represented the supreme ancient authority of the Temple administration, the chief spokesman for the nation and ultimately the most important Jew in the eyes of the Romans. Yet, largely because he remained in office solely at the pleasure of the procurator, the High Priest was no longer regarded by the people as the symbol of Jewish pride and hope, or irrefutable living proof that Judaism was superior to all religions. Many saw him as a puppet and a collaborator, a quisling who clung to the most sacred of Jewish national and religious posts through simony. Pilate realised that if Caiaphas misjudged the mood of the people over Jesus, no matter how strong the provocation or how certain the High Priest was of his facts, there could still be trouble. That would involve the use of Roman force. The procurator well knew how easily aroused the masses became over anything that threatened or offended their religious susceptibilities.

After his first visit to Jerusalem, Pilate had decided to replace the unadorned standards raised over the Antonia Fortress. He felt they did not reflect the authority of Rome. He already knew it was a basic and sacred precept of Judaism, clearly stated in the Book of Exodus, that '*thou shalt not make unto thee any graven image or any likeness of any thing that is in heaven above or that is in the earth beneath*'. But, determined to show his power over, and contempt for, such hallowed belief, something no previous procurator had done, Pilate went ahead with implementing the Roman custom of displaying, on all public buildings and monuments, standards and insignia which bore the face of the ruling emperor. These were raised overnight, Pilate gambling that, once in place, the Jews would allow the image of Tiberius to flutter beside the Temple. Dawn saw the full force of Jewish rage. A deputation, led by no less than a thousand priests from the Temple, marched to Caesarea, demanding the removal of the offensive emblems. Pilate refused.

For five days thousands of Jews had surrounded his palace, chanting prayers and squatting on the ground in an act of peaceful civil disobedience. The procurator had turned a legion loose on them; the Jews were driven at sword-point into the local hippodrome where gladiators fought once a week. Pilate ordered the soldiers systematically to beat the Jews. Hundreds of lacerated bodies littered the arena. Still the demonstrators refused to concede. Finally, Herod Antipas had arrived and suggested to Pilate that such important emblems warranted a more deserving site than Jerusalem could offer and would be better displayed at the magnificent Temple of Augustus in Caesarea. Pilate had at the time reluctantly admired the tetrarch's face-saving solution. The offending banners were removed from Jerusalem, and Herod Antipas attended the dedication ceremony which saw them raised over Augustus' Temple. He had then sent a report of the incident to Tiberius. When Pilate had thankfully thought the matter forgotten, from Capri had come a stinging rebuke. Pilate's instinct had been to move against the tetrarch as he had successfully done before with local opposition, but Claudia Procula cautioned against action. Her Roman sources had already told her about Herod Antipas' favoured position in the emperor's eyes. Not for the first time Pilate had been grateful for his wife's advice.

It was an autumn morning when Pilate had stepped ashore from an imperial galley and stood for the first time on the soil of Judaea. His dark deep-set eyes had surveyed the guard of honour and, beyond, the silent, watchful throng of Jews. No doubt he knew they were measuring him. The conquered always did; trying to gauge whether he would be strong or weak, fair or unjust, a meddler in their affairs or indifferent to their ways. The first moments of a new posting were always like that. Each time he had tried immediately to stamp his personality on the onlookers, showing them the way he intended to behave.

Less certain can be the motive for the action ascribed to him on that blustery day in Caesarea. After inspecting the drawn-up cohorts, the procurator had walked to the huge sun-dial on the jetty. Under a cloudy sky it was useless. He ordered it to be removed and replaced with a water-clock.

Later he had ordered checks to be made on the *clepsydrae* in Roman law courts throughout Judaea. They had been installed to curb the speeches of lawyers who were paid by the hour. The clocks governed the length of time permitted to prosecutors, who had two hours to state a case; defence counsel were allowed an extra hour. For grave offences – the murder of one Roman by another or Jews being tried for insurrection – the prosecution was permitted six hours to present their facts while the defence were entitled to a full nine hours to call rebuttal evidence. Trials could be conducted – if a Jew was involved – in Aramaic and Greek; but judgements were always recorded in Latin. Jews condemned to death had brief details of their crimes nailed in all three languages to their crosses. Such attention to detail was in the best tradition of the Roman administrative class – and had ensured Pontius Pilate was even more hated in the eyes of the Jews. A lifetime in imperial service, hoisting the standards of Rome over distant colonies, hardened him to such responses.

Pontius Pilate had a distinctive physical characteristic, the result of an imperfectly healed shoulder injury suffered when he had been rescued from a sinking war galley driven on to the rocks of Sicily during one of the sudden storms that made the Mediterranean so treacherous in winter. His skin had been darkened by desert sands and blistered in icy mountain passes. Born and bred in the colder uplands of the Apennine mountain spine south-east of Rome, he possessed the racially classical round head of antecedents who, centuries before, had migrated from Asia Minor over the Alps. His family name was a distinguished one among the Samnites, the clannish mountain people who, since the First Punic War – twenty years of fearsome battles – had provided Rome with administrators to rebuild and exploit shattered lands and peoples. Before governing Judaea, Pilate had seen service in Spain, Greece and Gaul. In all these territories – in spite of his reading and other knowledge – he had displayed, along with his punctuality, a massive indifference to local culture and customs. For him the social mores of the long-haired Gaul were no different from the peculiarities of Spaniards or Greeks. They were all subjects of Rome.

He would have preferred the governorship of a province where the seasons were more pleasing than those of Judaea: two abruptly divided periods of a long broiling summer and a winter when the nights were so cold that the law of the Jews required a creditor to give back any clothes, taken as a pledge, before darkness. During Adar, the third month of the Hebrew calendar, there was heavy frost at dawn, sweltering heat at noon, and at dusk ice once more rimmed the ornamental ponds in the grounds of his palace. No one had warned him of the winds. His Homeric scrolls had spoken of wafting breezes, little more than zephyrs. While it was true they made the heat of high summer almost tolerable, there was also the winter *qadim*, howling from the east, icy and dry, cleansing the air and chilling the bone marrow with its blast. Most unbearable of all was the *khamsin*, roaring in from the desert filling the sky with a gritty greyness that could bury a horse and its rider in an hour. A squadron of Rome's finest cavalry had vanished for ever on border duty beyond the Ghor, swallowed by drifting sand. Then there were the rains. A year's downpour fell in a few days, storms so severe that entire villages were washed away. Afterwards, the sun would settle in the sky and the temperature would rise dramatically, leaving the ground fissured over large tracts.

Only in certain parts, especially in Galilee, was the land fertile and forested, a place of fragrant acres of brushwood, where myrtle, broom, lentisk and acanthus grew. Where these had been cleared were fields of mustard and the smaller cultivated patches of mint, camomile, cummin, flanked on either side by meadows grazed by sheep. Here, too, grew the staple olive, the fig tree, the grapevine and the exquisite almond whose early flowers signalled another spring. Cereals, nuts, pomegranates, dates, lentils and beans, onions and peppers: all thrived in Galilee.

Several times in the past year, claiming she was bored with the garrison-town atmosphere of Caesarea, Claudia Procula had visited Galilee, travelling with a handful of servants and a small escort of soldiers. She had assured her husband that no one – not even the most fanatical Zealot – would attack her retinue, let alone kill her: Jews did not slaughter women. Pilate could have assumed the agents of

110

the High Priest and tetrarch had observed her and no doubt Herod Antipas would have reported the matter to Rome. Yet no reminder had come from the emperor or Sejanus that such behaviour was not in keeping with her position. Pilate had not asked her why she had gone – let alone whom she may have seen or met. That could only have led to an embarrassing confrontation with her. Within their relationship the procurator had learned that there were some matters best left unexplored.

Among the black-eyed Semitic women, her Romanness, like that of her husband, was unmistakable. Claudia Procula came from a military family which for over two centuries had supplied tribunes and legates to command legions. Her life had been punctuated by fine funerals for uncles and cousins killed in action. When her father died some believed the loss had killed off her own soul, leaving intact only her ambition and lust for position and power. She was lean, strong-jawed and forthright, and had ruled the domestic side with a grip as steely as Pilate's. On one occasion a slave she caught stealing had been sent to the great stadium in Caesarea, to die in its arena in combat with a lion – such a spectacle always drew huge crowds of non-Jews. The slave's amulet had been left hanging in her servants' quarters as a reminder of the fate awaiting all miscreants.

In Jerusalem further flocks of animals were being driven through the Sheep Gate. Traders' stalls were beginning to line streets, so narrow that two donkeys laden with panniers could not pass at the same time. From the maze of alleys and lanes people were emerging, almost all on foot; only the very rich could afford litters. Already, legionnaires – each man in his crested helmet and cuirass, red cloak worn on the shoulder – had begun a new day of patrolling.

Pilate would not leave the Antonia Fortress until it was time to return to Caesarea after Passover. From his vantage point he could stare down upon the Temple courts. He firmly believed an acquiescent Temple with firm control

111

over its people was a prerequisite for effective Roman governance.

Yet, at the last Feast of Tabernacles, there occurred an incident showing Caiaphas had backed away from ruthless action as far as Jesus was concerned. Incomplete and no doubt distorted, as such stories always were, Pilate's spies had emphatically reported that Jesus had suddenly emerged in the Temple and claimed his right to teach, and had caused a great stir with His astonishing attack on the priests over their hypocrisy in allowing circumcision on the Sabbath yet condemning Him for healing on the same day. From the rapidly growing crowd in the courtyard had come protests that here, indeed, was the man whom the Temple agents had sought – yet He was being allowed to speak freely with no one making a move to apprehend Him. Jesus had silenced the cries with a furious and extraordinary phrase that His '*time had not yet come*', and calmly walked past the guards and out of the Temple.

Pilate had little difficulty in assessing such behaviour: Jesus had simply been carried away by religious fervour. These past years the procurator had heard of numerous examples of such behaviour by itinerant preachers. What interested the procurator now was the truth of yet another report – that Herod Antipas was finally going to act against Jesus.

FIVE

The Tetrarch

Go ye and tell that fox,
Behold, I cast out devils
and I do cures today and
tomorrow, and the third
day I shall be perfected.
— Luke 13:32

The vast caravan of Herod Antipas and his entourage stretched back through the Wilderness of Judaea and skirted the shores of the Dead Sea. While its rear echelon was in the shadow of Masada, the most impregnable of all his father's fortresses, the vanguard was in sight of the Kidron brook that spewed winter rains from the Mount of Olives outside Jerusalem into the still waters of the vast lake, so heavy in minerals that no one could sink beneath its surface. Curious to prove this point, the tetrarch had once ordered a group of slaves to be slashed with swords, bound hand and foot, and thrown into the Dead Sea. They had remained floating, screaming in agony from the salts penetrating their wounds before they finally bled to death.

Herod Antipas transcended mere folklore, and his instability makes plausible the claim that for months he had plotted the death of Jesus for the stinging insult of branding him a fox. Ezekiel had called the false prophets of Israel foxes for ruining the nation, and no doubt Herod Antipas relished the prospect of subjecting Jesus to the torture the

113

tetrarch's numerous executioners devised. But after delivering His rebuke Jesus had once more mysteriously vanished from Galilee.

Herod Antipas' strong sense of survival must have been a constant reminder that Jesus should have been dealt with like any other activist and killed when His followers had numbered scores, not thousands. Then, His devotees would have done nothing. They were country people, far from Jerusalem, well beyond the centre of influence. Now Jesus was expanding His power base.

He had attracted growing support from the Pharisee party – the committed religious opponents of the Saducees, who were seen as collaborationists for accepting official posts under the Romans. Caiaphas was a Sadducee, the only bond he shared with the tetrarch; and just as Herod's relationship with Pilate was at a nadir, his contact with the High Priest was strained since the death of John the Baptist. Caiaphas had begun to speak about the tetrarch having abandoned himself to a purely licentious life. Herod Antipas had sent word to the Temple not to meddle in his morals. The warning was a reminder that the Herodian dynasty had always controlled the High Priesthood for its own ends. But the tetrarch knew Caiaphas was more devious and adroit than many previous holders of his office. That could explain why he had not acted against Jesus. Caiaphas was merely biding his time, wanting to be absolutely certain that any action he took would not involve the Romans.

The Sadducees were bent on keeping Judaism simple, intending it should remain centred on the bulwarks of Scripture, the Priesthood and the Temple. All other matters – particularly economics and politics – should be kept out of the religious arena. Sadduceeism had created a holy, dead relic of Judaism, though the party's conservatism had given it a natural appeal to the rich and powerful. Its doctrine had a strong attraction for both the Romans and Herod Antipas: it made for easier rule.

The Pharisees argued that the Torah applied to the whole

of Jewish life – and that included the right to express a strong political commitment. They had become the natural critics of the Roman occupation. When the Herodian dynasty was founded with the connivance of Rome, and later the compliant High Priesthood of Caiaphas came into force, the Sadducees became further natural enemies of the Pharisees who, for all their vociferous opposition, still only numbered around six thousand, mostly in Galilee.

The Pharisee party lacked real leadership. Many of its members increasingly felt Jesus could provide it, that He would unite the many paradoxes which surrounded them: the desire to be both traditionalist and reformist; the wish to be at the same time the core of national religious authority and the centre of political dissent; the belief they had a sacred role to perform as critics of society and the protectors of the faith of Abraham. Jesus was the authentic voice of their kind of Judaism; His teaching was a brave and honourable defence against tyranny and misused power, coupled with a well thought out appeal for the return of the old standards of decency and compassion; His words held the strongest possible attractions for the oppressed masses to whom the Pharisees increasingly appealed. Jesus was literally their God-send. To murder Him could be the precursor to a Pharisee uprising. But with Jesus alive and at their head, any insurrection would also end in unsurpassed bloodshed as hundreds of thousands of other Jews would seize the chance to try to overthrow the Herodian dictatorship and drive out the Romans.

There were a couple, Chuza and Joanna, husband and wife, somewhere in the midst of the caravan who had a special interest in what action Herod Antipas would take against Jesus. Chuza was the tetrarch's chief steward; Joanna was housekeeper to the royal household. In the past year they had become devout followers of Jesus. In their privileged position of personally cooking for and serving Herod Antipas they would have overheard more than most in his vast entourage. The more the tetrarch had dismissed the reports of cures and healings by Jesus the greater had grown Chuza and Joanna's belief in their validity.

Seated astride his magnificent horse, a birthday gift from Herodias, the tetrarch knew that the vast inheritance from his father – military powers no other Jew held, a string of fortresses, theatres where he could enjoy some of the finest tragedy and comedy in the empire, amphitheatres and stadiums for contests-to-the-death – in the end was in the gift of Pontius Pilate. For all his Roman education and embracing of its customs, to Pilate the tetrarch was still a barbarian, someone whose background had never been formed by the great cultural influences of Athens, absorbed and adapted by Rome.

To kill Jesus before or during the coming Passover would virtually guarantee a riot leading to Roman intervention. The tetrarch certainly knew how serious that would be. The procurator would not hesitate to use an uprising as an excuse to end the Herodian dynasty. Already Pilate could confiscate any Herodian property as punishment for any of a wide-ranging number of infractions of Roman law: criticism of anything Tiberius had ever said or done; wearing garments which resembled imperial robes; carrying a ring or coin bearing the emperor's image into a brothel; accepting any honour that had ever been voted to Tiberius.

As well as being a natural survivor Herod Antipas inherited other paternal attributes. He was hard and unforgiving, raised to know the value of cunning, deviousness and brutality. Shedding the blood of others without remorse was something he learned in infancy probably when he first witnessed Herod the Great slice off the head of a slave who failed to show proper servility. The tetrarch lived as he rode, without fear, knowing his lance or his arrow rarely missed, inspired to emulate his father.

King Herod, when still only a young Jewish nobleman, became embroiled on the side of the Romans in one of their periodic skirmishes with the Parthians. His small army had been quickly routed and pursued to the safety of his Masada refuge, situated on a plateau overlooking the Dead Sea. He had erected the massive fortifications, palaces and storehouses some years before. He had left his family in this redoubt and continued with a handful of men across the Sinai Desert to Alexandria. From there he sailed to Rome. Grateful for his support, the Senate appointed Herod King of Judaea and provided him with two legions to protect his title. The first of Rome's vassals in the province, he showed considerable political dexterity in pleasing his imperial masters, yet retaining his position as absolute monarch by ruling with viciousness, using murder and banishment to impose his will. There had never been a more cruel Jewish despot, at heart a pagan and filled with an unshakeable belief Judaea would be ruled by Herodians for Rome until the day came when its leaders would destroy each other, leaving the country ripe for total Herodian domination. His son had been raised on this creed.

However, Herod Antipas was not born to be a natural ruler. Lacking an important requirement – patience – he had not taken time to work out his relationship with the Romans: when to be deferential; when to recognise that something could not be achieved without their help and favour. Instead he had a strong conviction in his destiny, one which included a preternatural acceptance that he was meant to be preserved from the dangers that beset others. Behind his impetuousness, unreasoning anger and wild rage – that could degenerate into terrifying madness – was a highly developed sense of superiority. Jesus was a threat to that entrenched belief; the authentic voice of opposition to the tetrarch's violence, corruption and dishonesty. Jesus' was the one clarion call that rocked the very core of the festering rottenness prevalent in the Jewish establishment. Yet the tetrarch's instinct to kill Him with the same lack of compunction he displayed as a huntsman had been checked by the growing fear such a move could set in motion a reaction that would wreck his ambition to go down in history as a figure greater than his father.

Riding past Herodium the issue of Jesus again bore upon

117

him like a physical burden. The tetrarch's caravan approached Jerusalem from the most incomparable vantage point of all, coming up through Bethlehem to the top of the Mount of Olives. The mound offered a view which never failed to impress him. Across the Kidron Valley Jerusalem looked as unassailable as always, a fortress city defended by a wall that rose from sheer bedrock to nearly two hundred feet. This barrier was topped by towers rearing a further hundred feet into the blue sky. Behind them was the Temple, its golden spires rising a full three hundred feet above its cyclopean foundations. On its northern flank stood the massive square block of the Antonia Fortress from each of whose four towers fluttered Pilate's standard, unadorned in deference to Jewish demands. To the west, the tetrarch's destination, stood his palace, an imposing conglomeration of fortified walls and, behind them, colonnades and towers. As Herod Antipas began the descent from his vantage point, his entourage still tailed back to Bethlehem. Even now he could not be certain what had happened there over forty years ago when he had been a small boy, living at the top of Masada with his maternal grandparents.

★ ★ ★

When he first heard the story Herod Antipas had been enthralled by a saga that held all the ingredients of a superb fantasy, and guaranteed to excite the mind of any child, one in which the mystery of the heavens combined with earthly power and wealth.

It had centred on a star that appeared and vanished at will, on wish-fulfilment and a glorious dream of expectation which ended in a slaughter. It had been recounted by his grandparents, seated high above the silent Judaean Wilderness, in the moonlight over Masada, while far below them the Dead Sea sparkled, and it had indeed been possible for him to accept that a celestial sign had foretold a special birth.

118

Simple and believing nomads, they had said that Herod the Great personally witnessed the star over Bethlehem. It had appeared, the king's astrologers had confirmed, in that year when Jupiter was in conjunction with Saturn, and Herod Antipas had been close to his eighth birthday. Such a conjunction, the astronomers added, normally only came every eight hundred years. His father, so the story developed, had questioned them relentlessly, finally getting them reluctantly to admit that the star might be the long-awaited portent for the birth of the *Messiah* – that indeed He might have already arrived on earth.

His grandparents, their voices very likely as hushed as the heavens above Masada, had explained how his father had asked: where and when might the Expected One have been born? The astronomers had been unable to answer exactly but had suggested that Bethlehem was the most likely place – which would account for the overhead presence of the star. They had reminded their master of the old biblical prophecy: '*A star shall rise out of Jacob and a sceptre shall spring up from Israel.*'

Shortly afterwards three visitors had arrived at his father's court. They said they were astronomers from the East, members of the ancient cult of the Magi. The elderly couple had told the boy – and in doing so gave further lustre to a story he already found fascinating – that the Magi were really Melchior, king of the Persians; Gaspur, ruler of all the Indians; and Balthazar, leader of the Arabian nations. Later, in another retelling, they had confided that the trio were really Japhet, Shem and Ham, descendants from Noah. The young Herod Antipas had not paused to wonder why leaders of pagan nations would come all the way to Judaea to celebrate the birth of a Jewish baby. Instead, he had continued to be gripped by the unfolding tale.

The Magi had travelled over mountains, rivers and deserts to be present when the star had suddenly twinkled, brighter than all the others in the night sky, over Bethlehem. Then it had vanished. They had come on up to Jerusalem to seek the help of the Temple priests in solving the mystery. The High Priest had quickly referred them to King Herod. The men had crossed the city to his palace, where he sat racked with uncertainty over what his own astrologers had said. Their arrival, according to the account passed down to his son, had galvanised the king. Their first question had stunned him. *'Where is the newborn king of the Jews?'* Herod the Great had suppressed his natural instinct to torture his visitors for information. Instead, he had questioned them politely. They told him of their thousand-mile odyssey, and of their fear that they had arrived too late: that the *Messiah* was already born.

Tormented by such news, his father had suggested they rest before speaking again. Then he had summoned the High Priest and all the leading Scriptural scholars in the city, even the hated Pharisees and the diffident Essenes. They had consulted their holy books and concluded that, according to the fifth chapter of their scroll of Micah, the *Messiah* would, when he came, be born in Bethlehem. King Herod had sat transfixed while the High Priest read: *'But thou Bethlehem Ephratah, though thou be little among the thousands of Judah, yet out of thee shall He come forth unto Me, that is to be ruler of Israel, whose goings forth have been from of old, from everlasting.'* Bethlehem, the city of David, was then clearly the designated Saviour's birthplace.

An already exciting story had taken yet another twist. While the king consulted with his seers, the Magi had slipped away from the palace – heading back for Bethlehem. It was again nightfall when they reached the small hillside city ten miles from Jerusalem. There the star had once more appeared. They had followed its rays as it led them across fields, where shepherds kept watch over their flocks on a late summer's night. Finally the star had brought them to a cave. Inside, the trio had found a man, a woman and a Baby. Their quest was over.

Kneeling, they paid their respects to the Holy Family, and then presented the Boy Child with gifts usually given to new-born royalty in the Orient: gold, the symbol of divinity; frankincense, the potent incense used solely on religious occasions; myrrh, a spice used to embalm the dead. Herod Antipas was too young to know that myrrh was also sometimes given to those men and women his father ordered to be crucified. The Magi had explained to the Holy Family that they had left Herod's palace after a divine intervention ordered them to return to Bethlehem and warn Mary and Joseph that the king intended to kill the Boy Child. His grandparents had not explained how they could possibly have known all this. But in answer to his questions, they had told Herod Antipas that the Magi had somehow escaped back to the east, before his father's troops had slaughtered every male child in Bethlehem under the age of two years. To a Herodian prince raised in an atmosphere of continuous blood-letting, that was a satisfying end.

He had subsequently never been able fully to convince himself all this had really happened – that it was no more than a fable. His father had steadfastly refused to discuss it right up to his death. Now there was nobody willing in Bethlehem or among his courtiers who could have confirmed the veracity or otherwise of the story that all these years later had returned to haunt the tetrarch. According to rumour, in spite of the wholesale killing, the Holy Family had somehow escaped into Egypt. What troubled Herod Antipas now was whether they had later secretly returned to Judaea and their child had grown up to be Jesus.

* * *

Approaching Jerusalem in a great cloud of dust Herod Antipas' caravan – a procession of hundreds of horses, camels, donkeys and flocks of lambs to be slaughtered – passed workmen repairing bridges and roads and whitewashing tombs so that the devout would avoid them and not be contaminated before Passover. In an enclosed litter sat Herodias and Salome. The court flunkeys, slaves and eunuchs had made the entire journey on foot. All were protected by the tetrarch's personal bodyguard of nomad horsemen and three thousand Thracian, Germanic and

Gallic troops, the mercenary army Rome permitted him.

At the Golden Gate, Herod Antipas dismounted, leading his stallion into the city and past the Temple. It was his token of respect for the forthcoming festival.

On foot, in his protective armour and headgear, Herod Antipas appeared more than ever as a squat, powerfully muscled figure with protruding eyes darting constantly from side to side. He knew moments like these were the most dangerous for him in this city which he hated – and whose people regarded him with similar loathing. Its population saw him as paramount among collaborators. In the wake of his father's death, when the people had risen against the hated Romans, the insurrection had been contained long enough for the legions to arrive from Syria and Egypt, Herod Antipas in the meantime having used his forces to defend the beleaguered garrison in the Antonia Fortress. That had been the terrible week in which Jew killed Jew on behalf of the pagans – a crime the people of Jerusalem would neither forgive nor forget. Even now somewhere in the milling crowd could be an assassin, a man or woman prepared to plunge under the flanks of his escort's horses and attempt to drive a weapon into the tetrarch's body. He could have thought of a thousand or more persons who would die happily knowing they had killed him. They were the relatives and friends of his victims. He had lost count of how many he had ordered to be put to death. Winding his way through the narrow streets, into the Upper City, he knew that waiting in the dungeons of his palace were more prisoners. It was not difficult to imagine their fear at the sound of his approach.

The palace loomed over the Upper City, forming part of its boundary walls. His father had told him it was built on the exact spot where King David had sung his psalms, and spies of Herod Antipas had reported that some of Jesus' followers claimed He was descended from the royal family.

The tetrarch would have known that in Judaism the use of the word *Messiah* did not automatically bestow divinity. Though he had not chosen to do so, he could have used the title from the day he was appointed tetrarch. Caiaphas had claimed the ancient right of all High Priests to attach the word after his name; it meant *anointed*, a reminder that his inauguration had been blessed with holy oil. The ritual had been introduced by King David, who was first to be known as *Messiah* or, in Greek, *Christos*, Christ. Equally, *Messiah* also held another and far deeper significance to all devout Jews: the concept of a divine deliverer who would rescue them from centuries of subjection which had culminated in the horrendous oppression of Rome. Descending from David, would one day assuredly come, with the miraculous help of God, a very different *Messiah* than the title cheapened by Caiaphas. It was popular belief that the Expected One would liberate and return the Chosen People to their rightful place as the proud unfettered descendants of the most beloved of all biblical dynasties, the Davidic one, which had ended six hundred years before. The Scriptures contained numerous prophecies that the *Messiah* would be heralded by a precursor. John the Baptist had repeatedly claimed that role.

Often on those balmy desert nights, in Machaerus at the onset of the Baptist's incarceration, Herod Antipas had crept away from the bed of Herodias and ordered the guards to unchain the strange man in the dungeon and bring him to the tetrarch. Squatting on the floor before piles of sweetmeats, nibbling as he spoke, Herod Antipas would recount the first reports of the ministry of Jesus: Cana, exorcising the demons and even the unlikeliest claim – the healing of the son of a Roman centurion at long distance. The child had been dying and his distraught father had sought out Jesus, reaching Him after a lengthy walk around Galilee. He had begged Jesus to return with him to help his firstborn. Jesus had told the soldier there was no need for Him to come, that when the Roman went home he would find his son cured. The officer had indeed found his child out of bed and playing. The tetrarch would ask John why a Roman had behaved like that. The Baptist had confined himself to

123

repeating that the *Messiah* would one day rule as David had done as the unchallenged King of the Jews, except that He would not only be a human figure, but would exercise power as God Himself and all people would accept Him and His Temple in Jerusalem.

For all their support for Jesus, the Pharisees were essentially opposed to the prospect of a *Messiah*. He would be a stumbling block in their republican ambitions to abolish completely the Jewish monarchy. Part of their religious philosophy was based upon the timeless words of Isaiah that the day must come when swords would be beaten into ploughshares and the wolf would dwell with the lamb. It was enough for them to live by the old Scriptural adage that God was *already* their Ruler and Lord. There was no need for Him to appear before them to reinforce this clear-cut understanding.

Nevertheless they would still support anybody who could trace his lineage back to David and unite the Jewish forces into a single army. To achieve victory the Pharisees would willingly grant such a person the right to assume the full glory of David's original title. Scriptural belief insisted that the Expected One would be recognised because He would possess prophetic powers not seen since Solomon's reign. He would perform miracles unequalled since Moses had fed the people in the Wilderness. He would, like Elisha and Elijah, be able to bring the dead back to life. Jesus fitted all these expectations.

The tetrarch's palace was the most magnificent of all Jerusalem's dwellings. It was twice the size of the Antonia Fortress and dominated by four massive towers, huge enough for a hundred spearmen to stand on each of their ramparts. Three of the towers bore the names of the few people Herod the Great had really loved. The one overlooking the Serpent's Pool was dedicated to his friend, Hippicus. The adjoining tower, with a clear view across the roofs of the Lower City, was named after Phagael, an uncle of Herod Antipas, who had perished fighting the Parthians.

124

Facing Herodium, the monolithic fortress-tomb his father had built in the prime of life to house his remains, was a tower higher than the others, rising a full one hundred feet above the battlements. King Herod had erected it in memory of his wife, Mariamne. He had put her to death when he believed she, too, was plotting against him. A perpetual flame burnt on top of the tower in her memory.

Far below in the dungeons other fires were kept constantly alight to heat the variety of rods and branding irons used on prisoners. The tetrarch would spend hours watching men and women being not only branded, but also scourged by whips or suspended from hooks with weights attached to their feet, soles barely clear of the ground.

Like Pontius Pilate, the tetrarch had come reluctantly to Jerusalem for Passover. Herod Antipas possessed a desert dweller's dislike for its crowded alleys and their unpleasant smells, enjoying instead the windswept landscapes, broken by chalky hills whose reflections dazzled the eyes, and the narrow *wadian*, valleys which after a while broke the spirit of anyone but a nomad used to traversing them. His spies had reported that Jesus, born and bred in the verdancy of Galilee, had once spent forty days and nights testing Himself in the Wilderness. It seemed a supernatural feat.

* * *

The Wilderness stretched, total and defeating, from the banks of the Dead Sea to the mountain chain in the far distance. Between lay the burning sand. The heat would have risen through the soles of Jesus' sandals, first blistering the skin, then forming callouses. After a while the sand would have become bearable. The further He penetrated into the desert, the sparser grew the vegetation. Finally, nothing, not so much as a blade of grass, was visible in this area where once the people of Sodom and Gomorrah had lived before the fire and brimstone of Yahweh had engulfed their immoral souls. Here, a man could indeed commune with God, trudging over the salt-encrusted earth,

125

the silent dark desolation broken only by a jackal howling in the mountains; or from the Dead Sea the sudden unnerving sound of a massive chunk of asphalt breaking free from the lake bed and shooting to the surface.

From remembered times prophets had gone to the Wilderness to purify their bodies. Desolate and terrifying though the vast empty quarter was, a person could still survive there. Beneath the sub-soil were edible roots and also wild honey was to be found.

When Jesus had come close to the mountains, His followers said He had met Satan. The Devil had asked Him to turn lumps of rock into loaves of bread to prove He was the *Messiah*. He had also invited Jesus to climb to the top of a mountain peak and hurl Himself into space in the belief that His angels would stop Him crashing to the ground. Jesus had rejected the challenge.

★   ★   ★

For the tetrarch any claim that Jesus had out-manoeuvred Satan would be important evidence that He believed Himself so exalted He could confer without fear with the Devil. The holy books taught that only God could do that. Such a blasphemy would bring Jesus to the notice of the Temple. Then it would be up to the religious authorities to deal with the matter.

SIX

The High Priest

---

*All things are delivered unto
me of my Father and no man
knoweth the Son, but the Father.*
— Matthew 11:27

Each day for fifteen years Joseph Caiaphas had made his
way from deep within the Temple towards the most famous
of all its inner barriers, the towering Nicanor Gate. Ninety
feet high, double-doored, each a foot thick, fashioned from
pure silver and gold, it was so heavy that to open and close it
required the efforts of twenty guards. They would be
already waiting, Jonathan, the captain of the Guard,
towering over them, ready to obey any order of the High
Priest. Behind his sanguine blessings Caiaphas was a man of
whiplash power, driven by some inner force to keep the
great machine – the Temple – grinding relentlessly forward
on its ponderous way. There was a hard-rim interior to the
man that matched his commanding look and the authority
in his voice. It would make him all that Scripture intimates.

Once the High Priest positively identified a crime of
blasphemy – or adultery – it was crushed by the ancient
capital punishment of stoning. The condemned would be
led to the place of execution, a cliff beyond the city walls,
specified in a tractate to be *the height of two men*. There the

doomed person was forced to the edge and suddenly hurled backwards, so that the fall either stunned the victim or broke his or her back. Caiaphas often threw the first boulder, aiming it at the heart. He then motioned the crowd to continue stoning until he was satisfied life was extinct. The mangled remains were left for birds to pick over, as it had been first ordained in Deuteronomy. The exact interpretation of Scripture was something the High Priest cherished.

In the turbulent closing years of Herod the Great's reign, Caiaphas had also learned where to be servile, and how to appear accommodating – when he was at his most dangerous. Under the tutelage of his father-in-law, Annas – High Priest for nine years – he had learned the most valuable asset of all: never to make a move without being certain of victory. Almost certainly Annas had only retired to live in his palace adjoining the Temple when he was absolutely certain all these lessons had been fully absorbed, and that his son-in-law, his anointed successor, would continue to protect the greatness of the Temple.

Not for a moment would Caiaphas have forgotten that one sacred and paramount responsibility. In all his decision-making would be one overriding consideration: that God's Chosen People would once more be divested of their position if anything threatened what the Temple ultimately represented – the miracle of faith for millions, down to the poorest Jew in the farthest corner of the Diaspora. He had promised to sacrifice anybody and anything to maintain this solidity. A hundred High Priests before had made a similar pledge on taking office. That was why Caiaphas paid Pilate bribe money. It was a small price to remain in God's highest office. That was why he had also done nothing about those reports of his agents that placed Claudia Procula on the edge of the crowds Jesus attracted in Galilee. She was no threat; she was a despised Roman who would one day leave Judaea with her husband. Nor had Jesus been a threat at first.

But at some stage the High Priest's other highly attuned quality had surfaced. He could sense trouble the way

128

animals smell prey. There was much he still did not understand or believe about Jesus, but the scent was there from the last Feast of Tabernacles. Caiaphas had been in his office when a commotion from the Court of the Gentiles had interrupted him. From the shelter of a colonnade he had watched Jesus addressing a crowd. Every word He had shouted remained engraved upon Caiaphas' mind from that moment when one of his own rabbis had challenged Jesus to explain how He dared to say He had more knowledge than the scholars of the Temple. Caiaphas knew the question was meant to unsettle Jesus, to mock and cow Him and make Him look foolish in the eyes of the crowd; his priests were expert at such tactics – it kept lunatic preachers at bay. Jesus had rounded on the rabbi. *'My doctrine is not mine but his that sent me. If any man will do his will, he shall know of the doctrine, whether it be of God, or whether I speak of myself.'* Other rabbis, drawn by the excitement, had shouted threateningly at Jesus to explain. The demand had provoked a further outburst. *'Ye both know me, and ye know whence I am: and I am not come of myself, but he that sent me is true, whom ye know not.'*

No word had come from Caiaphas: if he had felt some private humiliation it had never been allowed to surface. Only when Jesus was out of sight had he moved. The High Priest had turned on his heel and walked back to his office, as if nothing had disturbed the unique balance of obedience and authority through which he ruled.

He could no doubt have rationalised his behaviour: to apprehend Jesus in such a throng could have provoked a violent response; no one knew how many supporters Jesus had in the Temple that day.

The High Priest and his escort crossed another courtyard. The darkness hid the colonnades, and the Temple's outer gates: the Water Gate, through which the flagon of blessed liquid was carried for the libation at the Feast of Tabernacles; the Mourner's Gate, restricted to the recently bereaved to come and worship; the Bridegroom's Gate, reserved for the newly wed; the Eastern Gate, through which the ark had first come into the Holy of Holies. That most sacred of all the divine places in Judaism – a sanctuary of which it was said *'wherever it is written in the Bible "before God"'* – was protected by the Nicanor Gate. In daylight its appearance would have been overwhelming except for proportions in such perfect symmetry. Beyond where the money-changers and purveyors of sacrifices traded, were the courtyards for the women and the Gentiles and a clerical bureaucracy. There was no way for anyone confined to those outer limits to begin to imagine what high responsibilities and cruel tensions existed within the Nicanor Gate.

It was in this inner keep that Caiaphas had deliberated upon the words of Jesus and begun to prepare the legal groundwork, shaping the questions which would entrap Him: about His parents and ancestry; about His meaning of calling Himself *the Son of Man*; about the deeper significance of the curing of the paralysed and the resuscitation of the dying. Caiaphas was not a man in a hurry. Speed was not the road to a guaranteed conviction, but slow and careful deliberation, with each question tested in the light of Scripture. That was the only way.

The High Priesthood had always been in the gift of a few Sadducean aristocratic families whose private fortunes could meet its high costs: each encumbent purchased his personal religious vessels, tableware of silver and gold, and made generous donations to the Temple. This created a natural social barrier with the masses, further emphasised by sheer numerical size: Caiaphas ruled over almost twenty thousand men. Immediately beneath him were over a hundred chief priests who held equal status with the three treasurers who administered the Temple finances. Below them came seven thousand two hundred ordinary consecrated priests. Next came the Levites, who helped with the sacrifices, baked the shew-bread and had general custody of the Temple, acting as clerks and administrators and ushers to the Sanhedrin. There were over ten thousand Levites.

Jonathan had a force of five hundred guards. There were almost a thousand singers and musicians.

There was a separate group, about six hundred in number, who also worked for God – but in a very specialised role. They were the doctors of the law, the scribes, who devoted their days exclusively to studying and explaining the many complex questions of religion. They traced their authority back to the Book of Nehemiah, when Ezra established himself as the first scribe. Five hundred years later the scribes were accepted without demur as the arbitrators of sacred dogma. Proud of their position, they generally distanced themselves from priestly intrigues and saw themselves as the authentic intellectual power of the Temple. There were a number still alive from that day when Jesus, on the verge of manhood, had debated and often challenged them to the point where they had gone to their books and found His interpretations were both new and strikingly original.

Even Caiaphas' most careful questioning of these scribes had been frustrating. The incident had happened a long time ago, and all that they could recall with certainty was that the boy had been exceptional in His command of Scripture, and clearly His knowledge had been based on a strong and devout upbringing. Enquiries in Nazareth had produced no more. Jesus' teacher was long dead and His mother, brothers and sisters had instinctively drawn away from any probing stranger except to admit that Jesus had worked as a young man in His father's carpentry shop and upon Joseph's death had become the family breadwinner until the other children came of age.

Jesus and his four younger brothers were in Nazareth when Judas of Gamala had marched through the town on his way to capture Sepphoris, four miles to the north-west, and make it the Zealot capital of Galilee. The rebel had urged every able-bodied Galilean to join him. Scores had, only to die under the swords of the Roman legion which had routed Judas. The Romans had crucified all the insurgents who surrendered and razed Sepphoris to the ground.

131

Herod Antipas had persuaded Tiberius to allow him to rebuild the ruined town. The tetrarch had constructed within its keep an open-air theatre, a massive semi-circular building with seating capacity for over four thousand, a stage a hundred feet wide, an orchestra pit for sixty musicians and a resident company of players. When Herod Antipas began to spend most of his time at Machaerus and Masada the stage had become a forum for criticising religious and political leaders; the continual lampooning of authority was reluctantly tolerated by the authorities as a safety valve for the oppressed – providing it stayed within limits.

There can be little question that the destruction of Sepphoris and its emergence as a platform for political protest had a powerful effect on Jesus. The sight of men and women, among them no doubt His friends and neighbours, suffering excruciating pain on crosses lining the roadside from Nazareth to Sepphoris could only have increased Jesus' yearning to see His people liberated. Later, His own ministry, as well as increasingly placing Him in direct confrontation with the Temple, was firmly set in the radical tradition of the Sepphoris theatre. Assembling his case, Caiaphas may at least have considered whether the success of Jesus as a public orator was based on time spent with those professional actors and actresses who baited the High Priesthood. If His parables and stories could be exposed as deriving from Sepphoris it would be another way to discredit Jesus, to place Him firmly in the role of political agitator.

Joseph Caiaphas would never forget when he had been *set apart* from other men and received into the priesthood. The day had begun with a ritual bath in perfumed water. Afterwards he had dressed in white linen and was led by the High Priest to make three animal sacrifices: a bull and two rams. Before slitting their throats Caiaphas had placed his hands upon the beasts and asked Yahweh to accept them. Their blood was mingled with holy oil. The High Priest had used the mixture to anoint Caiaphas, receiving him into religious life with prayers that went back to the days of Moses. Intoning them, he had daubed the solution on Caiaphas' right ear, right thumb and right foot; ram's fat, unleavened bread and a cake baked from flour and oil had been carefully placed on his open palms and exposed thighs. These offerings were afterwards consumed in the altar fire.

When he became High Priest, the ceremonies were even more solemn. Annas had anointed him with the most costly scents; the ritual sacrifices were spread over seven days – each killing accompanied by a reminder that in embarking upon supreme religious office Caiaphas must continue to conform to strict rules. He must never eat game or drink wine before services or trim the corners of his beard. He accepted these restrictions and the sacred robes in his fifty-first year after a long rabbinical apprenticeship which had taught him how to balance the affairs of religion and state. No one, least of all Jesus, would be allowed to disturb things, in any way to weaken the authority of the Temple and so divest Joseph Caiaphas of his position as the personal representative of God on earth, ruling in Yahweh's name over a vast cluster of buildings that made Jerusalem greater than all other cities in the eyes of devout Jews.

This spring morning marked one of the most important occasions in the Temple: the approach of Passover, the *Pesah*. It was the holiest, most fervent and ancient feast in the religious calendar, an occasion which combined gratitude for escaping from Egyptian bondage with a reminder that there was only one God. The rites of celebration were laid down in the twelfth chapter of Exodus where it is recounted that Moses instructed his people on how they must behave if they were to avoid the angel of death who had come into their midst to destroy their enemies. Once more, the paschal lambs – countless thousands of them – would be sacrificed and the blood from each animal daubed with a branch of hyssop upon the lintel and frame of every outside door. The law prescribed that all who possibly could must come to the Temple to have their animals

133

sacrificed. Each family brought an unblemished yearling lamb for the ritual meal that was one of the high points of Passover.

His feet encased in hand-tooled sandals, Caiaphas walked through the final narrow covered courtyard leading to the Nicanor Gate, carried forward by the unshakeable sense of destiny he had never lost and that men like Pontius Pilate and Herod Antipas would never possess, let alone understand. The High Priest was as certain of that as he was that God had chosen Jerusalem to be the sanctuary for all spiritual life and that from here His voice would be heard *'till the ends of the earth'*. It was foretold that three days before the Day of Judgement God would return to redeem Israel, appearing as the *Messiah*, and Elijah the prophet would appear on Mount Hebron.

That could be the logical explanation of why Caiaphas had been so dismissive of those first accounts of the sermon Jesus had preached on Mount Hattin. Some of what He had said brooked no argument; it was rooted in the best tradition of Judaism. But to imply as Jesus had that redemption was at hand was to arouse expectations cruelly. Then there had been His revaluation of the Mosaic Decalogue – the commandments which ruled all decision-making in the Temple – over such clear-cut matters as murder and adultery. Jesus had taught that not only killing but also an angry outburst must be punished. But what scale of retribution was to be applied? What kind of angry words merited a greater punishment than others? Jesus had not explained. Instead He had delivered further maxims which, under existing Jewish laws, were impossible to follow: *'Judge not and ye shall not be judged'*; *'condemn not and ye shall not be condemned'*. But society could not survive without judgements being made and condemnations being delivered. In the High Priest's world, the holy tractates already formed the bases from which a systematic and orderly code of civil law had grown. Rabbinical teaching provided commentaries and explanations of the biblical texts. These were embraced in almost two score scrolls; a precise listing of crimes and misdemeanours, ranging from the rape of a betrothed girl or the public cursing by a son of his father, to the removal of route-marking stones and using rigged weights. The punishment for all those offences was death. Stoning was also prescribed for many other crimes: a man convicted of masturbation or sleeping with a menstruating woman; a priest's daughter who became a whore or a bride who concealed previous sexual experience. Taken to its ultimate folly, Jesus seemed to want to do away with the existing legal framework.

To a High Priest nurtured in rabbinical literature, as well as in the rich oral tradition of ethical casuistry, a combined corpus of received ethical, devotional and legal precepts, Jesus' message seemed contradictory: on the one hand He was careful to distance Himself from violent action, on the other He insisted the new life He proclaimed could only come through suffering. But who would suffer most in the world Jesus foresaw? To Caiaphas the answer may have become increasingly self-evident: the established order he headed. He could be forgiven for wondering if Jesus was cleverly encouraging others to launch a violent liberation movement, and, if it succeeded, He would proclaim Himself its leader. Was that what lay behind His repeated statement that man could not live by bread alone? Judaea was filled with its starving. The words could be a signal to them to appease their hunger by overthrowing the present system. Again Jesus had consistently preached that for those who accepted the Kingdom He envisaged there would be protection. Was that another subtle call to insurrection? There were thousands of young Jews who might see it as such.

Educated in a quasi-systematic tradition of Scriptural commentary, and elaborate and meticulous oral jurisprudence, the High Priest could only have been horrified at some of Jesus' proposals – such as giving a litigant even more than he asked: '*And if any man will sue thee at the law, and take away thy coat, let him have thy cloke too.*' But rabbinical lawyers in the Temple had used scrupulous care in formulating the rules for assessing damages. There was a vast library of scrolls, going back to Solomon, which covered such important issues as property ownership, loans and debts.

If only because he had taken no immediate action against Jesus it seems most likely that Caiaphas had initially regarded His teachings as the foolish, but harmless, idealism of someone who had no grasp of the practicalities of life. Israel had seen more than its share of those men during the High Priest's reign. They peaked for a while, then faded as their followers drifted to a new claimant for religious immortality. Caiaphas' policy had been to ignore them; to take action would only have prolonged their presence and enhanced their reputation. But something had urged Caiaphas to keep his agents on Jesus' trail. In the past months the reports had grown more alarming, culminating in the one which described in detail the paralytic rising and walking out of that almost roofless house in Capernaum. That may well have been the moment when Caiaphas realised he could no longer dismiss Jesus as another harmless religious fanatic; if there was truth in what was being claimed for Him, the matter must be handled with the greatest of care. To hurry unprepared against such a man would be to face a public outcry and certain defeat.

A complicating factor was the uncertainty about how great Jesus' influence was within three of the four main Jewish religious groups. Caiaphas' own party, the Sadducees, would continue automatically to oppose Him. The position of the Pharisees was more difficult to judge. Recently they had shown signs of dissent over Jesus' attitude towards religious observances; for His part He had made some stinging references to Pharisee doctrine. Yet Jesus shared with the rank-and-file Pharisee a working-class background; Caiaphas knew that, for all their religious purity, they could still rise in His defence. Even more difficult for him to establish was the position of the Essenes. Numbering only a few thousand, and living in strict isolation on the edge of the Wilderness, they, too, believed that

136

God would overthrow the powers of evil and inaugurate a new Kingdom. Jesus had visited them on a number of occasions. The High Priest had sent his most skilled rabbis to the Essene community beside the Dead Sea only to have them turned away by the sect's leaders. They would not openly commit themselves either way on Jesus – at least so far. But if they felt He had been unfairly treated they might march to Jerusalem and, magnificent debaters that they were, cause havoc within the Temple. Finally, there were the Zealots. Battered and bruised by repeated encounters with Roman troops, the Zealots were no longer the force they once were. But they still posed a threat. Suicidal though it would be, they could be driven to launch an uprising to save Jesus. All these factors required the most careful consideration.

Then, on a recent Sabbath, Jesus had once more slipped unexpectedly into Jerusalem with the Disciples. Instead of going to the Temple they had walked through the twisting streets in the Lower City. Near the Square of the Butchers, Temple agents had spotted Jesus. Preaching as He walked, unfolding once more His vision of salvation. Under cover of the growing crowd – word always spread swiftly when He was among them – the agents had worked their way close to Jesus.

A blind man had stumbled from an alley into His path. One of the disciples had posed a question. '*Master, who did sin, this man, or his parents, that he was born blind?*'

Jesus' response had been to say: '*The works of God should be made manifest in him.*' Then He knelt and spat on the dust from which he kneaded two pellets. Rising, Че placed these upon the sightless eyes and ordered the man to go to the Pool of Siloam and wash off the mud. Since King David's days Siloam had provided the sacred water used in Temple ceremonies; no one could use it without prior permission from the High Priest.

One of the agents had followed the man; others had remained with Jesus, to memorise any further extra-ordinary statements.

Shortly afterwards, incredulous cries came from the pool's direction, then into view, running unaided, came the man. '*I can see*,' he kept shouting, '*I can see*.'

The agents had hurried to the Temple. Jesus had not only broken the Sabbath once more by working, but had almost certainly been party to trickery. The wretch had feigned blindness; beggars did it all the time. This single episode in the hands of someone as skilful as Caiaphas could be fashioned into an unchallengeable case of sustained blasphemy.

When they reached the end of the final courtyard leading to the Nicanor Gate, Caiaphas' escort stopped, watching as he climbed the three steps to a dais rimmed by a thin balustrade of solid gold. Like everyone else, he stared up towards the very tallest of the Temple towers, a cone-shaped minaret with a doorway leading to a tiny balcony, his thin hands gripping the rail, the style of his vestments unchanged since Joshua had led the first High Priest into Canaan.

Caiaphas wore puffed-out pantaloons and a tunic made from a single piece of linen, open at the neck and held in place with silk shoulder strings. Over this was a sleeveless violet surplice, the lower half embroidered with pomegranates. Between each fruit were suspended bells made of pure gold and designed to repel devils. The sacred stole, unlike any other in the world, cut from silk dyed crimson and sewn with gold thread, was draped around his shoulders. This was held in place by ties made from onyx engraved with the names of the twelve tribes. On his breast attached to the stole by rings of gold was the pectoral, a box inlaid with twelve precious stones on the outside and containing the holy relics of the High Priesthood: dice-shaped badges embossed with hallowed engravings. His head was covered with a cone-shaped turban; attached to it were two wide ribbons, scarlet like his stole. Wound round his waist was a wide purple sash. Caiaphas had once more collected this regalia from the Antonia Fortress to wear for Passover. How the High Priest felt about this demeaning control over his office was also something he shared with no one.

In time to come, just as the physical appearance of Jesus and Pontius Pilate would be described – and disputed – so Caiaphas, who might otherwise have disappeared through the trapdoor of history, would be remembered as the High Priest whose splendid robes did little to enhance his appearance. There was a serpent-like quality about his puny body and narrow head. The years had ravaged his skin, leaving it slack at the jowls and neck. But as the light lifted, bringing with it the first warming wisps of spring wind, it was the look in the High Priest's eyes which would also have made it easy to misjudge the man; their watery appearance suggested weakness; the rheumy look of a man who knew that long ago he had lost the universal regard his office demanded; that his simonistic behaviour allowed Pilate to squeeze the nerve ganglion of Jewish religious independence. To all suffering Jews he was another collaborationist who had sold out. They failed to see his more deadly qualities.

Rejection did not trouble him. Caiaphas possessed an intellectual's belief – or contempt – that the masses had no real interest in the subtleties of religious dogma. Within the Temple, Pharisee scholars and Sadducee priests worked side by side, if not always in Scriptural harmony, at least bound by a common understanding of the necessity to show a united front to the Romans. The sophisticated Temple Pharisees understood the meaning of self-interest and were far removed from their country cousins with their wild talk and aspirations. If it came to the crunch Caiaphas could have felt confident that these scholars would yet curb their Galilean brethren from protesting at any move against Jesus.

Nevertheless, there would still be another formidable barrier – persuading the Great Sanhedrin that it should put Jesus on trial. Though the supreme court was the ultimate legal authority – responsible for the interpretation of all Jewish civil and criminal law – and, as High Priest, Joseph Caiaphas was its president, it rarely involved itself in trials except those of national concern. While the Great Sanhedrin had total autonomy and authority in all cases which came before it, and the Romans would not break with precedent and become involved, the court was protective of its position; it would not wish to see its authority diminished by conducting a trial that in the end could turn out to be of little importance; nor had it previously been asked to judge an itinerant preacher like Jesus. The daily jurisdiction in such matters was in the hands of the Small Sanhedrin; these lower courts were established in all the major towns in the country. But to bring Jesus before a Small Sanhedrin in Jerusalem was a risk. That court could decide that any charges against Him were not only offences against religion but crimes under the Roman code. He would then have to be sent to the imperial tribunal presided over by Pilate. The problem that created would be manifestly clear to the High Priest. The Romans would inevitably condemn Jesus to death. He would then become the martyr the oppressed masses needed.

Yet if the Great Sanhedrin could be persuaded to hear the case and if Jesus was convicted *purely* for offences against Scripture the people could be convinced of the justice of the verdict. Nevertheless, to bring the case before the Great Sanhedrin would require a great deal of skill on the part of the president. While Caiaphas could count on the votes of the Sadducee judges, he could not be absolutely certain how Pharisee members would vote; at the end of the day, they might still be unconvinced of the gravity of the charges. Without their support not only was an overwhelming conviction impossible but the chances of convincing the people of its righteousness would be totally lost. Once they realised there had been an unsuccessful attempt to kill Jesus the population could easily be aroused into action by His enraged followers. Then the Romans would step in. Jesus would have brought about the situation that Caiaphas, like the tetrarch, feared the most.

On the minaret balcony a dark shape had appeared. At the first sign of daybreak, a priest-trumpeter raised his long-stemmed silver instrument and blew through its fluted opening three distinctive blasts. As the first one, the ear-piercing *thekiah*, broke the silence, Jonathan, the Captain of the Guard, ordered his men to remove the beam that barricaded the gate. Then came the *theruah*, a series of long blasts from the musician, so clear that the holy books record that when the Israelites captured Jericho – until then one of the oldest seats of moon-worship – similar blasts had carried thirty miles eastward from Jerusalem and bounced against the walls of that pagan city, causing them to crack. Jonathan's men opened first one, then the other half of the gate. They completed the task as the trumpeter delivered a final *thekiah*.

Beyond, Caiaphas could see the first supplicants and animals entering the Temple. Another day had begun. As he did every morning, stepping down from the dais, he was led by Jonathan and his guards and his priest escort, to make his way through the Nicanor Gate to show himself to the people, to remind them again that he personified the living God and the Temple was His home on earth. All he surveyed was proof of that – the filigree on the gleaming marble around the roof into which were mounted spikes gilded with gold, designed to prevent birds from perching; the interlocking courts with their colonnades sculpted in the style found in Babylon and Athens; the massive outer walls, with their sheltered porticoes roofed in cedar and floored in coloured stone; the religious courts where the doctors of the law debated and pronounced. The ritual over, the procession returned into the inner courts leaving behind the din of pilgrims bargaining with the money-changers and sellers of sacrifices. At the Nicanor Gate priests waited to receive the animals.

Within the gate, beyond the narrow courtyard which Herod the Great had erected, was another large enclosure, almost three hundred feet in length and two hundred feet wide. Around it were various sanctums, including the chamber where the Great Sanhedrin met. In the centre of the square stood the altar dedicated to burnt offerings, a block of unhewn granite, each side forty-seven feet long and rising to a height of thirteen feet, its four corners formed in the shape of horns, symbolising the *shofar*. Cut into the block were a series of gutters which carried the blood underground to the Kidron.

The lambs to be slaughtered were tethered to one of the rings set in the ground before the altar. When their turn came to die they were pushed up a ramp to where the sacrificers waited with their sharp knives. The air was already beginning to reek with the stench of burning entrails and fat thrown on to the altar fire.

Beyond this scene of ritual butchery stood the actual Temple, reached by the twelve steps, each one representing a tribe of Israel. The colonnade which embraced the main building was a full ninety-eight feet high and a hundred and forty-seven feet wide. Rising above this were the unbroken walls of the building and its roof covered with gold.

At this point Jonathan and the escort halted, allowing Caiaphas to continue alone into the Temple within which Jews everywhere evoked Solomon's prayer: '*Yahweh, Thou should ever be watching, night and day over this place of Thine, the chosen sanctuary of Thy name. Be this the meeting-place where Thou wilt listen to Thy servant's prayer. Whatever requests I, or Thy people make shall find audience here; Thou wilt listen from Thy dwelling-place in Heaven, and listening will forgive.*'

The focal point of these preparations was the High Priest's small office. It guarded access to the *debir*, the Holy of Holies, the most sanctified of all places in the Temple. There was no door to the *debir*, only an opening screened by two heavy curtains. No natural light ever penetrated this sanctum; illumination was provided by the soft glow from a seven-branched candelabrum. Only Caiaphas could replace the tall tallow sticks in the *debir*, which was strikingly different from all others throughout the Diaspora. Apart from their candelabra they were empty. But the *debir* of Jerusalem had in its centre a large rock – precisely placed to cover the mouth of the abyss out of which the world had grown. This was the Foundation Stone upon which King David had discerned the name of Jehovah. The letters had disappeared before his gaze – and since then it had been accepted that anyone who stood before the stone and '*pronounces the Name letter by letter will destroy the world*'.

Caiaphas had a lawyer's mind, but he was not a stubborn and inflexible legalist. Only too clearly he saw that some of the evidence which his agents had thought so damning would almost certainly fail to impress the Great Sanhedrin. There was the accusation that Jesus had transgressed normal custom and often did not wash His hands before eating. While that could be certainly construed as anti-social behaviour, equally Jesus could also argue that with the shortage of water often acute, especially in Jerusalem, it was a crime to waste it on such a small matter as hand-washing. More important, there was nowhere in Scripture that made it obligatory to do so before dining. Again, the often reported charge He had levelled against many rabbis of being hypocritical could be defended. Caiaphas could well imagine that Jesus' judges, being men of the world, might be persuaded to see His accusation as no more than the over-heated passion of someone who only wished further to improve the quality of religious life. There *were* priests who were tinged with hypocrisy; everyone knew that. No doubt Jesus had intended to be insulting – but what He had stated was hardly a capital offence. Again, on closer examination, much of what He preached, such as a need to banish evil and bring back the faithless from the edge of darkness, was unexceptionable.

There were difficulties in challenging claims Jesus made about His healing powers. Every Jew swore upon God's omnipotence – and therefore accepted His right to choose, however unfathomable, the instrument to carry out His will. Jesus could argue that He was only doing that; He could even make a case that it would – in Scriptural terms – be blasphemous to *deny* God's right to help the incurable in this way on *any* day, even the Sabbath. Jesus had also often said to the cured that their sins had been forgiven. But He

143

could also vigorously defend such a potential blasphemy on the grounds that Scripture *did* contain indications that God forgave sins in many ways. The truth was that so much of what Jesus said could be argued as being no more than a warning that divine retribution would come unless there was an overall improvement in religious attitudes. That would almost certainly strike a sympathetic chord with the supreme court. Many of its members had repeatedly expressed concern that once more the Chosen People had forgotten the terms of the Covenant. Nor did Scripture forbid prophesying; Jeremiah had done so centuries before.

The most promising avenue for the High Priest to pursue would be the references Jesus had made to Himself as the *Son of Man*. It was a perplexing phrase – unless once more it was meant really to mean that Jesus saw Himself as in some unique relationship with God. The High Priest would have recognised that the key word was *Son*. It was an integral part of the Covenant; it gave the Chosen People their sonship with Yahweh. In the Book of Exodus was the sentence: '*Thus saith the Lord, Israel is my son, even my firstborn.*' The Book of Hosea contained the words: '*when Israel was a child, then I loved him and called my son out of Egypt*'. In that sense the use of the word *Son* meant somebody completely united with God in an exceptional manner. Was that why Jesus had been so careful always to refer to Himself publicly as *the Son of Man* to avoid the charge of blasphemy? Again, there was the way He used *Father* when referring to God. He used it in a personal sense, once more as if His relationship with God was very different from anyone else's. More recently Jesus had reportedly even begun to refer to '*My Father*' and '*No one knoweth the Father except the Son*'; and '*I and the Father are one*'. That was, in the written law of the Pentateuch, blasphemy. Yet to launch a prosecution on such grounds alone was no guarantee of success. Jesus had only to deny the allegation for the case to collapse.

Then came news that could only have given the High Priest sudden and renewed hope. A Temple agent had rushed with it from Bethany. Jesus had a second home in the tiny village two miles to the west of Jerusalem. Whenever He came to the capital He invariably stayed with two unmarried sisters – Martha and Mary – and their brother, Lazarus. All three were among His earliest followers. More than one agent had spent time trying to establish the nature of His relationship with the sisters and the other young woman in Jesus' life, Mary Magdalene. For a while they had pursued the promising lead that Jesus had enjoyed a full sexual relationship with both Mary Magdalene and Mary of Bethany. If that could be shown it would be possible to convict Him of licentiousness – punishable by stoning. But no satisfactory proof had been forthcoming.

It appeared that Lazarus, never very robust, had been struck down with a sudden severe illness. Mary and Martha had nursed him, praying that Jesus would soon return. When Lazarus showed marked signs of deterioration the worried sisters had sent a trusted man friend to ask Jesus to help their brother. After days of searching, the man had found Jesus and the Apostles on the outskirts of Emmaus, a small town deep in western Galilee. They hurried to Bethany. Well before reaching the village Jesus suddenly stopped: *'Our friend Lazarus sleepeth; but I go that I may wake him out of sleep.'*

The Disciples had looked puzzled. One said: *'Lord, if he sleep, he shall do well.'*

Jesus' reply had stunned them. Lazarus was dead. Then He delivered a further pronouncement equally astounding: *'And I am glad for your sakes that I was not there, to the intent ye may believe.'* With that, He had turned on his heel and strode ahead of them, without saying another word.

Approaching Bethany they had been met by Martha and her equally grief-stricken neighbours; Lazarus had been a popular figure in the community. Through her tears, Martha said her brother had been dead for four days. Mingling with the mourners, the agent heard Martha upbraid Jesus for not coming sooner. Jesus had gently

145

taken her arm and said that Lazarus would rise again. His sister, her face ravaged by grief, had nodded numbly. Finally, she had forced herself to speak. '*I know that he shall rise again in the resurrection at the last day.*'

Jesus had held both her hands, willing her to look at Him, forcing her to raise her eyes and stop crying. When He had succeeded He delivered a shattering statement. '*I am the resurrection and the life: he that believeth in me, though he were dead, yet shall he live.*' Silence, sudden and total, greeted the words. Eyes still intent on Martha, Jesus raised His voice so that everybody could hear. '*Whosoever liveth and believeth in me shall never die. Believest thou this?*'

Filled with sudden hope, Martha had responded: '*Yes, Lord. I believe that thou art the Christ, the Son of God, which should come into the world.*'

Jesus told her to fetch her sister. Mary came running out of the house, and fell at His feet, weeping that Jesus had come too late. He gently lifted her up. He asked where Lazarus was buried. Mary and Martha led the way to the tomb, Jesus walking between them, murmuring words of comfort, His eyes filled with tears. Behind came the Apostles, villagers and the Temple agent. All around him, between the sobbing, the spy heard the questions – asked but never answered. Why had Jesus, who had cured others, not done so in the case of Lazarus? Were His own tears from grief or guilt? Why were they going to the grave?

Lazarus had been laid to rest in a cave set in a hillside beyond the village, and a boulder covered the cavern entrance. Jesus told Martha to roll away the stone. She protested. '*Lord, by this time he stinketh.*'

Once more, Jesus gently reminded her. '*Said I not unto thee, that, if thou wouldst believe, thou wouldst see the glory of God?*'

On Martha's command some of the village men reluctantly rolled back the boulder. Then fearful of what they had done, for no one tampered with the resting place of the dead, they withdrew down the hillside. Even the Apostles backed away.

Jesus walked to the mouth of the tomb. Then He raised

His head to the heavens and cried out: *'Father, I thank thee that thou hast heard me. And I knew that thou hearest me always: but because of the people which stand by, I said it, that they may believe that thou hast sent me.'*

There was a long moment of silence. The first breeze of evening sighed, carrying the odour of the sepulchre in the air. Then, in a thunderous voice Jesus shouted into the cave: *'Lazarus, come forth.'* There was another long moment. Then a movement came from within the cavern. Slowly, bound in his shroud, unfolding it as he emerged, and removing the burial cloth which had covered his face, Lazarus walked into the daylight. Jesus turned to the open-mouthed crowd: *'Loose him and let him go.'*

As Lazarus embraced his sisters, the agent began to run to Jerusalem to tell Caiaphas what had happened.

The High Priest knew there was now no time to ponder the finer points of evidence to hand. By raising Lazarus from the dead, Jesus would have finally proven Himself in the eyes of the great majority who would come to hear of the story.

Throughout the Diaspora was the spreading expectation that the *Messiah* was imminent. Millions *could* be aroused by the followers of Jesus, and even Himself, to march on the Temple and demand His recognition as the Expected One. They could bring Lazarus with them as proof of His divinity; Jesus could perform further feats to support that claim. And if they were then still refused they could take matters into their own hands. Jonathan's guards would be trampled out of the way. The forces of Herod Antipas would be no real opposition for such an aroused mass. Even Pontius Pilate's legions might not be able to contain the fury of the mob.

Recognising the full peril, the High Priest saw only too clearly that he, and he alone, would have to move swiftly. The slightest show of panic or uncertainty on his part would be disastrous. In the action he planned, Joseph Caiaphas, with the connivance of a few others, was condemning untold future generations of Jews to unparalleled hatred.

147

The Passover Plot

My soul, sit thou a patient looker-on;
judge not the play before the play is
done. Her plot hath many changes:
every day speaks a new scene: the
last act crowns the play.

— Francis Quarles
(epigram: Respice Finem)

SEVEN

With Intent to Murder

Ye are my friends if ye
do whatsoever I command you.
— John 15:14

Jesus and the Apostles continued to pick their way over scree and down the sides of ravines before climbing again. Ahead was the Mount of Olives, adjoining it their next landmark, the massive outcrop of *Ha-Zoafim*, Hebrew for The Overlooker. The hill dominated the landscape to the east of Jerusalem. In choosing this escape route from Bethany, Simon the Canaanite knew that no one would expect them to come so close to the city walls. He had led them past the place where Joab had first found a way into Jerusalem, allowing King David's army to capture it. Almost ten centuries later, Jesus, his descendant, edged past the site of the royal tomb towards the ground where, in the wake of David's death, another Jewish king, Manasseh, had sacrificed children to appease the pagan god Moloch. Few pilgrims encroached into the Valley of the Slain. Simon led them round the isolated pocket of land before they were once more engulfed in the crowd.

Redolent with animal and human odours the air was also awash in noise: a confused din of pedlars and public criers, herders and tradesmen, animals being driven in and out of pens and the rhythmic hammering of construction vying with repetitive psalmodic choruses. It was an unbelievably crowded atmosphere where the hurly-burly of commerce mingled with religious piety. Both the Temple guards and the tetrarch's troops recognised the futility of searching in this mêlée; the Romans would not be so foolhardy as even to consider entering the area. But for Jesus and the Apostles to remain within the crowd's protective cover had meant climbing *Ha-Zoafim*, a test of stamina. Beyond lay another of Judaea's desert-scapes; a legion would not easily find anyone there.

They all knew that the threat of arrest *had* become very real after the resurrection of Lazarus. The action of restoring life only properly belonged to God. By demonstrating He had that power Jesus had opened a far more dangerous phase in His career. When word spread the Jewish people would flock to Him. While He had made clear His sympathy for their desperate plight He also wanted them to realise His purpose was not to lead an apocalyptic movement, that His Kingdom would not be fashioned from bloodshed – except the shedding of His own. That was the sole purpose of a life He must prolong a little longer. He had fled with the Apostles from Bethany to gain further time to explain the realities of the plan He had first revealed on Mount Hattin: to show them that their grace would only come through participating in His; that the redemption He would win and the Eternal life He offered were infinitely possible.

Yet, in spite of all His efforts, they continued to see Him in human terms, identifying many of His responses with theirs. They could very easily have believed that He, like them, had been genuinely attracted to evil before taking the hard and worthwhile decision to reject it. Being young and healthy themselves, they had undoubtedly speculated whether He was sometimes sexually drawn to the women He seemed so often to go out of His way to attract, and whether He did so to show them it was possible to have

152

control over the demands of the flesh. They still regarded Jesus as a man of God, not as the Son of God.

Judas, in particular, had displayed increasing signs of real misunderstanding. Culturally and politically more sophisticated than his fellow Disciples, imbued with a high-minded thrift about money – the slightest expenditure had to be justified – he was above all a man of action and had become convinced that in any confrontation with the existing powers – whether Roman or Jewish – Jesus was certain to emerge victorious. Who can therefore doubt that the treasurer would have regarded Lazarus' resurrection as further proof that the *Messiah* was among them. The Apostle's bewilderment would have been understandable when Jesus abruptly led the flight from Bethany. To Judas it must have seemed as if Jesus was once more avoiding His responsibilities to launch the Kingdom. Finally, Jesus had delivered a gentle rebuke: '*But of that day and that hour knoweth no man, no not the angels which are in heaven, neither the Son, but the Father.*' But the time was drawing close enough for Jesus to have realised He must take urgent action to show the Disciples His very humanity was deliberately designed to lead them deeper into self-knowledge; through Him they would learn their own new relationship with God: through them the world would savour salvation.

They made their way through another encampment. Tied to a stake outside each dwelling was a *mezuzah*, a cylinder holding replicas of the commandments God gave Moses. Women ground corn between millstones carried from distant parts of the Diaspora and pummelled the dough in wooden kneading-troughs whose shape had remained unchanged since the Exodus. The air was pungent with cooking, including the distinctive smell of locusts being fried in oil or boiled in brine. Yet, within a month, the last pilgrim would have departed and the ground cleaned of the carrion from the execution mound of Golgotha, where the birds picked at the crucified, extracting eyeballs and pecking away fleshier parts like lips and genitalia.

153

Jesus spoke often nowadays of His own fate. Again the Disciples stared at Him: in the eyes of Peter that familiar look of honest fear; Thomas perplexed; Judas' face a controlled mask; the others openly confused. Even James the Less, his blood brother, it was clear, had not fully realised that to bring forgiveness to the world Jesus must allow His earthly mission to end only in one way if He was to demonstrate God's full pardoning of man – through His death.

Yet, after almost three years of continuous teaching, during which He had consistently revealed Himself as the creator of a new religious ideal, they saw Him as earthbound as they were.

Their misapprehension was also understandable. In some ways Jesus' behaviour fitted a popular concept that the Expected One would reveal Himself in the guise of a brilliant strategist; that He would appear and strike unexpectedly, a dazzling figure who would consecrate anew the lives of all those on earth He touched. Nevertheless, outside a faithful coterie, mostly around the Sea of Galilee, few still even knew what Jesus looked like. The Temple agents and the other spies who dogged His footsteps, had, when pressed by their masters, no doubt found it hard to describe Him as being different from other practising male Jews: He had no distinguishing facial blemishes; His long hair, beard and curling side-locks, far from setting Him apart, were typical, so were His clothes. At table, He behaved like any other man, using only His right hand to eat a staple diet of fish and bread washed down with goat's milk; roasted lamb never passed His lips from one Passover supper to another. Jesus' command of languages was not unusual: Aramaic for everyday conversation; Hebrew while preaching and interpreting the liturgical language of the Bible. That He understood Greek and Latin was no more than a mark of diligent days at school.

In the years preceding His ministry Jesus had spent time with a group of Pharisee teachers in Galilee; the sect was the only one which educated the poor. Under their tutelage He had become a superb preacher. But it had also become

154

increasingly clear that in spite of the vividness of His teaching – which frequently drew upon such homely examples as sowing and harvesting to try to describe His concepts – even the Disciples failed fully to understand He was not in any sense a military leader.

Yet the strong anti-Roman feeling of the great majority of Jews could only be satisfied by the Expected One leading an armed insurrection. The death of John the Baptist had increasingly placed the onus for triggering that deliverance squarely upon Jesus. Like Judas, many of the Baptist's followers said Jesus must take *action* to support words which they interpreted as meaning He intended to fulfil the prophecies of Isaiah, Joel and Zachariah, who had envisaged a great climactic battle in which the *Messiah* would lead the nation to victory. The more Jesus tried to explain this was not His mission, the more the belief had spread that He would perform such a feat. A desperate people had cast Him in the role of a very different type of Deliverer than He intended to be. To convince them otherwise first required the Disciples to understand that only His death would inaugurate the Kingdom and bring a very different kind of victory.

As they followed Him past one tented family after another, such ready examples of human life made it natural for them to put into a purely earthly context His views on such issues as sex, marriage, divorce, virginity and celibacy. Time and again, since delivering that manifesto on the slope of Mount Hattin, Jesus had returned to those topics, patiently answering their questions, reminding them, for example, that those whom God had joined together, no man should attempt to put asunder. Did that mean, they had pressed, that marriage was such a risk that it was better to remain celibate? Jesus offered a response meant to make each Apostle think the matter through for himself. '*There are some eunuchs which were so born from their mother's womb and there be eunuchs, which have made themselves eunuchs for the kingdom of heaven's sake. He that is able to receive it, let him receive it.*'

The linking of the forthcoming Kingdom with such human functions as marital relationships and the problems of everyday living made it difficult for them to grasp the reality of His repeated and growing proclamation that He must sacrifice Himself. Frequently struggling to understand their Master's exact meaning of redemption, there was no Scriptural precedent of a *Messiah* having to suffer for the salvation of the world.

In many ways the Apostles were still conditioned by the Mosaic laws. Until Jesus had called them, those laws had provided a matrix which they accepted without equivocation. There was a religious commentary for everything: how they must dress, eat and work; how they should behave in every relationship, whether in the family or in the larger community. For them, despite having witnessed stunning examples of His power, the Kingdom of Heaven, when it came, would appear in surroundings with which they would be reassuringly familiar. Nowhere in the Torah or any other holy book was there one word which said the *Messiah* would come to die to ensure the birth of His prophecies. The Apostles could still not fully grasp that this was the one fundamental factor which placed Jesus apart from all other religious authority: He saw His fate as a deliberate sign of contradiction – but never one of defeat.

The miracle of raising Lazarus had, in some ways, changed everything, yet on the other hand it had not. Bringing a person back from the dead was undoubtedly the most dramatic of all His feats – made all the more vivid by the event's proximity to the Temple and a direct affront to the stated dogma of its High Priest that resurrection was an impossibility. But many Jews would not have been entirely overwhelmed by the happening because they no longer believed in the claim that when the angel of death put the '*deep and bitter gall*' upon the lips of the dying, the soul was carried away to some mysterious region that Scripture often called *Sheol*, identified by Job as that '*place of darkness and of the shades of death*'. The Psalmist described it as '*the dwelling of silence*', located so far from earth that Job, again, had recorded that even '*the anger of the Lord*' could not penetrate into *Sheol*.

Jesus had explained to the Apostles that His meaning of resurrection went far beyond what was essentially a Judaic belief in reincarnation. He was talking about a unique transcendent power – His – which would make His ministry so different from all other faiths. He had already spoken of that authority in His words to Martha: '*I am the resurrection and the life.*'

He had meant them not only to comfort her but to provide another lesson for the Disciples. He wanted them to absorb it as the core of the faith they would spread for Him; only then could they be His witnesses. In raising Lazarus He had demonstrated the full hopelessness of the existing human situation He had come to save; He had to make the Disciples understand that dying should hold no terror when contained within a belief in all He represented. Jesus had hurried from Bethany to continue to prepare them for His bitter fate – a prerequisite to launching His message. He had to make them all absolutely accept that, while by birth and upbringing He, too, was a son of the Covenant; that while He was capable of loving and being aroused to anger as a man; that while He accepted His people had their own place and destiny in history; that while He supported all the Mosaic laws; that while all the touchstones of the faith He was born into were encompassed in His teaching, including a total and imperative acceptance there was only one God: that while all this, and a great deal more, He held to be absolutely true, He still had more, so much more, to offer to all those who wished to perfect their own way of knowing and seeing God. His Apostles must be completely convinced that He was concerned with more than satisfying the longing of hundreds of years of Jewish expectation. The salvation He was bringing was for all mankind. Unless they understood that, they would never be able to go out into the world and properly continue His work. He would gladly pay for that clear understanding with His life.

157

The time of supreme sacrifice was not quite at hand. After Lazarus had embraced his sisters, Jesus saw it as the sensible precaution for them to leave the village before word spread of what had happened; the Temple agent racing off towards Jerusalem clearly forebode trouble. Mary and Martha, supporting their still dazed brother, headed south, probably to the safety of caves where Amos, the misogynous shepherd-prophet, had prepared his thunderous denunciation against rich women. The villagers would keep secret the route He and the Apostles had taken.

Simon the Canaanite had shaded his eyes against the sun whenever there was a glimpse of the track which led from Jerusalem to Bethany after he spotted the column of guards racing from the Golden Gate towards the village. He switched direction several times, taking them through the larger camps, where in the turmoil people would be less likely to remember a group of men moving with unassuming purpose. From the crowded top of *Ha-Zoafim* Simon saw the guards trudging slowly back towards the city. For the moment Jesus and the Apostles were safe. They continued to pick their way along yet another track, heading north, away from Jerusalem. Jesus led them as He had on that day when, hungry, thirsty and tired, a similar path had brought them into a small Judaean village. It was a day Matthew would never forget.

* * *

Matthew, in spite of immediate acceptance by the others, found it hard at times to shake off his past. For years he had been a Roman tax gatherer, a Jew to be despised, whose circle of friends had been restricted to other outcasts: alcoholics, vagrants and prostitutes, the reviled and rejected. Then Jesus had passed his collector's booth in Capernaum and commanded Matthew to follow Him. He had obeyed without hesitation, bringing to an end days spent counting coins and poring over schedules of tolls.

When previously Matthew entered this village to collect

imperial dues, the children had tormented him with jeers that he was a paid thief. Now, at the end of another of Jesus' long and exhausting treks, these unhappy memories surfaced when a group of urchins raced towards them. Recognising their old enemy behind the beard he had grown, they began to cat-call. Matthew ran towards them, waving his fists, followed by Peter, who could be quick-tempered, and Philip, anxious to defend the dignity of his best friend. The children backed away, keeping out of reach of the dust-smeared trio. Jesus strode forward and stopped the pursuit with a firm rebuke. '*Suffer little children and forbid them not to come unto Me. For of such is the Kingdom of Heaven.*'

Watched by the shame-faced Disciples Jesus walked over to the boys and asked their names. Then He beckoned the Apostles to join Him. When they gathered around, He addressed the children, reminding them of the proverb in Holy Writ which said everyone must keep to the course he had begun; even when he grew old he must not deviate from that chosen path in life. Jesus looked into the children's suddenly serious faces, smiling gently as He put the questions. Did any of them wish to depart from the rule their fathers had given them? The one about showing respect to their elders? Did they want to forget that was as important as all the other maxims of Holy Law? One by one the children shook their heads. Then they turned and bowed bravely towards Matthew.

That evening Jesus and the Disciples were supper guests of the *hazzan*, the village school teacher who greeted them in turn, giving each the kiss of peace, and led them to an inner courtyard where the girls in his family waited with bowls of water to wash their feet. Afterwards Jesus motioned the Apostles to stand and, wrapped in their prayer-shawls, to face in the direction of Jerusalem, a reminder that the prophet Daniel had done so every time he had prayed throughout the long exile in Babylon. They knelt, outstretched their arms and recited the *Shema*, the ancient and uncompromising promise they would never

159

forget they were the people of the Book, and other prayers, a haunting repetition of low chants which glorified God and this land of Abraham and Jacob. Finally, as they did before each meal, they repeated the Our Father.

The guests stretched out on cushions, each supporting himself upon the left elbow, using the right hand to pick at the food. Jesus, as usual, had the place of honour – facing the gap in the dining area through which the women came and went from the kitchen. The *hazzan* served them in strict precedence, offering the dishes to Jesus first, then the Apostle on His left, Judas: being at His elbow was deemed to be the safest place for the man who carried the money that paid for their board and lodging. The host worked his way around the group until he finally returned to serve Peter, at Jesus' right elbow. Each Apostle followed Jesus in taking a handful of food on to a tin plate; earthenware was ritually unclean. The host poured goat's milk for Jesus and wine for the others. The fare was simple: fish, locusts, fruit and bread. Passover was approaching and it was a time for frugality before the greatest of all celebrations.

Throughout the meal Jesus touched upon themes never far from His lips: those who suffered insults and persecution in His name would have a rich reward in Heaven; those who followed Him would be seen as the salt of the earth. They were familiar allusions to the problems they would face and the rewards for dispelling the gloom of a sombre and uncertain world. During the discourse villagers had crowded into the courtyard to listen, including several of the boys who had earlier mocked Matthew. Jesus motioned one of them to come forward. He sat the child on His lap and began to speak again. '*Whosoever shall humble himself as this little child, the same is greatest in the kingdom of heaven.*'

He waited, the pause of a natural story-teller, eyes no doubt sweeping the circle of Apostles, drawing the boy closer, the way a father would hold his own son, the Disciples staring at their Master clasping this child clothed in rags, bare-footed, constantly brushing flies from his eyes

160

and skin, no different from all the others. Jesus emphasised that the only way people would understand the true meaning of His teaching would be to acquire the innocent mind of a child. This boy, He continued, had yet to assume his elders' selfish ambitions, privileges and position. Anyone who hoped to enter the Kingdom of Heaven must first relinquish them. He sent the child back to His friends.

Jesus returned to another familiar theme: social justice and the disparity between rich and poor. Staring at the intent faces before Him, Jesus reached into their farming background to illustrate His meaning. '*Which of you, having a servant plowing or feeding cattle, will say unto him by and by, when he is come from the field, Go and sit down to meat? And will not rather say unto him, Make ready wherewith I may sup, and gird myself, and serve me, till I have eaten and drunken; and afterward thou shalt eat and drink? Doth he thank that servant because he did the things that were commanded him? I trow not. So likewise ye, when ye shall have done all those things which are commanded you, say, We are unprofitable servants: we have done that which was our duty to do.*'

By such analogies Jesus tried to show the Disciples how His message should be taught; that, when the time came, they must also explain to others that the choice being imposed was a deliberately hard one to accept. People could either let their lives remain as they were – '*make ready wherewith I may sup*' – or they could make a clean break and hope for Eternal salvation. There was no easy promise; to achieve redemption would demand a consistent application of new, hard-to-live-by standards.

Jesus had been about to embark upon further explanations – no doubt once more searching for an example with which his audience could identify – when into the courtyard came a stranger. He wore an expensive *chadlock*, a garment which signified his social position. Only a wealthy landowner could afford a coat of embroidered silk squares. Hands hooked into its belt, the man halted before Jesus.

'*Good Master, what good thing shall I do that I may inherit eternal life?*'

Early on Matthew had noted that, almost more than any other pre-condition, Jesus made rejection of material possessions the prerequisite of salvation. Throughout the Sermon on the Mount, His commitment to social and economic equality had been clearly proclaimed; without it there was no redemption. Salvation was beyond anyone who did not realise that material wealth was potentially an instrument of corruption.

'*Why callest thou me good?*'

The man looked perplexed.

Jesus explained: '*There is none good but one, that is God. Thou knowest the commandments . . .*'

The man interrupted. He insisted he had kept the law, each tenet of it. What more could he do?

Jesus would not have needed a rueful smile to explain. '*One thing thou lackest: go thy way, sell whatsoever thou hast, and give to the poor, and thou shalt have treasure in heaven: and come, take up the cross, and follow me.*'

Understandably, the wealthy man stared at Him, his face working, his voice unquestionably filled with baffled regret: he could not possibly follow Jesus' advice. He *needed* to keep his possessions; they were an inheritance and an insurance for the future of his family. His wife and children depended on him. Motioning towards the crowd he said, his voice rising, that *his* money and *his* position ensured *their* future. He turned and walked out of the courtyard.

Matthew also noted the next words: '*It is easier for a camel to go through the eye of a needle than for a rich man to enter into the kingdom of God.*'

Peter broke the silence. His intervention was also understandable. Indicating his companions he said that surely *they* would enter because of what they had already given up: their families, homes, their fishing boats and land. They had forsaken all, and gladly, to follow Him. Could there be any doubt about their reward? Would they not have precedence over those who continued to enjoy worldly pleasures throughout their lives and only sought redemption at the very end?

Jesus, who had spent so much time trying to explain the real meaning of forgiveness, would have seen only too clearly the human concern and failing behind Peter's question.

* * *

Caiaphas waited for the return of Jonathan's men from Bethany. Their orders were to arrest and bring Jesus to the Temple before word of Lazarus' resurrection spread. The immediate threat He posed would then be reduced. In the meantime, Annas was discussing the *prima facie* grounds for a trial with the Court's seventy-one judges, arguing that Jesus had set Himself up as a direct opponent to God's delegate, the High Priest, and Moses and his laws. Therefore, Jesus opposed Yahweh Himself, the Ten Commandments and all their attendant corollaries, the 613 obligations, 365 of them negative and 248 positive, that guided the behaviour of the Chosen People. Caiaphas could have been well satisfied with such a strong holding charge pending the formation of even greater accusations.

The guards had returned empty-handed. No amount of threatening on their part could persuade the villagers to talk. A proposal from Jonathan to send his patrols into the crowded hills would have been a logical response; its rejection in keeping with the High Priest's pragmatism: even if the guards were able to pick up His trail, bringing Him through the pilgrims was now fraught with risk. As word spread about Lazarus any move against Jesus and His followers would certainly attract attention and very likely provoke resistance. An insurrection could flare in sight of the city and precipitate a Roman involvement.

However, with Lazarus and his sisters gone from Bethany, the danger seemed somewhat reduced; without the physical presence of a body returned to life the story would be that much harder to believe.

Jesus and the Apostles found that beyond *Ha-Zoafim* the crowds began to thin. For the moment the crenellated walls of Jerusalem were out of sight. Below was the road that led northwards into Galilee, the oldest of all the caravan routes, following the backbone of the land. In the distance was a ring of hills. To reach them meant crossing a desolate landscape broken by dried-out beds of streams and *wadim* plunging a hundred feet, and more, to their boulder-strewn floors. They made their way into the desert, moving under the cover of one gulch to another. They finally reached the hills with the sun setting behind them. There was no sign of pursuit.

They continued past shepherds tending their flocks, to the tiny village of Ephraim: no more than a handful of houses grouped in pairs around a common courtyard, each yard with its mill for grinding corn, a clay oven for baking bread and a fig tree providing shade against the fierce noonday heat of summer. In the centre of the village stood its most imposing building, rectangular-shaped, with stone ashlars and an open staircase along one wall that led to a gallery. Its façade was faced with a double row of Corinthian pillars, and the lintels above the entrance and window were decorated with various religious motifs. Everything about the building proclaimed its importance in the life of the community. It was the village synagogue.

Jesus led them towards the entrance, the door surmounted by a window designed according to Scripture to face the source of all light and wisdom – Jerusalem. In every synagogue throughout the Diaspora there was an identical opening. In contrast with its ornate, almost flamboyant façade, the interior was surprisingly bare; the floor of plain flagstones; columns supporting the gallery where the women worshipped. When their eyes adjusted to the light Jesus and the Apostles saw the familiar frieze, with its images and symbols set within medallions.

In size and shape the synagogue was similar to the one in Nazareth. None of the Disciples would forget that first and only occasion when Jesus had brought them there; His reputation was already beginning to be established around the Sea of Galilee and He had told them he wanted to carry the good tidings to where, as a child, He grew up with His brothers and sisters, watching their father work with wood, and the tanners and potters cut and mould objects of lasting beauty.

★ ★ ★

Jesus had been the first of Mary's children to go to school, and sit in a circle and repeat after the *hazzan* in a loud chorus the Scriptural verses to be learned by heart. When His brothers and sisters came of age they had squatted beside Him; if they stumbled He had corrected and encouraged them, the way any older brother would. Their mother had thoroughly indoctrinated each of them about the role of religion in the home. Everything was sacred; the smallest and most insignificant act required thanks to be given to God. Every morning they recited the first *beraka*, a blessing for the day; another for the clothes they wore; the sandals they laced; the food they ate. They even learned to repeat blessings for natural bodily functions. '*Blessed art thou, O Lord, who has fashioned men with wisdom and hast created in him apertures and outlets.*' After school they had gone into the countryside to watch the women tilling, planting and harvesting and discovering how to distinguish the differing calls of the shepherds. All this most definitely had influenced His approach to His ministry. It had to be clear-cut enough. to reach the uncomplicated minds of His people.

On their memorable visit the Disciples with Jesus had reached Nazareth before sundown on the eve of another Sabbath, and had gone to His mother's home to wash. Mary and her daughters were completing the preparation of food to last for the duration of the holy day, during which no fire could be lit or cooking done. As dusk approached she had lit the oil lamps which would burn continuously, untouched by hand, for the next twenty-four hours; His sisters had drawn enough water from the village well for domestic needs. Then, while His mother and sisters went to the

165

women's gallery, Jesus led the Apostles through the main entrance of the synagogue.

Its flag-stoned floor was crowded with men and boys. They stared attentively at the *tebah*, a simple platform lit by a single oil lamp standing close to a lectern. A legend was to grow that before he died Joseph carved the ambo. On it rested the holiest object in the synagogue, a copy of the *Sefer Torah*. The handwritten parchment scrolls had been removed from the wooden ark kept in a small room behind the *tebah*, and placed on the lectern. It was dressed in the garments appropriate for the rites: a mantle protected the scrolls from public view; filials, decorated knobs, had been mounted on to the staves around which the parchment was rolled.

With the villagers Jesus and the Disciples watched two figures standing before the ambo. One was the *hazzan*, the other a boy, limbs still developing, voice unbroken, eyes respectfully following the *yad*, the pointer, in the *hazzan*'s hand; during the reading of the Torah it is forbidden to touch the parchment. The boy repeated each sacred line in a high-pitched voice, demonstrating that when the time came he would be able to read the *Parashah*, the first public profession of his faith, the audible proof that he was fully prepared to partake in the greatness and the fate of the Chosen People. Every Friday night in synagogues throughout the Diaspora boys stood before their elders and chanted the blessings and readings of the law.

(On the threshold of his thirteenth birthday, shortly before His trip to Jerusalem where He bemused and startled the scholars of the Temple, Jesus stood on this same *tebah* repeating every gesture and intonation of His teacher, showing His proud family He was capable of officiating and praying in public.)

When the boy's instruction ended and the Friday evening service began, Jesus and the Apostles recited the blessings designed to concentrate minds upon the timeless world of the Sabbath. Afterwards they all walked home to His mother's house, built by Joseph on a shoulder of a hill and with a magnificent view towards the distant plain where Elijah slew the prophets of Baal. The dwelling had changed little since Jesus lived there: the thick interior walls of mountain stone that much blacker with smoke; the number of sheep, goats and chickens penned near the front door that fewer now with the children growing up and moving out. But otherwise the house would be as He always remembered it: an earthen ground floor leading to a platform at the rear, supported on stone pillars and reached by a wooden staircase. This was the heart of the household, a spacious area of bare floorboards where the family ate and slept. An opening led to the flat roof, itself designed to slope to one corner so that rain drained into a covered stone trough for those long summers when water was scarce. Jesus and the Apostles slept on the roof beneath the stars.

On Saturday morning they had returned to the synagogue. The main service of the week began with prayers that brought together the truths of Abraham's religion: respect for the Creator, a full understanding of the Law and the role of the Chosen People as the true representatives of the entire human race.

The rabbi then invited a member of the congregation to read the first of the one hundred and seventy-five verses of the *Parashoth*, the portions of Holy Writ. Jesus strode to the lectern where the rabbi handed Him the *yad*. The parchment was open at the Book of Isaiah. Jesus began to quote: ' "*The Spirit of the Lord is upon me, because He hath anointed me to preach the gospel to the poor; he hath sent me to heal the brokenhearted, to preach deliverance to the captives and recovering of sight to the blind, to set at liberty them that are bruised. To preach the acceptable year of the Lord.*" '

His voice ringing with certainty, Jesus uttered the first prophetic words of commentary. '*This day is this scripture fulfilled in your ears.*'

It was not difficult to comprehend the shocked murmur which swept the congregation, or that men began to murmur to one another. Matthew would remember voice after voice joining the chorus of accusations and hands perhaps

167

gesticulating first at Mary and her daughters, and then where Jesus' brothers stood in embarrassed silence. A worshipper turned to a neighbour and demanded: *'Is not this the carpenter's son? Is not his mother called Mary?'* Another voice shouted that Jesus could not possibly claim any right to fulfil Scripture; God alone did that. . . .

Jesus' exasperation survived along with the angry grumbling. *'Ye will surely say unto me this proverb. Physician heal thyself: whatsoever We have heard done in Capernaum do also here in thy country.'*

Tumult broke out. Men and women yelled in fury. How dare He come here with such blasphemy? They all remembered Him as a boy who had worked alongside His father, who had prayed here with them, a devout Jew linked in a special way to the faith of His forefathers. What gave Him the right, the madness, to pretend He was now endowed with gifts from God? They had heard the stories about how He had supposedly given a cripple back the power to walk and a blind man sight; that He had driven out demons and sent life coursing through those mentally stricken. They had heard, they shouted, and they didn't believe. Let Him show *them*! There was a man newly blinded in the town. They would fetch him – and He would show *them* if He could restore sight! There was a woman dying – show *them* how He could cure her! The taunting challenges came from all sides. *'Show us! Son of Mary – show us! Show us – son of Joseph! Show us – and your brothers and sisters!'* Jesus raised His hands to silence them.

'Verily I say unto you, no prophet is accepted in His own country!'

He reminded them of the fate of those in the past who had refused to believe: women who became suddenly widowed; lepers who had been left uncleansed. God had Himself momentarily withdrawn from His people in the face of their religious intolerance and prejudice.

The full fury of mob violence swept the building, and before Simon the Canaanite, Peter, Andrew, Philip and even the puny Judas could make their way to their Master a

168

core of men bundled Jesus from the platform and dragged Him through a side door, screaming and shouting that He must die for such heresy. His mother, brothers and sisters were swept aside as they struggled to reach Him; Thomas and Thaddaeus paused to help them while the other Apostles fought their way through the crowd, urged on by James the Less who knew where they were taking His brother: the sheer cliff face at the northern end of the town, where as boys they had looked out towards Mount Hattin. James knew what the mob intended to do: hurl Jesus headlong to the rocks far below. Of the Disciples he was the closest to Jesus as the crowd reached the cliff. Then, before their eyes, He was gone. No one could say how. The stupefied onlookers stared at one another in disbelief. They veered away from the Disciples as if they, too, were charged with paranormal capabilities. But all the Apostles could say to a relieved Mary was that Jesus '*passing through the midst of them went His way*'.

The Disciples had found Him the next day in Galilee. Jesus never explained how He reached there. His very lack of discourse and elaboration would reinforce the authenticity of a happening beyond all human capability. It had been an event of divine intervention, defying any earthly criteria.

* * *

In Jerusalem after the evening offering, during which the priests had led the faithful in reciting the *Shema*, a procession emerged from the Temple. Led by Jonathan, a contingent of his guards formed a phalanx of shields and swords forcing people and animals to one side. Next came a group of robed chief priests creating a circle around Caiaphas. In preparation for Passover he had undergone a seven-day period of purification, during which he had given up all physical contact with his wife and moved into bachelor quarters in the Temple. The priests were there to ensure that Caiaphas particularly avoided any risk of defilement through contact with the dead; the route across the city had been checked to ensure they did not pass a house where a corpse awaited burial.

Nobody could remember when a High Priest had last ventured forth into the filthy winding streets of Jerusalem before a festival and, to emphasise the importance of the occasion, Caiaphas had exchanged his turban for a golden diadem engraved with the Hebrew words: *Glory to God*. Jonathan led them down a long flight of steps which divided the Upper from the Lower City, and on past the royal palace of the Asmonean dynasty which had been ruthlessly destroyed by the father of the man upon whom Caiaphas was calling. A detachment of Herod Antipas' soldiers waited to escort the procession into a heavily fortified enclave. There were two main palaces and a score of lesser buildings, banquet halls, baths and accommodation for a thousand guests as well as extensive servants' quarters above the notorious dungeons. Groves of trees stood between canals and small lakes studded with bronze fountains. The tetrarch's private quarters were in the Hippicus Tower, the most secure site in the complex. Herodias and Salome lived in the tower his father had dedicated to Mariamne – the wife the old tyrant had executed.

Drawn up in a courtyard was a contingent of the household bodyguard, caped and armed in Roman style, each man a slave who had been given his freedom after pledging undying loyalty to Herod Antipas. With them were several black-garbed chamberlains holding lanterns to show the way. They brought the Temple entourage to a reception hall where courtiers were grouped around the tetrarch's secretary. Caiaphas advanced to receive the reverential welcome from the official, who then conducted the High Priest through several smaller reception rooms and across courtyards surrounded by colonnades, a watchful soldier before each pillar, a brazier beside him to lessen the chill of guard duty.

The tetrarch's audience chamber was a perfectly square salon reached through double doors with a throne at the

170

opposite end that Herod the Great had installed. His son preferred to receive visitors while seated on cushions on the floor. The room was lit by oil lamps on low tables. Outside the doors the high chamberlain greeted Caiaphas and escorted him across the marble floor to where the tetrarch had risen and stood waiting. Courtesies over, they settled themselves cross-legged on the floor and sipped from tiny cups of mint tea served by Chuza. The two most powerful Jews in the world began discussing plans to murder Jesus.

After sleeping out in the hills around Ephraim, a precaution to reduce the risk of discovery, Jesus continued to demonstrate He would be forever remembered as the greatest of all teachers. From the beginning of His ministry He had shown that His message must be permanently memorable to all those who could neither read nor write, which included the majority of the Apostles. Just as Jesus had been educated by rote and example, He used the same approach to lodge in their minds sayings which bore the mark of blinding reality. Seated in the cool morning air – the sun rising over Jerusalem in the distance, its rays reflected against the gold roof of the Temple and radiating off its snow-white walls – He reminded them again of epigrams which held a very different kind of truth than taught at Judaism's prime religious centre. They repeated after Him words of a supreme quality. He asked them: '*What shall it profit a man if he shall gain the whole world and lose his own soul?*' And when their voices had cho0rused the words He had put the next question. '*Or what shall a man give in return for his soul?*' Phrase by phrase, as Jesus did every morning, He reinforced in them the principles He held so dear. '*Whosoever exalts himself shall be abased, and he that shall humble himself be exalted*'; '*a man's life consisteth not in the abundance of the things which he possesseth*'; '*he that findeth his life shall lose it, and he that loseth his life for my sake shall find it*'.

He demonstrated that worldly standards of greatness and power could be destroyed in a sentence; that in a few words

171

values could be forever redefined; that what may sound incredible and unreal, on reflection, could not be denied; that to succeed in spreading the Word they must be willing to unshackle their listeners from their religious roots by every available means: hyperbole, the overdrawn language of poetry, the use of metaphors and humour – anything which would jerk people bolt upright, forcing them, even against their will, to see the new truth. They had, He continued, travelled a long and difficult spiritual road. Now there must be soon a physical parting of the ways. Once more Jesus had looked at them and added that they must take comfort from the ever more rapidly approaching Kingdom. Then staring deeply into each face He added: *'There be some standing here which shall not taste of death till they see the kingdom of God.'*

Jesus had first spoken those words when He was only too aware of the hostility He was attracting and He knew that, in human terms, His enemies must take away His life. Even then, in the second year of His ministry, the certainty of the Cross was inevitable. To earn a temporary respite from the pressures, He had taken the Apostles far to the north of the country, to the mountain citadel of Caesarea Philippi, where the Greeks believed their gods once lived and from where, in a cavern, the Jordan began its long journey south. Towering over the city was a gleaming white marble temple, erected by Herod the Great in memory of Julius Caesar.

In its sight Jesus had told Peter, in Matthew's hearing, that His first Apostle would have *'the keys of the Kingdom of Heaven'*. As a reward for being the first Apostle to have recognised Jesus as the *Messiah* he had been promised the post of a faithful steward who would symbolically open the door of the Kingdom by being the Founder of its Church. Jesus had once more spoken bluntly of the suffering that lay ahead for Him. Peter had reacted violently, shouting this would never be allowed to happen. The Apostle's response was, for Jesus, no doubt deeply touching. But it was also a further reminder of the problems He faced in trying to convince the Disciples that His going to the Cross was essential. He had not wasted words soothing the distraught Peter. Matthew caught the anger in Jesus' words. *'Get thee behind me, Satan, thou art an offence unto me; for thou savourest not the things that be of God, but those that be of men.'* Peter had confronted Jesus with a temptation similar to the one He had faced in the Wilderness: the easy road to power. Peter out of love had tried to weaken Jesus' resolve.

Now, on the hillside overlooking Ephraim, Jesus had the joy of knowing His ministry was secured because at least Peter, John and James the Less finally understood. The realisation came through an event on Mount Hebron regarded as ultimate proof of God's approval for Jesus' work.

* * *

After his appointment of Peter, Jesus had led the Apostles still further north from Caesarea Philippi to the foothills of Mount Hebron, the only mountain in Judaea coated with deep layers of ice all year round. Near one of the ruined villages of the Hittites, the tribe Joshua had overcome to complete the conquest of Canaan, Jesus ordered the others to make camp while He took His brother, Peter and John on up towards the summit.

Several of the Disciples had been concerned by their flight from Caesarea Philippi; they may indeed have thought His ministry effectively over. However, after his Transfiguration they must have seen that Jesus was revitalised, filled with renewed zeal, purpose and a certainty that the course He was embarked upon *was* fulfilling the will of God. The Apostles felt a renewed and deeper loyalty to Him and to each other. He had promised them that when He descended from the mountain they would journey together to Jerusalem to hasten the coming of the Kingdom.

Let there be confrontation, Judas had cried in his guttural desert patois; the enemies would be swept aside. In his voice could still be heard the authentic longings of Jewish Messianic hopes, dreams and expectations. He still clung to the dangerously misguided idea that Jesus was the all-conquering hero – and never destined to face the lonely agony of the Cross.

Watching the Master he adored disappearing up the mountain the first seeds of what he must do had been planted in the deluded treasurer's mind.

The three men following Jesus had an easy climb. In spite of its height, about ten thousand feet above sea level, the Hebron slopes are gentle. The ascent began in mid-afternoon. By the time they reached the half-way stage the sun was sinking. They paused by one of the many streams tumbling icy water from the snow-level, and joined Jesus in once more kneeling on the grassy stubble beside the brook to pray. When they opened their eyes Jesus was already a few yards away. He turned and faced them. Not only did His face assume an ethereal appearance, but His robe glowed with a light so white, and intense, that they had to shade their eyes. Then, as they remained kneeling, too awed to move, two figures appeared on either side of Jesus. They were Moses and Elijah.

Peter, clutching to something he could understand, stammered: '*Lord, it is good for us to be here; if thou wilt, let us make here three tabernacles, one for thee and one for Moses and one for Elias.*'

Jesus made no response. As they watched, the Apostles were convinced the two figures spoke to Him. A cloud rolled down over the mountain obscuring Jesus and His companions. Throughout the history of the Chosen People the concept of the *Schechinah*, Hebraic for the Glory of God, had often been expressed in the form of a cloud. During their forty years in the Wilderness a cloud, in the shape of a pillar, had led them to safety. God had emerged to give Moses the law from a similar cloud; it was present at the dedication of Solomon's Temple. The glorious cloud had always been at hand on the most significant occasions. When it dispersed the Disciples saw that Moses and Elijah had vanished. Then came a mysterious voice, the one Peter and John had heard after Jesus was baptised. Once more it boomed out, its rich timbre bouncing off the rock, filling the Apostles with understandable awe as it proclaimed: '*This is My beloved Son, in whom I am well pleased; hear ye Him.*'

Prostrate on the ground, hands over their ears to keep out the unearthly voice they believed was God's, the Disciples felt Jesus gently shake them, telling them to rise. When they did so He stood among them, putting His arms around their shoulders, calming and reassuring them with His words. When they recovered, He cautioned that what they had seen and heard must be divulged to no one until a certain condition was met. Jesus, by their own account, administered the oath of silence in words which once more could only have reawakened an old anxiety. '*Tell the vision to no man until the Son of man be risen again from the dead.*'

He said that those who were supposed to teach the old prophecies, the Temple scholars, had not recognised that the spirit of Elijah was the guiding force behind the ministry of John the Baptist. Jesus added, somewhat cryptically, that John had died violently to fulfil part of those prophecies which the scribes taught but had not grasped and that His own death would complete a sacred prediction.

Coming down the mountain, united by the so-far most important advance in the history of Jesus, the Apostles were convinced that in that one dazzling incident they had, through Him, witnessed the greatness of the Jewish past uniting Him with the even greater challenges of the future. They had been asked to accept there was a direct line which led from Mary's annunciation to the Transfiguration they had just witnessed of the Son of God she had been chosen to bear.

In his office Caiaphas, Annas and a number of other Sadducee judges listened carefully as the Temple crier read aloud from a parchment scroll. He would repeat the words throughout the streets of Jerusalem and at every encampment on the surrounding hills.

175

'*Anyone who has information on one Jeshu Hannosri, especially his whereabouts, let him declare it to the Great Sanhedrin. Anyone who can speak let him come forth and do so to the same body.*'

Jeshu Hannosri was Hebrew for Jesus the Nazarene.

Because He would be facing criminal charges, prosecution witnesses must be found. There was every possibility that among those who would come forward there could be someone Jesus had offended or disappointed. In the hands of Caiaphas they could be tutored to carry off a role which otherwise held its own special risks. An accuser was invariably stoned if his evidence was false. Yet until persons were found who were willing to testify before the supreme court there was no legal way of proceeding against Jesus.

EIGHT

Hosanna

---

*Sufficient unto the day
is the evil thereof.*
— Matthew 6:34

Puzzling though some of the Apostles must have found the
lack of pursuit after their headlong rush from Bethany, they
raised no recorded objection when Jesus announced they
would leave Ephraim and return there. It was on Simon's
advice that they would head for Zorah, where Samson was
born, bringing them south of Jerusalem before they would
turn east towards Bethany. The route was across rugged
terrain barely patrolled by either Roman or the tetrarch's
troops. To reach Bethany would be a day's hard walking; if
it was safe, they would stay in the village which had become
their traditional base for the past three years before going on
up to the festivals in Jerusalem. Their hope was that
Martha, Mary and Lazarus would have by then returned
home. There was the usual good-natured grumbling about
once more having to live with Martha's domestic routine.
Her sister was dreamy and easy-going, content to hover
around Jesus, a born listener.

Further discussion ended with Jesus preaching one of
His longest sermons since Mount Hattin. He began with

the story of the rich man who gave his servants money, and how all but one, through hard work, multiplied the coins. The message was clear: common sense and effort were prerequisites for the new life. The parable was an immediate and arresting way to get attention for the *euaggelion*, the gospel of good news, Jesus was intent on bringing. He wanted them to understand that to remove injustice and help the underprivileged was a continuous challenge: hardship, opposition and the utter rottenness of so much of human behaviour had to be dealt with unflinchingly. To follow in His footsteps, He kept on reminding them, needed not only a total devotion to God but also having to conquer temptation within themselves. Until they could achieve that they would not be fully committed. Becoming like Him meant not only being able to serve others but also being of service in God's name.

The five who had stood on the bank of the Jordan listening to John on the day Jesus was baptised could only have been struck by how different His approach had become to the Baptist's. To the end, John's ministry was based on perpetual threat: fires consuming non-believers; the axe hovering over their heads; wholesale destruction of all kinds. For all the *qadosh*, holiness, of John's teaching, there was an unapproachability about the God he perceived. Jesus, on the other hand, spoke continuously of a self-revealing God, whose paramount desire was to be known by everyone, and whose message was based on love.

They had all recognised His teaching ministry and healing miracles were often at their most powerful after He had spent prolonged periods praying. Those who had been with Him from that day when they were convinced they had heard the words of God – *'This is My beloved Son in whom I am well pleased'* – had accepted that His sense of intimacy with the Almighty remained unique. For His part, He continuously promised them they would all share in it, though there could be no short-cuts. Jesus had made that trenchantly clear.

As He spoke about clothing the naked, visiting the

178

imprisoned, nursing the sick and feeding the hungry, He was really describing a God committed to help every human situation, a selfless God who wanted to share Himself with all mankind in a totally different way from what they had known before. He was saying that the love of God could forgive any sin providing there was genuine repentance. He reminded them He was again describing a God who was not only inviting and forgiving, but also more meaningful. The Temple scholars taught that a sinner who came on hands and knees to seek public forgiveness, who loudly proclaimed his contrition and remorse in the presence of priests, who made sacrifices and paid penalties, might be forgiven. But the God Jesus spoke of asked none of these things; His God did not wait for penitents to come to Him, but went out in search of the fallen and openly appealed to them: *'Come, follow Me.'*

They listened, magnetised anew by the sheer brilliance of His concepts. There was a warmth and vitality about His words which matched the morning sun on their faces. The trio who had climbed Hebron with Jesus and witnessed the Transfiguration particularly noticed the boundless energy which had sustained Him from then on: they realised that plainly the event had been His Coronation. Those words of God – *'This is My Beloved Son'* – had their echo in the ancient anthem chanted at the crowning of every Jewish ruler since Saul. An important feature of the ceremony was that it took place on a mountain and that the Twelve Tribes of Israel must be represented. Well could James the Less, Peter and John believe they had been chosen to fulfil that role. When they saw the Transfiguration in that light they were understandably thrilled that among the Twelve they were still the only ones who knew how close Jesus was to launching His Kingdom.

Here, on a hillside above Ephraim, He reminded them all of an earlier saying of His: no one could survive in isolation; that everyone needed someone to complete himself – and that God was the forging link. That was why God had created the world and populated it, so that they could love

179

each other – and that was why God was willing to make any sacrifice to bring man to that realisation.

Shortly, Passover would begin – and during it '*The Son of Man is betrayed to be crucified*'. Jesus reminded them of the glory which awaited Him and them – life eternal. Unlike many of His parables – where the details were not meant to be closely examined and each line given its own significance – He wanted them to understand first the brutality of what lay ahead – and then the joy beyond. He impressed upon them they must never see Him as a victim; rather, that He was ready to lay down His life; that from the beginning He was only a chosen instrument in a drama whose every twist had been under the direction of God – just as would be its culmination. They should not weep. They should rejoice.

Heading west across Judaea towards Jerusalem the full impact of the words struck them. For the first time Jesus had indicated He would be betrayed. But how? Who would do such a thing? Clearly he or she would be motivated by Satan; Jesus never tired of saying that just as God had need of them, so the devil was looking for willing hands. Ulti-mately, it would not matter whether it had been left to Thomas or one of the others to synthesise the situation, no one could be used without co-operation, everyone could keep out the devil. The betrayer would have to be someone with a sufficient lack of faith to succumb to temptation. No doubt they were certain Jesus could not have meant any of them. They were now at last a close-knit unit, a fusing of very differing personalities. Thomas was noticeably less prickly; John, since coming down from Mount Hebron, more content to listen and not jostle for Jesus' attention. Bartholomew's last signs of reluctance over whether he should be tramping the countryside in the footsteps of Jesus had gone. Andrew and Thaddaeus, separated by a score of years, who had sometimes argued over trivialities, were inseparable. Simon the Canaanite, next to Peter, was the most amiable among them. No brother was more devoted than James the Less, and the behaviour of Philip, Matthew and the portly James was also above reproach. While some of the Apostles had found Judas' fanaticism a tiresome trait, clearly no one doubted his loyalty. Following Jesus over the broken ground, they had sensed a certainty which matched His stride – that His message would survive and that a world far beyond this parched landscape would come to know and accept it. In the past He had predicted so many other extraordinary events which, if they had not witnessed them, they might well have not believed. Matthew could certainly vividly remember a very different journey they undertook during that first year of Jesus' ministry.

* * *

The sun had been slipping across the sky when Jesus asked Peter to find a boat to ferry them from the small port of Dalmuntha to Kursi on the east shore of the Sea of Galilee. It had been another long day of preaching and healing, not made easier by the constant interruption from Temple agents, including a rabbinical lawyer. He had shown himself more skilful than Simon the Pharisee, his cultured Jerusalem accent posing questions which Jesus had answered in His broad country dialect. The attorney had joined the crowd at Dalmuntha, edging his way to the front, biding his time, waiting for Jesus to reach that now already mandatory point in His teaching: the promise of life ever-lasting. The lawyer asked how he could be granted such a privilege. Jesus calmly replied by asking the heckler how did he interpret the law. The lawyer ignored the riposte and the crowd had fallen silent sensing another theological battle was about to commence. The lawyer asked Jesus to remind them of the First Commandment. Jesus had not hesitated. '*Hear, O Israel; the Lord our God is one Lord, and thou shalt love the Lord thy God with all thy heart, and with all thy soul, and with all thy mind, and with all thy strength: this is the first commandment.*'

The lawyer asked Jesus to evaluate the various stages which had led to this definition. Matthew recognised that behind the exchange lay a deadly legal trap. The lawyer

181

must have hoped Jesus would insist all the Commandments had equal importance. That could have led to a complex discussion over the position of each of the prohibitions and positive amendments to the basic Mosaic tenets – a minefield of tractates in which the agent would have tried to ensnare Jesus. The subtleties of the law were not only rooted in the greatest antiquity but highly developed in every Jew; to misconstrue a point was a grave offence. No man entered adulthood without knowing that, while the Bible was at the root of all legal interpretation, it contained three distinct codes laid down in what was called the Book of the Covenant – chapters twenty to twenty-three of Exodus, five chapters of Deuteronomy and the Book of Leviticus. During the previous five hundred years the Temple scribes and scholars had continually refined this already extensive jurisprudence, adding to and rewriting it so that the original Commandments were hedged within a jungle of legal caveats. But, better than most, Jesus well understood the gulf between the ideal and application, and He dismissed the lawyer, saying the man had a contempt for the humanity of justice and was only interested in debating esoteric points.

When the crowd dispersed, Matthew saw how exhausted Jesus was. Though He was able physically and mentally to continue far beyond the limits of anyone the Apostle had known, the strain did sometimes show. While it was clear to Matthew that it was already beyond anyone's power to eliminate Him from all future history, the Apostle knew that continuously preaching the Gospel of God was a draining process, even in Galilee, among people Jesus could speak to in their own way because He understood their character and temperament and shared their history and hopes. Though there was an intrinsic chivalry and politeness about Galileans, they could be persistent – especially when it came to a stunning message summed up for Matthew in one unforgettable sentence: *'Repent ye, for the kingdom of heaven is at hand.'*

Jesus had asked for a boat to bring them across the lake to

take a brief respite from the continuous demands on Him. On board He had curled up and fallen asleep. The crossing to Kursi normally was a short one. But the Sea of Galilee, as Peter and the other fishermen knew, could be unpredictable. The lake bed was littered with wrecks and the caves in the surrounding hills filled with bodies of sailors who had been victims of sudden storms. Departing from Dalmuntha the forecast seemed set fair: a prevailing southerly wind, barely strong enough to ripple the surface, one that would carry them smoothly and quickly to Kursi.

As they often did when Jesus slept, the Disciples spoke quietly among themselves about such pressing issues as the disparity between the rich the and poor, a chasm which Jesus had attacked from the outset; about the way the priestly class deliberately separated itself from all others, and then, within itself, divided again so that there were only eight families with the privilege of filling the office of the High Priest; about the fact that while slavery was officially frowned upon there were still wealthy Jews who kept them and how the law made a clear distinction between pagan and Hebrew slaves: the former had far less protection unless they agreed to be circumcised. These factors had contributed towards a society which, while outwardly unified, was internally riven. The hostility between the classes was a tangible matter. The rich and powerful gravitated towards the protection of Rome, becoming often paganised in the process. The desperately impoverished had only their faith to cling to. Integral to their belief was the conviction that rescue would come. Looking at the slumbering man in the stern, they realised what a huge responsibility Jesus carried. On His slim shoulders rested the hopes of the down-trodden, the despised and overlooked. It was upon these He had concentrated His ministry, and it had spread, rippling through the base of the economic strata, gnawing away at a crushing system of taxation, at the foundations of the Temple, at the Herodian dynasty, at Roman domination, above all at a narrow Jewish religious life that Jesus realised was no longer sufficient and which He, single-

183

handedly, was determined to supplement with an altogether wider vision.

It was, the Apostles agreed, one far removed from the two existing centres of worship: the Temple and the synagogues. Jesus had told them that before He would conquer the Temple He must first secure the synagogues. The Temple existed solely for sacrifice, prayer and music. Within its liturgy there was no room for Him easily to spread His word. That had to be done through the synagogues. From the earliest time, when ten or more Jewish families had chosen a spot to settle, the law of Moses decreed a synagogue must be erected to deliver the word of God. Jesus had brilliantly exploited the well-established custom that at a certain point in the order of worship, the reading and interpreting of Scripture, anyone with a message from God could deliver it. He had begun to do so in the synagogue at Capernaum and, apart from that occasion in Nazareth, He had continued teaching and preaching in every synagogue without hamper. The following morning He intended to do so in the tiny one at Kursi.

At some point the discussions were interrupted by the stars vanishing behind scudding clouds and the wind direction veered and strengthened, sending the bow-wave crashing into the boat. Peter ordered sail to be reduced. It made no difference. The waves continued to wash over the sides. The Apostles frantically bailed. Water slopped around their ankles. Jesus, still asleep at the stern, remained oblivious to the serious crisis developing. Repeatedly Peter tried to get the boat to run before the storm, but this stretch of water was among the most unpredictable in the world; the wind changing capriciously in all directions defeating even Peter's seamanship.

Judas, born and raised far from such a frightening sea, was the first to panic. He crawled on all fours to the stern and shouted at Jesus. '*Master! Carest thou not that we perish?*'

Jesus slept on. Another wave broke over the boat, send-

184

ing water surging from prow to stern, settling the craft even lower. Peter stumbled past the man clinging to the mast and rigging and grabbed Jesus by the shoulder, shaking Him violently. *'Lord, save us! We perish!'*

Jesus opened His eyes and stared about Him sleepily. Peter shouted to make himself heard above the pounding seas. *'Master, master, we perish!'*

Jesus rose to His feet, somehow managing to stand unaided, something no one else in the now rapidly foundering boat could manage. He spread His hands towards the heavens and then the sea. But His words were for the men in the boat. *'Why are ye fearful, O ye of little faith?'* Then, in the same powerful voice that later would command Lazarus to emerge from his tomb, Jesus ordered the storm to abate. The wind and sea instantly dropped. The Disciples bailed out the water, rigged the sail and reached Kursi under a moonlit sky, marvelling at Jesus' miraculous intervention.

Not only had a storm been stilled on a lake but a more important one calmed in the hearts of the Apostles. Jesus had restored belief in those closest to Him. The fishermen among them were necessarily men of natural courage, used to confronting the elements and taking their lives in their hands. That required its own act of faith. They knew all about the business of surviving. That came also through faith. Yet, at the crucial moment, as Jesus had said, and Matthew would record, their faith in Him had faltered. It had taken Matthew a long time to realise that, in rebuking them, Jesus had felt they had not enough faith in His mission; that they had failed to understand that His Kingdom was not in some invisible heaven but here on earth – or out on that storm-tossed lake. If they had completely accepted that, His words implied, they would have felt no fear. It was a brilliant exposition of the glory and mercy of God being expressed to show His love for man.

Making his way to Bethany, Matthew had no doubt that whatever lay ahead his belief in Jesus would never again weaken. That was why he could be sure any betrayal must come from outside the group.

★   ★   ★

Along the arid path which would eventually bring them to Zorah, a small village on their route to Jerusalem, Jesus preached as they walked, His face reflecting the inward struggle and determination not to flinch from what must soon happen. Yet there was no pessimism, despair or hopelessness in His voice. Instead, His words sustained an abiding conviction that while man was a helpless sinner he was also capable of redemption which would bring him close to God. He reminded them – and it was one of the first lessons Matthew had noted – that they must be *'perfect as your Father which is in heaven is perfect'*.

As they wound their way around hillsides, forded streams and passed through hamlets so tiny they would never appear on any Roman map, He taught that among the greatest challenges they faced was helping to remove sin from themselves and others. Jesus repeated – because that was His way – that, no matter what else a person lacked in life, he was equipped to cope with sin. Each one of them should remember that it was rooted in an absence of love, pity and respect, but they must never forget the infinite capacity in every person to fight temptation. Even more serious was the sin committed by anyone who set out to trap others through words and deeds and offered bribes and promises to gain their own ends. That was the path that eventually led to the worst of all sins – sinning against God. In these past three years, if they had learned nothing else, He had given them repeated examples of those who insisted on doing this; men and women who could not recognise God's voice when they heard it – or His presence when faced with it. They were the ones who still failed to see He had been sent by God, come to fulfil far more than the ancient prophets had envisaged in their wildest dreams; that above all He was the harbinger of mercy: mercy for the

186

spiritually captive; mercy for the spiritually poor; mercy for the spiritually blind. And, He reminded them, it was all being offered as a promise, without threat or inducement. Yet already they had seen, in His very home town, how such an offer could be cruelly misunderstood by those who saw in Him a terrible threat because He challenged their conformity and the prejudiced way they clung to the conventions of their upbringing. They hated Him, He said, because they hated themselves: there was no room in their hearts for the grace and love of God. Not yet, anyway. That was why He was going to Jerusalem.

There had been that day, He also reminded them, even hotter than this one, when they had numbered only Himself, His brother, Peter, Andrew, John, James and Philip. John the Baptist had just been arrested, leaving his followers in disarray. All along the Jordan there was talk that Herod Antipas, in the full fury of his madness, was about to round up every travelling preacher. To reach Galilee and the safety of its forests and caves Jesus elected to travel through Samaria, following a trail which passed near Shechem.

John for one would never forget how fearful his fellow Apostles had been. Because they were men of human judgement, they had applied that quality to the route He had chosen. To them it had seemed as if He was taking an unnecessary risk. The feud between the Samaritans and the Galileans was old and particularly deep, going back over centuries when the Samaritans had first collaborated with occupiers long before the Romans arrived. Since then the other tribes had continued to look with contempt upon the people of Samaria and no self-respecting Jew would now willingly choose to pass through their midst.

Jesus led them to the well Jacob dug, and sat down in the shade of its stone walls telling the others to go into Shechem to purchase provisions. When they hesitated He assured them there was nothing to fear. On the way into town they passed a young woman balancing a large empty pitcher on her head. What Jesus described had happened between them remained for John highly significant. He had invested the encounter with a sense of pure drama.

★ ★ ★

Jacob's Well was rimmed with a wall twenty feet in circumference and a metre high. The woman looped a rope, fastened the jug and lowered it into the well. With the water drawn she glanced up – and found Jesus looking at her across the parapet.

He pointed to the brimming container: *'Give me to drink.'*

She stared at Him, stupefied. The words were enough to reveal He was not from Samaria. But what was a God-fearing Jew doing breaking the adage which said that anyone *'who takes bread or water from a Samaritan is like him who eats the flesh of swine'*? She asked why Jesus would consider breaking the rule.

He smiled at her. Ever since He was old enough to understand, He had heard, in one form or another, prejudice expressed towards Samaritans. His mother had told Him that, when she and Joseph went to Bethlehem for the census count shortly before His birth, they avoided Samaria just as they had done at each Passover. Later, in the streets of Nazareth, He had seen that when the boys momentarily tired of playing Zealots and Romans they switched to Galileans fighting Samaritans. Once more Jesus indicated the water.

'If thou knewest the gift of God, and who it is that saith to thee, "Give me to drink", thou wouldest have asked of him and he would have given thee living water.'

The woman stared open-mouthed, incredulous that she, with a full pitcher, would seek water from this stranger, and not just well water – but something called 'living water'. She recognised His accent was unmistakably Galilean. Like all Samaritans she had been brought up to believe that her northern neighbours were often stricken with a form of madness arising from a determination never to marry outside their community. She looked around her; there was ı help in sight. The sun was overhead; the women of Shechem had forsaken their work in the nearby fields and orchards. She decided to try to humour the Stranger.

'*Sir, thou hast nothing to draw with, and the well is deep. From whence then hast thou that living water?*'

Jesus walked around the well and stood before her. Tapping the jug He pronounced: '*Whosoever drinketh of this water shall thirst again. But whosoever drinketh of the water that I shall give him shall never thirst; but the water that I shall give him shall be in him a well of water springing up into everlasting life.*'

Trying to contain her growing alarm at words that made even less sense, she replied: '*Sir, give me this water, that I thirst not, neither come hither again to draw.*'

Jesus peered into her face. Finally He made another astonishing request. '*Go, call thy husband.*'

The woman clasped the jug to her body, flustered. Finally she stammered: '*I have no husband.*'

Jesus brought His face close to hers, His voice was gentle but His words made her shiver. '*Thou hast well said, I have no husband. For thou hast had five husbands: and he whom thou now hast is not thy husband.*'

The woman slumped against the parapet, her voice weak. '*Sir, I perceive that Thou art a prophet.*'

The silence between them stretched. Then Jesus spoke. '*They that worship Him must worship Him in spirit and in truth.*'

She nodded, the first glimmer of realisation on her face. She, too, had heard what John the Baptist had proclaimed. '*I know that Messias cometh, which is called Christ. When he is come he will tell us all things.*'

Jesus stepped back from her. '*I that speak unto thee am He.*'

Not trusting herself to answer, the woman grabbed the pitcher and ran, sloshing water as she went.

The full significance of the encounter only came to John after the Transfiguration.

Jesus chose to reveal His identity to the woman because even then He had been preparing the way for the fate awaiting Him shortly in Jerusalem; He had chosen to announce Himself to her, knowing she would never be able to keep secret their encounter, accepting that eventually word of it must reach the Temple. Yet on hearing of this encounter, John could no longer feel afraid – not after what he had witnessed on Mount Hebron. There Jesus had received God's double benediction: He was to wear a crown no other Jewish king had before worn and gladly go forward to His death.

*　　*　　*

At noon, like all high-born Roman women, Claudia Procula prepared for another of the several baths she took every day. Almost a quarter of her waking hours were spent in water. Dressed in a full-length white robe, the procurator's wife left her bedroom accompanied by her retinue of slave-women and descended a wide marble-stepped staircase within the Antonia Fortress's east tower. The attendants carried jugs of oils and jars of spices and bath salts. One carried a *strigil*, a soft claw-like leather instrument with an ornately carved handle embossed with the crest of the Augustine dynasty. It was to massage her mistress's skin and remove dead epidermis.

Claudia Procula had never understood the attitude of Jewish women to personal cleanliness. While their menfolk bathed daily, many of the women simply doused themselves with scents and renewed the henna in their hair. For them a weekly bath often sufficed. On her visits to Galilee she found it unpleasant to be surrounded by women reeking of camphor, storax and the pungent aroma from the crushed horny operculum of shellfish. One of the decisions she made after her first visit to Jerusalem was to order an architect to be brought from Rome to design a new bathroom for her use in the fortress.

The staircase led to an enclosed passage, its fresco depicting Vesta and the Vestal Virgins guarding the undying fires, symbolism which played an important role in the mythology of Roman life. The passage ended in a tiled courtyard, open to the sky but designed so that it was not overlooked. Between the Corinthian columns rising from pedestals of solid marble stood the statues of Rome's gods, dominated by Romulus, founder of the city, and the triad of Jupiter, Mars and Quirinas. Guarding the arched entrance to the bathing area were the goddesses Juno and Minerva. Set in the wall above the arch was a large medallion depicting Janus, a handsome bearded figure with two identical heads joined at the neck, ever on the lookout instantly to aid any Roman.

The designer had spared nothing on cost or attention to detail in the bathing area. The room was almost forty feet long and thirty wide, with marbled floor and walls. At one end was a changing area, concealed by curtains made of gold threads; at the other were the warm and sweltering chambers, with baths rimmed in solid silver, their temperature regulated by floor vents and hypocausts. In the body of the room were five separate baths each of varying size. The one closest to the hot rooms was a cold douche. Next came a vapour bath, its oil of camphor strong enough to bring forth tears. In the centre was a spacious circular pool with a pure bronze fountain in the middle providing an endless cascade of sparkling water. Close by was a massage block, a body-length sculpted slab of unblemished white marble. Two further baths were sunk into the floor. The water in one was slick with oil; the other perfumed with various salts. The walls of the salon were decorated with pure gold mosaics inlaid into the marble; they included Apollo wearing a radiate crown and driving a four-horse chariot through the sky and Dionysos, the god of fertility, embracing his consort, Libera.

Completely naked, surrounded by women soaping her body and rubbing it with ointments and spice-water each time she moved from one bath to another, the procurator's wife was the epitome of a rich and pampered imperial woman.

191

She was the closest living female relative of the Emperor Augustus who had laid the foundation of a dynasty that, through no fault of his, had been short-lived, but which now, in troubled Rome, was being recalled as the golden age of empire. She was imbued with her grandfather's unrivalled relentlessness and cunning, and remained one of the most powerful voices in the imperial world in spite of her husband's relatively modest status. Yet, over the past year, her behaviour would have appeared to any Roman as inexcusable and inexplicable. She had put Pilate's future, and perhaps her life, in jeopardy.

Claudia Procula had spent endless hours in her equally magnificent bathing salon in Caesarea, pretending and prevaricating, unable to understand what had first taken her to Galilee. Partly it was frustration with the petty, restricted and isolated life in Caesarea; partly no more than arrogance which originally drew her to stand on the shore of the Sea of Galilee and initially be filled with the overwhelming certainty that no man could offer more than Rome did.

But, as she had listened to Jesus, understanding almost nothing of what He said in Aramaic, let alone when He quoted Scripture in Hebrew, His compelling manner and the compassion in His voice had attracted her. She had returned with a servant who spoke His language. Standing at the back of the crowd, dressed like any wealthy Jewess, brightly bangled and beaded and her hair held in place with combs, the full and troubling import of His message reached her. Back in Caesarea she had tried to shake off the vivid images Jesus had created of a world so different to the one she knew – a place where love not violence was the ultimate weapon. Just as her husband continued to immerse himself in Jewish religious customs, so she had begun to study their beliefs. That could only have led to another startling discovery: the future Jesus proclaimed was so often at variance with Judaism; that He was indeed a new and tremendous force for good.

From then onwards Claudia Procula accepted that Jesus had entered her life and that He had begun to influence her outlook towards all that Rome held holy: its gods, rituals and customs, the very trappings she had been raised to believe were sacrosanct.

It has been suggested she had learned that a new threat had now emerged against Jesus, that she knew of the High Priest's plan to bring Him to trial, or that while the slaves kneaded and pummelled her body on the massage block, she was preoccupied with the question of what she could do to save Him. Apocryphal or not, that possibility would be enough for her eventual veneration as a saint by the Greek Orthodox Church.

Jesus and the Disciples reached the vicinity of Bethany without incident. Simon had gone ahead and returned with the reassuring news that the Temple guards had not returned, but Lazarus and his sisters were back home. Jesus led the way down the winding path which descended from the desert through a *wadi* into the village. Like many other Jewish settlements the hamlet was too small to have a protective wall and gates which could be closed at night with sentries posted on the battlements. Its workmen's houses and unpaved streets huddled round a couple of wells. The community numbered too few to warrant its own court of law and a judge; all crimes were referred to the Small Sanhedrin in Jerusalem. No one could remember when that had last happened; the people of Bethany were hard-working, God-fearing and law-abiding. Yet, despite its lack of size, it was still a noisy place from early morning to late at night; only in the heat of the day were the alleys and courtyards peaceful.

The arrival of Jesus was a matter of further excitement, following on the heels of the return of Mary, her sister and brother. Virtually the whole village followed Jesus to the house where they waited to greet Him. He climbed the stairs to the flat roof, picked his way over Lazarus' tools, avoiding the washing spread out to dry. Many times these past years He had used a roof to emphasise a point. '*That which ye have spoken in the ear in closets shall be proclaimed*

193

upon the housetops.' Jesus thanked the villagers for the welcome and asked for their understanding; in the morning He
must go to Jerusalem, tonight He wanted to be with his
three friends in their home. The onlookers saw the
emotional significance of the request; the word 'home' had
a strong biblical connotation; it was a reminder that the
Chosen People had ceased their wandering and no longer
lived in tents but had sent down permanent roots.
Respecting His wish, the gathering dispersed.

Lazarus had built a house for his sisters and himself
around a central courtyard with sleeping accommodation
and other small rooms leading from it. During the evening
Mary the mother of Jesus, and Mary Magdalene arrived.
The women had walked from Galilee for another Passover;
His mother had not seen Him for months. Since that clash
in the synagogue He had never returned to Nazareth. As
they greeted each other, the recognition of the redemptive
sacrifice He must make was already seared into her face.
But there, too, was the realisation that she must accept it –
that the reality of what He must soon experience was, in
part, designed as a test of her faith in His messianic mission.
What passed between them was more than words: it was an
understanding that He would not be able to help her
struggle between her feelings as a mother and accepting that
she had borne Him for this one purpose.

Apart from His mother one other woman enjoyed a
special intimacy with Him. Mary Magdalene had been
among the very first to understand the true purpose of His
mission, and she knew now that the hours were shortening
before He must enter resolutely upon His sorrowful task,
that a journey which began in Cana was almost over.

The younger Mary went to the room she shared with
Martha and returned with an alabaster jar. Judas stared at
it, calculating aloud its worth. While the other women
stood in the kitchen doorway and watched, Lazarus'
younger sister knelt before Jesus and opened the jar.

The warm evening air was filled with the fragrant essence
of nard, the same perfumed cream Mary Magdalene had

used to anoint His feet in the home of Simon the Pharisee. Now Mary of Bethany, eyes shining with devotion, sprinkled some of the costly lotion on to the palm of her hand and, using a finger, began gently to rub it first into His feet, then on His face, refreshing and softening skin dried by sun and wind. Tipping more of the pale brown lotion into her palm, she worked it around Jesus' lips and into His beard. Placing her hand on the back of His head she gently pulled it down, close to her, so that she could massage the cream into His scalp.

She was a virtuous and unworldly young woman whose contacts with men were very limited. She had not yet learned the art of disguising her feminine feelings. From their first encounter she had made no secret that she was increasingly attracted by Jesus yet it would never have entered her head that the adoration she so freely displayed towards Him would be unkindly misunderstood by others. Martha, on the other hand, was more experienced in the ways of the world; she knew about the potency of sexual attraction, perhaps only too well aware what lay behind the looks she still drew from men in Bethany. She finally stepped forward and tried to attract her sister's attention, to signal with a glance that this kind of behaviour was causing unease among the Disciples. But Mary was intent upon her task. At last Martha called out to Jesus: '*Lord, dost thou not care that my sister hath left me to serve alone. Bid her therefore that she help me.*' But Jesus, with His eyes closed, and relaxed under the soothing caressing, had failed to see the excitement in Mary's eyes – just as He did not comprehend the anxiety behind Martha's words. Like the kneeling woman, He, too, saw nothing improper in what was happening. He responded: '*Martha, Martha, thou art careful and troubled about many things. But one thing is needful: and Mary hath chosen that good part.*'

When she completed her work, Mary lifted the pot, turning it upside down to show Jesus it was empty. The rapt silence in the courtyard was broken as she deliberately dropped the jar to the ground, smashing it into pieces.

Judas leapt to his feet, trembling with sudden anger. Pointing an accusing finger at Mary, he shouted to ask why had she wasted a jar of very expensive ointment – worth at least three hundred shekels. He pointed to his money-bag, yelling that it was almost empty; that the money from the sale of the jar could have gone towards feeding and clothing the Apostles. Frightened by the unexpected outburst, Mary had started to move backwards, to crawl away from his screaming voice.

Jesus stopped her, placing His hand on her head, soothing her trembling. Then He looked up at Judas, standing beside Him, still convulsed with rage. '*Let her alone. Against the day of my burying hath she kept this.*'

Jesus had looked around the circle of seated men. '*For the poor always ye have with you; but Me ye have not always.*'

On that prophetic and sombre note supper began.

At sunset Jonathan's guards herded the last pilgrims, money-changers and vendors of sacrifices out of the Temple. Its outer gates were secured and patrols posted at each one. Teams of Levites raked out the fires in the sacrificial altar and the ovens where the shew-bread was baked, and swept up the refuse in the courtyards. Then the Nicanor Gate was shut. Normally the inner court would be deserted, the rabbis and scribes at their evening meal. But hundreds remained under the colonnades, their attention focused on the *Liscat Haggazith*, the chamber where the Great Sanhedrin was in session behind closed doors.

When the Temple crier had returned without news of Jesus' whereabouts, or without any witnesses, Caiaphas had summoned the seventy-one judges to the windowless cavern at short notice. They sat in a wide semi-circle on carved seats on either side of him, ranged in order of seniority, their faces lit by oil lamps, wrapped in their heavy woollen blue robes against the chill. The court's walls and domed roof were built from polished stones, cut and positioned when King Jannaesus had ruled; in the suffused light the stones glinted like stars. Normally the court assembled on Tuesday and Thursday afternoons and twenty-three judges were sufficient to provide a *hulikka*, a verdict in a non-capital case. If a capital case extended beyond sunset, no sentence of death could be passed on conviction; the prisoner had to be brought back at dawn, after the trumpeter had sounded the start of a new day, escorted from one of the cells below the Court of the Gentiles. When the accused was standing in the circle of justice, placed immediately before the president's chair, the judges, flanked by beadles and scribes, would file in from the Court of the Priests.

In this case there had not been a pre-trial inquiry by the court's two senior secretaries. These experienced lawyers normally had divided responsibilities in preparing a case: one framed the appropriate charges; the other drew up the scrolls containing a broad rebuttal of the accusations. Appended to each set of documents were the appropriate sources from the legal tractates. A quorum, chaired by the president, then met to consider the evidence; the slightest doubt over its admissibility meant the charge being dismissed. Jewish law was deliberately biased in favour of defendants. Evidence could only be given by witnesses of exemplary standing; sinners or suspected sinners were excluded, along with women and children. Agents of the Temple could only give testimony in corroborative support. Any defendant could compel the production of testimony in his favour. The verdict had to be a majority one.

According to some early Christian writing, what happened next in the chamber began with the intervention of a long-standing member of the court. From his seat a few places to Caiaphas' right, Judge Nicodemus, a Pharisee, demanded to know why there had been no preliminary inquiry. He quoted from the tractate *Makkoth* and its insistence that '*the spirit of God must shine upon the Beth Din, the home of judgement*'.

Caiaphas assured him it would; that he, too, would never forget that the basis for Jewish law was appeasing a God angered by wrong-doing. He had convened the court purely in the spirit of that other biblical command, '*be holy as I am holy*'. Because of the circumstances, he had dispensed with a pre-trial inquiry in favour of addressing the court on the grave threat facing the Temple – and very likely the nation. He was clearly speaking of insurrection, an uprising which could mobilise the millions within the city and beyond its walls, an unstoppable rebellion the like of which had never struck before. The High Priest had paused, knowing he had their full attention, letting his words form their own fearful images in the old and clever minds around him, before he had continued to lead them through excerpts from the sixty-three tractates of the law that dealt with blasphemy, profanation of the Sabbath and sorcery and then reminded them they were appointed to represent the common conscience of the people, but they all knew the masses could be fickle; seditious or factious forces could arouse them. That was the danger now at hand.

In building his case the High Priest could hardly have overlooked how Jesus had claimed to have raised Lazarus from the dead. That was sorcery, punishable by death. If they had been true to form any one of the Pharisee judges would have objected. Where was the evidence? Who were the witnesses? Had they been interrogated by the High Priest and his staff? Had they been put under oath? If so – which one: by God, by Heaven, by Jerusalem, by the Temple? Had Lazarus been interrogated to establish he had not been party to a trick? Had testimony been taken from his relatives? Why had the court been convened when even these rudimentary steps had not been taken? Was the case based on this solitary incident? Such questions would have been routine for Pharisees with no liking for the rigid literalism of a Sadducee High Priest.

Unperturbed, Caiaphas replied that now was not the time to raise such questions, that he had brought them together simply to vote on whether or not Jesus had a case to answer. With Passover about to begin, the matter was certainly urgent. He could well have set out to demonstrate that the incident involving Lazarus, coupled with all the other claims Jesus had made, must be seen as a trigger factor, one powerful enough, when the news spread, to arouse the ill-informed to action. They must all perform their duty to protect the mob from the consequences.

Nicodemus intervened to ask what evidence was there that the admittedly extraordinary event involving a Bethany man had taken place – let alone been received seriously?

Caiaphas explained that Lazarus and his sisters had fled. In spite of the efforts of the Temple guards they had not been found. When they were they would be interrogated. But the real threat was Jesus. He could proclaim that what He had done gave Him divine authority. It would be enough to turn already excited pilgrims into a rampaging mob. That was the threat which must be averted. That after all was why they were here to support his demand for Jesus to be put on trial.

How had Jesus exactly set out to encourage rebellion? Nicodemus challenged. Who were His supporters? How were they equipped to launch such an uprising?

Caiaphas explained: Jesus had given ample proof of His powers of sorcery; that His support had spread as He more openly practised His magic; that He had predicted wholesale death and destruction unless He had His way. The High Priest reminded them of the day Jesus had brought His crusade into the Temple itself at the Feast of Tabernacles—

Nicodemus interrupted once more. Why had Jesus not been arrested then? Surely what He had said on that occasion had been evidence enough?

Caiaphas was reproving. Had the learned judge now changed his mind? Only a moment before he had been among those who had said that the court should not hear a case of such gravity based on a single incident. But in Jesus' case there were any number of such offences. Together they comprised evidence for a trial.

A judge of Nicodemus' calibre would most certainly have

pressed: What was the quality of that evidence? Was it totally independent and sufficiently strong to withstand rigorous professional scrutiny? As a Pharisee, he taught both oral and written law. Would any evidence tendered satisfy the court on both counts?

Another Pharisee, Judge Gamaliel, one of the court's outstanding legal and religious experts, has been popularly assumed to be the one who returned to the critical question of Jesus planning an insurrection. Rebellion was an offence against Rome. The case should therefore be referred to Pilate.

The aged jurist Annas rose to his feet and turned to face his fellow judges. Better than any of them, it has been claimed for him, he knew the inherent risks of involving the Romans. In his long life he had seen how the Romans eventually laid any threat at the door of the Temple. He had not forgotten how many priests had been brutalised when they had marched to Caesarea to protest over Pilate's pagan emblems being erected to overlook the Holy of Holies. Nor had that horrific day faded from his memory when the procurator's troops had actually come into the Court of the Gentiles and slaughtered innocent Jews they suspected to be revolutionaries. Further, he would never forget the bloodbath Pilate had unleashed after he sequestered money from the Temple treasury to finance an extra water-supply for the city. Hundreds had died or been seriously maimed trying to defend that sacred money. No: to involve the Romans would be the worst possible move. Pilate would seize the opportunity to tighten the imperial hold on their people. That could lead to the very situation they wished to avert – a national uprising. There was, in any event, cause for concern that Pilate would welcome such confrontation as a chance to crush for ever the spirit of their people. But to do so he would have to weaken, if not totally destroy, the Temple's paramount influence in Jewish life.

It was perhaps a sign of the rift between the Pharisees and Sadducees in the Great Sanhedrin that Gamaliel is credited in some accounts with conceding that, while all this was undoubtedly true, and that he needed no reminding of Rome's brutality, the nagging central question still remained: what was the precise nature of the revolution Jesus was planning? Was it solely against the Romans? There were hundreds of thousands of Jews who would acclaim such a move. Where was the exact threat to the Temple?

Annas no doubt chose the words attributed to him in the Gospels with care. *'He hath spoken blasphemy; what further need have we of witnesses? behold, now ye have heard his blasphemy.'*

Nicodemus, cast in the role of popular defender, made a further intervention. Had Jesus actually said He was the Son of God? If He had, then he would support a move for trial; indeed, he was certain every judge present would.

Annas was the focus of silent attention. Finally, the former High Priest accepted, he could in all truth do no less, that Jesus may not have used the actual words – but that in all He said was His implicit belief that He was the Son of God, that He had chosen it as a compendious title to enshrine all He claimed to represent: *Son of Man* was designed to conjure up a ready vision of the *Messiah* for the masses, without risk to Himself.

Nicodemus protested. He did not share such a contempt for the people. Like him, he was certain that many knew that the title Jesus had taken was in the Book of Daniel; He could argue that He was only carrying on the prophet's work. Where was the proof that Jesus intended the title to be a rallying point, a clarion call to insurrection?

Caiaphas could have insisted that when the time came the evidence would be there: all he wanted was approval to go to trial. Again, the Gospels would recount that the High Priest addressed the Court and told them that this man was the son of Joseph the carpenter and was born of Mary, but that when He said He was the Son of Man, He really meant He was the Son of God. Moreover, that he polluted the Sabbath and wished to destroy the law.

Other voices took up the refrain about whether this was

still circumstantial evidence or based on eye-witness accounts. The discussion switched among the seated judges, with Caiaphas following the cut-and-thrust of the debate intently. Gamaliel once more had the floor. He reminded them that the Great Sanhedrin was not only a court of law but also a theological forum, that in this very chamber the legendary Rabbi Hillel had debated and for-mulated some of the regulations that at the time had been considered revolutionary but which were now accepted. Would it therefore not be reasonable and proper that Jesus should be invited here, of His own free will, and allowed to argue His claims? Only then, if they were found to violate the legal code, should He be brought to trial. Such a propo-sal must only have increased the tension. Caiaphas, outwardly at least, showed that he would consider it most carefully. It would also, of course, mean deferring a vote on bringing Jesus before the court.

The sound of the Temple trumpeter carried to Jesus and the Disciples in Bethany. Some of them were still heavy-eyed, having fallen asleep late, kept awake by the troubling epi-sode with Judas. As soon as they had breakfasted and said their farewells to Lazarus and the women, Jesus and the Disciples set off for Jerusalem. There was about Him the deep courage of someone who had thought long and hard, who saw with chilling clarity what lay ahead. He had calcu-lated the cost in human terms, and had to go on.

Early though it was, the hills were alive with other pil-grims heading for the city, the air filled with singing and with the bleating of animals about to be sacrificed to obtain forgiveness of a sin, to excise an act of ritual impurity, to offer thanks for a birth, to remember the special pact between God and Abraham. Few would have spared a second glance for the group plodding up towards the Mount of Olives. By the time they had reached the base of the hill Jesus had succeeded in getting the Twelve to join Him in chanting the ancient hymns; Judas' shrill voice raised loud-est of all in praise to the special pact between God and

Abraham. Jesus now took the final steps to end that old alliance.

He ordered Matthew to accompany Judas and follow a track around the hill; this would bring them to Bethphage, the first suburb of Jerusalem on the eastern side of the city. If Matthew recognised the irony in being asked to go to where Jerusalem's main customs house was located, he was too busy following the explicit instructions Jesus gave on what to do when they arrived at Bethphage. '*Straightway ye shall find an ass tied, and a colt with her: loose them and bring them unto Me. And if any man say ought unto you, ye shall say, "The Lord hath need of them".*' The sun was still low in the sky when Matthew and Judas returned with the donkey.

Guided by Jesus, the Apostles used their cloaks to form a saddle, lashing it in place with their *hazons*. As they worked people began to stop and look: a handful grew to scores, then hundreds. Soon there were thousands of pilgrims standing and staring at the ass with its improvised saddle with Jesus beside it. Old men reminded their younger companions that the *Messiah*, the liberator of their people, would enter Jerusalem on the back of an ass. Every school child knew that; it was one of the first Scriptural lessons they learned. As word spread more people paused on their way into the city, lining either side of the track that led to Jerusalem. The crowd remained silent and watchful, yet united in some mysterious and inexplicable realisation that here, at last, was the moment they had all waited for.

As Jesus mounted the donkey, a huge cry went up, surging over the Mount of Olives and down the other side, sweeping on across the Kidron Valley finally to resound against the walls of the city which for so long had not only been the capital of the nation, but the very heart of its belief. The cry faded. There was a moment's silence then it repeated itself, louder than before. It died again. But this time the interval was briefer until the cry once more erupted. Then there was no gap, just a sustained roar.

'*Hosanna!*' – *Save us!*

Jesus began to edge the donkey towards Jerusalem,

deliberately choosing to ride upon the ass of peace rather than on the horse of war. His ultimate offer of love was contained in the dramatic decision to enter Jerusalem in this way.

'*Hosanna! Hosanna!*'

The avenue of people extended all the way to the gate King Solomon had built for the day of the *Messiah*.

'*Hosanna! Hosanna!*'

Jesus was finally ready to implement the continuous entreaty roaring out around Him.

'*Hosanna! Hosanna!*'

NINE

Pressing Matters

If they have persecuted me,
they will also persecute you.
— John 15:20

The Small Sanhedrin was in session. The lower court shared the *Liscat Haggazith* with the Great Sanhedrin, hearing cases every morning except on the Sabbath. Caiaphas often presided when they were of a purely religious nature, like the one in which a husband had caught his wife in the act of adultery. There was no possible defence; only one sentence. The High Priest pronounced death by stoning and the court *hazzam*, its gaoler, stepped forward to pinion the woman's arms. Then the first tumultuous roar reverberated through the courtroom. *Hosanna!* The continuous sound confirmed that Jesus was coming into Jerusalem under the best possible protection – that of an adoring crowd.

Joseph Caiaphas motioned the *hazzam* forward. After receiving instructions the gaoler escorted the woman from the court.

The incessant wave of noise swept over the battlements of the tetrarch's palace, drowning the screams from the dungeons – and brought a sense of overwhelming relief to

Joanna, Herod's servant. She had told Chuza she was ready to die for Jesus. Together, as they had heard Him do, husband and wife stood in their room and recited the Our Father. As the din from the direction of the Mount of Olives drew closer, they gave thanks to God that Jesus was coming to rescue not only her but all others who were suffering.

Pilate stood with Claudia Procula at a window in the eastern tower of the Antonia Fortress watching the hundreds of thousands of pilgrims who formed an avenue. The endless cries rolled back and forth along the ranks. Guards emerged from the Temple, swords unsheathed, escorting a bound woman and a group of priests. They forced a passage through one side of the avenue, breaking its solidity for a moment and allowing it to re-form so that anyone who approached along its length would have to pass beside the execution site. The woman was positioned on the edge of the cliff. Pilate had stood at this window before and watched the ritual which had always begun with the High Priest casting the first stone. But there was no sign of Caiaphas. Nor had anyone moved to hurl the woman backwards. She, like her executioners, stared towards the Mount of Olives. Over the summit, came a figure mounted on a donkey. Pilate could not identify the rider. But, not bothering to keep the excitement from her voice, Claudia Procula uttered the Greek word – '*Christos.*'

In the palace dungeons Herod Antipas observed the daily round of torture. At the centre of this fiendish place was a pit with steep smooth walls, scorched black. Close by was a large trough filled with inflammable liquid, a blend of lamp-oil and raw alcohol. Naked prisoners, men and women, were dragged through the mixture and thrown into the hole. When it would hold no more the tetrarch signalled for a gaoler to dip a cresset into the trough, ignite it and toss the flaming torch into the pit, while he remained watching, intent on seeing who would scream the longest and be the last to die in immeasurable agony. Surrounded by his soldiers Herod Antipas rushed to the battlements to observe Jesus descending the Mount of Olives followed by a handful of men. The mighty chorus continued the repetitive chant.

'*Hosanna! Blessed is he that cometh in the name of the Lord.*'

'*Hosanna to the Son of David!*'

'*Hosanna in the Highest!*'

Then, once more: '*Hosanna! Blessed is he that cometh in the name of the Lord.*'

The tetrarch began to laugh uncontrollably, and it took the men around him a while to recognise that relief lay behind this outburst. Jesus and His group appeared not to have a weapon between them. Nor did anyone in the crowd seem to be armed. What possible threat could they be? Reassured, they watched Jesus coming down the hill, unaware of the significance of the slow and certain tread of a donkey bearing a rider who gave no response to the crowd.

A few yards behind the donkey walked the Apostles, their faces dazed and unable to comprehend fully what was happening. Astonishment further deepened when someone ran from the crowd to lay a cloak in the path of the beast. In moments a score more garments were strewn across the avenue, then hundreds, until Jesus and the Disciples were advancing over an unbroken layer of cloth; tens of thousands of robes covered the earth in a multi-coloured quilt which stretched to the Temple gate. Not satisfied with this obeisance, the crowd offered further homage. They cut boughs from the balsam, acacia and tamarisk trees which grew on the lower slopes of the hill. But, above all, they hacked off fronds from palm trees. The branches were placed over the garments, creating a bright green sward. In the meantime hundreds of women and children were fashioning bouquets and nosegays from the profusion of wild spring flowers. These were also placed in the donkey's path. The adulation surpassed even that glorious day when King David had escorted the ark to its final resting place. As Jesus crossed the floor of the Kidron Valley the chanting took on a new resonance.

'*Blessed be the kingdom of our father David!*'

'Blessed be the King that cometh in the name of the Lord!'
'Peace in heaven and glory in the highest.'

Then thundering forth came the now familiar climactic cry.

'Hosanna in the highest!'

The crowd surged forward, blocking the avenue, forcing Jesus to rein in the ass. The singing faded, and men, women and children stared at Him in silent awe. They had travelled far, across mountains and seas, by camel and on foot, just to be here for Passover, to commemorate again the night when the Lord, smiting the first-born of Egypt, had protected the homes of His children. Now, on this day, he was among them again, ready to join in prayers, the offering of the sacrificial lamb and the eating of unleavened bread. Yet, in spite of the rumours down the centuries which had sustained their hopes and deepened their longings, their stunned faces showed only too clearly they simply were unable fully to accept He was here, astride a donkey, finally fulfilling an ancient prediction. They stared at Jesus, not daring to believe, but wanting to, so desperately.

Judas, his eyes shining with excitement, was the Apostle who traditionally stepped forward and asked the crowd to let them pass. Slowly, and with a reverence the treasurer had certainly never seen before, the people did as he bid. Galvanised, Judas ran from one side of the avenue to the other, urging the onlookers to sing even louder, quoting Scripture to them, reminding those who could hear that God Himself had chosen Jerusalem above all other places as where He would be worshipped, and that the city was linked with every happening in their history – as it was on this bright spring day.

Jesus once more edged forward. He travelled only yards before unmistakable Galilean voices cried out.

'Master! Master, we have two blind men here. Give them back their sight.'

The pair were brought forward, stumbling over the strewn branches, and Jesus reached down and placed a finger on their eyelids and commanded them to open.

208

Moments later the men were gazing upon the stunned crowd. One of them called out: '*I see the Son of David!*' His companion cried: '*Blessed is the King of Israel.*'

The procession had assumed a royal importance, reaffirming another hallowed prophecy.

'*Rejoice greatly, O daughter of Zion; shout, O daughter of Jerusalem: behold, thy King cometh unto thee . . . lowly, and riding on an ass.*'

The hosannas soared. The Apostles saw that the avenue had merged behind them and a great wall of humanity spread towards Bethlehem on one side and Jericho on the other. Beyond it lay the Gate of the Messiah.

If Pilate was not quite transfixed by the approaching procession, there can be no doubting his wish to get a closer look at Jesus. At last the procurator could see His face. He may well have seemed older than Pilate had imagined, thinner, almost gaunt, and the Roman may also have wondered if this was really the man he had been warned about in Jewish literature. Isaiah had predicted the *Messiah* would assume a certain form. '*There is no beauty that we should desire Him. He is despised and rejected of men; a man of sorrows and acquainted with grief.*' Almost certainly Jesus in no way fitted that description. He was handsome enough and far from being rejected. Spies had indeed told the procurator that Jesus had increasingly shown symptoms of strange traits such as His frequent disappearance into the desert, almost as if He was driven by wanderlust and a need for isolation; that He was sexually impotent, which would account for the way He rejected the obvious advances of women. Yet, watching Jesus draw closer, there was nothing in His face to show what sort of man He was; all the procurator saw was an inflexibility and certainty he had not seen in any other Jew.

Standing behind Pilate and Claudia Procula was the garrison commander, awaiting instructions. Though untutored in the finer points of Hebrew, he had been stationed long enough in Jerusalem to recognise the ecstatic

209

behaviour of the crowd as a clear act of rebellion against Rome. The commander was a man of action and proven valour. Jesus and the Disciples should be seized and brought to the fortress while soldiers threw a cordon around the Temple, forbidding all entry, and then began systematically to drive back the mob. A show of such strength and determination would quell the most excitable Jew, dashing hopes as swiftly as they had been raised.

From the balcony of the minaret where the trumpeter sounded the start of a new day, the traditional vantage point of a High Priest, Caiaphas stared at an unbelievable scene. From every pilgrim site people were still converging on the city, waving branches and bunches of flowers as they scrambled over the scree. It would be pointless to order the Temple gates closed to keep Jesus from entering and asserting his authority over the very heart of Judaism. No gate was strong enough to keep out such a crowd; it would batter its way in, its fury rising at every charge. The only course was to let Him enter; the only hope that somehow He would over-reach Himself.

In these past three years a great number of Jesus' miracles had been performed before small groups; often no one had been present except the Apostles. Even the raising of Lazarus had taken place before a handful of people. Finally, Jesus had given striking proof of what He had often said: that men could close their eyes to His message, but when the time came they would not fail to see.

Judas could well have been convinced that through that miracle of once more restoring sight Jesus had finally launched a bid for supreme sovereignty over the throng around Him and the city ahead. He was approaching Jerusalem as a literal rather than a spiritual King of the Jews. With the procession drawing closer to its unbroken curved walls of golden-brown stone, its formidable tower forts and reinforced gates, Judas' conviction could only have deepened that victory had been achieved without a drop of blood being shed; that Jesus would not after all have to die: the crowd would see to that. In the Apostle's bedazzled mind that would have been a reasonable explanation of why they were being allowed to advance unopposed. Jesus had flung down His challenge; the enemy had crumbled.

At the Temple gate Jesus turned and faced the crowd. He asked them to be patient; they should return to their encampments and make their preparations for Passover. When they started to disperse, He dismounted and walked into the Temple's immense outer Court of the Gentiles. A silence spread through its length, all two hundred and fifty yards of flagstones, and colonnades, every inch of floor space crowded all the way to the Royal Porch where the doctors of the law debated, and Solomon's Portico, where pedlars went about their business. Only the bleating of animals and the cooing of sacrificial doves broke the sudden tension. People stared expectantly towards the Holy of Holies, waiting for the stone they believed miraculously hovered in the sanctuary to come crashing to the ground. It would be the final proof the Expected One was among them. The silence stretched as Jesus surveyed the scene. Then He turned and walked out of the Temple.

Judas was too stunned to move. While the other Apostles slowly followed Jesus, the treasurer remained rooted. If there was a single instant when Judas moved from committed follower to the path of infamy, that was the moment. Around him pilgrims whispered in disappointment that the great stone must still be hovering.

In the *Liscat Haggazith* Levites lit oil lamps and replenished the jars of water from the Temple's underground well.

Instead of occupying the formal semi-circle of seats, the High Priest, Annas and the other Sadducee members of the Great Sanhedrin sat on cushions at the rear of the chamber. They had been together since early afternoon, after Jesus had departed and a Roman officer had arrived at the Temple to deliver a warning from the procurator that there must be no repetition of the morning's scenes. Caiaphas had sent back a reassuring message: he would take all necessary steps to reinforce his authority over his people. Caiaphas had told the judges that to avoid the full fury of Rome being unleashed it was vitally important to convince their Pharisee colleagues that they must place the preservation of their own position above all other considerations. The High Priest suggested how this could be done.

In recent months Jesus had singled out the Pharisees working in the Temple for special attack: He had accused them of abandoning their roots, of showing hypocrisy, contempt, selfishness and unscrupulous behaviour. He had taunted them about their punctilious observance of the Sabbath and attacked their teaching. He had accused them of plotting with Herod Antipas to kill Him. On one Sabbath in Capernaum He had treated '*a man with the dropsy*' and challenged the Pharisees to show cause why He should not do so on the day of rest. In the synagogue of Bethabara He had devoted His entire commentary on a portion of Scripture to assailing the Temple Pharisees. At Bethsaida Jesus had used a parable further to revile them: '*What man shall there be among you, that shall have one sheep, and if it fall into a pit on the sabbath day, will he not lay hold on it and lift it out? How much then is a man better than a sheep? Wherefore it is lawful to do well on the sabbath days . . .*' Around the Sea of Galilee He had regularly condemned Pharisees as vipers, fools and obdurate legalists protecting empty ritualism. In Nain He castigated them as '*the children of them which killed the prophets*'; in Jericho with '*extortion and excess*'; in Tyre He referred to their '*hypocrisy and iniquity*'; and in Sidon accused them of '*evil thoughts, murder, adulteries, fornications and thefts*'. At every opportunity Jesus had heaped maledictions upon their colleagues.

The men around Caiaphas listened attentively, the anger in their faces deepening, as he argued that, in attacking the Pharisees of the Temple, Jesus was destroying their own divine authority to teach and interpret God's will and word. The High Priest urged his listeners to stress the danger to their colleagues, bringing an end to the division which had wrecked the last meeting of the Great Sanhedrin. Further discussion ended with the arrival of Jonathan to announce that Herod Antipas was waiting in the Royal Porch.

From the roof of Lazarus' home, Jesus and the Apostles continued to watch the increasing groups of men camped out around Bethany. Simon had gone to them and returned with the news they were Zealots and their supporters, there to provide protection. As the night cooled they lit fires and sat talking or occasionally making music, plaintive sounds which carried to Jesus and His companions.

Judas kept his distance, once more his brooding self. Over the meal he finally turned to Jesus and demanded to know why He had not claimed His Kingdom. Why had He once more walked away from what had been His for the taking? Why had He not done what the prophets promised and destroyed His enemies? Why was He back here when He could be occupying that throne He had spoken so much about? But before any of the Apostles could rebuke Judas, Jesus had quietly reminded him of that evening on the Sea of Galilee when the treasurer, like the others, had been frightened, until He had spoken to them. Soon the faith they had kept since then would be realised. Judas had lapsed once more into sullen silence. After the meal he abruptly excused himself and left the courtyard. Jesus watched him go, saying nothing. The treasurer had not returned before the men on the roof had fallen asleep.

Caiaphas and Annas let Herod Antipas rant on without interruption in the Royal Porch. Jesus, he roared, had come to take away his throne; He had already proclaimed Himself king. For that alone He must die. There was no longer a need for covert ambush. Jesus would be cut down in public before His people. If they protested they would also be slaughtered. There was a madness about the tetrarch which might well have reminded the two priests of the last days of Herod the Great: his son displayed the same demented stare and ferocious gesture.

213

Then, while Levites replenished their wine, they began to reason. Jesus had not actually proclaimed He *was* King of the Jews. Until He did so, however offensive His behaviour, it would be hard to get a conviction. But to move openly against Jesus without the support of the law could have dire results. His followers would obey any instruction He gave: they had quietly dispersed when He told them; they could just as easily be mobilised to full-scale fury. Point by point Caiaphas and Annas had carefully cooled Herod Antipas' blood-lust. The safest and surest way, concluded the High Priest, was to allow the Great Sanhedrin to find grounds to convict Jesus legally. Herod Antipas reluctantly accepted their arguments and left.

After Annas had retired to his palace, reaching it through an underground passage from the Temple, Caiaphas went to his temporary quarters near the Holy of Holies; it would be a further six days before he could return to his own palace, his wife and children. At some point during the night he was awakened by Jonathan, who had himself been aroused by the officer of the watch with urgent news. The Captain of the Guard recognised it was of sufficient importance to awaken the High Priest. Caiaphas had dressed and, using another of the labyrinth of underground passages, had emerged with Jonathan in the Court of the Gentiles. Standing there, firmly gripped by the officer of the watch, was a man. Jonathan held the burning taper close to the face of Judas.

As noon approached all male adults, those aged thirteen years and upwards, in the Court of the Gentiles, as in all the other courts of the Temple except one – the Court of the Women – prepared to pray. Women, children and slaves were excused the obligation. Each man wrapped himself in a *tallith*, his prayer shawl, and secured with thongs to his forehead or the palm of his right hand a *tefillin*, a small square black box made of the hide of kid or camel and containing identical parchment excerpts from Exodus and Deuteronomy. As the hour approached Caiaphas stood on

214

the podium before the Nicanor Gate. The High Priest, along with everyone else, turned towards the Holy of Holies. In the streets of Jerusalem men did the same; in the hillsides still more rose to their feet and faced in the direction of the Temple. At the farthest point of the Diaspora where an adult Jew was located, that Jew would be performing the same precise ritual. It was a compelling example of religious conformity.

Inside the Court of the Gentiles all commerce halted. The most rapacious traders, who had haggled with customers until the last possible moment, hurriedly threw around their shoulders *talliths*, the pure white silk often the most expensive garment they possessed, allowing the ritual fringes to fall around their waists. Caiaphas uttered the first word of the *Shema* – 'listen'. Voices, piping and deep, wavering and resolute, joined together to recite the phrases of the most famous prayer in their religious life, the one that brought each of them once more into the presence of his Maker.

The consecration over, the trading din resumed, the air a cacophony of sacrificial animals being sold and rates of exchange quoted by the money-changers. From his dais Caiaphas looked upon a scene that caused him no offence. Yet the Temple was being desecrated; traders regularly stored their goods in the sacrosanct porches, an offence grave enough to be singled out in the Book of Leviticus. Along the length of Solomon's Portico men hawked and spat and trailed their soiled clothes and feet through the sacred area, profaning its purity.

From the far end of the Court of the Gentiles came a sudden and increasing commotion from around the main trading area. The sound of something crashing to the ground reached the High Priest, followed by a flock of doves fluttering into the air. Guards ran towards the disturbance. There was another mighty crash as a money-changer's stand was hurled out of the portico, its frame splintering and its contents scattering over the courtyard.

Caiaphas saw Jesus, whip raised in one hand, the other

215

holding a cage of birds. One of the men with Him opened it and sparrows flew over the Temple walls. Jesus threw the cage from Him and brought His whip lashing down on a money-changer's table, toppling it under the sheer force of the blow.

Jonathan appeared at the foot of the podium urging Caiaphas to let him arrest Jesus. The High Priest pointed towards the court's gate, through which scores of pilgrims were pouring to cheer on Jesus as he upturned another vendor's table, and very sensibly commanded the captain to hold back his men: the Temple was the last place for a pitched battle. Twenty-three years ago, he could have reminded Jonathan, when the captain was a lowly guard, he had helped to drive out Samaritans who had behaved improperly in the Temple. They had been only a handful, yet it required the entire Temple police force to evict them. While Jonathan ran into the courtyard to order his men back, Caiaphas was faced with the truth that once more Jesus had unerringly calculated the mood of the people.

The commotion interrupted Pilate's reading of a scroll which contained good news from Rome. In the Senate the campaign against Sejanus was mounting. The procurator sensed that the time had come to make discreet contact with Agrippina and her elder son, Nero, once powerful voices in the capital before they had been exiled by Sejanus to small islands off the Italian coast. Their supporters had recently borne Agrippina's standards into the Senate to rousing cheers, a certain indication she and her son would shortly be back in the city. Expressing support for them now could have incalculable benefits later. Nero was the sort of man who could pluck someone from the ends of the empire and install him at its centre. The shouting from the Temple courtyard certainly interrupted such pleasurable speculation.

From his window the procurator could have watched Jesus striding through the portico, using His whip to clear the way, pausing only to topple over stalls selling grain, salt, wine, incense and oil. Thousands of birds were being set free; hundreds of sacrificial animals were stampeding around the courtyard. Pilate would not only have heard, but seen the rage in Jesus' face. The calm certainty of yesterday, when He had steadfastly ignored the acclaim for his triumphant entry, had given way to naked fury. The procurator found this reassuring: an angry man could also be a frightened man. And no Roman god had ever shown fear.

Recovering from the sheer speed of the onslaught, the dealers began to vent their own anger, screaming at Jesus, demanding what authority allowed Him to behave as He had.

Jesus picked up another table and hurled it at the traders, shouting: '*It is written my house shall be called the house of prayer, but ye have made it a den of thieves!*'

Escorted by the throng Jesus continued on His path of destruction. The Temple guards kept pace but made no effort to intervene. Jesus was surrounded by the same men who had followed the donkey along the processional avenue. Eleven, Pilate would have seen, were also helping to wreck the merchants' tables, booths and seats. But one, a tiny swarthy-faced man, clutching a *punda* to his chest, was taking no part. Could this be the same man his spies had trailed from Bethany to the Temple during the night and who had only reappeared hours later after spending the time with the High Priest?

Jesus reached the northern end of the portico; flushed from His exertion He leant against a pillar, whip in hand, surrounded by the Apostles. They had been as stunned as everyone else by His actions. On previous visits to Jerusalem He had ignored the vendors and their squalid dealings. The traders angrily demanded to know again what authority Jesus had to disrupt their living.

The question held a deeper meaning. The key word was *authority*. Jesus was not a member of the Temple hierarchy, armed with formal *authority* to interpret the law within its walls: it could therefore be argued that His actions fitted the

217

Scriptural definition of *a blasphemous and rebellious elder*. That carried its own penalty – stoning. Once more the question was put. *'What sign showest thou unto us, seeing thou doest these things?'*

Jesus' reply must have silenced all in earshot. *'I am able to destroy the Temple of God and to build it in three days.'*

Without further explanation He led the Apostles out of the courtyard. Only when they had left the Temple was the baffled question asked by one trader to another: how could any man possibly destroy and raise a building in three days – especially one which had taken so far forty-six years to erect and was still in the process of construction?

They did not grasp that Jesus had spoken of a very different *temple*: His body.

But the face-value of the words fitted into the choreography Caiaphas was creating.

By the light of the stars Jesus and the others saw movement among the men guarding the track which led from Jerusalem to Bethany. The cordon could only attract rather than lessen trouble: neither the Romans nor Herod Antipas would tolerate it for long. Anxious to avoid exposing Lazarus and his sisters to needless risk Jesus had asked Simon to find a new and secure place where they could sleep, then instructed Peter and John to go to Jerusalem in the morning to make preparations for Passover. On previous occasions they had been guests of relatives and friends. Jesus told the Apostles that this time they would dine together as a group with no others present.

He had also explained that His fury with the vendors arose directly from contradiction of the law. Isaiah had defined the Temple as *'a house of prayer for all nations'*. But its priests shamelessly supported the fanatical aims of the Shammai religious cult which had emerged in the wake of Herod the Great's death and was dedicated to promoting a radically pure faith. As part of that creed the sect had also banned the long tradition of non-Jews offering gifts to the Temple at the great festivals. Yet many traders still

218

accepted the tribute and divided it with the priests.

What had enraged Jesus was not only a passion for social justice – the traders *were* swindling scoundrels battening on the pilgrims – but the recognition that they were only a part of a corrupt structure. From the High Priest to the lowest Levite, there was a thriving involvement with the sale of sacrifices: they imposed inspection fees to make sure each bird and animal was unblemished; they received bribes from each money-changer and every purveyor of goods permitted to operate within Solomon's Portico. In deliberately challenging these arrangements Jesus intended to hasten a confrontation which went far beyond a condemnation that ritual slaughter could never be the substitute for the true love of God. Further, in speaking of '*His house*', Jesus also made it once more clear that He identified His action as being that of God.

Some of the men guarding the track were in the street below, calling they had brought a visitor from the city. Matthew was the first to recognise the figure in a *chalouk*, a knee-length tunic, and a *tallith*, the cloak draped around his shoulders. It was Judge Nicodemus. The Apostle's duties as a tax collector had sometimes brought him to the Small Sanhedrin which sat in Sepphoris, one of the country's five main provincial law courts. For a while Nicodemus had presided over the Sepphoris judiciary, and shown himself to be a fair but firm upholder of the law. Matthew introduced their visitor and John asked what '*a leader of the Jews*' wanted with them.

Nicodemus apologised for the lateness of his visit – strangers rarely called after the supper hour – explaining he had used the cover of darkness so that he would not be recognised. Jesus asked, no doubt more politely than John, why a member of the Great Sanhedrin was here.

'*Rabbi, we know that thou art a teacher come from God.*'

There was no guile about the words. Nicodemus was merely using a judge's right to refer to himself in the plural rather than indicating that a body of support existed for Jesus within the Temple. Indeed, if pressed, Nicodemus would have had to admit that any such support had been eroded among even the most liberal of the Temple Pharisees in the wake of the stinging rebukes Jesus had recently directed at them.

Jesus addressed Nicodemus. *'Except a man be born again he cannot see the kingdom of God.'*

Conditioned by many years of court work never to show surprise, Nicodemus nevertheless could not control his bewilderment. *'How can a man be born when he is old? can he enter the second time into his mother's womb, and be born?'*

In a Jerusalem street, the same questions had been put after Jesus had restored sight to yet another blind man. Then they were meant to trap Him. Now they were put genuinely to seek enlightenment.

Jesus said that only someone born again *'of the spirit'* could enter the Kingdom.

Nicodemus, as he would have done in the Great Sanhedrin, pressed politely but firmly for a more detailed explanation.

Jesus provided it. *'That which is born of the flesh is flesh; and that which is born of the Spirit is spirit. Marvel not that I say unto thee, ye must be born again. The wind bloweth where it listeth, and thou hearest the sound thereof, but canst not tell whence it cometh, and whither it goeth. So is every one that is born of the Spirit.'*

Nicodemus clearly found the answer still confusing.

Jesus could not hide his irony. *'Art thou a master of Israel and knowest not these things?'*

Then, once more acknowledging he had come for no other purpose than to learn, the judge asked Jesus to explain where His teachings differed from the existing law. Had Jesus come to offer a new explanation for the written and oral law of the Pentateuch, to tear down the elaborate structures which had stood the test of centuries?

Jesus repeated a now familiar refrain. He had not come to replace or destroy. He had come to fulfil the law. There were many, He accepted, who would remain wedded to their faith. It should be so. What He had come to do was to

220

reveal a new truth, one that not only absorbed all the commandments of existing holy writ, but went beyond them.

Jesus spoke about His meaning of faith; that the time was fast approaching when the sovereignty of God would extend beyond the Promised Land, beyond all other lands, conquered and free, to rule over Rome itself and all the other pagan centres on earth. One age – the one which Jews gave cognisance with their concept of being God's chosen People – was about to end and a new one begin. It would be one in which the God of the past, present and future would be unified and the Kingdom would be within each person, placed there as God's gift to each of those He had created. To receive the gift was both a simple and, at the same time, an extraordinarily demanding process. It required a sense of what was instinctively right and wrong, an ability to forgive, a readiness to offer and accept love. A child found that easy but an adult more often than not difficult. The richer a man, the harder for him to accept God's gift; the greater the stake in worldly life, the more difficult it was to see the larger rewards beyond.

Nicodemus had asked, perhaps with a hint of exasperation, if all those with money, land and authority over others were precluded from receiving this gift.

Once more Jesus gently chided him. *'Verily, verily, I say unto thee: We speak that We do know, and testify that We have seen.'*

He promised the Kingdom of Heaven would allow Nicodemus to be in direct communication with God. There was no other way to describe it.

The stars were fading when Jesus invited the judge to join Him and the Apostles in the Lord's Prayer, so that Nicodemus could repeat words which so perfectly demonstrated what he had been told: that God's purpose would be fulfilled on earth as it was in heaven.

In the east tower of the Antonia Fortress, Claudia Procula prepared to spend another day in her salon. The Jews had the streets to themselves. Her husband had confined all Roman patrols to barracks to reduce possible friction. The centurions sat around the fort, drinking *sheckar*, the local beer, and complaining it was a poor substitute for a Roman brew. The incessant noise from the Temple only aggravated her own mood.

At some point in the morning, from one of the salon windows overlooking the Temple she had seen the throng around the Eastern Gate part to form a corridor through which walked Jesus.

Two chief priests forced their way through the crowd. The first addressed Jesus in the polite and circumlocutory language of the high-born. *'Master, we know that thou art true, and teachest the way of God in truth, neither carest thou for any man.'*

The second priest fished in his robe and produced a silver coin, a Roman denauris, and asked: *'Is it lawful to give tribute unto Caesar or not?'*

To any Jew the Roman tribute was a reminder of their subjugation to a heathen power. If Jesus confirmed the propriety of the levy, the word would most certainly spread swiftly that Jesus supported one of Rome's most hated impositions. His credibility would be destroyed; there was every possibility that the same crowd that had praised Him would kill Him. The priest asked again if it was lawful to pay.

Jesus put out a hand. *'Show me the tribute money.'*

The rabbi handed over the penny. Jesus held it between thumb and forefinger, inspecting it carefully. On one side was the embossed head of Tiberius and the letters: *TI CAESAR AUG D F AUGUSTUS – Tiberius, Caesar Augustus Divi Filius Augustus*: Tiberius Caesar Son of the Divine Augustus. On the other side was an engraving of the empress Julia Livia, with a sceptre and flowers and the letters: *PONTIF MAXIM – Pontifex Maximus*: High Priest.

Jesus pointed at the emperor's head and asked whose image and inscription it represented.

222

The first priest replied impatiently: *'Caesar's.'*

Jesus handed back the coin. *'Render therefore unto Caesar the things which are Caesar's, and unto God the things that are God's.'*

Applause and delighted laughter from the crowd greeted the epigram. The discomfited priests left to report to Caiaphas.

Towards the end of the day the High Priest received another visitor. The man followed a pre-arranged route, a traditional one for informers, entering through a door in the part of Annas' palace which extended into the Lower City. From there he had been brought underground into the Temple, emerging near the *Liscat Haggazith*, from where he was escorted to the High Priest's office. Caiaphas had greeted Judas.

* * *

What passed between them would leave unanswered tantalising issues. Was Judas now primarily motivated by mental confusion and disillusionment? Was he obsessed with the belief that he, and he alone, must *still* bring Jesus into open confrontation with the authorities, not because he wished to see His Master die, but because he clung to the belief that Jesus was invincible? Did he *still* think that Jesus primarily intended to topple the authority of Rome – and, when the Temple realised that, its full authority would support Him? Had Judas, in spite of being more culturally and politically aware than the other Apostles, with the possible exception of Matthew, *still* not realised what the High Priest's intentions were after that first nocturnal visit? What had prompted him to return? Had Caiaphas used coercion – threatening to unmask the treasurer unless he continued to co-operate, knowing that exposure would be enough for the crowd to kill Judas? Was that why Caiaphas had reduced Judas' role to one he could more easily understand and manipulate – that of paid informer, offering him money, the thirty pieces of silver? They only raised still further questions. Zechariah had spoken of receiving a similar amount for doing the Lord's work. Had Caiaphas, ever the expert manipulator, persuaded Judas – whose judgement would have almost certainly been further clouded under the tension and danger of what he was about – that he was performing a similar divinely approved function?

*　*　*

After darkness had fallen, Joanna left the tetrarch's palace, wrapped in an *isomuklia*, a heavy outer robe which kept out the chill of the Jerusalem night, and she made her way through the Upper City, along a maze of narrow unnamed streets, many of them stepped, all crowded with pilgrims. Her destination was a house close to the Antonia Fortress. Despite its modest exterior of roughly hewn stones and a door made of cedar wood, it was the home of the most prosperous businessman in the city, Joseph Haramati, a Galilean who had come south to make his fortune. He was now wealthy enough to have a private burial tomb reserved for himself and his family. It was close to Golgotha.

History would suggest that a year before, on a visit to Galilee, Joseph had encountered Jesus preaching and become a devout follower. He had seen in Jesus many of the virtues of his other religious hero, the Jewish teacher Rabbi Ben Hillel. They both encouraged healing through prayer, did not place undue stress on religious ritual, emphasised the need for giving and receiving spiritual love, and displaying humility, and made no distinction between Jews or Gentiles in God's eyes. To the deeply religious Joseph, Jesus offered still more – the promise of life beyond the grave. Joseph had come to know His mother and friends, and in the past they had sometimes stayed in his home, holding prayer meetings. At one of these Joseph had met Joanna and, on learning of her position in the palace, he realised that she could bring any information to him of moves the tetrarch was contemplating against Jesus. Joseph listened with mounting concern to Joanna's latest news about the tetrarch's attempt to have Jesus murdered.

On the afternoon of what the Jews called the fourteenth of Nisan, but which Pilate preferred to reckon as the fifth day of the first week of the fourth month of the sixteenth year of the reign of Tiberius – and which would become known as Thursday, the sixth day of April in the year of Our Lord 30 – the procurator prepared another report for the emperor. It would have to take account of how Jesus had provoked such alarm in the High Priest and tetrarch, and how the spies of Herod Antipas were out in force fruitlessly combing the city and hillsides.

The irony of the situation must have appealed to the procurator because it confirmed that the best way to rule the Jews was to keep their leaders divided. If relations between the tetrarch and the Temple had been anything other than icily polite, Herod Antipas would know that Caiaphas had learned from Judas of the new hiding place of Jesus and the Apostles within hours of Simon selecting the cavern among the thickly planted groves on the Mount of Olives. It was used to store and squeeze the fruit and accessible only through a small and easily disguised entrance. Locally it was known as *gath shemane*, the olive press – Gethsemane.

The Christian Coptic Church would enshrine such details, and interpret them to allow Pontius Pilate to be included in its calendar of saints on the premiss that he was '*already a Christian in his innermost heart*'. It would certainly be one explanation for behaviour which would become increasingly baffling to a pagan Roman.

Late in the afternoon Simon bought an unblemished yearling lamb and brought it to one of the priests standing at the Nicanor Gate. Passing inspection, the animal was taken to the sacrificers at the great altar. It was despatched in seconds, one of ten thousand lambs an hour slaughtered in the week before Passover. With the gutted carcass slung over his shoulder and the lamb's hide in one hand, Simon made his way through the throng into the Lower City.

225

Several times he slipped down alleyways, through courtyards, up open flights of stairs and across flat roofs before descending again into streets some distance from where he had begun his evasive action.

The sun was setting when he finally reached Zion, the oldest part of the city, a casbah of souks, sunken courtyards, roof terraces and passages too narrow for a Roman soldier in full armour to negotiate. Simon entered a house which belonged to one of Joseph of Arimathea's servants. Peter had arranged to borrow it for the Passover meal and in return had promised to leave the hide as a traditional form of thanksgiving.

Peter was already waiting in the courtyard, tending the fire he had lit beneath the oven in a corner. Near to it was a well. Checking again that none of the lamb's bones had been broken – an examination required by the Passover tractate – the two men placed it on a grid in the oven. Then they inspected the upper room which John had been preparing. It was a low-roofed chamber supported by heavy beams in the wall and ceiling. On the floor were rattan divans and a low square table. It was set for thirteen, each place denoted by a goblet and platter. Tall candles in clay holders were placed around the table. They would be lit to mark the start of the most important meal in the Jewish liturgical calendar, the *Seder*.

Caiaphas addressed the judges seated around him in the *Liscat Haggazith*. He asked again that the Great Sanhedrin should order the arrest of Jesus. There was a demand from the Pharisees present, perhaps once more led by judge Nicodemus, to hear the evidence, know the name of the witnesses and their standing in the community, whether they were personally acquainted with Jesus and had their testimony already been formally taken under oath. If so, could the court study it and, if need be, question the witnesses before coming to a decision? That would be the normal procedure.

It would not have needed Nicodemus or Gamaliel to

226

remind the others that, when they had last assembled, Caiaphas had warned that insurrection was imminent. But there had been no sign of any uprising. Indeed, Jesus had actually ordered the crowds to cease their acclaim. Under such circumstances, the senior Pharisee judges clearly saw no cause to rush to judgement.

Not for the first time the Supreme Court would have broken up in disorder with the High Priest walking out of the chamber – the ultimate sign of displeasure at his disposal.

Through the darkness the Apostles arrived one by one in the courtyard. Each went to the well, drew water and carefully washed away the dust of the road.

Peter tended the oven, basting the lamb in its own juices. Normally the women in Jesus' entourage would have supervised the cooking, but His insistence on only the Twelve being present meant the oldest Apostle was responsible for filling the tiny beakers with drops of salted water which they would all sip before the meal to commemorate the tears of their forefathers, blending the *hazareth*, the red sauce into which the unleavened bread would be dipped, and preparing the bowls of crushed bay leaves, marjoram, basil and horse-radish, the *bitter herbs* of the tractate, eaten as a further reminder of their past as slaves in Egypt. While Peter worked John and Simon maintained a vigil at the courtyard entrance. At every knock John peered through a crack before nodding to Simon to open the door. Each arrival was warmly greeted and gave the assurance he had not been followed. Eventually eleven men were in the courtyard. Still to come were Judas and Jesus.

The men in Caiaphas' office would have carefully considered what Judas had said before formulating a plan. At some stage the High Priest would have needed to address Jonathan over how many men would be required to capture Jesus. On the captain's part, tactical consideration would have made him hesitate over any attempt to do so in the city, especially in such a volatile quarter as Zion; it was a fore-gone conclusion that Jesus would have innumerable followers among the predominantly working-class people who lived there. If every one of the five hundred Temple guards were deployed, there could be no guarantee they would be able to extract Jesus without a fierce running battle; an even greater danger was that resistance would not be contained within Zion – the entire city could become embroiled. No doubt Caiaphas and the other priests present had persisted, determined this time not to be thwarted. If the Temple guards were reinforced with sufficient numbers of the tetrarch's soldiers, opposition would be contained and overcome in the casbah; there were enough troops for a cordon to be thrown around the entire area. Such a proposal was still not without risk. The more men involved, the greater the chance of advance warning: the casbah was renowned for its street intelligence: word would travel its length long before any troops were in the area. By the time they would have undoubtedly had to fight to reach the house where Jesus was, He and the others would have long gone.

Very possibly still furious over his failure in the Great Sanhedrin, Caiaphas wanted agreement on a viable plan to bring Jesus to the Temple.

That may well have been the moment that Judas chose to ask what would happen then.

Caiaphas, in the mood of the moment, would not have bothered to hide the contempt in his voice. Judas would be paid for his work. When Jesus was captured he would receive thirty pieces of silver.

The amount was equivalent to a labourer's income for four months.

Caiaphas continued questioning Jonathan about his strategy. If he could not take Jesus in Zion, where would he capture Him? Before deciding, Jonathan needed to know from Judas where Jesus and the Disciples would go after the Passover meal ended. The treasurer, anxious to appease the High Priest's anger, replied that the most likely place would be back to the cave on the Mount of Olives. Jonathan would need to be told the exact position of the cavern and what cover there was for his men to approach undetected. Satisfied on those counts, the captain came to a decision. He would capture Jesus in the cavern or its vicinity.

A thought struck Caiaphas. How would Jonathan recognise he had captured the right man, out there in the darkness on the Mount of Olives? Judas said he would identify Jesus by giving Him a traditional kiss of peace.

John and Simon greeted Jesus with relief at the courtyard door; not only had He arrived without incident, but also old tensions had surfaced among the Disciples. This time the squabbling was over the seating arrangements for the meal; arguments had broken out when John had led the other Disciples to the upper room and indicated their places. They returned to the courtyard and immediately began to accuse him of favouritism. James the Less reminded John he had always sat close to his Brother: now he was placed farthest away. Thomas objected at where he was seated. Thaddaeus complained at being seated several places below Judas. Philip and Bartholomew both argued they should be closer to Jesus. In vain John had explained that these were places of honour. Peter, because he had organised the occasion, was automatically entitled to preside over the part of the table to Jesus' right. Andrew, because of his seniority, was next to his elder brother. John had placed himself beside Jesus because He had requested it.

The arrival of Jesus put a stop to the acrimony. While Jesus washed, Peter removed the lamb from the oven, placing it on a large plate which he carried upstairs and set in the centre of the table, surrounding it with piles of unleavened bread. Peter then went to the well and cleaned himself.

In uncomfortable silence, the Twelve followed Jesus to the table. He lit the candles and invited them to stand at their places. After some hesitation they did so and joined Him in prayer. When they were all settled, Jesus reached for His beaker of salt water, blessed it and addressed the table.

'*With desire I have desired to eat this passover with you before I suffer. For I say unto you, I will not any more eat thereof until it be fulfilled in the kingdom of God.*'

They sipped their salted water. Jesus blessed one of the jars of red wine. Then He rose and filled the first of the four goblets they would drink from during the meal: for *Kiddush*, the sanctification; followed by the wine for *Haggadsh*, the celebration of the lamb; the third glass would be drunk after the prayers of thanks; the fourth to accompany the closing prayers. The goblets symbolised the kingdoms which the Book of Daniel identified as having oppressed God's People: the Chaldeans, Medes, Babylonians and the Romans.

Jesus once more spoke. '*For I say unto you, I will not drink of the fruit of the vine, until the kingdom of God shall come.*'

The words were deliberately meant to give the banquet His own unforgettable seal. They were more than a blessing of the good things they were about to eat and drink; within them lay a declaration of gratitude that He had at least been allowed sufficient time to partake in this sacred repast: He wanted them to know He was a condemned man yet one who could sense the closeness of salvation. In those words Jesus had removed the *Seder* from its ancient meaning and bound it for ever to His identity. He wanted them to understand that when next they met they would partake of the imperishable nourishment of eternal life. Beneath His allegorical nuances He was saying they would all meet Him in the Kingdom of Heaven. He excluded no one – not even Judas. Instead, he was appealing to all of them to be conscious that, through Him, they would ensure the survival of the Kingdom. They must see this meal from now on as His own celebration. In time it would become known as the Eucharist or Holy Communion.

John could sense the bickering starting again; a whispered niggardly resentment had resumed over the seating. John looked at Peter, who was visibly upset that, having all heard such words from their Master, there should still be such unseemly behaviour. Only Judas seemed so moved that he sat with head bowed.

Jesus passed the bowl of spicy red sauce to John, who tore off a piece of bread, dipped it into the *hazareth* and then handed the chalice to Andrew. The sauce-boat was halfway round the table and the grumbling showed no signs of abating.

Jesus abruptly rose to His feet and went downstairs. In the upper room the argument intensified. Below in the courtyard Jesus stripped to His *nikli*, a short undergarment, and wrapped Himself in one of the towels the Disciples had used to dry themselves. He drew a pail of water from the well. Carrying the bucket upstairs, He stood for a moment in the open archway listening to the complaining men, then walked over to where Peter reclined and, placing the bucket on the floor, knelt in front of the Apostle. He began to wash Peter's feet, saying nothing but making His point as powerfully as any of His words.

Peter, recovering, tried to move his feet away, protesting. *'Lord, dost thou wash my feet?'*

Without looking up, aware that all eyes were on Him, Jesus spoke. *'What I do thou knowest not now, but thou shalt know hereafter.'*

Peter tried again to stop Jesus. *'Thou shalt never wash my feet!'*

Jesus looked at the Disciple. *'If I wash thee not, thou hast no part with Me.'*

Peter's voice became eager. *'Lord, not my feet only, but also my hands and my head.'*

Jesus sighed. *'He that is washed needeth not save to wash his feet, but is clean every whit; and ye are clean, but not all.'*

He continued to bathe Peter's feet. Once more, at this late hour, He had to show them what He expected. He deliberately chose Peter because he had not been one of those bickering. Yet Peter, in many ways, had responded no differently from the others. He had initially not accepted what Jesus wanted to do; Peter had shown an obstinacy and

231

stubbornness in insisting he would *not* allow his Master to wash his feet. Then, realising that Jesus was totally intent upon His task, Peter had tried to prolong His personal attention, asking for his hands and head to be bathed. Just as much as the others with their argument over the seating plan, Peter had failed to understand the true purpose of this feast. It was not a Passover, but a farewell meal; yet it was not a time only to remember the past but an occasion to look to the future. By spending time in cleansing Peter's feet Jesus wished to make it clear that there was no time to be wasted on the petty matter of who sat where. When Jesus finished, He walked slowly from the silent room, the sorrow in His face plain.

Dressed, Jesus returned to the table and the meal resumed. He ate little, still preoccupied in driving home that, with the dignity of being His Apostles, went the responsibility of working together in harmony: not one of them was greater in His eyes than the other. He wanted to remind them that He, as their Host and Master, was privileged to serve them – as soon they must serve others.

Around Him the Twelve at last began to realise the extraordinary significance of what was taking place. Jesus had brought them to this table not only to express his gratitude for their loyalty – He offered no indication that Judas was specifically excluded from this benediction – but to give them in trust a task of the utmost importance: the future religious guidance of the people. The meal progressed while He continued to urge that the only worthwhile authority was achieved through humility; that the essence of greatness was found in the depths of modesty; that to be of service was the noblest thing they could do: to each other, to others and, above all, service in God's Kingdom. It would require at times hard decisions. But to judge without flinching was the only way to govern over the new Kingdom.

Overwhelmed by what he had heard, Peter burst out that he, for one, was ready to follow Jesus unto death. Jesus looked at the Apostle. Peter: the very first one He had picked on that hot day on the banks of the Jordan; who had given Him a home in Capernaum; who had never wavered in his faith; who had been foremost in recognising Him as the *Messiah*; who had been given specific instructions about the future of His ministry – the Peter who would one day be the Rock on which a new Church would rise.

There was sad acceptance in His voice as Jesus finally spoke. '*I tell thee, Peter, the cock shall not crow this day, before that thou shalt thrice deny that thou knowest Me.*'

Peter was too shocked to speak. There was not an Apostle who did not sense the troubled mood of Jesus.

Some time during the evening Pilate learned of the plan to arrest Jesus. However, the matter was still purely a Jewish one. The procurator had no grounds upon which to intervene: no evidence to suggest insurrection was at hand; no proof that the High Priest intended to do any more than hold Jesus in custody until the end of Passover; no hint that a trial was in the offing. In such cases his orders were clear: the Jews had full autonomy in dealing with religious offences. To involve himself in the matter could be to put at risk what he and his wife wanted – a speedy and smooth return to Rome.

Claudia Procula would have been unable to offer a countermanding argument to such reasoning. She might well have retired to bed – perhaps indeed burdened with the foreboding her papers of canonisation would subsequently insist.

The *Seder* continued along its precise way. The appropriate portion of the Hallel – Psalms 113 and 144 – were recited, praising the Lord and recalling when the People of the Book left Egypt. Each Apostle then drank. The bowls of bitter herbs were passed around along with the platter of roast lamb, every man taking a handful of meat with his right hand. When they were all served Jesus continued to address them, His face more pensive, His voice as sad as the surviving fragments of the original Gospels were to suggest. As He

233

spoke, John, seeking to be comforting, stopped eating and laid his head against Jesus' chest. Suddenly the Apostle sat bolt upright, stunned even more than Peter had been. Around the table equally stupefied men stared at Jesus, unable to believe what He had just said. '*One of you shall betray Me.*'

Eyes flashed around the table. These men who thought they knew each other intimately, who had shared danger and joy, stared with sudden suspicion at one another. Simon was half-crouched, ready to deal with any move that might threaten Jesus; following the revelation, he appeared to expect the traitor immediately to take action. Nobody moved: James the Less frozen-faced; Matthew's eyes darting back and forth, looking for a clue in the eyes of others; Andrew turned sideways, transfixed, goblet halfway to his mouth; Thomas repeatedly shaking his head, even more than the others, refusing to believe. Philip, Thaddaeus and his father looking stricken; Judas calmly staring at Jesus. Peter broke the terrible silence. '*Master, of whom speakest Thou?*'

If there was a traitor in their midst he wished to have him named. It was a matter of urgent security. Like Simon, Peter no doubt feared the man would strike without warning.

Jesus ignored Peter's question.

Around the table shattered men were regaining their composure, whispering to one another, turning to those with whom they felt closest: Matthew to Philip, Thaddaeus to his father, Andrew to Peter, Bartholomew to Thomas. John was half-leaning across Jesus, offering his body as a protective shield. Jesus gently pushed him away and broke off a piece of bread. Those who saw the gesture felt relieved. Whoever the traitor was, Jesus clearly did not fear him; rather He was intent on continuing to perform His role. It was a custom that the host at the *Seder* should offer his guests a piece of bread dipped in a sauce: the gesture went back to the first Passover, when Joshua celebrated the arrival of the Chosen People in Canaan, and he had used it to express gratitude and friendship to all those who survived the Exodus with him. Since then the ritual had been observed with full ceremony. Jesus steeped the bread in the sauce.

John repeated Peter's question. '*Lord, who is it?*'

Concentrating upon what He was doing, Jesus gave no answer. When the bread was sufficiently coated, He held it delicately between thumb and index finger and turned to Judas. His voice almost certainly did not carry beyond the treasurer. '*He it is, to whom I shall give a sop.*'

Judas' response was equally low, meant only for Jesus. It was the reaction of a man who very clearly feared he would never leave the room alive if the truth became known. Leaning into Jesus he murmured: '*Master, is it I?*'

Jesus placed the morsel of bread on the treasurer's lips. '*Thou hast said.*' His words were so soft that no one, not even the vigilant Simon, seated beside Judas, heard them. The treasurer's treachery remained between him and his Master. But that brief exchange signalled the onset of a new phase in the drama. Jesus, in refusing to name Judas publicly, had willingly allowed the betrayal to proceed. After Judas swallowed the bread, Jesus, His voice resigned, the tone of a man who had always accepted He must be the availing victim, spoke once more to the treasurer. '*That thou doest, do quickly.*'

Judas rose to his feet and left the room, clutching his *punda*. John was among those who thought Jesus had sent him to give alms to the poor.

In the tetrarch's palace the celebration had deteriorated into debauchery. Herodias sat on one side of Herod Antipas, Salome on the other. The girl wore a diadem the tetrarch's mother had used at her wedding. Herod Antipas had given it to Salome after spending another afternoon in her company; it was common gossip he had begun to share alternately the beds of mother and daughter. Before them, close to five hundred guests ate and drank in saturnalian revelry. From the rear of the vast hall servants brought

235

more food and wine, while others moved behind the guests, sprinkling them with perfumes. Intent upon draining goblet upon goblet, Herod Antipas did not see Jonathan enter the hall, only aware of his presence when Chuza whispered in his ear. Jonathan stooped and spoke to the tetrarch. Finally comprehending, Herod Antipas nodded. Satisfied, the captain left. He had received permission to include in his force a *centuria* of the tetrarch's troops. It was Caiaphas' idea: if anything went amiss, the High Priest could attempt to place the blame upon Herod Antipas' men.

The departure of Judas had the immediate effect of relaxing Jesus. The tension left His voice and face; He was His old tender self. His mood communicated itself to the others. They watched respectfully as He blessed the last of the wine and refilled their goblets. While they sipped, He called them *'little children'*, and said with the poignancy of someone who realised that He would soon be going to where they could not follow, that they must continue to love one another as He had loved them. There was about Him – though those present would only see this later – an air of martyrdom: God so loved them, and all those beyond the walls of this room, that He was ready to sacrifice His only begotten Son. Then, in one magnificent sentence, Jesus anticipated His own glorification with the familiar confidence He had always shown when discussing the bond between Himself and God. *'Now is the Son of Man glorified and God is glorified in him. If God be glorified in him, God shall also glorify him in himself, and shall straightway glorify him.'*

Jesus fell silent for a moment. His look of deep concentration reminded both Matthew and John of that time just before He had raised Lazarus. John sensed a radiation emanating from Jesus' body, as if spiritual energy was coursing through it. They all watched as, once more, He selected a piece of unleavened bread, blessed it and then broke it into eleven pieces. He went from one to another giving each of them a portion before returning to His place.

236

Then he spoke words which would hold a timeless significance. '*Take, eat, this is My Body*.' Once they had all swallowed, Jesus lifted His goblet, which had remained untouched throughout the meal, and sanctified it. As Matthew would later record, Jesus passed the cup to John with these words: '*Drink ye, all of it. For this is My Blood of the new testament, which is shed for many for the remission of sins.*'

Each drank in turn until the goblet was returned to Him, empty.

They looked at Jesus in awe. In a few moments, as if it were the most natural action, Jesus had created a unique new rite which would perpetually remember Him. Not since Yahweh had persuaded Abraham to go forth had there been such a comparable moment. From His hands and lips had come a sacrament of the deepest possible meaning. Pieces of the same bread He had given Judas had now become part of His Body; an ordinary working man's goblet turned into the chalice of the Lord. With simple commands – '*take, eat*' and '*drink ye*' – Jesus had shown them that each time they repeated the ceremony they would be at His table, remembering Him, awaiting His return.

He looked around, smiling reassurance, reminding them of other truths: those who believed in God believed in Him; that in His father's house there were many rooms, each of which He was as familiar with as the one in which they were seated. He was certain there would be one for each of them. He would never have asked them to have travelled so far with Him unless that was an absolute truth. When He had made all the arrangements He would return for them. In the meantime they must always be prepared for that moment; He could give them no advance warning when that would be. But it would happen.

Jesus stood up, allowing them to sense His pure joy at being with His friends. Finally, in a resolute voice He said: '*Arise, let us go hence.*'

The moment had come to take the final steps in delivering Himself to the hatred of the world.

★ ★ ★

Moving in single file, Jonathan led his force out of the Temple. At the Golden Gate, as arranged, the tetrarch's *centuria* waited. Its officer formally placed his men under Jonathan's command. At this late hour the area was deserted, the pilgrims sleeping after the repast. The men moved at a trot into the Kidron Valley, picking their way past the tombstones of the Jehoshaphat cemetery. Reaching the brook beyond the graves, they found themselves knee-deep in a sluggish flow of blood and animal entrails from the Temple's altar. There were curses and groans as they slithered through the cloying mess and its overpowering stench. The crossing effected, Jonathan led them south, using the tomb of King David's son, Absalom, as a navigating point. There was yet no moon and few stars. Opposite the tomb they paused for Jonathan to divide the force. A sensible strategy would be for the tetrarch's men to continue down the valley a little further and shelter in the rocks there. Once Jesus and the Disciples passed over the bridge which formed part of the track between the olive groves and the city, the soldiers were to occupy the crossing, and stop all access. As they left, Jonathan led the Temple guards towards the olive trees. They moved slowly, careful not to awaken the pilgrims in the encampments further up the Mount of Olives. When they reached cover Jonathan motioned them to lie low while he edged forward, pausing from time to time to check his bearings, using the Temple as a reference point. At some point within the trees he waited, hand on sword handle, the chill of the night forgotten. Judas had arrived, turned and led the Captain of the Guard further into the groves. Finally the treasurer pointed out the entrance to the cavern. Shortly afterwards, Jonathan began to deploy them in a circle around the cave with instructions that no one must move until his command.

Jesus insisted upon being the first to leave the courtyard. When Simon and His brother protested He firmly said there was to be no argument and disappeared into the darkness. Moments later Matthew followed: then one by one the other Apostles hurried through the lanes. Simon and Peter left together, quietly closing the courtyard door behind them, Simon scanning the alley for any sign of movement. It was completely deserted.

Moving swiftly Simon led the way to the Golden Gate. It was wide open and there was no sign of the watchman or the Roman patrol which usually stood sentry duty inside the portal. The gate had been left open for Passover, the Romans confined to barracks, and the watchman was at his *Seder*. They followed the trail the others had taken to the olive groves, crossed the bridge and climbed over the scree to the trees.

Jesus waited at the cavern entrance. He greeted the three men and led them inside. He asked Peter to remain with Him and beckoned John and His brother to join them. Jesus told the other Apostles He was going outside to pray and they must stay in the cave.

Moving through the trees He suddenly turned and confessed to His companions: *'My soul is exceeding sorrowful unto death. Tarry ye here and watch.'*

The Disciples sat down against tree trunks and watched Jesus walk on. They whispered among themselves that He seemed once more so deeply troubled as to be on the verge of collapse. Through the murk they heard His anguish. *'Abba, Father, all things are possible unto thee; take away this cup from me: nevertheless not what I will, but what thou wilt.'*

Already tired and emotionally spent from all that they had heard and observed in the past hours, these were words far beyond the comprehension of even men who had come to understand the mystery of the Transfiguration. They were unable to grasp that, having been His witnesses on Mount Hebron, Jesus wanted them to see the painful torment which filled Him on the lower slopes of the Mount of Olives. By exposing Himself so openly at the onset of His Passion, He wished them to remember for ever the enormity of the suffering He would soon have to bear. He wanted them to realise that He could sense the fearsome pain ahead and He knew He could not escape it: instead, He accepted that through His forthcoming agony lay redemption for all those beyond this landscape of gnarled trees.

As they watched Jesus once more fall to the ground, they heard His plea that '*the hour might pass*'. His was a cry filled with supreme courage and understanding. How long He remained out there, alone, in the first throes of His Passion, the Apostles would never know. They fell asleep. Jesus awoke them, reproaching Peter in particular. '*Couldest not thou watch one hour?*' He then moved back into the trees, once more falling to His knees, remaining prostrate before dragging Himself to His feet, hanging on to a branch for support, praying all the time. Returning, He had again found them asleep. Jesus admonished them once more and then continued with his Agony.

For the third time Jesus found the trio asleep. This time He knelt beside them, shaking them in turn, His voice gentle, without a trace of his previous disappointment. '*The hour is come. Behold, the Son of Man is betrayed into the hands of sinners. Rise up; let us go; lo, he that betrayeth me is at hand.*'

They could see Judas standing behind Jesus. From nearby came a shouted command, then racing through the trees were men with drawn swords.

Struggling to their feet the three Disciples, sleep banished, prepared to defend Jesus. But before they could move Judas stepped forward and kissed Him on the cheek.

Jonathan shouted at the guards to seize him.

A dozen pairs of hands reached to grab Jesus.

240

Hours of Trial

O Judgement! thou art fled to brutish hearts,
And men have lost their reason.

— Shakespeare
(Julius Caesar)

TEN

Beyond Arrest

Jesus answered: My kingdom
is not of this world.
— John 18:36

Jesus' words halted everyone: Judas, the touch of his lips
damp upon his Master's cheek, arms around His shoulders,
the traditional embrace of a friend, yet who would be
judged as plumbing the depths of human depravity; Peter
struggling to remove something from under his cloak: John
and James the Less beginning to move to His side; the
guards reaching forward but not yet touching Jesus. His
words, delivered without a trace of surprise, were
addressed to those who had swooped out of the night and
who, in spite of Jonathan's command, seemed uncertain.
'*Whom seek ye?*'

The tableau dissolved, Judas stepped back among the
Temple guards. Peter produced a knife he once used for
gutting fish. John and His brother sprang forward and
stood fore and aft of their Master, warding off the first
grabbing hands.

Peter's was the typical response of an impulsive personality. He had been the first to give up his livelihood to
become an Apostle; the one who, convinced he saw Jesus

walking on the water in their first year together, had stepped over the side of the boat and nearly drowned. His companions had also acted in character. John was naturally self-assertive; James the Less, when aroused, had the formidable temper of a physically small person used to defending by force all he held dear.

Jonathan's words cut through the darkness.

'*Jeshu Hannosri!*'

Jesus responded at once. '*I am He.*'

The guards, confronted by three aroused men, not knowing what reinforcements were close by, perhaps overcome by the authority of His voice, or feeling sudden doubt about arresting someone who faced them so calmly, drew back, stumbling on the scree and protruding roots before falling to the ground.

From behind Jonathan, Judas again shouted. '*It is He! Hold Him well!*'

The words would forever damn the treasurer. Yet was it the cry of a man who again believed that Jesus was about to exercise His extraordinary powers and literally disappear in front of them? Did Judas feel that Jesus was going once more to avoid the confrontation the Disciple had always felt was required to prove his Master's invincibility, a final prelude to the launch of the Kingdom? Had Judas' thinking become so warped that he had failed to understand what Jesus meant by that final command at the *Seder* – '*What thou doest, do quickly*' – and took it as a positive encouragement actually to produce confrontation?

Jonathan ran forward, roughly ordering his men to their feet, and roared again at Jesus to confirm His identity. Through the trees, led by Simon, came the other Apostles, speed carrying them through the Temple ranks towards Jesus. Simon's reaction would have been that of a bodyguard who had been taken unawares. He, above all, should have sensed the presence of danger after years of being hunted by Roman and Herodian forces in the hills of Galilee. Simon would also have quickly realised that the Apostles were heavily outnumbered. Those he had led from the cavern had followed him blindly. Seeing Simon's surrender and the bewildering sight of Jesus doing nothing to save Himself, they could only have felt helpless and terrified in the presence of such menace.

Jesus motioned all eleven to stand behind Him before answering Jonathan. '*I have told ye I am he.*' Jesus pointed to the Disciples. '*If therefore ye seek me, let these go their way.*' It was His last act of service to them. Knowing they, like Him, were in mortal danger, He had not revealed their identity, so fulfilling a promise made during the first part of His Passion: '*Of them which thou gavest me, have I lost none.*' Jesus stepped towards Jonathan, open hands extended, a display of willing surrender, a man going into captivity voluntarily.

It would be understandable if Jonathan hesitated. He would have heard so many tales about this man: that He possessed mysterious powers enabling Him to control the wind and sea; that once He had fed five thousand people with a few loaves and fish; that He could cure the terminally ill, restore sight and raise the dead. Whether such facts had all been the work of sorcery, as the High Priest insisted, or something else, Jonathan almost certainly had no way of telling. But his own experience as a law officer cautioned him that no one gave up so calmly, knowing the outcome must be certain death. The captain ordered Jesus to stand still.

The guards were still scrambling to their feet when Peter made another impulsive move.

Possibly Judas' words provoked it. The treasurer had finally confirmed Peter's suspicions, and he could, in that mercurial mind of his, have intended to murder Judas for his betrayal. Then, realising that to reach the treasurer he must cut down Jonathan, Peter had lunged at the captain; perhaps intending to drive his blade into Jonathan's neck. With Jonathan dead Peter may have presumed his men would be less inclined to press any action. In the uncertain light, he misjudged his aim. Matthew and John were both in a position to agree that Peter '*smote off the ear*' of the captain.

Jesus' response was swift as the blow. He sharply ordered Peter to put away the knife, reminding all within earshot that '*they that take the sword shall perish with the sword*'. Then Jesus touched Jonathan's wound, healing it instantly. It would be His last miracle in aid of another – and an act of mercy which would also raise questions. Why did Jonathan not respond to the assault? Was he constrained by Caiaphas' strict order that only Jesus was to be apprehended? Did he fear that if he arrested Peter the others, believing they were also about to be taken, would have launched an attack violent enough to arouse pilgrims sleeping not too far away? Was Jonathan even aware that he had lost an ear and that a moment later Jesus had miraculously replaced it? If he did know what had occurred, had he seen it as striking confirmation of Jesus' powers of sorcery – and had the captain been too frightened to act against Peter in case He evoked even more awesome powers? Jesus' next words certainly left them all in no doubt that He believed ample help was available should He require it. '*Thinkest thou that I cannot pray to my Father, and he shall presently give me more than twelve legions of angels?*'

The threat to summon over seventy thousand angels might well have seemed to Judas that his Master had lost none of His power – that the Kingdom was a mere flap of celestial wings away.

Jesus dashed any such hope. '*But how then shall the scriptures be fulfilled, that thus it must be?*'

The treasurer turned and ran through the trees, his place in historical infamy secured, through misunderstanding to the very end what Jesus had meant.

Jesus' promise of divine help was clearly designed to reassure the Apostles, to remind them that, surrounded by enemies, He was giving Himself into the care of God. Jesus was telling them that even now, if He wished – just as He had done when threatened in Nazareth, calming the tempest or raising Lazarus – He could once more have called upon God to help Him: He had not done so because that would save Him from His chosen path. But, even as He spoke, the Apostles were fleeing. It would not matter in which order: whether Thaddaeus went before Thomas, or Philip followed Bartholomew, or James took flight with His own brother, or if Matthew preceded Andrew and if it was finally Simon, John or Peter who was the last one to bolt. But they fled and He understood. The sudden invasion of armed guards, their brutal questions and cursing, followed by the foolhardy gesture of Peter: all this would have panicked the Apostles, sending them racing in all directions into the night. It was very human.

Jesus reproached Jonathan and the guards. *'Be ye come but as against a thief, with swords and staves? When I was daily with you in the temple, ye stretched forth no hands against me. But this is your hour and the power of darkness.'* He fell silent, letting them bind Him, offering no resistance. They led Jesus down through the trees towards the bridge where Herod Antipas' soldiers waited, dressed and equipped like Roman centurions. That simple coincidence would stir intense controversy.

* * *

The fleeing John, his mind filled with a kaleidoscope of impressions, identified the tetrarch's men as a *cohort* – normally a force of six hundred Roman centurions led by a tribune. Aside from the fact that guarding the bridge was a *centuria*, only a hundred men, the Apostle's subsequent eye-witness account did not attach the crucial word *Roman* to his *cohort*. Its absence would not stop apologists from suggesting the arrest was a joint undertaking between the Roman and Jewish authorities and that the Temple hierarchy, in all such matters of common concern, were subservient to imperial control: therefore, the all-important actual *authority* for the arrest should be laid upon the occupying power. The salient weakness of the argument is that it overlooked that the Roman criminal code required a formal indictment before a person could be detained. In fact no warrant had been made out by any competent authority against Jesus. The Great Sanhedrin had been unable to issue one owing to the objections of Nicodemus and Gamaliel. The Romans had not been asked to provide one. Jesus was being frog-marched towards the Golden Gate solely upon the order of Joseph Caiaphas. His decision to act outside all legal parameters was further exemplified by his command not to arrest the Apostles. In law, if their Master had a case to answer, so did they as accessories directly supporting His teaching; if Jesus proclaimed heresy, then they were His appointed instruments in spreading it. But involving the Disciples in such charges would require, under the law, further investigation, proper testimony and independent witnesses. Caiaphas was no longer concerned in working within such a legal framework. The High Priest, from whom all hallowed dignity and piety had long gone, for whom only the circumambient ceremonial trappings remained, and even then the most important of those, his robes, the Romans kept in custody, was intent upon subverting the law. The irony would be that John – who hated the existing Temple authorities more than any other Apostle – should be the one who would give unwitting credence to the myth that the Romans were ultimately responsible for bringing Jesus through the Golden Gate.

* * *

Jonathan very probably was concerned that the flight of the Apostles presaged an attempted rescue. He would have deployed his forces to reduce the threat using a standard tactic in which the tetrarch's troops would have been divided, half going ahead, forming a solid wall of shields, the remainder acting as a rear-guard, with the Temple guards forming a cordon around Jesus, swords and staves drawn. In their midst would be Jonathan and a guard, holding Jesus by the arms. The force would have properly abandoned silence for speed, and Jesus, bound hand and foot, was half-dragged over the rocky terrain. On the lower slopes they had been hidden by the darkness. But climbing towards the city walls, the moon, which had only been rising when the operation began, was now directly overhead – at the crucial time when the steepness of the ascent slowed their progress. Their presence would have awakened pilgrims in the surrounding encampment: there were shouts; cries of who was there, what was happening. Jonathan no doubt urged the men on. If Jesus stumbled He would have been hauled to His feet. Every breathless step brought the force closer to the sanctuary of the Golden Gate. The advance group of the tetrarch's men may just have passed through the massive portal when a figure raced from the shadow of the city wall, darting among the guards, trying to reach Jesus. Jonathan would have had no more than a glimpse of a boyish face and a body wrapped in a white cloth. One of his men grabbed at the lad, holding fast to the cloth. The youth ducked and twisted, unravelling the sheet, and raced away down the valley, naked. Years later, when he had grown to full manhood and dedicated his life to Jesus, he would include the incident in his account of this night. It would form part of the Gospel of Saint Mark, based also on Peter's experiences.

The moment his force was inside the gate Jonathan ordered it to be closed and left the tetrarch's men on guard. He gave his own men new directions. At a brisk trot they moved through the streets to a gate set in a high wall and with a covered grille. Upon Jonathan's knock the cover drew back, a face peered out, the gate was opened by a waiting manservant and Jesus was bundled into the grounds of the palace of Annas. The gate closed behind prisoner and escort: its grille would come to bear the name of a Judas window. The treasurer had used the gate for those secret visits to the Temple.

The High Priest, Annas and a few Sadducee judges were in the palace library when Jonathan arrived with news that Jesus had been brought to an outer courtyard. No doubt they eagerly questioned the captain on everything Jesus had said and done, noting His threat to call upon angels. Caiaphas must have viewed it as a further example of His sorcery. He ordered Jonathan to remove Jesus to an underground chamber and the judges resumed their task of finding ways around the formidable obstacles of the law they were charged with upholding.

No Sanhedrin, Great or Small, could commence criminal proceedings once darkness had fallen; no person could be tried on a criminal charge during a festival. There was also the old problem of the absence of, at the very minimum, a pair of lawfully qualified witnesses who would testify they had, independently of each other, warned Jesus of the criminality of His actions and the penalty they would invoke. The Book of Deuteronomy could not be more insistent on those points.

Annas might well, as some accounts were to insist, have pointed out that the case would almost certainly stand or fall on establishing a clear offence in Scriptural law, and that he directed each of them to read silently the appropriate paragraph in the Book of Leviticus. The scroll was handed from one legate to the next. Only the occasional movement of lips barely visible behind flowing beards and a sudden intake of breath betokened realisation that here were the words that could lead to Jesus' death. '*He that blasphemeth the name of the Lord he shall surely be put to death, and all the congregation shall certainly stone him: as well the stranger, as he that is born in the land, when he blasphemeth the name of the Lord, shall be put to death.*'

God's sanctity was an article of faith from the day Yahweh had called forth Abraham, and it had remained the ultimate source of Judaism, the axiom upon which everything else depended. No Jew was permitted to compromise this hallowed principle. Only the High Priest in the sanctity of the Holy of Holies could utter God's name. For anyone else to associate himself in any way as equal with God was a capital offence.

For a prosecution to succeed on the grounds that Jesus had committed such a crime it would be essential to have Him repeat before a court His claim to *Messiahship*. If Jesus could be forced into doing this in the presence of judges of the Sanhedrin, His conviction would be assured.

The Leviticus passage, being written Scripture, formed part of the old Sadducean legal system and central to its doctrine was that men could be punished solely on their own confessions. The murderer of Saul was executed after confessing to David; Achan had been stoned after his confession to Joshua. These were impressive precedents. Equally important, there was no legal barrier to a solely Sadducean-based court being convened to apply only Sadducean law – particularly in a time of emergency. Those present in the library would have needed no persuasion of the gravity of the situation. There had been Jesus' triumphal entry, His decision to release the adulterous woman, His threat to destroy the Temple. If Jesus had not been apprehended, it would have boiled over into insurrection, and indeed His supporters might yet attack the Temple to rescue Him. These were the strongest possible reasons to despatch Him as swiftly as possible by the most convenient means available – in this case the law of the Sadducees. Caiaphas would have needed little persuasion to convince the other judges that Jesus had violated the code. For example, His claim to be able to summon angels at God's will was blasphemy – clearly defined in the eighteenth chapter of the Book of Deuteronomy: 'There shall not be found among you any one that maketh his son or his daughter to pass through the fire, or that useth divination, or an observer of times, or an enchanter, or a witch, or a charmer, or a consulter with familiar spirits, or a wizard, or a necromancer.' The High Priest could indeed have argued that Jesus' entire ministry was a prime example of the magical arts: He had interfered with the dead, the elements and the natural laws. Under Sadducee code these were offences that made it imperative to deal with Him urgently – if needs be, even without the normal due process of law being applied.

There was a precedent for such action. Some hundred years previously eighty witches in the city of Askalon had posed a sudden and grave threat to the Temple. There had been no time for a trial. Instead the High Priest of the day had exercised the executive authority invested in his office and the women were promptly hanged. Caiaphas could have little difficulty in convincing the men around him that the behaviour of Jesus fitted into that criterion. Yet almost certainly the High Priest had not requested unilateral power – by which he would simply despatch Jesus to Golgotha without trial. That would be altogether too risky – turning Jesus into a martyr and perhaps even providing His followers with an excuse to attack the Temple. What the High Priest wanted was agreement to bring Jesus before a court composed only of Sadducee judges who would examine Him, tease out the evidence and obtain the necessary confession.

Caiaphas reiterated that Jesus was a Jew, threatening Jews, and He must be dealt with by the Jews chosen to represent the people, and the finer points of whether it would be possible in every accusation against Him to establish a conviction based upon eye-witness testimonies did not apply: there was ample circumstantial evidence. Nor should they concern themselves that there was no precedent for holding an immediate trial at night, or at a time of festivities. The *ultimo ratio* of Jewish law allowed an emergency to override all such considerations. Such an argument could have concluded with a confident Caiaphas predicting that their Pharisee colleagues and the Great Sanhedrin would support their action.

One by one, the men around him agreed on what must be done. First there would be a preliminary examination, with Caiaphas forgoing his right to conduct it, saving his interrogation for later. The initial questioning was assigned to Annas. Attended by his secretary the old priest left the library. Caiaphas summoned Jonathan and ordered him to deliver the prisoner to a nearby room.

Having run from the olive groves, Peter and John sought shelter amongst the tombs of Jehoshaphat where another terror faced them. From the Vale of Hinnom – where Moloch was once offered human sacrifices and which had

252

become the city refuse dump, still a place of evil and smouldering fires – a figure moved towards them. Only the devil or his acolytes roamed Hinnom at night. John and Peter acted in concert, rising to their feet to flee once more. A voice, filled with its own boyish fear, stopped them. They turned and faced the naked Mark.

John gave the boy his *haluk*, an under-shift, and Peter ordered Mark to continue through the Kidron to try to find the other Apostles.

Then, no doubt in considerable fear, the two men entered the city through the nearby Gate of the Fountain and made their way towards the sounds of activity around the palace of Annas.

Jonathan, still anticipating a rescue attempt, had turned the palace and adjoining Temple into a fortress. His entire force, five hundred heavily armed men, patrolled inside the Temple walls and the palace perimeter. In the palace courtyards and gardens the guards lit fires and ordered servants to fetch food and wine. The entire area was a hubbub of action as figures flitted through the shadows. Realising it would be a focal point for any impending attack, Jonathan withdrew the tetrarch's soldiers from the Golden Gate and posted them as sentries around the outer walls of the palace. To facilitate easier contact between the troops and his guards, the captain had the palace servants' gate, used for reaching the street, left open. Soon there was a constant milling of domestic staff and soldiery around the portal. No one challenged Peter and John as they edged their way into the palace.

At some point, Claudia Procula awoke in her bedroom adjoining that of her husband. She drifted back to sleep, no doubt hoping her troubling dream would not return. It had been about Jesus.

Another of the unexplained mysteries of this night of unsurpassed drama was how Matthew, whose closest encounter

253

with Claudia Procula may have been no more than glimpsing her on the edge of a Galilean crowd, and who at this very hour was somewhere out in the Kidron Valley, hiding in fear of his life, should come to know about a dream filled with foreboding and ominous reality. More easy to accept is the judgement of Nicodemus in his Gospel that she was by now a '*a pious woman of Jewish tendencies*'. Less convincing would be the claim that in her premonitory dream Socrates appeared to Pilate's wife and urged her to intercede on behalf of Jesus.

Dressed in the regalia of a judge of the Great Sanhedrin, Annas sat on a high-backed wooden chair, a symbol of his further authority as a doctor of the law. His secretary squatted on a stool, tablet and stilus on his lap, beside a lamp on a metal stand, its flame bright, a sign that its oil was refined, not like the rancid-smelling liquid burnt by the poor. On the edge of the pool of light stood Jonathan, gripping Jesus by the arm. His feet had been cut in several places during the journey into the city; the hobbling rope around the ankles chafed the skin; His wrists were similarly bruised.

Annas ordered Jonathan to remove the bonds before the questioning began.

He asked Jesus his name.

Jesus gave it. The secretary's stilus marked the wax.

Annas went straight to the point. He asked Jesus what work he did.

Just as the Temple vendors had hoped to trap Jesus by questioning His *authority*, so did Annas. Establishing Jesus' lack of Temple-approved *authority* was an essential step towards a conviction. Behind the word lay a range of accepted public manifestations of Jewish religious life: the *authority* of the rituals, the ceremonies, the consecration of every working moment. *Authority* was accepting the Sabbath as a day of rest as God had Himself rested on the seventh day of creation. *Authority* was recognising that any violation of this or any other divine commandment would

254

be punishable by death. *Authority* meant never to challenge the will of the men who sat in God's Temple.

But Jesus had consistently implied that, like John the Baptist, His *authority* came directly from Heaven; that He was the appointed link between God and man. Once that claim was established in this room His fate would be sealed. Annas put the question: on whose authority did Jesus work?

Jesus made no answer.

Annas would have known the value of keeping silent – and the psychological advantage he held. With His followers scattered, and Himself rushed through the night like a dangerous criminal and confined in darkness before being brought here, Jesus must have been unsettled. He continued to wait, studying Jesus, no doubt estimating His strength and weaknesses. Jesus remained silent and impassive. The deadlock stretched.

Inside the palace grounds Peter and John separated, each Apostle tagging behind servants carrying food and wine to the guards. Emboldened at being able to move without challenge, Peter drifted from one group of guards to another. Their talk could only have given him sudden hope: they feared that if rescue was attempted it would be impossible for them to hold off the throngs Jesus had shown He was capable of arousing. Peter set off to find John.

John had been hovering around the servants' gate, trying to get some idea of the number of soldiers patrolling the outside walls, critical intelligence for any rescue. Peter's arrival provoked questions. Should they both go in search of Simon – the Canaanite would certainly know where to find the men and how best to organise a rescue mission – or should one of them remain and try to locate exactly where the Master was being held in the palace? Any further discussion was interrupted by the gate portress – John would remember her as young – who broke off her badinage with the soldiers to point at Peter. '*Art not thou also one of this man's Disciples?*'

255

Peter vehemently shook his head and said emphatically he was not, glad no doubt that his face was in shadow.

The girl continued to stare at Peter trying to make up her mind. The light was poor; she could have made a mistake. They had both come from within the palace; they might even be Temple agents.

While she hesitated, John calmly steered Peter back into the palace grounds.

Annas had sent for several judges from the library. They stood along one wall, black-robed figures, staring fixedly at Jesus. Jonathan stood immediately behind Him. Annas was intent upon creating a threatening atmosphere – to break the iron will of the man who had so far avoided every pitfall in His path. Jesus had said little apart from confirming the number of His Disciples, where they travelled and the synagogues He had preached in.

Annas interrupted. He asked Jesus what he had taught there.

Jesus patiently explained that all the essential themes of Judaism were incorporated into His teaching.

Glaring at Jesus, Annas could not contain his frustration. What else had he taught?

Jesus could have included in any explanation the fact that, like any rabbi, He placed the highest value on moral purity; that, for instance, He believed that adultery was a cause for a man to put aside his wife, but that did not give him the right to take another. To do so was also an act of adultery. This teaching proclaimed His strong support for the sanctity of wedlock and condemnation of sexual licentiousness. Jesus concluded: '*I spake openly to the world! In secret have I said nothing.*'

The men along the wall murmured angrily. No prisoner had ever dared address a judge, let alone a former High Priest, in such a way.

Annas continued to probe, perhaps believing that the man before him – for all the absence of diffidence, humility, submissiveness and fear – could be irked to the point where

He would bear witness against Himself. What did he mean?

In that first year when He had selected the Twelve Jesus had told them: '*What I tell you in darkness, that speak ye in light; and what you hear in the ear, that preach ye upon the housetops.*'

He delivered a sharp rebuke to Annas. '*Why askest thou me? Ask them which heard me, what I have said unto them. Behold they know what I said.*'

The words were followed by Jonathan's savage slap on Jesus' face. The captain shouted in His ear: '*Answerest thou the High Priest so?*'

The judges could not contain themselves. They spat at Jesus. He looked at them stoically then turned to Jonathan, the mark of the blow clear on His skin. '*If I have spoken evil, bear witness of the evil. But if well, why smitest thou me?*'

For the best part of a Roman watch – the accepted way to measure time at night – Annas had tried every manoeuvre: alternately threatening and placating, being coldly dismissive and feigning politeness. He had asked a series of simple questions before smoothly inserting a deadly one. He had tried to establish that Jesus was the founder of a school of teaching that really was no more than a secret society, open only to the initiated. He had attempted to make the Kingdom sound like a form of *Sheol*. Yet, every time he had scented victory, Jesus had calmly removed Himself from danger. He had turned the claim of secrecy against his interrogator: there had been none on His part; it was the Temple which had behaved in an underhand manner, sending agents to listen surreptitiously when He would have been happy to come and explain openly. The more Annas had tried to defeat Jesus, the greater must have been the priest's sense of personal failure. Even Jonathan's slap had drawn forth a majestic rebuke. But it had also ended any pretence this was a legally convened preliminary inquiry. Annas ordered Jonathan once more to bind Jesus and take Him to the Lord High Priest. But first Jesus must be taught a lesson.

Thomas and Philip had fled the length of the Kidron Valley, stumbling through one pilgrim encampment after

257

another before scrambling down the slopes which led to the aqueduct Pilate had built to improve Jerusalem's water-supply. It had taken two full years to lay, and the hewn stones used to form the pipe were all double-flanged to make the joints watertight. The exhausted Apostles rested, their backs against the pipe, staring towards Bethlehem where His story, they believed, had properly begun and which, they could not yet grasp, was almost at its earthly end. Disorientated, convinced they faced certain death if they entered the city, they struggled to find common solace in what Jesus had said towards the end of the meal: He would return. But, in any event, they knew the way to where He had gone.

On that bleak hillside they continued to recall the certainty of His words: that He was the revelation of God and that as long as they accepted that they could face the future without His bodily presence.

John and Peter had separated, trying to establish where Jesus was being held. Peter passed beyond another arched portico into an open courtyard when he hesitated. Ahead of him a soldier was peering through a window opening. From inside came angry voices. Then, above all the shouting, clear and authoritative as always, Peter heard Jesus. The room where He was being held was deep inside the palace. There was no guarantee that rescue could be effected before He would either be moved or killed.

Peter set off to find John, walking as nonchalantly as possible through another courtyard, taking care to stay clear of the men warming themselves around a fire. Peter could not have forgotten that only a few hours ago Jesus had spoken of the unique bond which existed between Himself and the Disciples. Judas had already departed from the *Seder* – and how Peter now hated him – when Jesus finally pushed aside His plate. Then, leaning across John and Andrew, He addressed Peter about the mission the Apostle must fulfil. In the warmth and friendship of the room that had seemed easy to accept. But here, alone in the darkness,

258

surrounded by enemies, Peter knew he had already failed: that moment at the gate when he had made his denial still must have hurt deeply. Yet alongside the pain Peter could have drawn strength from how Jesus had described not only the immense task ahead but the victory which would be all the sweeter for overcoming the obstacles. As he entered another portico, staying close to the wall, a shadow to the guards moving restlessly around the adjoining courtyard, Peter could have begun to be certain that Jesus after all would have forgiven his denial.

Jewish legal procedure did not have an official prosecutor. Witnesses performed that function. Throughout the night a number of Temple vendors, as well as some of the guards in the arresting party and men who had shouted protests at Jesus when He forgave the adultress, had been brought to the palace to fulfil that role. Assured that they would face no penalty for bearing false testimony, all had co-operated. Caiaphas' only problem could have been the lack of time. Given a day he could without doubt make them word perfect. But, in their eagerness to please, the men continued to stumble over the details of the perjury the High Priest had added to the other illegalities.

John had concentrated his search upon the lower end of the palace grounds, an area of servants' quarters, chicken-pens, ornamental and vegetable gardens. He also began to sift impressions of this fearful night. What Judas had done was too despicable to dwell upon. John would never describe the treasurer's kiss; he would leave that to Matthew. Nor would he reveal his own feelings at having to run into the night as the guards seized and bound Jesus.

John suddenly heard Peter's voice shouting in protest, momentarily drowning that of a woman. He ran towards the altercation. Peter stood in a courtyard, surrounded by several men and women servants. A maid wagged a finger at her companions to emphasise her claim. She had been in the crowd when Jesus had ridden on the donkey. She pointed at Peter. He *had* been walking behind the animal.

Peter uttered an even louder denial. '*I do not know the man!*' He started to shove past the woman. The others blocked his path.

A manservant prodded Peter in the chest. '*Thy speech bewrayeth thee.*'

Peter roundly cursed him as a liar and trouble-maker, roaring that he did not know *the man* – once more putting a verbal distance between Jesus and himself: He was a stranger, someone Peter wanted them to believe he had never set eyes upon – *the man*. So vehement was his protest that the servants cowered. Peter undoubtedly had a country accent, but so did many of the spies of Herod Antipas – and he was infamous for punishing anyone who upset his men. '*I know not the man!*'

Peter stormed past the servants. John called from the shadows. As they hurried back into the Lower City a cockerel crowed.

The room was close to the palace library yet far removed from its scroll-filled elegance and had been chosen for one of the most shameful incidents in the Passion of Jesus, one almost certainly engineered by Annas and approved by Caiaphas.

Trussed hand and foot, Jesus stood while a guard slapped His face; next a judge spat in His face. The intention of His tormentors was to show Jesus the hopelessness of His situation and make Him realise they could do as they wished with Him; that here in one of the foremost palaces of His people He was regarded as scum, abandoned by everyone: once that penetrated His stubborn pride, He would confess. Another judge sent spittle dribbling down Jesus' face. A third Sadducee member of the Great Sanhedrin contemptuously delivered a further punch. Jesus stared calmly at the persecutors. A guard delivered another resounding clout. A trickle of blood ran from Jesus' mouth. Jonathan spoke to one of the guards, who hurried from the room. Yet another judge spat into Jesus' eyes and said He was a blasphemer. The guard returned with an empty grain sack. Jonathan thrust it over Jesus' head and down around His shoulders. The captain motioned for two of the guards to begin spinning Jesus around. As the grotesque pantomime began, judge after judge stepped forward and struck blows at his hooded head.

One of the guards shouted: '*Prophesy unto us, thou Christ, who is he that smote thee?*'

Raucous laughter greeted the sally. The blows continued, each strike accompanied by further abuse. Jesus bore it all without flinching.

Mark found four Apostles: Andrew, Thaddaeus, Bartholomew and James the Less. They huddled in the cold darkness of early morning near the tombs of Jehoshaphat. Jesus' mother and Mary Magdalene joined them. The women could have contributed little as they sat staring helplessly towards the silent city, listening to the men's accounts of Jesus' last hours with them – and how He had prayed for all who believed in Him, not only now but in the future. But the women would have had no trouble in imagining how Jesus had felt: deeply loved yet so little understood, and in the end deserted by all those who had been so close to Him. Yet they would also have accepted that what had happened showed the true greatness of His soul. Through the intensity of prayer Jesus had crushed His human self but left His spirit intact. They had every reason to believe that nothing or nobody could destroy that.

Simon and Matthew chose the same escape route – southwards, intending to reach the Wilderness; and after a few strides, realising they were not being pursued, Simon suggested heading for Bethany to break the news to Lazarus and his sisters. Mary was distraught, Martha practical. It would be perfectly in keeping if she had broached the possibility of rescue.

Protest by Matthew would have been meant for Simon.

Jesus had specifically ordered, after Peter's intervention in the Garden of Gethsemane, that there was to be no more violence. He had told them that the Kingdom could never come through armed force, that they must love their enemies. If Simon mobilised his contacts to march in their tens of thousands upon Jerusalem, then the whole purpose of the past three years would be destroyed.

While Martha and her sister prepared breakfast, the men sat on the ground, accepting the truth.

ELEVEN

Rush to Judgement

*He said unto them: if I
tell you, ye will not
believe.*
— Luke 22:67

The sound of the priest-trumpeter heralding a new day
carried clearly to Annas and the twenty-one judges assembled in the largest of the many magnificent halls in his
palace. Its lofty ceiling was supported by two rows of
Corinthian pillars. Between them were window openings,
their lintels decorated with moulded profiles of griffins and
capricorns, figures from Greek mythology. The consoles
flanking the wide entrance arch were in the shape of palm
trees. Above the arch, in relief, were a pair of lions. The
judges sat in a semi-circle of throne-like chairs in the centre
of the hall. Each was either a chief priest or elder of the
Temple. All were practising Sadducees. They included the
judges who had spat upon and assaulted Jesus. Behind
them were members of the permanent staff of the Great
Sanhedrin: beadles, ushers and Levites who would fetch
scrolls, summon witnesses and maintain order in the
spectator area, an enclosure to one side of the seated
judiciary.

Every effort had been made by Caiaphas to give the

263

setting the aura of the supreme court. He knew from long experience how intimidating that could be: accused sometimes fainted when faced with the row of silent robed judges, and witnesses had quaked even before being bound by oath. The High Priest recognised it was doubly important to create an overwhelming legal presence: Jesus was more than just another prisoner; under Jewish and Roman law the forthcoming trial would be a travesty. No witnesses had been sought to testify on His behalf. The Temple crier had not been sent forth on the previous day, the minimum notice required under the law, to announce all those who wished could attend and, if need be, give evidence providing their depositions had been properly sworn to beforehand. No formal evidence had been taken by the court in advance of the trial. No public notice had been posted in the Temple, an obligation under the Sanhedrin rules of procedure. No prior written notification had been sent to the Antonia Fortress – which would have allowed the procurator the right to send an *assessore* to the Jewish court and decide whether there was a need to intervene. When this intervention was exercised a new trial was mandatory before a Roman court, where Scriptural law was inadmissible. The ancient '*right of the sword*' was sometimes not always easy to discern. If a religious crime had elements which impinged upon Roman law – sedition, and any challenge to the emperor's divinity were high on the list – then, while a Jewish court could *pronounce* a death sentence, it had to ratify the verdict with the procurator before it could be *executed*. It was another reminder that imperial authority overrode all else.

The studied scene-setting to suggest this would be a serious investigation had the trappings of a carefully managed show-trial. Almost certainly there was not one genuine member of the public present in the enclosure; it was filled instead with priests, Levites and Temple vendors, virtually a hand-picked audience.

Caiaphas entered the hall in the wake of a procession of priests who sat among the spectators, while the High Priest took his place in the midst of the semi-circle of robed men. The two clerks of the court who would keep the official record perched on stools at his feet.

Attention focused on the arrival of Jonathan escorting Jesus. The captain led Him to a point directly in front of where Caiaphas sat; it was marked by a freshly made daub on the marble floor. Jonathan stepped back, coming to attention. He had taken no chance that a rescue might yet be attempted. Guards stood shoulder to shoulder around the courthouse, swords drawn ready. More armed men were in the archway. The tetrarch's soldiers had been withdrawn from outside the palace walls to surround the hall. It all strengthened the impression that even in custody Jesus was dangerous.

This was the moment when the *Balil Rib*, a court-appointed defence advocate, would have been asked to step forward and offer his services. None did so. Caiaphas should then have formally enquired whether Jesus intended to defend Himself or send for an attorney. The question was not put.

In the strengthening light all eyes in the hall continued to stare at Jesus. Here at last was the man who had stirred the imagination of thousands, who had offered Himself as the crystallisation of their hopes, the symbol of their burning nationalism. Spontaneously they had elevated Him to the level of the Expected One. But now He had to answer for Himself. The air seethed with suppressed excitement.

Jesus' bonds had been removed but the marks of violence were visible: bruised cheeks, swollen nose and lips, puffed eyes, dried blood on His beard and a welt around His neck from the halter. Yet His gaze was calm and quietly determined as He continued to meet the cold and hostile stare of Joseph Caiaphas.

At this point the High Priest should have formally reminded the court that the case would be tried under the tractate that specified *'Capital charges open with a verdict of "not guilty" and not with a verdict of "guilty".'*

Rather, what seems to have happened is that Caiaphas

265

rose to his feet, took a shuffling couple of paces towards Jesus, then turned and faced the judges. He said the accused, '*Yeshu Hannosri*', was brought before them on a capital charge grounded in the following clauses: not having the proper fear and respect of *The Name* in His heart but, having been moved and seduced at the instigation of Beelzebub, falsely and repeatedly claimed in this city and elsewhere to be endowed with authority and powers He did not possess; blasphemed against *The Name* and profaned the Temple; altered, subverted and overturned its appointed constitution; attempted to raise insurrection by various statements and actions against the Temple and the lord tetrarch, the sovereign temporal ruler.

Amid all his other activity, Caiaphas had supervised the formulation of the indictment. It was pregnant with implication, a combination of theological necessity and political convenience. It would allow for exploration of the purely Judaic offences that Jesus had presented Himself as being in kinship with God and that the superhuman powers He claimed came from demons and accounted for why He was a charismatic exorcist. Conviction on either of these counts carried a death sentence. At the same time Jesus was charged with having sought to bring the Jewish state into conflict with the rule of Rome by disputing the authority of its appointed representative, Herod Antipas. This was an offence against the imperial code, punishable by crucifixion. The underlying implication of the indictment was that, in attacking the priestly authority of the Temple, Jesus had challenged the mandate of Rome which had also appointed the High Priest and upon whose power the untroubled functioning of the Temple depended. Caiaphas would have total freedom in his indictment to raise any action which had been initiated by Jesus and supported by His Disciples and all those who had shown only too clearly that they believed Him to be the *Messiah*, the divinely designated King of the Jews. While the High Priest had based his strategy for the trial around that factor, and everything else would build to it, and lead from it, he knew that ultimately a conviction very much depended upon Jesus confirming He regarded Himself as the *Messiah*.

The reading of the indictment marked the formal start of the trial.

It was preceded by further breaches of procedure. There had been no roll-call of the judges. This was more than a legalistic formality. It was an integral part of the law that '*the spirit of God*' must always favour the defendant: anything which fell short of that ideal was not permitted. At the calling of his name any judge would stand down if the prisoner was personally known to him or if there was any other reason why he could not fairly try the case. Each, for instance, should have been asked if he had any prior knowledge of the charges. The judges had been at the meetings of the Great Sanhedrin and had supported Caiaphas in his attempts to obtain an arrest warrant; having participated in those proceedings, they were precluded from trying the case. A challenge from either Jesus or somebody on His behalf at this stage could have wrecked Caiaphas' carefully crafted plan. None came. The second procedural breach was that the *Shema* had not been recited before the indictment was read. This profession of faith held an even deeper meaning in a criminal case. It was an implicit oath that those who would give evidence and try the proceedings were bound by several sacred commands of truth and fairness; they would always speak, listen and judge by the strict rules of their religion.

Caiaphas addressed his fellow judges. In trying the case they must constantly have before them the national interest – '*our place and our nation*'. The words no doubt were chosen and spoken with care. Behind them was the spectre of Roman intervention which could have deprived everyone in the hall, excepting Jesus, of their position and seen the end of Jewish autonomy. The phrase was an emotionally charged reminder that the court should remember all those who had struggled and died to achieve a measure of independence; that no one must forget the still desperate hopes and aspirations of the people behind any threat to '*our place and our nation*'. In those words Caiaphas had conveyed an impression of Jesus cynically exploiting the masses with a new and dangerous teaching which masked a plot to destabilise the nation – and perhaps even destroy it. The High Priest had reinforced fear and anger.

Jesus made no protest. He remained perfectly still, an unprepossessing figure in His soiled robes.

Caiaphas returned to his seat and ordered a court usher to summon the first witness, so further straining the legal credibility of the proceedings. The *Sanhedrin* tractate stipulated that immediately after the charge was put the prisoner was entitled to have the court hear argument for an acquittal on the grounds that the charges were unsupportable. There was an impressive number of precedents for such dismissals. Jesus was not invited to challenge. The law also required that adequate time be allowed after the indictment was read for a prisoner to reflect whether he or she would prefer to let the case continue in the expectation that the prosecution witnesses would be unable to establish guilt and might themselves be punished for bearing false testimony. The prospect of exacting revenge was often a decisive factor. The *lex talionis* of the biblical command – '*an eye for an eye, a tooth for a tooth, a hand for a hand, a foot for a foot, burning for burning, wound for wound, bruise for bruise, life for life*' – still had a strong appeal, part of the general principle of vengeance being authorised by God. But until the accused indicated his or her intention, hearing of evidence for the prosecution could not begin. No one questioned a further lapse from normal procedure. Jesus continued to gaze impassively at the judges.

★ ★ ★

The various and flagrant breaches of the Jewish legal system would have serious and far-reaching consequences. Ultimately they would make it all the more difficult to establish what did occur in the pale light of a new day in that hall. Unravelling the facts, deciphering the many ramifications of the proceedings, requires a clear understanding of a number of separate yet inter-related factors.

The first, and the root cause of all subsequent difficulties, were to arise from early Christian doctrinal interests. Struggling to survive, then to expand, the faith of the Fathers of the early Church needed a focal point. Unable in the beginning, from a sheer lack of numerical strength, to apportion any blame upon the Roman imperial system whose evils had spawned a renewed yearning for the *Messiah*, and subsequently unwilling to do so – Rome, through the Emperor Constantine, eventually became the way for the Church to expand – it became an act of Christian faith that *the Jews* arrested Him, brutalised Him and staged undoubtedly the most celebrated show-trial in history. A web of vile circumstances, woven by a few, became the mesh from which an entire people would not be allowed to escape.

The stigma of collective guilt upon the entire Jewish people would form the source of the harassments, the humiliations and the pogroms which culminated in the Holocaust. Jews would be expelled, uprooted, looted, pillaged and vilified for what was done in their name in that palace in Jerusalem on a spring morning when anti-Semitism was already rife. The events in that courtroom would foster the great collision between one of the oldest religions of mankind and a lusty upstart of a faith which, in the spirit of the time, would have no compunction in distorting truth to give semblance to *the Jews* having collectively provided the true climax to a night of genuine horror for Jesus: all that followed would flow from that monumental misrepresentation.

The truth of what happened in that hall – between perjured witnesses and a handful of morally bankrupt priest-lawyers – would be further removed from reality by an understandable, yet seriously flawed, attempt to rebut the monstrous allegations against *the Jews*. The claim would be made that what Caiaphas and his cohorts intended to appear as a legally constituted full trial was in reality an *inquiry*. Such dangerous dissembling would be a crude attempt to

269

rewrite history that in a way is as historically improper as shifting the responsibility upon the entire Jewish people. But Jewish apologists would make much of there being no Christians in the courtroom, or that there was no likely way Christians could have had access to an objective account of the trial proceedings; that, in any event, followers of Jesus were primarily peasants with no grasp of the subtleties of legal procedures and would be unable to distinguish one kind from another. Such a multi-accusation has been disputed on the grounds there is no evidence that some of those in the courtroom did *not* subsequently become converts to Christianity; indeed the annals of the early Church are filled with accounts of Jews and Romans who embraced His teaching. On the matter of the trial record, again what may have happened is that as well as the official court clerks there were also certainly present the secretaries of the judges, keeping records for their masters; it would perhaps not be entirely fanciful if one of them had made available his account, to form subsequently the basis for the Gospel versions. More sustainable would be the argument that Matthew was far from being an uneducated peasant. As a tax collector he had been grounded in law and would certainly have known the difference between a *trial* and an *inquiry*. But what at least can only be a rough approximation of what happened could be lost in the welter of anti-Semitic polemics.

Early Christian calumny that not a handful of Jews but *the Jews* were implicated in the trial of Jesus would produce an intense and degrading hostility between two religions bound by an umbilical cord which cannot be severed: the Old Testament. The Gospels, Acts, the Epistles of Paul, right to the last verse of the Book of Revelation would grow from that earlier testament. All Christian claims for Jesus would be based in Scripture from that source; a belief in the primacy of its faith would be based upon the texts of the Pentateuch. Without the books of Israel there could be no meaningful testament of Christianity. Yet, because of what Jesus suffered on that night – shock, outrage and travail –

the understandable and righteous wrath of His followers, perhaps even their claims to vengeance, would be extended to far beyond those directly involved and solely responsible – a few Jewish notables who, out of ignorance and fear, set out to destroy a man who had done his best to help the afflicted and those with sin. The behaviour of the priests in that hall, acting secretly and illegally, could never, by any accounting, be taken as representing the legitimate will of the Jewish people, yet it would be presented as such.

A great deal of energy would be expended to try to establish discrepancies within the testimony of those not actually present: Matthew, Mark, Luke and John. Matthew and Mark would, incorrectly, set the trial as taking place during the night. Luke would indicate, correctly, that there were no proceedings during the hours of darkness. From this simple and relatively unimportant mistake would grow the Jewish argument that if the Apostles could be wrong on timing they could be in error in other areas. John's Gospel, the most anti-Semitic of the Evangelical accounts, would, for that reason, be called in defence of Jewish claims. Much would be made by apologists of John's omission of any mention of the trial in the hall. Why should he, of all the Apostles, would run the argument, miss this opportunity further to blacken the name of *the Jews?* It is an unattractive question which takes no account of how much else John excluded. His Gospel is the most selective; that does not give it any more, or less, historical authority. Equally the other accounts should not be treated with suspicion when measured against John's. His silence apart, they based them on what they discovered actually happened in that hall.

* * *

The first prosecution witness stood a few feet to the right of Jesus, facing the semi-circle. Defence witnesses would have given evidence from His left. Each witness in a capital charge had to be solemnly put on oath, have its significance

271

explained and be given a firm reminder of the punishment for false testimony. Caiaphas ignored the requirement.

At this stage Annas rose to His feet to begin establishing that Jesus was guilty of blasphemy, had threatened the Temple and planned an insurrection; it fits into what is known about Sadducee legal procedure, which allowed the most senior judge, next to the High Priest, to cross-examine. It was a task for which the old priest was well suited. In spite of his years Annas had retained a rhetorical delicacy, a mental capacity to juggle, to ridicule, and to make the most innocent action appear the product of an evil and calculating mind. His working life had after all been spent in continual meditation upon the *corpus divini* of the Jewish penal code.

Assuming he was no different from any advocate, the examination would have quickly developed its own pace, a litany of standard questions and answers. Where had the witness first seen the accused? On that day Jesus had arrived at the Eastern Gate on a donkey. Did he know the significance of that gate? It had been built by Solomon for the Expected One. What had people said when they saw Him on the back of a donkey? That He had come to free them. Why? Because they said He fulfilled the prediction of Scripture. Had He resisted that claim? No.

An interrogation along such lines would have been important to establish the expectations of Jesus being the *Messiah* and a liberation leader. Annas would then have had to confirm the popular concept of the *Messiah*: that His appearance would be preceded by a precursor – Elijah. The interrogation and responses continued. Had the witness seen any evidence that the prophet was once more among the people? No. But Jesus had been acclaimed? Yes. How could the witness explain that? Jesus had deceived the crowd. How? By His silence. An answer along such lines would have helped to imply that Jesus not only had a special relationship with God – but was determined not to deny it. The offence to Jewish religious susceptibilities had been rooted. The questioning continued. Before he had seen the prisoner had he heard of Him? Yes: His preaching was widely known to be about a kingdom over which He would rule and which only those who obeyed Him could enter; all others would perish. Did he believe that? No. Why not? It was talk that would arouse the Romans.

Annas would have needed to set about establishing a direct link between that dire prospect and Jesus' entry into Jerusalem.

What had the witness felt in the presence of such a throng? Coached by Caiaphas, the witness remembered. Fear. He had felt fear. Why had he felt fear? What had made him fearful? *Fear. Fearful?* The words echoed around the hall. The man expressed what some undoubtedly may have felt: an unease that Jesus *could* have such power. What had the mob shouted? Hosannas. That He was King. Words like that. Swiftly and smoothly, *fear* had been followed by *mob*, *shouted* and finally a claim to *Kingship*. The whiff of insurrection drifted in the air from the judges' semi-circle to the spectators and back to Annas. It is by such advocacy – if not the precise detail, then the substance – that men like Annas are remembered.

Jesus had been established as the harbinger of the long-awaited apocalyptic revolution. He had presented Himself as ready to overthrow the existing political and social order, end Roman domination and restore the Chosen People to their rightful place. Whatever the merits of such a vision, Annas had managed to imply such a role was reserved solely for the Expected One.

So it could have continued. When had the witness next seen the accused? In the Temple. Where in the Temple? Near his stall. What was the defendant doing? Destroying other stalls. It would only have been natural for Annas to let the impact of the scene once more settle over the courtroom. *Destroying stalls in the Temple.* No further repetition would have been needed: Annas' silence had its own telling eloquence; it seemed to say he did not have to remind them where matters would have ended if Jesus had not been brought to justice.

273

By this stage Annas had established what he had set out to do: not only had Jesus offered Himself as the Messiah but He had begun to fulfil the mob's expectations through violence; that beneath the teaching claims He made for his ministry – the nation would only be delivered from bondage if they followed Him – lay an altogether more dangerous intention.

To discover what that was required Annas to show that Jesus was familiar with Temple procedures and customs. His own mother had purchased a bird for sacrifice after His birth and he knew there were no legitimate grounds to attack the traders and overturn *'the tables of the money-changers and the seats of them that sold doves'*. What, then, had driven Him to do so a few days ago? Annas would have left the court in no doubt. Jesus' action was not against a handful of tradesmen, earning a legitimate living, but was directed at the Temple administration. It was a deliberate and premeditated attempt to gain control of the Temple and dispose of all those lawfully appointed to run its affairs. The first rumble of anger had come from the spectators as Annas wove a damning portrait which went far beyond any temporary interference with petty business transactions. Jesus had made the first probing move to launching wholesale insurrection.

The ensuing questions and answers were designed to confirm the extent of this sinister design: Jesus on the rampage; the posse of men protecting Him; the mob cheering Him on; the vendors, honest God-fearing men, helpless in the face of such evil violence.

Annas would have failed in his task if he had not turned and faced the semi-circle of judges and asked what clearer evidence did they need that an act of blasphemy had been established? Jesus had come in the guise of a pilgrim but was plotter-in-chief of a monstrous plan. Nor was there any question that He had behaved impulsively. What He had done had been a carefully prepared attack. The court should look upon His action as that of someone not only filled with evil intent towards the chief priests but falsely proclaiming His own Messianic mission. Who would deny that in the guise of religion He had not sought to take absolute power? How easy it is to hear the deadly trip of the questions and to accept the premiss of the judges staring at Jesus, waiting to see if He would offer any challenge.

Jesus remained silent.

The next witness was sworn; the same corroborative evidence. Had he been terrified at the destruction the accused had unleashed? He had. Had he been too terrified to oppose the violence? He had. Even when the defendant had destroyed his own stall? Yes. Had others been equally terrified? They had.

All the Gospels – not just the four evangelical accounts but the other books discreetly discarded by the early Fathers of the Church at their councils at Nicaea and Chalcedon – suggest that events in the great hall unfolded broadly along these lines.

Annas set about nailing down another plank. Had Jesus been alone? No: He was accompanied by His usual followers and some of the mob who had called Him the *Messiah* on the previous day. What had they done? Supported His actions. Once more Annas had cleverly exposed the threat of insurrection. He would have needed to return to Jesus' behaviour so as to leave no room for doubt. Did the witness remember what Jesus had said during this destruction? After being tutored by Caiaphas, the witness did: that the Temple was a place of thieves. Was there any basis for that reaction? No. Had he ever heard anybody else refer to the Temple activities in that way? No. Like any astute lawyer, Annas would not have overlooked a chance to bolster favourable testimony with the law; in this instance it provided for the Temple to offer a number of ancillary commercial services in conjunction with its religious role: the Temple was a bank and a treasury and it derived valuable income from such facilities. Any challenge to that could be construed as an attack on the sacerdotal authorities and seem as yet another step to the rebellion Jesus had plotted.

Again it is not hard to envisage Annas turning back to the witness. What else had Jesus said? He would destroy the

Temple. What had he taken this to mean? That Jesus would use magic to accomplish the feat; it was impossible by any other means.

Annas would not really have needed to remind the court that such a clear and carefully articulated prophecy could indeed only be construed as being aimed at the religious heart of the nation. The threat to Jewish survival had been buttressed. The spectator area seethed at this proof that Jesus had intended to commit the ultimate act of violence which gave further substance to the charge of insurrection.

Witnesses came and went, stitching together a portrait of a man who travelled the land working His spells by the power of Beelzebub. Inevitably there was one who testified to his shock at being told the accused had brought Lazarus back to life, and that it was either fraud or induced through sorcery; another said he had seen Jesus restore sight and was convinced it had been done through the power of darkness; a third insisted the look on Jesus' face when He had destroyed the money-changers' booths was of someone possessed by the Evil Eye. A guard who had been in the Gethsemane arresting party said he personally heard Jesus threaten to call upon a host of angels to help Him. What kind of angels? The messengers of the Evil Eye. Caiaphas would hardly have needed to remind the court about these fallen angels who made their lairs in trees, and went about their wicked work under cover of darkness. The inference was only too clear: what better place for Jesus to plot than among the olive groves of Gethsemane, with the evil hosts ready to do His bidding? Why, with their help, if He had not been seized, He would now be on the way to Galilee to gather the Zealots for an all-out attack on the Temple. In gilding the prosecution case, none had been more eloquent than Annas as he continued to enhance the image of Jesus as a dangerous revolutionary.

Jesus said not a word.

Yet another witness took the stand. It may have been a momentary relaxation on the part of the old priest, it may have been over-eagerness on the part of the witness: the reason would be lost – but not the effect. The man said he was sure Jesus had made the threat against the Temple on the *same* day He rode through the mob. Annas moved to head off disaster. He urged the witness to remember. Surely it had happened on the *following* day? The man looked doubtful. Perhaps. But he was certain of one thing: it had occurred *after* morning prayers. Think again, rasped Annas. Had it not been *before* morning prayers? The hapless man pleaded that the fear he had felt at the time had confused him. Perhaps it had been *early* in the morning.

A furiously disappointed murmur came from the spectators. This time the judges dared not publicly ignore the tractate that specified the slightest contradiction by witnesses for the prosecution rendered all previous testimony invalid.

Annas waved away the man and abandoned calling further evidence.

*   *   *

In spite of this spectacular failure the parade of witnesses must, inevitably, have made an impact – the more so because their perjury had passed without challenge. Ironically, Jesus, who had offered as the basis for His teaching the ideal *'Blessed are they which are persecuted for righteousness' sake for theirs is the kingdom of heaven'*, by that same silence which brought Him closer to His pre-ordained fate also ensured that countless millions of other Jews would suffer torment, degradation and persecution in centuries to come; they would find small consolation in those words He had spoken on Mount Hattin. *'Blessed are ye, when men shall revile you, and persecute you, and shall say all manner of evil against you falsely, for My sake. Rejoice and be exceeding glad: for great is your reward in heaven.'* Through accident or by intent the Christian monopoly of *truth* would ensure that the matter of responsibility for what was happening in that hall would be obfuscated, and all Jews forever blamed for a

277

trial whose ultimate and sole responsibility rested upon an old man and his son-in-law.

★   ★   ★

The Court of the Gentiles was once more filled with pilgrims come to make their offerings. Mingling with them were the usual *goyim*, men and women non-believers, come to meet a landlord, settle a debt or enter into a contract. Pagans and believers were united in discussing a number of puzzling features: Solomon's Portico was virtually deserted of traders; there was not a Temple guard in view; only a solitary priest stood vigil at the Nicanor Gate.

Those first through the Eastern Gate had noticed Caiaphas hurry from the podium and that he had not been seen since. Nicodemus and Gamaliel had arrived and gathered the twenty-three other Pharisee judges of the Great Sanhedrin into one of the courts of the Temple that led from the Royal Porch. Its door had been closed behind them. The more knowledgeable wondered if it marked the start of some new doctrinal dispute with the Sadducees. The absence of the sect's judge-priests caused further speculation; something had happened, or was about to; but no one could say what, or when it would occur.

Pilgrims who had camped on either side of the Golden Gate recounted the disturbance of the night and the glimpse of soldiers hustling along a prisoner. In the past few days there had been several arrests in the hills. The most notable had been that of the capture of a Zealot leader, an elderly warrior who could no longer out-run his captors. He was known as Barabbas of Galilee. He had been handed over to the Romans and languished in the Antonia Fortress; it was a foregone conclusion he would be crucified.

Travellers from the Bethany area reported there was still no sign of the man upon whom they had begun to attach so many hopes, the one they increasingly called the Expected One. Jesus had not been seen in public for the past twenty-four hours. The more cynical speculated whether He would

278

turn out to be another of those self-styled Messiahs. Old men in the courtyard would still have remembered those heady days when the Master of Justice of the Essenes had briefly claimed himself to be divine; there were those who recalled praying that either Judas of Gamala or Sadduck the Pharisee was the Messiah. Those who had experienced previous disappointments wondered if they were about to do so again; that, while Jesus had been more dramatic and direct in His impact, He could still turn out to be no more than a symptom of the national desperation.

Very likely no one paid any special attention to a trio of women, one old and frail, the other in her middle years, their companion younger: the courtyard was always filled with such anxious-faced pilgrims. Mary, the mother of Jesus, Mary the mother of two of His Apostles and grandmother to a third, and Mary Magdalene, who loved him with devotion and unconsummated passion, were filled with growing fear as they tried to discover His whereabouts. At Annas' palace, the portress at the servants' gate, hearing their broad Galilean accents, had very likely eyed them suspiciously. They had hurried to the Temple, the natural source for all news. But no one had answers for their diffident enquiries. No one probably noticed – why should they? – the man who walked through the crowd. Judas' presence would only be verified by what he was about to do.

Back in the hall, undoubtedly concerned to regain the initiative, Caiaphas needed to establish that Jesus had deliberately thrust Himself forward as the symbol of Jewish nationalism. To do so he asked a series of questions designed to lay out the historical situation of Jesus: how He had grown up in a milieu of alternating violence and tension; how His formative years had been influenced by the apocalyptic plans of terrorists like Judas of Gamala and later by visits to the Sepphoris theatre. Who could doubt that there, among the painted faces, He had learned how to make a continued attack upon established authority? Who could doubt that there He had developed His contacts with the criminal *kanna-im* movement, the Zealots? When Judas of Gamala had been executed, his followers had fled to the desert. Was that the real reason He had gone to the Wilderness? To make contact with the surviving criminals? Was it there He had first planned the assault on the Temple? Was it there He had prepared His attack on the existing legal system? Was it there that He had planned a social structure that would leave the legally appointed authority of the land helpless? Was it there that He had perfected His sorcery? Who could doubt there was a menace about the question that even Annas had not equalled?

There was no response from Jesus.

Caiaphas needed to introduce the arrest of Barabbas, to portray the Zealot who had been captured close to Gethsemane as a pitiless killer. Where had he and Jesus met? Where had they plotted? With Barabbas arrested, had Jesus been about to take over His followers? Were His own Disciples no different to the Zealots?

Circling Jesus, careful to keep a distance as if he might have feared contamination by coming too close, Caiaphas continued asking questions about the Disciples and their sobriquets. Was it not true that *Shi'mon* was a professed Zealot? That Peter was known in Capernaum as *Banjora* – Terrorist? That the brothers, *Ya'kob* and *Johanan*, James and John, were called *Boanerges*, Thunderers, because of their threatening behaviour? That the *son of Tolmai*, Bartholomew, had been a renowned fighter round the taverns of Galilee? That not one of the Apostles was a placid man, content to follow his faith like all good Jews? Were they not similar to the one called *lover of horses*, Philip, given to violence, even threatening the lawful agents of the Temple? Were they not like the one born with a Greek name, *Didymus*, who now called himself Thomas, but for whom no change of name could disguise a revolutionary nature? Had not even *Matthai* been seduced from his lawful work, however unpleasant those in the court would find such an occupation, to help launch a movement that from the beginning had been concerned with rebellion? The impact of the High Priest's examination was made that much more impressive by Jesus continuing to remain silent, staring fixedly ahead.

Caiaphas explored other matters. Had Jesus not reviled the lord tetrarch? Had He not claimed total authority over those who listened to Him? Then, once more, had Jesus not done everything to undermine the very citadel of the nation's authority, namely the Temple? The questions still failed to produce a solitary response or reaction.

The High Priest had to dispose of another matter. Jesus was *not* to be grouped with other itinerant preachers: for all their doctrinal fallibility, they were men of essential passivity. But they did not have a contempt for the Temple's authority, which was clearly stated in the Book of Deuteronomy: '*The man that will do presumptuously, and will not hearken unto the priest that standeth to minister before the Lord thy God, or unto the judge, even that man shall die.*' Jesus, imbued with His own authority as eschatological prophet, had refused to submit His teaching or Himself to the authority of the Temple. Moreover, from the outset of His ministry, Jesus had been preoccupied with action, at every turn determined to prey on the ignorance of people. Whatever else He could *not* lay title to, there could be no denying he *was* a political leader; that the purpose of His ministry was not primarily religious but to excite the crowd into accepting Him as their Deliverer. Even His teaching reinforced that. Caiaphas could have quoted passages his agents had noted which all amounted to one thing: Jesus was *not* a man concerned with doctrinal issues. He was preoccupied with action – action and violence were opposite sides of the same coin.

The interrogation conveyed only too clearly the obsessive fear that Jesus was imbued with demonic powers, whose most dramatic manifestation had been seen in the triumphal entry. That everything He had done had been in preparation for arousing the people on the eve of the *Pesah*. The consummate skill of the High Priest reminded them of the sound and tumult of that climactic moment. Jesus absolving the adultress was presented as a further example of His defiance of Scripture, a belief He had the right to reinterpret Holy Law. Yet, absolutely to ensure a conviction, Caiaphas constantly kept to the fore that, behind Jesus' visions and predictions, was a man who had inherited the sheathed dagger of Judas of Gamala, and was even more dangerous because He knew how to stir people with His claim to heal the sick and raise the dead. Performing such tricks to heighten public passions, and deluding people to the point of hysteria into allowing Him to enter the city on the back of an animal to fulfil a promise of *the Name*: what else was all that but a clear attempt to raise a rebellion? What had the mob called him? *The King!* They had heard the witnesses. All had agreed upon that. *The King!* That had been followed by physical assault upon the very Temple. How else could that be regarded other than as a prelude to insurrection? Were not He and His men *biastai*, the violent ones? Whatever of this kingdom He spoke of – did He not intend to seize it by force? And in proclaiming a kingdom He had set Himself up in direct opposition to the lord tetrarch, the Temple and, of course, the Romans. That was rebellion. Nothing would soften the hammer-blows. No one could deny what followed.

Caiaphas turned and confronted Jesus with yet another question. Dared he challenge one word?

There would be those who were not there who would claim Jesus looked at the High Priest '*calmly and with authority*', '*without a trace of fear*', '*knowing what He must say*'. Perhaps.

But His words would become a matter of acceptable record. '*If I tell you, ye will not believe.*'

Caiaphas stood closer to Jesus, an arm-length separating them, no doubt staring into His eyes, no doubt waiting.

There would be those who would recount that Jesus had '*stared back with certainty*', had '*never wavered in His gaze*'.

The certainty is that, when Jesus spoke again, the words were framed as a question, but offered as a statement. '*And if I also ask you ye will not answer me, nor let me go.*'

Everyone in the hall must only too clearly have realised a critical moment had been reached. Somehow Caiaphas had forced Jesus to remain silent no longer. His decision to speak, to reveal Himself, was all the more unexpected because Jesus had hitherto seemed untroubled by the relentless pressure of the examination.

Caiaphas weighed his words. '*Art Thou the Christ?*'

Jesus repeated what He had said. '*If I tell you, ye will not believe.*'

Caiaphas must have sensed how close he was. His last question had been delivered with the ring of metal striking metal. Jesus had hesitated for a moment. Now, without any prompting, He moved a sentence closer to the victory the High Priest sought. '*Hereafter, shall the Son of man sit on the right hand of the power of God.*'

Caiaphas held his breath.

Suddenly, Jesus was close to destroying Himself. Casually, and not at all declamatory, as if he was raising a question in a Temple debate, knowing he was master of the situation, the High Priest asked:

'*Art Thou then the Son of God?*'

Jesus did not hesitate. '*Ye say that I am.*'

A collective gasp came from the court. Jesus had done what no one in Judaea had ever done, what Abraham, Jacob, Moses, and all the other great prophets had never considered doing: He had made Himself the equal of God. He had made Himself God. There could be no greater blasphemy.

Caiaphas turned away, suddenly weary. Slowly he raised a hand and then ripped his tunic. The gesture was not a histrionic response to victory; it was the ritual prescribed for any priest who had heard a blasphemy uttered. Around him other priests were tearing their garments, not along a seam, but in the middle of the cloth so that the damage was beyond repair and the skin exposed over the heart, a sign of grief.

Caiaphas addressed the judges. '*He hath spoken blasphemy. What further need have we of witnesses? . . . What think ye?*'

Once more procedure was ignored. In capital trials voting was designed to avoid the senior members of the bench influencing their juniors. The youngest member voted first, then a verdict was given by each judge in ascending order of seniority. The High Priest would normally have been the last to cast his vote. But Caiaphas had made clear his own feelings on what the verdict should be. One by one, they gave the same answer. '*He is guilty of death.*'

The High Priest had a final matter to settle. He told the court that not only had Jesus been found guilty of blasphemy but He had also committed crimes punishable under Roman law. To claim divinity was a direct affront to the emperor and a capital offence. Imperial law also prescribed the death penalty for anyone convicted of threatening a sacred building, and that protection had been extended to include the Temple. Further, the court had seen how Jesus had refused to offer any defence to the many questions put to establish political crimes which were further offences under Roman law. Therefore Jesus must be sent forthwith to the Antonia Fortress to be dealt with by the procurator. The judges agreed.

Caiaphas left the hall, the bells of his regalia the only sound to break the silence. By sending Jesus to Pilate the possibility of a defeat within the Great Sanhedrin had been avoided.

TWELVE

Roman Responses

And Pilate asked him again;
saying: Answerest thou nothing?
— Luke 15:4

Since sunrise on the day that would become known as Good
Friday, Pontius Pilate had been at work in his salon. The
large room resembled a counting house as the collectors
responsible for tax gathering arrived with bulging *pundas* of
coins.

The procurator derived considerable satisfaction from
this most important task. There was the spur of showing
Rome that once more he had increased the amount of tax
gathered, something his predecessors had never managed,
and the challenge, one which required his total concentration, of dealing with the collectors: they were sharp and
devious and always ready to seize an opportunity to cheat.
But not even the most rapacious would dare to go about his
business during the forthcoming week. Judaea, in an
administrative, legal and commercial sense, would cease to
exist during Passover. Even Golgotha would be cleared of
its crucified by this nightfall. The two convicted thieves
being held in the fortress before carrying their crosses to the
mound would find their agony that much shorter when they

reached there. If they had not succumbed before sunset they would be killed by a centurion's spear.

Because of its importance – this salon was where her husband made all his administrative decisions and received visitors while in the Jewish capital – Claudia Procula had given extra thought and care to its decoration and furnishings. The stone walls had been chiselled to a smooth tawny-coloured finish and adorned with paintings and tapestries depicting scenes from Roman mythology. The furniture was the finest Rome could offer, including several pieces she had inherited from her grandfather's palace. A bust of the Emperor Augustus stood on a marble plinth behind the handsomely carved table which served as Pilate's desk. The sculpture was a reminder of her hope that one day he would also be sufficiently important to be immortalised in marble. Placed around the salon were divans and the statues of imperial gods and the floor was covered with rugs from Persia, India and China. At one end were wide stone steps that led down from the procuratorial sleeping quarters; a heavy curtain drawn across the upper stairway protected the bedrooms from prying eyes. The salon was ordinarily a magnificent example of Roman taste, surpassed only by that of his wife one floor below. Now it was the focal point of a sordid business.

At the outset of his administration Pilate had recognised how effective it was to gather taxes when the Jews were concentrated in one place and during the ten days the procurator had been in Jerusalem the collectors had combed the city and hills. Each man had his own team to reinforce demands; a few cudgel blows and the threat of more severe punishment were usually sufficient to quell resistance from any who hesitated to pay his dues. On the previous day a collector and his men had been working their way through an encampment on the road to Jericho when a force of Zealots led by Barabbas attacked them. One of the tetrarch's cohorts patrolling the area came to the rescue. There had been a skirmish in which several of the tax-collectors had been killed before the Zealots fled. In the

286

pursuit Barabbas had been captured and brought to the fortress. Pilate had not yet sentenced him to death.

That incident apart, the collectors had gathered their usual levies for income tax, poll tax, road tax, toll-bridge tax, house tax, boundary tax, market tax, meat tax and salt tax. There was even a tax payable by all pilgrims for the right to enter or reside in Jerusalem during the Passover period. It was a thorough system and one impossible to evade. After Passover the collectors would pursue any outstanding debt to the remotest corner of the country. They were encouraged to do so because an imperial edict allowed them to garner for themselves any additional money they could obtain; from this source they paid their own men and built often substantial fortunes. Impositions were so financially crippling that victims were frequently driven to flight or suicide. Their families were then invariably shipped to the slave markets of the empire by the collectors, who divided the purchase price with their Roman masters.

Before a collector left the salon he deposited a sum in Pilate's personal coffer. The amount was calculated against the official tax collected – the assumption being that the larger a collector's return the greater his own personal profit. This form of cynical exploitation was common throughout the procurator's staff. Each Roman official received payment from those who called at the fortress seeking imperial seals and signatures on documents granting permission to work in a garrison, to become a supplier to the occupying forces, to be exempt from an order to provide free grain and meat to a local fort or free transport for the army. There was a bribe payable for every service. The largest was for an exemption from having to deal with the Roman businessmen who roamed the countryside and cornered the harvest at often half its true value and then sold off the crop for substantial profits in other parts of the empire. A Jewish landowner could pay the equivalent of a worker's salary for a year to have one of Pilate's men provide a scroll which said his crop was reserved for the Judaean market.

If Pilate needed a pause from his scrutiny of the counting and apportioning of money, the windows of the salon provided views of the Temple courtyards, the Lower City, Herod Antipas' palace and the hills around Jerusalem and immediately below the huge fortress courtyard with its iron scourging post. The thickness of a mature cypress tree trunk and three feet tall, it stood in the centre of the courtyard. A prisoner would be stripped naked and fastened to shackles at the top and bottom so that his body was tautly arched against the post. He was then lashed with a scourge, strips of leather, each with a slug of metal or animal bone at the end; under Roman law the face and genitalia could also be beaten. There was also scourging to death, in which a man was cut to the bone, his skin left hanging in shreds and his innards spilt on to the ground. Julius Caesar had decreed that the scourging was too severe for Italian soldiers to administer; Pilate's entourage included two Syrian conscripts who shared the task. The Jews had a modified form of the punishment, using a rod for blows to the shoulders and buttocks, limiting them to the Scriptural *forty stripes save one*.

At this hour Pilate saw no sign of unusual activity beyond the fortress walls. Sentries patrolled on the tetrarch's battlements. Annas' palace seemed as deserted as it always did. Now that the vendors had appeared in the Temple courtyards, there was the usual bustle to buy last-minute sacrifices; by late afternoon the last of the unsold sheep and birds would be removed for Passover. In the hills pilgrims were on the move once more, and no doubt informers would have begun to report that priests were moving through the city and encampments spreading the word that, far from being the Expected One, Jesus had planned to attack the Temple with the help of Barabbas. Pilate would not have been surprised to learn that a groundswell of feeling against Jesus was developing: he had always said that Jews were even more fickle than those Romans who patronised the arena in Rome.

Nevertheless, it would be prudent for him not to ignore

warnings that Barabbas' compatriots could launch a reprisal attack on the procurator's column when it headed north to Caesarea in a week's time. While Pilate could have had little doubt that his vastly superior force – a full-strength legion, six thousand men – would be able to drive off even the most fanatical assault, there would undoubtedly be Roman casualties which would have to be reported. Administrators had been punished before for what Sejanus decided was an unnecessary loss of men. Rather than provoke confrontation Pilate would want to avoid it.

Very possibly, as the hagiography of the Christian Coptic Church claims, the procurator was once more interrupted by the return of the fortress commander asking for a decision on Barabbas.

The commander felt that Barabbas should be executed with the thieves. Probably not for the first time Pilate took the long view: if Barabbas remained alive for the moment there was a better chance the Zealots would hold off retaliatory action, perhaps even doing so in the hope that Barabbas might at least be spared the ignominy of the cross to die in the *zystus*, the Hippodrome built by Herod the Great, and one of the dominant features of the Lower City, with its outer walls rimmed with gold, silver and precious stones. Every week, except during Jewish festivities, gladiatorial shows were staged for the benefit of the Romans and the tetrarch's soldiers in which men fought to the death against each other and lions and leopards. Criminals were regularly sent to the arena rather than to Golgotha.

Any decision on Barabbas was overshadowed by the news that Jesus was about to be delivered to the fortress. Pilate's reaction was understandable, if only because already during his time in Jerusalem he had been confronted with what must have seemed arrogant demands. Pilgrims from Egypt had delivered a petition to the fortress reminding him that the Jewish community in Alexandria possessed total autonomous jurisdiction in *all* cases. Could not the same freedom be enjoyed by Judaean courts? A group of Jewish lawyers from Sardes had written that an edict of Julius

Caesar gave them civil jurisdiction over Roman citizens. Would the procurator support their proposed appeal to Rome to grant a similar privilege for the Jerusalem courts? Pilate had no doubt fumed that such arrogance only confirmed the more freedom Rome gave Jews the more they wanted. The impending arrival of Jesus furthered his anger with the Temple for daring to have proceeded without advance notice with a capital-charge trial and then arrogantly to refer Jesus for sentencing under Roman law.

Caiaphas, Annas and other Sadducee priests had prepared the scroll listing the tractates under which Jesus had been convicted. The parchment also indicated the infractions of Roman law. The paperwork would accompany Him to the Antonia Fortress. They were interrupted by the arrival of Judas Iscariot, whose attitude must only have confirmed Caiaphas' view that he had been right not to call the treasurer to give evidence. Judas was agitated. Caiaphas gave him a purse containing the thirty pieces of silver.

Judas put the bag on the table upon which Caiaphas had been preparing the scroll and lamented: '*I have sinned . . . I have betrayed the innocent blood!*'

It may have been Annas who picked up the *punda*, threw the purse at Judas and ordered him to leave.

Judas ran from the office, very probably still shouting in remorse and despair. As he passed the altar in the Court of the Priests he opened his bag and hurled the coins at the startled sacrificers and, still screaming, continued through the Nicanor Gate and out of the Temple by the Mourner's Gate, and on through the Lower City to the Golden Gate. He finally halted his headlong progress at an outcrop of rock high over the boundary-strewn Hinnom valley and its smouldering refuse fires. There were several trees growing on the outcrop. The treasurer chose one and climbed its trunk. Standing on a branch he removed the girdle from around his robe and, with some difficulty, fashioned one end into a noose and tied the other to a bough above his head. He then placed the noose around his neck and stepped into space. He may still have been alive when the girdle broke, sending his body plunging on to the rocks below. The Acts of the Apostles would recount how he *'burst asunder in the midst and all his bowels gushed out'*.

While the treasurer was plunging to his death, the sacrificers had recovered the money and taken it to Caiaphas' office. Once more the High Priest was forced to interrupt his work, this time to deal with a minor point of law. The silver could not be placed in the Temple treasury because it was contaminated. Equally, it would be unthinkable not to make use of it. After a brief discussion, it was decided that the coins could be used to purchase a plot of land near the Golden Gate as a burial place for pilgrims who died on a visit to the city. Caiaphas then summoned Jonathan and ordered him to prepare to take Jesus before Pilate.

Pilate was hampered in deciding how to prepare for the arrival of Jesus through a lack of information. He did not yet know what Jesus had been charged with or convicted upon. It would have been perfectly sensible for Pilate to have ordered a halt in the procession of collectors while he sent for the two *assessores*, the advocates who could advise him on any point of law in a Roman trial.

The lawyers were young and cautious. Jerusalem was a junior posting in the imperial legal service; their hope would be to complete their tour of duty without making serious mistakes and either return to Rome or be sent to a more congenial and important part of the empire. They would have tempered advice with caution, but no matter how hesitant they were in recommending any specific action they would know there was no precedent for the Jews to transfer a prisoner to Roman jurisdiction on the eve of the most important religious festival of the Jewish year.

Within their enclosure in the Temple, Nicodemus, Gamaliel and the other Pharisee judges heard nothing to reassure them there had not been a grave miscarriage of justice. The broad sweep of their discussion must have taken into

291

account that the conflict between Jesus and the Temple on doctrinal and politico-religious grounds required a full and proper examination. Caiaphas had been all too clearly wrong, in both a legal and a moral sense, to stop at the one question, *'Art thou the Son of God?'* He should have pressed the matter after Jesus', at best, ambiguous answer. It had not even begun to be established that Jesus had arrogated to Himself an exalted relationship with God which would satisfy any Pharisee judge. Further, the law contained the proviso that a *unanimous* verdict of guilt presupposed bias on the part of the court. In Jesus' case that should have meant His automatic acquittal. These were serious issues. The prelude to Passover was clearly not the time to probe them, and it would be far more sensible if the whole matter could be postponed for a later date, when both the pilgrims and Pilate would have left Jerusalem and the Temple judges and scholars could deliberate in their usual careful manner.

Such a laudable sentiment became irrelevant, as did the role of the Pharisees, with the report that Jesus was about to pass out of the jurisdiction of the Jews and into that of Rome.

Among the apocalyptic literary forms used to couch early Christian faith – writings, it must be added, that often reflect a naïve positivism – are accounts of Claudia Procula receiving her husband early on in the morning in her salon, no doubt an oasis of silk and perfumes in the midst of militaria. She immediately launched herself upon a further account of her dream. Her obvious distress would survive in her words; there was also a revealing passion about them. *'Have thou nothing to do with that just man: for I have suffered many things this day in a dream because of Him.'*

* * *

Her plea was grave and urgent and that much more important and significant because the dream must have lost some of its initial terror. She had had time to think and had become a woman deeply troubled and concerned to stop her

292

husband becoming embroiled in a situation she recognised as highly dangerous. Was this ambitious, wilful and highly strung woman purely concerned with *their* future – and only wanted to avoid any precipitate action that could affect it, especially at such an emotionally charged time as Passover? Her well-developed understanding of Jewish attitudes would have left her in no doubt that for the Romans to become involved with the fate of Jesus could have an effect on her husband's career; if civil unrest ensued, it was bound to bring criticism – or worse – from Rome. Was that the sole reason she had taken the highly unusual step of interrupting her husband at work and sending for him? Clearly, Claudia Procula was a woman desperate to get across the point that her husband must not, under any circumstances, involve himself with the case of Jesus. No longer did she bother to keep secret her own attitude. For her Jesus was a '*just man*'. Then she had added a poignant and wifely appeal: she had suffered, perhaps greatly, from what she had learned in the dream; only her husband could ensure she would endure no more. They were the words of a woman in torment; a virtual confession: she had come under the impress of His spiritual message and it finally had wrenched from her the admission that He *was* a powerful influence on her life – a '*just man*'. In accepting and admitting that, she had rejected all she had been taught to revere: paganism, emperor- and idol-worship, the indisputable authority of Rome. Hers were the words of someone suffering all the agony of withdrawing from the past into an uncertain future. A sentence of such brevity had conveyed so perfectly her position. The words were a determined effort to influence the fate of someone she had come, if only from afar, to know. In that one sentence she had mingled her aspirations for her husband's future with her love for Jesus.

* * *

Mary, His mother, and her companions only had a brief glimpse of Jesus as He was marched, bound like any

293

common criminal, across the Court of the Gentiles. The three women could hardly have recognised Him: His face was a blotch of bruises, His beard and hair matted with sweat, spittle and dried blood, and His robe ripped. After His conviction the priest-judges and guards had once more punched Him and spat and torn at His clothing, releasing their pent-up fury against the man who, throughout His ministry, had branded them as hypocrites and leaders of the blind.

This, then, was the Son Mary glimpsed. Even He had most definitely not warned her of this: the hatred on the faces of Caiaphas, Annas and the other Sadducee priests who led the way across the courtyard under the protection of Jonathan's men, swords unsheathed, shields touching to form a solid wall around Jesus. More guards stood at the Eastern Gate, parting only for prisoner and escort to pass before closing ranks again. Unable to continue, the three stricken women watched helplessly as Jesus disappeared from view.

Herod Antipas continued to follow the pattern of his normal day in Jerusalem, alternately plunging from the icy coldness of one tub into the steaming waters of another in the colonnaded splendour of his bathroom and its cathedral-like tepidarium. Naked and dripping, his skin flowing with renewed vigour, all signs of his hangover gone, the tetrarch had walked to the massage block to have his body pummelled and kneaded. He then went to his private apartment and breakfasted with Herodias and Salome.

The women represented a curious psychological parallelogram of forces. They undoubtedly sensed how delicately balanced was their position. That their master needed them both meant neither alone could satisfy him: one wrong move and they could both be forever banished. That prospect very possibly influenced their attitude to the arrest of Jesus. In the past they had encouraged Herod Antipas' wish to kill Him. They would almost certainly have seen the danger for them all if he now pursued such a plan. In the volatile atmosphere of Passover, His followers would retaliate; once more Jew would kill Jew. Rather than risk such a possibility, a wiser and safer course for them would be to urge Herod Antipas to allow the Romans to deal with Jesus. Even the most inflamed of His followers would hesitate over confronting the occupying power.

Advancing in wedge formation, shields and swords creating a menacing wall of metal which forced all before it, the Temple guards led Jesus through the narrow streets, heading eastwards, climbing as they went over the cobbles. Behind the wedge came rows of chief priests. They formed a further protective cocoon around Caiaphas. Behind him marched Annas and the other trial judges. Flanking them was a double line of guards which narrowed to form a further wedge at the rear of the force. In the midst of the formation was Jesus, held on one side by Jonathan and on the other by a guard. Behind the main group trotted several further ranks of guards, ready to stop any attempt to follow or get close to the prisoner. In all there were over five hundred people hurrying Him through the streets.

The size of this force would subsequently reinforce the fiction that '*the Jews*' were collectively responsible for handing Jesus to the Romans: it would be represented as the *vox populi* – the voice of *the people*. That accusation would form a further basis for the early Christian Church successfully to inveigh against the Jewish nation. Its people would be forever damned by the action of the closely bunched men taking Jesus to Pilate.

It was mid-morning and the sun beat down on their heads. The air was pungent with the stench of the hot grease of cooking and the sickening smell of rubbish rotting in the smaller alleys. Long before they reached its walls, the presence of the Antonia loomed over them. Built upon fortifications dating from Solomon's time, the citadel was only surpassed in height by the actual Temple. Its towers rose a full hundred feet above the main walls, themselves soaring fifty feet above street level. Rectangular in shape, the fortress was almost four hundred feet long by two hundred feet wide. They could see centurions in full battle dress assembling on the battlements, and beyond the walls came shouted commands and the distinctive sound of Roman soldiers running at the double in their armour.

When Jonathan's men swept round the corner of the south flank of the fortress to approach its main entrance they found themselves confronted by several rows of centurions blocking any approach to the portico. In the vast courtyard – three thousand square metres and paved with immense slabs of stone – the remainder of the garrison was mobilising. Almost seven thousand men and their officers stood poised for action.

The front wedge of the Temple force halted a few feet from the Romans. Jonathan went forward to consult Caiaphas. The fortress was a pagan place which no Jew, let alone the High Priest, could enter during the Passover period without resulting in legal impurity. But normally the Roman tribunal sat near to the whipping post in the centre of the courtyard; in that way its members could see a sentence of scourging performed without having to leave their seats. Caiaphas proposed that the tribunal should assemble in the vaulted gateway, the procurator and his *assessores* sitting inside the arch, while Jesus and His accusers remained out in the street. The High Priest gave the scroll to Jonathan, who marched to the portal, saluted and addressed the officer and suggested where the trial could be held.

The officer took the parchment from the Captain of the Guard and disappeared into the fortress. The silence stretched behind him.

One by one the Apostles had made their way back into the city and had taken up positions near the fortress. They were tense and nervous, whispering among themselves, not knowing what to do. With them were Mary and Martha of Bethany and Joseph of Arimathea. Whatever else they felt, they must have shared a common feeling of dejection.

Barely five days ago, Jesus had made His triumphal entry, been acknowledged as the *Messiah*. Now He was trussed and battered and covered with the spittle of contempt, waiting for His fate to be decided by the all-conquering Romans. It was an image they could only have found agonising to witness. As they stared helplessly there was sudden activity in the gateway. Soldiers were positioning three handsomely carved wooden thrones.

Wearing his procurator's cloak over his toga Pilate emerged from the east tower accompanied by the garrison commander and the *assessores*. Maniple after maniple came to attention as they passed. In his hand Pilate held Caiaphas' scroll. Crossing the courtyard they reached the west portal. The commander ordered the centurions to break rank and form an avenue on either side of the throne that extended to where the Temple party stood. The *assessores* took their seats. They would have no part in the proceedings unless Pilate sought their advice on a point of law. He would act as prosecutor and judge; upon him alone would rest the final judgement. While the commander took his place behind the procurator's seat Pilate continued to stare at the throng of priests and guards.

Caiaphas turned and spoke to Jonathan. The priests and guards divided so that Jesus stood alone. Jonathan nudged Him and he stumbled forward between the silent ranks of centurions. When He was a few feet short of the thrones Pilate motioned for Him to stop. Ignoring Jesus, the procurator addressed Caiaphas. *'What accusation bring ye against this man?'*

The second trial of Jesus had begun.

The question was put in Greek, the language commonly used within the imperial legal system, and had a special significance. Pilate now knew the charges under which Jesus had been convicted in Jewish law: they were in the scroll. It also contained a broad outline of the offence under Roman law of threatening the Temple and a summary of the questions Jesus had refused to answer. Pilate could have confirmed the judgement of the Jewish court and formally ratified the sentence. That would have been the end of the matter: a few words, a nod of assent could have concluded his involvement. Instead, by putting that question he had ignored the Jewish proceedings and verdict and indicated he wished to exercise his right to hold a completely new trial under Roman law.

Was it curiosity to know more about the prisoner which prompted him to take this course? Was he showing himself as the supreme arbitrator anxious to weigh the truth to the last gram? Did he recognise that the High Priest and his companions had behaved with the cunning dexterity of conjurors in that, having convicted Jesus, they wanted to use the cover of Roman law to have Him killed – so reducing the risk of any action against the Temple? How much had his discussions with his wife affected him? Did he anticipate that any accusation brought by the Jews would not be sustained in Roman law – and, having established that, he would leave Caiaphas with a difficult decision of whether to risk carrying out the Jewish penalty on the eve of Passover? Whatever its grounding, the question Pilate had put produced an immediate response from the High Priest. '*If he were not a malefactor, we would not have delivered him up unto thee.*'

Pilate considered the words. There was a wheedling certainty about them. But Caiaphas had not answered his question. The procurator came to a decision. Pointing at Jesus, he addressed the High Priest. '*Take ye him and judge him according to your law.*'

Caiaphas flinched as if he had been slapped. When he spoke, his next words had certainly lost their arrogance. He pleaded that the political offences Jesus had committed were outside the jurisdiction of the Jewish legal system and their seriousness transcended the purely religious crime of blasphemy upon which he had been convicted. Therefore, because Roman law superseded all other, '*it is not lawful for us to put any man to death*'.

Pilate considered the point.

Already emotionally drained and physically exhausted by the events of the night, several of the Apostles found it intolerable to continue observing what was happening at the gate. They began to slip away into the crowd that had begun to assemble. In the end only Matthew, John and Peter remained with Mary and Martha and Joseph of Arimathea. They all clearly heard Pilate repeat his question as to what were the specific accusations.

Caiaphas strove to keep his anger under control when he realised Pilate had cleverly out-manoeuvred them. In bringing Jesus before the procurator the High Priest had conceded the Temple's *jus gladii*, forgoing any further right to implement the sentence they had passed. But Pilate showed a clear reluctance to carry it out for them. Instead, he had given all the signs of being determined not merely to act as their executioner.

The High Priest broke into a furious torrent. *'We found this fellow perverting the nation and forbidding to give tribute to Caesar, saying that he himself is Christ a King.'*

Those words ensured Pilate could not, after all, escape. Caiaphas' accusations placed Jesus totally within Roman competence. The charges could not be more damning. *'Perverting the nation'* spoke of insurrection. *'Forbidding to give tribute to Caesar'* was a direct affront to the imperial mandate for taxation. Most serious of all was the accusation of kingship. If proven, that was high treason. The accusations did indeed supersede the charge of blasphemy under Jewish law and invested Jesus with the grave political offence of having set Himself up as a direct threat to the emperor. Whatever Pilate's original motives for prolonging the matter, he now had no alternative but to continue. The charges must be examined and, if proven, he must pass the only sentence possible – death.

Pilate rose to his feet and spoke to the garrison commander. Then, followed by the *assessores*, and ignoring the onlookers, the procurator walked back into the fortress.

The commander took Jesus by the arm and led Him

through the gate. Behind them the centurions re-formed to block the view of the mystified onlookers.

The window in Claudia Procula's salon provided a view of the courtyard. She would not have been the woman she was if she had not watched her husband and his prisoner passing through the ranks of centurions to enter the east tower. She had urged Pilate to have nothing to do with *'that just man'*. Yet he was bringing Jesus into the heart of the citadel. Could there be any doubt that her mind was filled with desperate hope?

Pilate himself settled behind the table in the salon. There would have been no time to remove the tax lists or the chests of coins. The *assessores* sat to one side of the procurator. The commander remained on guard at the top of the stairs. Jesus stood in the centre of the room. Pilate came at once to the core of the matter. He realised that the final part of Caiaphas' accusatory words – the reference to kingship – implicitly included the other charges of subverting the gathering of taxes and plotting rebellion. His question to Jesus was without equivocation. *'Art Thou the king of the Jews?'*

Pilate had tried to establish grounds for a simple confession or denial, a straightforward plea of guilty or not guilty. Jesus answered in almost the same terms He had responded to Caiaphas. *'Thou sayest.'* Yet the answer was steeped in philosophical distinctions. Where Jesus had showed no difficulty in affirming His status to Caiaphas as that of *'the Son of God'*, to say He was *'the King of the Jews'* was a different matter. Jesus did not want Pilate to think He was invested with royalty in any practical, earthly sense – any more than the Kingdom He would rule over was of this world. Instead, Jesus wanted the procurator to realise He had never intended there to be the misunderstandings which had filled His fellow Jews with unrealistic expectations and the Romans with unnecessary fears.

Jesus now began an exchange which would prove to be of supreme importance. He amplified his response with a question of His own. *'Sayest thou this thing of thyself, or did others tell it thee of me?'*

300

He wished to establish a basic fact before going any further: was He going to be judged on hearsay, or receive an impartial hearing? It was an extraordinary display of confidence. In spite of all the punishments and insults, Jesus had effortlessly taken command of the situation. There was a natural dignity about His words that could not fail to have moved His listeners: here was a man of noble stature, who knew how to conduct Himself in the face of death. They could well have thought of no higher tribute than to say He was behaving like a Roman. Nevertheless, realising he was being disadvantaged, Pilate displayed impatience. *'Am I a Jew?'*

The procurator wished to make clear he would not be drawn into discussing Judaic doctrine – let alone his own view on the accusations. His next words were a sharp reminder. *'Thine own nation and the chief priests have delivered thee unto me: what hast thou done?'*

Pilate wanted to bring Jesus back to earthly reality to defend Himself. But Jesus was determined to establish another reality; He returned to the main reason for His arraignment. *'My kingdom is not of this world; if my kingdom were of this world, then would my servants fight, that I should not be delivered to the Jews.'*

Pilate must have sensed that once more he was being dragged into a doctrinal debate beyond his competence to judge. He made a further attempt to regain control of the situation. *'Art thou a King then?'*

Jesus might well have paused, perhaps even sighed and wondered how He could make His position clear. *'Thou sayest that I am a king. To this end was I born, and for this cause came I into the world, that I should bear witness unto the truth. Every one that is of the truth heareth my voice.'*

Even in confessing to kingship, Jesus had manifestly tried to make Pilate understand the one salient reason they were having this dialogue; that He had been born solely to bear witness to a great new religious truth; that His Kingdom was in the minds of all those who sought it; that His royalty was spiritual; and His empire no smaller, or greater, than the willingness of each person to hear His teaching, become His Disciple, a citizen of His kingdom. He had given *truth* a new grandeur, one that was totally divine in its concept. Finally, he had issued a personal invitation to Pilate and the others in the room: they were part of His *every one*; if they wished, they, too, for all their pagan Roman ways, could enter His Kingdom. It only required that they should embrace the new *truth*.

Did Pilate ponder, even for a moment, the idea of accepting the invitation? Or was he already so blunted by the limitations of his life that there was no room for such a revolutionary vision? Or did his scepticism once more surface and take control? Was that why he put the question *'What is truth?'*

Pilate rose and ordered the commander to take Jesus back to the gate. Accompanied by the *assessores*, the procurator led the way.

Matthew and John, the sisters from Bethany and Joseph of Arimathea must have been alarmed by what was happening around the gate. More priests had come from the Temple to occupy the entire frontage of the fortress. There were many hundreds of them, black-robed and silent, eyes fixed on the portal. When Pilate and the advocates appeared, the throng began to chorus the accusations Annas had made. Ignoring them, Pilate turned and beckoned into the courtyard. The commander led Jesus before the men seated on the thrones. The tumult increased so that the Apostles had difficulty in hearing the procurator's words.

Pilate leaned forward and raised his voice to make himself heard above the crowd. *'Hearest thou not how many things they witness against thee?'*

Jesus made no response; His silence was filled with an innate sense of propriety; He did not wish to quarrel with His countrymen before the Roman tribunal.

Pilate, undoubtedly vexed by what was happening, recognising that he was being used, addressed Caiaphas. *'I find in him no fault at all.'*

302

The High Priest raged that Jesus had incited the people; that He had intended to raise rebellion through the country from that first day He had appeared in public in Galilee—

Pilate interrupted. The mention of Galilee provided a solution that would absolve him from any further involvement. Jesus was a subject of Herod Antipas. He should be sent to the tetrarch for judgement. It was a satisfying Roman response.

THIRTEEN

To Herod and Back

And Herod with his men of war
set him at nought, and mocked
him and arrayed him in a gorgeous
robe, and sent him again to Pilate.
— Luke 23:11

It is not difficult to imagine the foreboding of Chuza as he went to convey the news to Herod Antipas that Jesus was on the way. At this hour of the morning the steward would have known where to find the tetrarch and Chuza's sense of fear could only have increased as he descended a flight of stone steps to the palace dungeons. No sane person would willingly come to this place. The steward edged past the near-dead suspended from hooks, and the half-mad held in chains. Among them moved gaolers with whips and other instruments of torture. They cat-called and shouted coarse witticisms and abuse. There was an air of boisterous vulgarity that made it all that more frightening; the men in charge enjoyed their work. They went to and from a forge to heat branding irons used for burning into a forehead the dreaded *stigma*, marking for ever a man as a thief. Sometimes a gaoler thrust too hard and the white-hot metal burnt through a skull and cauterised a victim's brain. Men were being destroyed by the *furca*: each bore a heavy wooden yoke across back and shoulders. Unable to move because their arms were chained above their head, the sheer weight of the *furca* would eventually wrench limbs from torsos, leaving prisoners to bleed to death. There were treadmills and racks from which death was almost a merciful release. One of the most feared punishments was the crusher in which a man's body was placed between two thick planks. These were then inexorably tightened by other prisoners turning ratchets until first the shoulders and hips were crushed by the pressure then the rib-cage and finally the head pulped. It could take hours. The stench was over-powering: excrement, vomit and the pungent body odour of men and women in mortal terror. The women were kept in a separate cage. They were regularly raped – though none would live long enough to give birth. The life expectancy of all those consigned to the dungeons was weeks rather than months.

Herod Antipas must have appeared an incongruous figure as he strode back and forth through the dungeons in his regal garb that included a splendid purple silk cloak which had once belonged to his father. He could spend hours discussing with his turnkeys the merits of a specific torture before ordering it to be carried out. He would stand at the edge of one of the pits filled with slurry and watch a man being lowered into the cesspool and drowned; he would wait patiently for a tallow-coated stake to be impaled in someone's upper and lower jaws and then lit, so that the wood burnt away the lower part of the face. He would sometimes inspect the hand of a woman caught stealing before it was severed. He could stare, his eyes bulging in excitement, watching the desperate struggle of a man being garrotted by a rope held by two warders pulling on either side. Even then his craving for witnessing punishment was not satisfied. He would watch the specialists at work who pulled off fingernails one at a time, who gouged out eyes with a hook, who disembowelled a living man with a few cuts of a knife. At the end of a spell in the dungeons the tetrarch would emerge sated and cheerful and at his most unpredictable. On this day after sunset there would begin a

305

week's pause in the torture, for Passover. However, in the past he had come down here on holy days and personally killed a prisoner to appease his blood-lust.

Upon receiving his steward's news the tetrarch left the dungeons to prepare to receive Jesus.

Pilate resumed his business with the tax collectors. They could well have looked at him with sudden curiosity. His behaviour was by any reckoning beyond anything they would have known: men in power, whether Romans or Jews, did not behave as the procurator had done. First he had hesitated over Jesus; now he continued to prevaricate over the fate of Barabbas.

Jonathan had re-formed the wedge-like formation around Jesus, Caiaphas, Annas and the chief priests. But there was no way his guards could encompass the other priests who insisted on accompanying them across the city. There may have been three thousand members of the Temple marching upon the tetrarch's palace.

In trying to understand why the High Priest and his cohorts were probably angry and close to panic a number of factors must be taken into account. They had confidently gone to Pilate expecting swift confirmation that Jesus should be executed. Instead the procurator had created a precedent in having a Roman court hand back a Jew to the Jewish authorities. Further, because there had been no time to consult the appropriate texts, they would be almost certainly in some doubt whether Herod Antipas had any legal right to hold a trial after the Temple had done so. There was, in fact, no precedent for such a hearing. More alarming still would be the thought of the tetrarch hearing the case and then acquitting Jesus. That would leave the High Priest and his cohorts in a dangerously exposed position. They would then either have to bring the case before a full plenary session of the Great Sanhedrin – or else release Jesus. Both prospects were fraught with risk. The supreme court might not come to a verdict before sunset, when it would have to rise to observe the Passover. If that happened it would not be able to meet for another week. In the intervening period there would be no knowing what could happen.

In this increasingly uncertain and anxious mood they reached the palace entrance. Caiaphas ordered the chief priests and guards to accompany him into the palace with Jesus while the others were to maintain a silent vigil at the gate – a brooding presence which held its own menace.

Inside the palace hundreds of court officials had hurriedly assembled, probably in the banqueting hall from where, on the previous night, the tetrarch had been carried out senseless with drink. They stood on either side of the hall forming a corridor which led from the closed double entrance doors to the empty throne of Herod the Great brought from the tetrarch's own salon. A measure of the importance of the occasion would have been the presence of Herodias and Salome, seated on adjacent thrones, the women formally caped and robed, possibly even with diadems in their hair. Chuza waited before a curtained alcove. A hush, part curiosity, part anticipation, fell upon the massed courtiers.

The Temple procession and its escort of palace soldiers were greeted by the tetrarch's high chamberlain, secretary and other senior officials in an ante-chamber near the hall. The high chamberlain formally asked why they were here. Caiaphas explained. Perhaps it had been left to the tetrarch's secretary to demand that Jesus should be untied, and any protest would have been met with the explanation that Herod Antipas never received anyone who was not a free person: it was a way of demonstrating that in this palace he alone decided when a person's freedom should be restricted. Caiaphas reluctantly told Jonathan to remove Jesus' bonds. Only when the work was completed did the high chamberlain order the hall doors to be opened.

Beyond, over a hundred paces away, was the still empty

throne from which Herod the Great had dispensed judgement on so many of his subjects.

Pilate's anger was understandable. The counting had already been seriously interrupted and it was almost certain this could not now be completed before sunset, which in turn would mean carrying over the process beyond Passover, an unwelcome prospect. The departure for Caesarea would have to be re-scheduled and the port authorities would have to delay the galley carrying the money chests to Rome. That must provoke questions from the imperial treasury and perhaps even from Sejanus. Under these circumstances the last thing the procurator would want would be any further distraction.

Jesus walked through the densely packed assembly. Ahead strode the high chamberlain, immediately behind came the tetrarch's secretary. These were the positions they normally occupied when escorting an important dignitary into the presence of Herod Antipas. They were followed by Caiaphas who was flanked by Jonathan and Annas.

The chamberlain halted before the empty throne then stepped back to stand on one side of Jesus while the secretary moved forward to stand on the other. Chuza drew the curtain and Herod Antipas emerged wearing his father's cloak and crown and smiling that dangerous and demented half-smile which made him look so uncannily like his father as he sat on the throne.

Earthly ruler and subject stared at one another; a king with a kingdom beyond this world faced the most powerful Jewish ruler on earth. The tetrarch's half-smile was followed by a courteous greeting. It drew suppressed laughter from the courtiers. Herod Antipas stared about him, eyes darting, the smile more lop-sided than before. There would be those who would say that the smile was the clue to what followed.

* * *

The meeting between Jesus and Herod Antipas would become one of the most hotly debated, and contested, events of His Passion. Disagreement would start over whether it was an impulsive whim which made the tetrarch receive Jesus in this extraordinary manner, or whether he was driven by some deeper compulsion to humiliate the High Priest and his cohorts. Had the tetrarch, caught in the grip of one of his fantasies, decided to show that, in spite of being a vassal of Rome, he was Pilate's equal in judicial power – at least when it came to dealing with a Jew? Or had he, in that devious and disabled mind of his, prepared this charade to show contempt for the way the Temple had mismanaged matters?

Yet, where Caiaphas had at least attempted to create an impression of legality, there was no question of Herod Antipas doing so. What he was embarked upon was neither an informal inquiry nor a trial. There had been no time for the tetrarch to prepare for either. What followed – though it would be called the third trial of Jesus – was beyond all known jurisprudence.

* * *

Sifting possible fact from pure legend, what happened in the hall unfolded something like this.

Having received no response from Jesus to his words of welcome, Herod Antipas addressed the audience. They had all heard a great deal about this man, and those miraculous happenings. He came before them with impressive claims and they should all be properly impressed. But who among them had actually *seen* Him perform a single feat?

The courtiers would have been less than their grovelling selves if they had not dutifully laughed at the tetrarch's baiting.

He asked a further question. Who would like to see Jesus perform just a single miracle which would show that He was, after all, the *Messiah*?

The mockery was now a full-throated roar which had its echo in that Sabbath when Jesus had stood in the synagogue in Nazareth. Once more He was assailed by the same demand to prove himself.

Herod Antipas, signalling for silence, addressed Jesus. Would He tell them first how He performed His sorcery? Would He then show them? Perhaps He would once more turn water into wine? Maybe He would wish to have a broken body to heal?

Who could doubt that once more raucous laughter erupted.

Jesus maintained complete silence.

Herod Antipas rose to his feet, the smile on his lips, if anything, more alarming and dangerous. He unclasped his cloak and walked up to Jesus. He asked him a further question. '*Thou art the King of the Jews?*'

Jesus gave no flicker of response.

The tetrarch draped the cloak over His shoulders and stood back to admire the effect. He addressed the hall. Surely now, with a king's robe around His shoulders, they could expect Him to behave like a king? The tetrarch bowed mockingly before Jesus. The courtiers did the same. The low chanting began.

The tetrarch's mocking banter gave way to a sudden surge of anger. He began to attack Jesus, reminding Him of the defamatory words He had used. *A fox!* He had called His lord tetrarch that! *A fox!* Why had He done so? What gave Him such a right to do so? The questions tumbled forth in a furious spittle-laced torrent of words. There was madness in the air.

Then, as abruptly as it had begun, the abuse ended. Perhaps exhausted by his tirade, Herod Antipas returned to his throne, slumped in thought. Finally, indicating Jesus, he once more addressed the gathering. Did they think that even in a king's robe He looked like a king?

They chorused they did not.

The tetrarch at last spoke to Caiaphas. He reviled Jesus and ordered the High Priest to return Him to Pilate.

As the High Priest began to rage Herod Antipas walked from the hall. Herodias and Salome followed him.

Emerging from the palace – Jesus once more bound and wearing the ridiculous and demeaning cloak and surrounded by furious priests and Temple guards – Caiaphas and Annas only too well recognised they had reached a supremely critical moment. Twice they had failed to have others put Jesus to death. For themselves to order carrying out the sentence of the Sadducee court was still fraught with risk. The Pharisee members of the Great Sanhedrin could intervene and force a postponement; that would be perilously divisive and seriously damaging to the authority of the Temple. But, more serious still, the longer Jesus lived the greater was the threat He posed of public opinion being aroused against the priesthood. All He represented would be seen by the masses to be *right* and the Temple shown to be *wrong*; if His teaching prevailed, then the Temple and all its functions would be regarded as totally irrelevant and would be cast aside. That would see the end of the priestly life of privileges and perquisites that included the second bird used in the ritual purification of a woman after childbirth; the portions of each animal presented to the sacrificers at the great altar; the *terumah*, the choicest gathering of all fruit and vegetables; the *challah*, the giving of one twenty-fourth part of the dough used in any baking; the *tithes*, one tenth of every other item which could be used for food. These gifts ensured that, from the High Priest down, the Temple employees were a highly privileged and pampered group in a nation where poverty was rampant. It was human for men like Caiaphas and Annas not willingly to wish to surrender their rewards.

Most serious of all, Jesus was a direct threat to their position which placed them between believers and God. The law insisted that sacrifices must only be offered at the Temple and only through its priests, and that they alone had the authority to decide the penalty to be exacted to restore a supplicant to good standing with God. Jesus threatened this supremacy. Caiaphas and Annas realised they faced a simple and clear choice: either they destroyed Jesus – or He ruined them. If Jesus lived, He would remain a constant threat to their life of power and luxury and their position as the ultimate arbitrators in all spiritual matters. He must die.

Standing outside the tetrarch's palace, the sun high in the sky – a reminder of how little time they had left to act – the High Priest gave instructions to Jonathan.

Some time before the change of the morning watch, Pilate came to a decision over Barabbas. He would send him to Golgotha, with the two thieves. He had barely made up his mind when he received word that the Temple hierarchy was back at the west portal with Jesus and demanding to see the procurator.

Pilate's full fury burst upon Caiaphas when he reached the gateway. *'Ye have brought this man unto me, as one that perverteth the people: and, behold, I, having examined him before you, have found no fault in this man touching those things whereof ye accuse him. No, nor yet Herod, for I sent you to him; and, lo, nothing worthy of death is done unto him.'*

It was an exemplary summary of events to date. In the procurator's view nothing had changed; his angry words contained the explicit reminder that under the Roman *Lex Julia* – the Roman law originally enacted by Julius Caesar – Jesus had not caused any injury to the majesty of the emperor. The definition of an offence under *Lex Julia* was so far-reaching that it included virtually anything the emperor or, in this case Pilate, would regard as diminishing the authority of Rome.

Standing before the massed ranks of the Temple, the procurator had so far kept his nerve – perhaps it had been bolstered by the restraining influence of his wife. Nevertheless he must also have sensed that the seething priests would *not* relent – any more than they had done so that time when they had marched to Caesarea to protest about the Roman insignias fluttering next to the Temple. There was certainly about the men before him the same grinding and growing opposition he had witnessed before – and all that more dangerous with Passover almost upon them; they were torn between a need to prepare for the *Pesah* and their self-evident determination to obtain some imperial action. Notwithstanding the presence of his numerically superior troops, Pilate made a decision which would forever implicate him in the fate of Jesus. '*I will therefore chastise him and release him!*'

He ordered centurions to take Jesus into the courtyard. Under Roman law 'chastising' meant scourging – and that form of punishment generally formed part of a Roman death sentence. There was no precedent for releasing a prisoner *after* such a whipping. Caiaphas and Annas must have been filled with sudden hope.

Mary, His mother, Mary Magdalene and the elder Mary had found their way to Joseph of Arimathea's house. There they found Mary and Martha, Joanna, John and Peter. They sat quietly, weeping, occasionally asking questions. The legend would take root that it was here that His mother said she would make every effort to be with her Son as the end approached.

Pilate was making his way across the courtyard to go back into the fortress when he was stopped by a momentous and growing new chant. '*Crucify him! Crucify him!*' He returned to the west portal. The crowd of priests had grown and their demand bounced off the fortress walls. '*Crucify him! Crucify him!*'

The cry rose and fell, an echo of that very different tumult six mornings earlier when Jesus had made His triumphal entry into the city. Now, instead of Judas leading the hosannas, Caiaphas and Annas were at the forefront of a very different roar. '*Crucify him! Crucify him!*'

Once more events overtook Pilate. Standing there, uncertain and perhaps even a little afraid, the procurator was interrupted by the arrival of one of his wife's servants.

She handed over a scroll written by Claudia Procula, again urging her husband not to become involved: that even now he must not be swayed by the vociferous urging of the crowd. '*Crucify him! Crucify him!*'

Pilate strode out into the street, centurions flanking him, swords drawn and shields extended, ready to do battle at his command. It was a dangerous and ugly situation. The procurator halted a few feet from the High Priest. Pilate turned and indicated Jesus, standing between two centurions inside the fortress gateway. '*What evil hath he done? I have found no cause of death in him. I will therefore chastise him and let him go!*'

They were the words of a man who had fallen prey to some inner force. As a sop to the howling mob, he was going to subject Jesus to the cruellest punishment possible, short of crucifixion, and then release him. It was unprecedented.

In the courtyard the priests could see the two thieves and Barabbas being prepared for the journey to Golgotha. Once more Caiaphas and Annas motivated those around them. Hundreds of hands pointed at Jesus and an even more thunderous roar assailed Pilate. '*Away with this man and release unto us Barabbas!*'

Pilate stood transfixed by words which would spark one of the bitterest controversies to divide the two faiths represented before him: Judaism and Christianity.

★　★　★

The argument would stand or fall on two questions. Was there *privilegium paschale* – a Passover pardon? Did Pilate have the authority to implement it?

Both in Roman and Jewish law there existed specific and clear grounds for granting an amnesty on the occasion of the onset of great festivals. The Romans had inherited the custom from the Greeks and had refined it to two kinds of pardon. There was the *indulgentia*. Only an emperor could grant this and it was normally only extended to a conquered enemy leader who had shown exceptional courage in the

314

face of defeat. There was also the *abolitio*, which was an integral part of the Roman legal code; this pardon could be granted at any point *before a Roman sentence was passed*. An *abolitio* ended proceedings and freed a prisoner before his guilt or innocence had been formally established. The prerogative was in the hands of the chief imperial administrator in a province. Under Roman law both Barabbas and Jesus would qualify for an *abolitio*: the Zealot leader had not been tried; Jesus had been adjudged not guilty of any offence.

The Jewish tractate, *Pesahim*, allowed at Passover for the release of a prisoner from either Jewish or Roman custody – providing he or she was *not guilty* of a religious crime; those charged or condemned for secular offences – including *any political crime* – could be freed. The custom of granting a prisoner freedom at Passover and other great Jewish festivals dated from those turbulent times when the Hasmonean dynasty ruled over Jerusalem, civil war engulfed the nation and the number of purely *political* prisoners dramatically increased; anyone who opposed the Hasmonean king was deemed to be *politically motivated*. Hundreds, perhaps thousands of such prisoners had filled the city gaols. To ensure a measure of peace during the Passover, the Hasmonean king regularly pardoned and released an inmate. The gesture was underpinned by a strong commercial consideration. The dynasty included a large number of princes who were Temple priests whose income virtually depended on the number of pilgrims who came to Jerusalem. Granting freedom to one man was a small price to pay to encourage pilgrims from the Diaspora to accept they would not be embroiled in the civil war if they came to the city. The custom became a recognised ritual. When the Roman occupation began, the imperial power consented to it continuing – seeing it as a shrewd way to reduce the extra emotional tension always present at times like Passover. In an equally calculated move Caiaphas had used it to try to force Pilate to heed the will of the Temple.

Barabbas still clearly qualified for release under the

tractate. Jesus, who had also been convicted of blasphemy, did not.

* * *

The tumult engulfed the procurator. He had been repeatedly confronted on his doorstep, an unpleasant and draining experience. Added to this was the realization he would now be definitely forced to remain after Passover in a city and among a people he hated. His personality was most probably ill-equipped to deal with such vagaries; the essential and reassuring links which governed his life were being strained over the fate of one man. The relentless cry bore in on him. *'Release unto us Barabbas! Crucify Him!'*

It was too much for Pilate to cope with: the unconscious forces previously held back finally burst into his consciousness. The shouting was coming dangerously close to violence. In a moment he would be engulfed in an uprising – trampled to his own death by the crazed mob of aroused religious fanatics. The procurator's sense of self-preservation overcame all else. Once more he walked over to Caiaphas. They stood feet apart, divided by religion and social mores, but linked by a loathing which was mutual and vibrant. A gradual silence settled over the crowd. Pilate's question cut through the hush. *'Whether of the twain will ye that I release unto you?'*

The response was immediate.

'Barabbas!'

Pilate's next question showed the increasing strain he was under.

'What shall I do then with Jesus which is called Christ?'

That question marked the formal abdication of his prerogative as impartial judge. It saw the end of what skills he had in handling a complex and perplexing situation, of showing that Roman justice, for all its severity, could not be misused and exploited. Now, in the face of a mob of aroused priests he had capitulated, sunk to the point where he had asked *them* for advice. He had accepted the rule of the mob. It roared at him. '*Let him be crucified.*'

The procurator turned and walked to the gateway. Beside it was a drinking fountain for the sentries. Pilate washed his hands in water. Then, standing near Jesus, he addressed the Temple cadre. '*I am innocent of the blood of this just person. See ye to it.*'

The words were lost in a renewed chant, no longer furious but triumphant. '*Crucify Him!*'

Pilate ordered Barabbas to be released and Jesus to be taken to the scourging post. Then he returned to his salon. In one sense the trials of Jesus were over. In another they were about to begin.

Beyond the Cross

Vicisti, Galilae – *Thou hast conquered, O Galilean.*

— Julian
(*alleged dying words*)

FOURTEEN

The Place of the Skull

To give light to them that
sit in darkness and in the
shadow of death.
— Luke 1:79

Led unprotesting into the courtyard and through the ranks of centurions, hardened men largely indifferent to what was to happen, Jesus knew His brief mission was almost over. He would face an excruciatingly painful ritual death knowing He had done all that had been asked of Him; that it had always been intended He would go to His earthly end without any idea of the efficacy of His teaching, miracles and cures. The one certainty had always been that after He had planted the Word all that was required of Him was to die.

The more He sowed, the closer it came, and these last three years had been an accelerating race towards death. He had lived all His public life in readiness for this and had announced His fate to those closest to Him as an inevitability. If they could see Him approaching the scourging post He would have urged them, as He had done so often in the past, not to regard what was about to happen as either a disgrace, a failure or the inevitable consequence of His actions. The destruction of His body – though not His soul

321

– had always been intended as the climax to His mission on earth.

Crossing the courtyard under the scrutiny of men wedded to other gods; watching Barabbas, freed and making his way to the west portal, where the Temple cadre continued their triumphant chanting; passing the two thieves who had just been scourged and were bowed under the crosses they must drag to Golgotha: Jesus saw and accepted it all.

The two Syrian conscripts waited at the post. The ground around it was slippery with the blood of the thieves. Each held a *flagellum*, made of strips of leather soaked in brine, and a *flagrum*, whose thongs were studded with pieces of bone and small metal spheres with spiked surfaces. The choice of whip rested on the garrison commander standing beside the post. The thieves had been brutalised by the *flagellum*. He ordered the *flagrum* for Jesus.

One of the conscripts stepped forward and ripped Herod the Great's cloak from Jesus' shoulders and handed the garment to the commander. The two Syrians then shoved Him, face forward, against the post, shackling His hands and feet. Using a knife, one of them slashed His robe from the neckline to the hem and yanked it free. Another stroke cut away His undergarment. Jesus was as naked and defenceless as the day He was born. The Syrians stepped back, each measuring his distance, expertly flicking his whip so that for the moment the thongs only caressed His skin. From beyond the west gate came another roar. *'Crucify Him! Crucify Him!'*

The commander ordered the punishment to commence.

The first Syrian stepped forward and delivered a lash, the *flagrum* opening the skin, the first slivers of flesh torn from His body and His blood starting to spurt on to the flagstones, mingling with that of the thieves. A further roar came from the priests as the second blow landed.

Each *flagrum* made a whistling sound as it snaked through the air, then a dull thwacking as the strips of reinforced leather struck home. Jesus was being steadily cut open from

322

the back of His head to His heels. After every few lashes the commander stepped forward to estimate how much more He could bear. Each time he motioned for the shameful torture to resume.

* * *

Matthew, Mark and John would all limit themselves merely to recording the punishment. The Apostles, like every other Jew, had grown up with scourging: they well understood the shame of its nudity, the unbearable physical pain and, above all, the infamy of Jesus being condemned to a punishment normally reserved for slaves and criminals. Their understandable discretion would be used by the early Church to argue that the punishment was too horrific to be recorded; further, that in not protesting at it, *the Jews* tacitly accepted a barbarism far crueller than any kind of ritual slaughter.

The claim would be made that Pilate had inflicted this revolting suffering upon a man in whom he had found no fault at all, as a last resort to appease the bloodthirsty clamouring of *the Jews* and it was they, not he, who wished Jesus to be punished in this vile manner. The story would flourish that the whips made by Romans, wielded by Roman conscripts, on the authority of a Roman commander and procurator, which curled and coiled across the body of Jesus, did so at the behest of *the Jews*.

The scourging would produce its own grim literature: eventually a library of several hundred books devoted to the subject would occupy a gallery in the secret archives of the Vatican detailing the history of the torture and the precise method of manufacturing its weapons – '*the pieces of bone came from previous victims*' – and how scourging came to be part of the Jewish penal code. In these books can be found claims that the flogging lasted between three and five minutes; that it produced widespread subcutaneous haemorrhages on His body and that throughout the ordeal His lips seemed to be moving in prayer, as if Jesus '*forgave the*

323

Jews who had instigated all this'. There were numerous descriptions of how Jesus must have been a pitiful sight when the Syrians – much would be made of their Semitic background – finally set aside their whips and wiped the perspiration from their brows. His chest, neck, shoulders, back, hips and legs were slashed as if with knives and streaked with blue welts and swollen bruises. Even his face was cut and disfigured by the lashes that had rained down upon Him. Having recovered their breath, the Semitic Syrians, with no more feelings of compassion than the priest had for the lamb with its head through the rung, unshackled Jesus. He was in such a state that He could scarcely have been recognised even by those who knew Him best. The scourging had exposed the mechanism of His flesh, even to the very veins and arteries.

What had happened was indisputably appalling – but so was the subsequent shocking accusation that *the Jews* had brought it upon Him: that they were somehow collectively responsible for the gruesome sight of Jesus lying at the foot of the scourging post, unconscious.

From the west gate came the ceaseless chanting of the High Priest and the Temple cadre continuing to demand His crucifixion.

★ ★ ★

One of the conscripts picked up a pail of water mixed with salt and sloshed it over Jesus: the stinging brine was a routine way to revive a victim and help to stem the flow of blood. Jesus was hauled to His feet and held upright until He could feel some return of strength. His body ached with pain, which grew in intensity as full consciousness returned. The blood matting His body hair, He stood shivering in shock. These were standard responses to a scourging. What followed added cruel insult to torture. The soldiers – no doubt bored and certainly without pity – began to taunt Jesus. Any fear they may have felt in His presence had gone; with it went the respect normally

324

accorded to a man who had survived the *flagrum*. He now became the plaything of the centurions. While Jesus struggled to reclothe Himself as best He could, they addressed Him with mocking gallantry, finally draping the purple cape of Herod the Great over His body. One of them fetched a faggot of dead thorns used as firelighters from a pile stacked in the courtyard. The soldier shaped it into a *pileus*, the oval-shaped hat Romans often wore when attending festive occasions. He placed the plaited ring on Jesus' head. Another stripped a branch of its spikes and shoved it in His hand.

The centurions knelt before Jesus, each on one knee, and bowed their heads, their chants matching the cries from the west gate. '*Hail, King of the Jews!*' The mockery which Herod Antipas had begun was complete.

Obtaining no reaction from Jesus, the soldiers became more unpleasant. They rose to their feet and approached Him, one at a time, as if to bestow a kiss of peace. Instead, they spat in His face. One grabbed the stick and used it to beat Him. He handed it to a companion who repeated the process. The cane was passed from one hand to another to strike Jesus. He gave no response. A centurion drove the crown of thorns into His lacerated scalp. Jesus stoically bore this further pain. The soldiers grew increasingly furious, kicking and punching as they chanted: '*Hail, King of the Jews!*'

Beyond the gate the priests screamed that Jesus must be crucified *now*: the sun was already directly overhead. Time was running out if He was to experience the full agony of the cross. In the courtyard the soldiers, tired of their savagery, began to shove Jesus towards the east tower. Propped against its wall was the cross intended for Barabbas.

John, unable to bear the strain of not knowing what was happening, had risked his life to return and stand among the priests. Suddenly they fell silent. Through the fortress gate came Pilate followed by a small detachment of soldiers with Jesus in their midst, bedraggled and bloody, the crown

325

of thorns rammed into His skull, the robe hiding his terrible injuries; prisoner and escort remained inside the gate. The procurator addressed Caiaphas. '*Behold I bring him forth to you, that ye may know that I find no fault in him!*'

Pilate motioned for the soldiers to bring Jesus out of the shadow of the archway and expose Him to the bright sunlight. John and those around him saw the brutality Jesus had suffered. Pilate spoke again. '*Behold the man!*'

Caiaphas' response was immediate. '*Crucify Him!*'

Thousands of other voices took up the refrain around the anguished Apostles.

* * *

That brief exchange, recorded by John without comment, would foment further tension between Jews and Christians. The tableau at high noon outside the fortress would be explored and exploited. Pilate, who *had* ordered the scourging, but almost certainly not the subsequent mockery and brutality of his soldiers, would be presented as determined to make a last desperate plea to *the Jews* to recant and let Jesus go; that the words '*behold the man*' were a straightforward appeal to the compassion of the priestly cadre: the procurator was saying that Jesus had already suffered enough, and that He stood before them, bloodied and physically broken, an object of derision, no longer a threat to the Temple. What more did they want? There would be others who would see in the words an even more profound meaning by capitalising the word '*Man*'. It would become a sentence used to portray the procurator in a still more appealing light – in spite of the fearful whipping he *had* ordered. '*Behold the man*' would be seen as meaning: 'Behold Him; here was a Man unique among men; one filled with mystery; humbled He retained an indefinable grandeur.' It could have been a description of the *Messiah*.

Pilate would be presented, in that moment, as having regained his integrity and become once more the dispenser of imperial justice, a proud ruler who could hardly restrain himself from saying to *the Jews* that their behaviour disgusted him; that he would no longer involve himself with their injustice. Instead, *the Jews* had continued with their raucous demand. '*Crucify! Crucify!*'

All that is certain is that in doing so the High Priest and his staff brought further odium upon their people.

*   *   *

Pilate finally did not bother to hide his displeasure. '*Take ye him, and crucify him: for I find no fault in him!*'

John would record that *the Jews* – though almost certainly it was Caiaphas – answered: '*We have a law, which by our law he ought to die, because he made himself the Son of God.*'

Originally Jesus had been brought to the bar of Roman justice on a charge of treason. Now Caiaphas was attempting to reintroduce the religious charge which had no counterpart in the imperial code; he was clearly casting about for anything that would persuade Pilate to have Jesus crucified.

The procurator put a question to Jesus far beyond any geographical significance. '*Whence art thou?*'

Jesus caught the uncertainty in Pilate's voice. He was asking Jesus to explain what He stood for, to amplify those values Jesus had hinted at earlier, when they had spoken in Pilate's salon and Jesus had said His Kingdom was not of this world.

Jesus did not reply. But His silence was not purely that of suffering; He wanted to see if Pilate could grasp for himself the answer to his question.

'*Speakest thou not unto me? Knowest thou not that I have power to crucify thee and have power to release thee?*'

Pilate was saying, perhaps even pleading, that even *now*, after all that had happened, he would still free Jesus – and no doubt arrange for His safe conduct through the hostile mob of priests. All the procurator wanted were explanations he could understand.

Jesus put aside any thought of freedom. '*Thou couldest have no power at all against me, except it were given thee from above; therefore he that delivereth me unto thee hath greater sin.*'

Jesus wanted Pilate to understand that not only did He sympathise with the procurator's position of having a very limited earthly authority, but that Jesus was speaking of a far more exalted power – God's and His own. Both were interchangeable and equal. Then almost as an afterthought He had firmly apportioned blame for those who had brought them *both* to this situation: Caiaphas and his priests.

Their renewed shouts interrupted further discussion. The High Priest shouted into the gateway: '*If thou let this man go, thou art not Caesar's friend: whosoever maketh himself a king speaketh against Caesar!*'

In final desperation the High Priest had been driven to invoke the emperor; to proclaim that the High Priest of the Jews was more loyal to a system he hated than was the procurator he equally loathed. Pilate, whatever action he may have been contemplating, now had no alternative. He must show that he, too, had no loyalty other than to Caesar Tiberius. The procurator ordered the cross to be brought to the gateway. He summoned a secretary. When the man arrived Pilate dictated a sentence to him in Latin, Greek and Aramaic. '*Jesus of Nazareth. The king of the Jews.*'

Pilate ordered the inscription to be nailed above the crosspiece of the cross. Then, his voice filled with all the bitterness the Gospels would imply, he spoke to Caiaphas. '*Behold your King!*'

The High Priest, as he had done at the end of the trial in Annas' hall, sensed victory. It would have been natural for him to stare at Pilate, waiting. In keeping with his entire behaviour the procurator uttered a last despairing question. '*Shall I crucify your King?*'

His victory complete, Caiaphas replied: '*We have no king but Caesar.*'

Pontius Pilate nodded to Jesus' escort and walked into

the fortress. Claudia Procula's *just man* must, after all, die on Golgotha, the place of the skull.

★ ★ ★

Pilate's question was the last recorded words he spoke, leaving unresolved a tantalising issue. The procurator was certainly a more complex person than the Gospels would accord: their failure would be to offer any plausible explanation why Pilate – who had previously shown insensitivity to those he governed – should have gone to such exceptional lengths to save Jesus before being finally driven to *deliver* Him – and then only in the face of that threat to report him to the emperor.

The threat was hardly enforceable. Caiaphas had no avenue to report anything directly to Rome; his channel to imperial authority was through the tetrarch. After the latest behaviour of Herod Antipas there was no way the High Priest could have been certain that any complaint he made would be forwarded. And, if it did reach Rome, there was no guarantee it would be treated seriously. Caiaphas could have been under no illusion about the contempt in which he was held in Roman circles. Finally, before daring to protest about the procurator to the emperor, he would need the full backing of the Great Sanhedrin: High Priests simply did not act unilaterally in such grave matters. That would almost certainly have led to further fierce debate. Pilate, then, should not have been unduly troubled by the threat.

But had he acquiesced to it for a very different reason? In his conversations with his wife he would not have failed to grasp something of her feelings that Jesus was in every sense an exceptional person; his own conversations with Him could only have reinforced that view. Could it, then, be that Pilate finally realised that Jesus not only *had* to die – but that He was actually prepared to? Could the procurator have come to believe that the last service he could perform for Jesus was to hand Him over to be crucified as King of the

329

Jews? Could it be that Pilate had, after all, at least an inkling that nothing could stop the coming of His Kingdom?

★ ★ ★

Once Pilate agreed to the crucifixion and disappeared into the courtyard, the scene at the gate took on a military precision. The commander detailed one of the officers to act as *exactor mortis*, responsible for taking Jesus to Golgotha.

It was a coveted duty: the *exactor mortis* had first choice of the clothes and any other personal effects of the condemned. Three soldiers were ordered to complete the death watch that would remain at the execution site until Jesus was dead. The commander took the unusual step of sending a *centuria*, a further hundred troops in full battle-dress, to accompany them: undoubtedly it was a precaution against any attempt to intervene in the proceedings.

The officer ordered the men to dismantle the cross, made from two balks of roughly hewn timber, the vertical span a standard ten cubits tall, fifteen feet. Assembled it weighed around three hundred pounds, beyond the strength of even a physically fit man to carry to Golgotha, and an impossible feat for someone who had been severely weakened by a scourging. The *patibulum*, the cross-beam, weighed over fifty pounds.

With the officer pulling forward Jesus' head, the beam was lowered on to His neck and shoulders. Then Jesus' arms were extended and tied to the span. Fresh blood seeped from the wounds on His body. The *exactor mortis* unfastened the Herodian robe: he had made his first acquisition. He ordered the crown of thorns to be removed; it had been part of private sport and had no place in the ritual of the Roman crucifixion.

The soldiers hoisted the upright on to their shoulders while the officer fastened a rope around the waist of Jesus which he then tied to the back of his own belt; sometimes a condemned man had to be dragged to his execution. Attached to the belt was a hammer, an awl, a pouch of nails

330

and a flagon. In one hand he carried two stout poles, forked at the top; in the other a pair of wooden shovels.

It was early afternoon when the procession formed up. First came five ranks of centurions, ten abreast, followed by the execution party, then a further five rows of soldiers. Caiaphas and the priests along with Jonathan and his guards walked behind them. The public followed; in all there may have been already close to four thousand persons going to see Jesus die. Among them was John. But he would write nothing about that journey; like the kiss of Judas it was almost certainly too awful for him to record. Around him were those who would provide details for Matthew, Luke and Mark; like the best of reporters they would confine themselves to simply relating what they learned happened.

The distance to Golgotha was short, no more than five hundred yards to the north-west of the Antonia Fortress. To reach the mound required passing through the business quarter, a warren of shops which largely depended on the Temple for their livelihood. As the procession wended its way the priests ordered the shopkeepers to follow; scores did so, swelling the monotonous chanting. '*Crucify. Crucify.*'

Climbing towards the gate which led from the city towards the execution hillock, Jesus finally began to falter. The officer ordered a halt, almost certainly not from pity but of necessity; if Jesus died before being crucified there would be disciplinary proceedings. Coming through the gate was a peasant, Luke's Simon, '*coming out of the country*'. He was ordered to take over the burden of the *patibulum*, and made to walk behind the soldiers carrying the upright.

The procession restarted but only went a few more yards before there was a second and equally dramatic intervention. During the changeover of the spar a number of women had managed to infiltrate the escort; seeing His pitiful state they began to weep and wail. There would be subsequent speculation that they included Jesus' mother and the other

331

women from Joseph of Arimathea's house. More likely they were members of an organisation of pious women who devoted themselves to helping the condemned along this final stage.

Freed from His crippling yoke, Jesus spoke to them. '*Daughters of Jerusalem, weep not for me, but weep for yourselves and for your children. For, behold, the days are coming in which they shall say, blessed are the barren, and the wombs that never bear, and the paps which never gave suck. Then shall they begin to say to the mountains; fall on us; and to the hills; cover us. For if they do these things in a green tree, what shall be done in the dry?*'

He had spoken in the timeless manner of the great prophets. His phrases may well have been broken by gasps of pain; almost certainly He had not strength left to deliver a sustained discourse. Every word must have cost Him dearly, draining further His steadily diminishing strength. Yet they contained all the sobering eloquence of a visionary: Jesus was once more peering into the future and what He saw was apocalyptic: a world where it was better not to bear children, a time of great catastrophe. These were crushing predictions, a series of paralysing images through which He wanted everyone who could hear clearly to understand that ahead lay great misery if they had the courage still to follow Him. It was unflinching and without a shred of compromise: the way of the cross was essential to enter His Kingdom.

The *exactor mortis* ordered the women away and the procession continued through the city gate. To the left rose the ramparts of the tetrarch's palace; the screams of his prisoners must have carried clearly. A mere hundred feet ahead and slightly to the right rose the skull-shaped mound of Golgotha. The two thieves were already suspended from their *cruxi*. The *centuria* were instructed to form an outward-facing circle around the hillock and let no one pass. The officer led Jesus forward. Behind came Simon and the trio carrying the upright. They moved among the centurions who had accompanied the robbers, and who,

332

their work completed, sat on the ground, sharing out their possessions.

The three men dropped the balk and began to prod the ground around the erected crosses. Finally they selected a spot between and slightly forward of where the naked and very likely semi-conscious thieves were suspended. Two of the soldiers used the shovels to dig a hole; when they judged it deep enough they positioned the upright, wedging the post firmly in place with rocks, forming a cairn of stones around its base so that it would not sway and fall under the load it must bear.

While they worked the *exactor mortis* untied the rope which bound Jesus to him and stripped Jesus of all His clothes; the officer chose what he wanted and left the rest to be divided among the squad.

★　★　★

The early Christian Church, understandably anxious not to remind its members that Jesus was going to His death as a circumcised Jew, would go to considerable lengths to suggest that He wore a loincloth; volumes would be written arguing that *naked* could mean *relative as well as total nudity*; that the Romans made an exception of Jesus and allowed Him to retain an undergarment.

But Roman practice considered that part of the penalty of crucifixion should include total degradation of the victim: the only permitted concession was that women were crucified facing the cross – though they, too, were completely nude.

★　★　★

Once the upright was firmly positioned and Jesus was naked the squad began the task of attaching Him to the crossbeam. After Simon laid the *patibulum* on the ground near the upright he was dismissed from the mound, his chance encounter with history over, his place in Christian

333

lore forever assured. Jesus was ordered to lie on His back so that His shoulders were resting in the centre of the beam. A soldier grasped each of His arms and stretched them out on the wood. The *exactor mortis* then used the point of his spear to make a scratch mark near each wrist. Jesus' arms were momentarily raised above His head while the officer used the hammer and awl to make a hole in the timber so that it would receive a nail more easily. Jesus' arms were then repositioned, the soldiers holding them taut. A nail was hammered through His wrist into the wood. The other hand was similarly pinioned. This was standard Roman procedure; what followed had been absorbed from Judaism.

The *exactor mortis* uncorked the flagon and offered Jesus a drink to ease the pain: the Apostle Mark was sure it was the usual mixture of wine and myrrh, a potion which produced a quick-acting narcotic effect, dulling senses and pain. The Romans had, almost certainly reluctantly, been persuaded to offer this relief to Jews: the Book of Proverbs and the Talmud both contained instructions to ease the suffering of the condemned. Jesus allowed the drink to moisten his lips but He would not swallow a drop. In the Garden of Gethsemane He had accepted that His passion must be borne without any relief: that He must sacrifice Himself in full possession of his faculties, including those which stimulated His terrible physical pain.

The ground around Golgotha was crammed with onlookers, now silent; even the Temple cadre at last showed a sense of respect for what was being done at their behest.

The four Romans bent over His body, working efficiently. Ignoring the involuntary twitching of His body and the fresh blood oozing around the nail wounds, they began the most difficult part of any crucifixion – raising and attaching the *patibulum* to the upright. Jesus was now a dead weight and unable to assist them – and so perhaps make it easier for Himself. Two of the men grasped either end of the beam, the third held Him around the waist while the officer supported the back of His head. At his command they lifted Jesus on to His feet and positioned His back against the upright. The officer handed the two men supporting the beam each a pole. They placed the forked ends under the beam close to His body. The third soldier grasped Jesus, this time around the knees. At a further command from the *exactor mortis* the soldiers with the poles raised the beam while their companion supported Jesus' body as it inched up the main spar. When they had lifted Him several feet, the crossbeam slipped into a notch already cut into the upright. The officer took a stout peg with a metal spike at one end and hammered it into the wood between Jesus' legs. The weight of His suspended body was now divided between His arms and crotch. His feet were then nailed to the wood, two nails driven through each tibia.

The squad's work was over. They sat on the ground a few feet from the cross dividing up His clothing and, in Luke's sparse yet chilling graphic account, '*cast lots*' for the raiment as they kept watch.

The priests reminded the onlookers that the Book of Deuteronomy said there was a curse upon any man hung from wood – such a person '*was not the elect of God*'. They should therefore not feel any sympathy – let alone have any lingering thought that Jesus could be the *Messiah*. After a while the crowd began to disperse, no doubt influenced by crucifixion being a drawn-out affair in which little appeared to be happening.

Looking down from His cross, dying, Jesus must have experienced the very depths of rejection. He had been betrayed, denied and forsaken. His flesh had been torn and pierced and His blood had flowed copiously. He had been hoisted up from the earth in a final barbaric operation, placed between two common thieves, the parchment proclamation above His head a derisive reminder of His failure. As He looked down He would have noticed the crowd thinning – though it would be uncertain whether He would have still been able to see His mother, Mary Magdalene, Mary the mother of two of the Apostles, and Joanna. With them were Mary and Martha, Nicodemus and John.

They could only wait.

Below the *cruxi* the soldiers played with dice made from knucklebones, drank *posca*, a vinegary wine, and haggled over the meagre spoils of the three men suspended above them. From time to time a centurion rose and walked around the crosses, trying to judge how close was death by the swarm of flies settling on the bodies and the number of carrion birds circling in the blue sky. In this manner an hour, perhaps longer, passed. It may have been the effect of the *posca*, boredom, or the innate cruelty of any death watch. Whatever the cause they began to mock and insult Jesus.

Caiaphas heard the jeers from the mound and began to shout: '*He saved others! Himself He cannot save!*'

Annas and the other priests took up the refrain. '*Let Christ the King of Israel descend now from the cross, that we may see and believe.*'

After the outrages they had perpetrated what came from them now was a miserable evil.

At some point during the torrent of abuse, Jesus found the strength to turn His head to the men on either side of Him and encourage them to bear their suffering. Then, with what could only be a superhuman effort, He raised His voice so that His words reached the chanting Temple cadre. '*Father, forgive them; for they know not what they do.*'

They were genuinely heroic words – an unforgettable contrast between the behaviour of the availing victim and His executioners. Jesus was actually praying for all those who had brutalised Him; He wanted to bestow upon them His limitless pity, charity and forgiveness; He wished them to know that whatever they had done, or must do, would not ultimately matter if they came to understand who He was. It was a haunting and thrilling reminder of what He had said on Mount Hattin. '*Love your enemies, bless them that curse you, do good to them that hate you and pray for them which despitefully use you, and persecute you.*'

336

His forgiveness of those who had treated Him so grievously would forever ennoble the sombre horror of Golgotha.

While the priests continued to behave shamefully John had started delicate negotiations with the officer commanding the *centuria*. The Apostle explained that Jesus' mother and His closest friends wanted to go to the foot of the cross to be near Him when the end came. What passed between the two men would forever be uncertain: there would be suggestions of bribery, of John handing over money; others would say that the stricken beauty of Mary Magdalene stirred something in the officer; or that it was His mother's dignity which finally influenced the Roman. Whatever the reason, he allowed to pass through the cordon Jesus' mother, the elderly Mary, Mary Magdalene and Joanna. John was allowed to accompany them. The four women and the Apostle picked their way up the mound.

When they reached the foot of the cross they knelt and averted their eyes: they had been raised with a proper sense of modesty; to be exposed completely naked in public was a humiliation almost beyond equal. John was beside Mary, His mother; he could sense her resolve, knowing she only wished to encourage Him in His sacrifice, to let her Son understand she supported this total submission to the will of God. In centuries to come that would be the moment that the Church would say she became blessed among all women.

Jesus called down to her. '*Woman.*' The word was filled with formal respect, the way He had always addressed her in public since that evening in Cana when she had asked Him to perform that first miracle and He had said, '*Woman,*' and that His time had not yet come, but they had both known and accepted even then it would come to this. '*Behold thy son.*' Jesus wanted her to know He would not turn away from the sacrifice; that while He would shortly no longer exist in this world they would next meet in a better one. In the meantime, she must be protected. Jesus turned his gaze to John. '*Behold thy mother.*' He was asking John

337

not only to take care of her – but to remember always that through Mary His presence would always be there: she had been chosen to give birth to Him; she still possessed the sacred authority to make Him live in her.

Peter, to whom Jesus had chosen to give the keys to the Kingdom, may well, as the Catholic Church still insists, have made a deliberate decision not to come to Golgotha, and sent John to bear witness for him. It would be a suggestion that neither enhanced Peter's position nor diminished the role of John. Of the Twelve he alone continued to show himself as worthy of that original invitation – *'Come follow me.'*

The mocking voices were now joined by another. One of the thieves began to curse and revile Jesus for not using His power to save them. It was the understandable and desperate reaction of someone embittered by his fate, and who, sensing his own end was very close, wished somehow to distract himself from its torment and terror. His companion delivered a rebuke. *'Dost not thou fear God, seeing thou art in the same condemnation?'*

The robber wanted to urge the other thief that, while they were both irretrievably doomed, he should not behave like those who had condemned them. Then, with another glance and a movement of his head, all he could manage, he continued to remind his companion of reality. *'We receive the due reward of our deeds. But this man hath done nothing amiss.'*

The honesty of the words was the more moving under the horror they were all enduring; through them, that petty criminal, uncouth, roughened and hardened by a life of sin, had found grace. Having shamed and silenced his companion, he now called out to Jesus. *'Lord, remember me when thou comest into thy kingdom.'*

In confessing his own sins and proclaiming a firm belief in the innocence of Jesus, the thief, with the simplicity of the untutored, had found the way to look beyond his own immediate fate. He wanted Jesus to know he believed in Him – and that he accepted His kingdom was only a few further tortured moments on earth away. This man, whose name and appearance would be lost for ever, asked for nothing except to remain in the memory of Jesus.

An endless and futile debate would ensue as to whether the thief could have known Jesus before they became brothers-in-misery. Rationalists could ponder whether his conversion was the climax of lengthy exposure to His teachings and that was why he had felt able to speak with such familiarity: *'Remember me.'* The most likely possibility was that the thief would have heard the discussions in the Antonia Fortress that had led to the release of Barabbas; he would have seen the parchment nailed to Jesus' cross; if he could not read, the robber would have learned of its meaning from the mocking taunts of the priests. Above all, he would have been a witness to His dignity, patience and overwhelming goodness and had heard Jesus ask God to forgive and pardon all those who had brought Him here. This had all helped the thief to receive the grace of God which alone could explain his immediate and total conversion. His profession of faith would have remained one of the most unforgettable events in history even if Jesus had not responded. But His reply would be incontrovertible proof that as earthly death drew closer for them both so did the threshold of Eternity. *'Verily, I say unto thee: today shalt thou be with me in paradise.'*

There was an urgency to the promise. Soldiers were prodding the other thief with their spears to confirm he was dead. Jesus knew that the man on His other side, who would simply become known as the Good Thief, like Himself, could not last much longer.

Until a short while ago the sky had been cloudless; now it grew steadily gloomier, almost obscuring Jesus and the men on either side.

The darkness over the land finally silenced the abuse. Caiaphas and Annas led the Temple cadre back into the city; the few remaining spectators followed. Jonathan and a handful of his guards remained on watch outside the ring of Roman troops.

The soldiers on Golgotha huddled together, shields over their faces. Of all the meteorological phenomena of Judaea, the one the Romans disliked most was the *khamsin*, the black sirocco which scooped up tons of sand in its swirling progress out of the Wilderness. In minutes it had once more obscured the sun and filled the air with a dark choking fog. It was widely believed by Romans that it was sent by the gods as a mark of grave displeasure. The centurions peeped around their shields at His cross, understandably suddenly fearful.

Mary, His mother, and her companions saw that Jesus was sinking rapidly. Blood dripped steadily from the wounds in His hands and feet. From time to time He had tried to redistribute His weight, attempting to ease Himself upward to relieve the agonising pressure in His chest; this only increased the pain in His legs. Jesus' movements were now more sporadic and weaker, little more than twitches. He was still alive, but barely. The sand of the *khamsin* coated His body giving it a strange greyish appearance as if He had already been turned to ash and dust. Then the wind passed, leaving a gloomy stillness.

Suddenly, Jesus pulled Himself once more against the upright, forcing up His body, gulping air into His lungs. He stared out over Golgotha and beyond, to the towers of the palace of Herod Antipas and further, to the Antonia Fortress, and finally to the Temple. Then He cried out: '*My God, my God, why hast thou forsaken me?*'

The mystery of those words would remain forever inexplicable unless they were seen as the *final proof* that Jesus wished to spare Himself nothing; that right to the end He would remain His own master and, with the help of His Father, become the immolated victim through which all those who accepted Him would be saved. Not for a moment was he complaining of rejection, though He well understood that everyone was quite alone at death; rather He was reminding Himself of why He had to suffer. He knew, and accepted, that in dying He *had* to sink to the depths before He would ascend to the peak of liberty. His words were *not* spoken in despair, or reproach, let alone anger; they were a reminder that He was about to be rescued from His present misery – just as a short while before He had saved the Good Thief.

The sky began to brighten, though the sun was still obscured. The centurions returned to their posts, staring at Him, openly incredulous that Jesus was still alive. From His lips came two words which showed how far His agony had gone. '*I thirst.*' No longer had He the strength left to speak loudly; almost certainly it was the barely audible moan of a man in the burning fever of death.

The words aroused something in the *exactor mortis*; he alone had the authority to intervene. He took the sponge used as a stopper for the flagon of *posca* and poured some of the wine into it. He placed the sponge on the tip of a spear and raised it to Jesus' lips. He sucked upon the sponge. When the officer lowered the spear, Jesus bowed his head. All those around the cross heard the next words. '*It is finished.*'

It was the beginning of the ninth hour, His third on the cross: the moment the sun once more appeared; the end of His suffering.

Even in dying Jesus had acted on His own volition. His head had not dropped on His chest *after* death. Instead He had bowed in acceptance that his physical life was finally over – and He acknowledged this before his spirit returned from whence it came.

But the *exactor mortis* had to be certain. He removed the sponge and drove his spear into Jesus' side, working its broad blade around the ribs and into His heart. He withdrew the weapon leaving a large hole. John and the others watched as from the opening came a mixed flow of blood and water. The lancing of the heart, itself almost a banal act, the pointless desecration of a victim already beyond further earthly destruction, would be given a special significance by the evangelist: he would see in the flow the image of Christianity itself emerging; the mixture would symbolise for John the two great sacraments, baptism and communion.

The spear thrust signalled the end of the Roman presence on and around Golgotha. The usual imperial custom was to leave the crucified exposed for a few days as a salutary warning: in that time they became the prey of wild animals and carrion birds. When the stench became unbearable the remains, still on their crosses, were dumped in the Hinnom Valley.

The centurions came down from the hillock leaving Jesus and the two thieves hanging. The *centuria* re-formed and marched back to barracks. The way was clear for others to join John and the women at the foot of His cross: Joseph of Arimathea, Nicodemus, Mary and Martha. There was both uncertainty and a sense of urgency mingling with their grief. In two hours' time the Passover Sabbath would begin. From then on it would be forbidden to remove His body under Jewish law – as this would violate the edict of not working on the Sabbath. But before Jesus could be buried they must find a sepulchre.

Joseph said he would go to Pilate and seek authority to have Jesus removed and buried in Joseph's own tomb. The sepulchre was close to where they stood and Jesus could still be properly laid to rest before the onset of Passover. With the accord of the others, Joseph hurried into the city.

He was back on the mound as the sun began to dip beyond the Temple. With him was Mark. The boy carried what would be described in his Gospel as *fine linen*, which Joseph had purchased in the city to provide a burial shroud. The only hint of what had transpired between Pilate and Joseph would be Mark's revelation that the procurator had expressed surprise that Jesus was already dead; he had sent for the *exactor mortis*, and only when the officer had confirmed the fact did Pilate agree to release the body.

In the face of the advancing afternoon there was grisly work to do. While Nicodemus went to the Street of the Perfume Makers to purchase embalming materials, John and Mark undertook the task of taking Jesus from the cross.

They began by pulling out the nails from His feet, most likely using the hook-like tool Joseph, like any other busi-

342

nessman, carried on him to remove stones trapped in the hoofs of his donkey. Then, with the women supporting the body, the men stood on the cairn and nudged the crossbar from its socket and lowered Jesus to the ground. The nails from His wrists were prised loose. Owing to rigor mortis there was undoubtedly a problem in placing Jesus' hands to His side; equally likely, it was resolved by forcing them into position and securing them with perhaps the cincture of a robe. Still completely naked, Jesus was carried by the three men, the women following, to the tomb.

Befitting a man of Joseph's position, it occupied a prime position among the burial sites in the vicinity of Golgotha. Barely a hundred paces from the execution mount, it was sheltered from its sights by being placed in the lee of another hummock and further protected by a low stone wall inside which had been planted trees and shrubs and the ground cleared of stones and seeded. The tomb had been carved from the hummock and was reached by rolling a boulder, shaped like an outsize millstone, in its groove: this provided effective protection against animals yet made it easy to gain access. Because the sepulchre was unoccupied the stone had been left moved back, exposing the entrance.

Jesus was laid on the ground before the opening.

The women in the burial party took over. Led by Mary, His mother – custom dictated no less as she was His closest relative – water was fetched from a nearby well and the body bathed. John and Mark were too overcome to report the undoubted horror they must all have felt as the full extent of His injuries became clearly visible when the thick coating of dust and caked blood was removed.

Nicodemus returned laden with sacks of myrrh, resin and dried aloes; they were standard burial preparations. John was astonished at the sheer weight the elderly judge had managed to carry – *'about an hundred pound weight'*. The load was not only heavy, but expensive: it required a very wealthy man to afford such homage.

The sticky myrrh was worked into the skin, coating the wounds with a thick light-brown covering. Afterwards the

343

sweet-smelling powder of aloes was sprinkled on the body. The men then wrapped it in the shroud, starting with the feet and winding the linen tightly. When they had covered up to His shoulders they paused so that all those present could view Him for the last time. Then the head was covered.

The sun was barely visible above the city wall. When it sank below the horizon it would be the Great Sabbath of Passover. Already, in the windows of the tetrarch's palace the first lamps were lit and over Jerusalem itself a hush was settling. The men carried Jesus into the burial chamber, stooping to pass through the low entrance. A ledge had been cut in the rock on one side of the vault. Jesus was placed in the niche. Then they left the tomb, pushing the great round stone in its groove to close the sepulchre.

The news that Jesus' body had been buried and not consigned to the Hinnom Valley did nothing initially to dampen the satisfaction in the Temple over his death. But at some point priests reminded each other that Jesus had actually promised to return: early on, when the agents had first set out to trap Him, Jesus had rounded on them and said just as Jonas had spent three days and nights in the belly of a whale, '*so shall the Son of man be three days and three nights in the heart of the earth*'. While Caiaphas did not believe Jesus could possibly rise from the dead, he became steadily convinced that His Disciples could remove the body – and claim Jesus had fulfilled the greatest of all His prophecies.

Next morning, in spite of it being the Sabbath, the High Priest and the judges who had tried Jesus hurried to the Antonia Fortress. Ignoring the law of purity, they demanded to be taken to Pontius Pilate. He received them in his salon, surrounded by money chests. The High Priest explained that any belief in Jesus' resurrection would be an even greater threat than He had posed in life as the promised *Messiah*. The procurator finally agreed to provide a detachment of centurions to guard the tomb. Joseph Caiaphas took great care in positioning the soldiers so that

344

no one could possibly approach the sepulchre. The High Priest finally left the burial ground, no doubt satisfied, and certainly unaware that what he had done would help to provide the most striking proof of the divinity of Jesus. Between them the High Priest of the Jews and the imperial procurator of Rome had helped the world to enter shortly into a new relationship with God through the Resurrection of Jesus which would make Christianity possible. No death, since or before, would achieve more. His had, indeed, been an inevitable crucifixion.

Explanations

Be not curious in unnecessary matters;
for more things are shewed unto
thee than men understand.

— Ecclesiasticus 3:23

FIFTEEN

Attitudes

---

*In the beginning was
the Word.*
— John 1 : 1

Shortly after I had begun research into the book you have
just read I had the good fortune to meet that renowned
Anglican theologian, Dr John A. T. Robinson, Dean of
Trinity College, Cambridge. When he heard that I intended
setting out on a rigorous personal search for the answer as to
why Jesus had to die, he diffidently suggested I could do
worse than take as a starting point the question that had
preoccupied him throughout his ministry: can we trust the
New Testament?

We sat in his room in Trinity on a damp autumn day in
1975 discussing the daunting mass of conflicting material
about His death. Dr Robinson leaned forward and, in that
careful and considered way that none of his students will
surely ever forget, began to read me a passage from some
work in progress.

'The first thing to recognise is that no scholar comes to
his work without his presuppositions. He does not start
with a blank mind but with one formed by all the influences, beliefs and convictions that have made him what he

is. In this way he is just like the rest of us. Hence it is not surprising that in the arena of religious scholarship, as in every other field of knowledge, experts differ widely. This is bewildering to the layman. A common reaction is not to know whom to trust and therefore to trust no one.'

He put aside the manuscript and, passing a hand over that great dome of a brow, continued.

'What you must write is a book which is an invitation to trust. Don't get side-tracked by the confusion of voices. Just remember that you can trust the New Testament when you approach it as providing a portrait of the human face of God. But a portrait is *not* a photograph. A portrait is an interpretation of the sitter by the artist or, in the case of Jesus, by many artists. And also remember that any book about Jesus, while depending on historical inquiry, will in the end require faith; that, in a purely historical sense, none of the answers will be more than extremely probable. What you must do is write a book that is rooted in proper Bible criticism – and by that I mean using your critical faculties *on* the Bible. Then, what you write will be totally positive, confirming rather than denying. It will be a book which is an invitation to trust.'

I have tried to keep such wisdom to the fore. That is why I did not write yet another survey of the conflicting opinions, trying to balance constantly opposing views and telling the reader where there is general agreement and where it is absent. That would only have added to what Dr Robinson rightly called a confusion of voices which has created a situation where many feel there is no agreed truth to arrive at.

The more I read and the wider grew my circle of distinguished interviewees and correspondents, a number of clearly stated and opposing positions emerged about the life and death of Jesus. What forcibly struck me was that considerable scholars in other fields were quite prepared to play fast-and-loose with the truth when they entered the Christian arena. Controversial claims were often buttressed by extensive references and quotations. Purely as an exercise I decided to run the normal checks and balances on one such work. To my astonishment it was largely based on a book published some eighty years earlier and long discredited. But its claims had become subsequently respectable because a professor had attached *his* name, *his* university and *his* degrees of academic distinction to them. A historian achieved considerable fame with his thesis that Jesus probably never existed. What I found as remarkable as that claim was that his book carried an endorsement from a professor of modern history whom I knew from previous contacts to be the epitome of caution. Yet he had allowed his name to promote the idea that Jesus was a creation of the early Christians.

Nor was I encouraged by my contacts with the exponents of religious fundamentalism. Its very conservatism seemed to have grown more entrenched in the face of the wilder excesses of some radical scholars. The problem of so much fundamentalism was neatly explained in the course of a pleasurable summer afternoon in 1980 that I spent with that formidable Catholic scholar, Franz Koenig, cardinal-archbishop of Vienna. In his view the classic dilemma of fundamentalism was Jesus' reported prediction about the end of the world coming in His generation.

'If that is what He said, and if we are to take His words literally, then clearly Jesus was wrong. On the other hand, I would not need much convincing that His words, at least on this matter, have been adapted and interpreted by the early Church for a perfectly understandable purpose, the propagation of faith. Of course that means that what Jesus said or meant is not exactly reflected in our Bibles.'

The thought struck me, and has remained, that if someone as eminent in the Catholic Church as a cardinal could even suggest such a possibility, then it was more than ever important to try to sift the truth that lies beyond so much fundamental thinking.

Around a year or so into the research I came across a judgement by the Oxford classical historian Professor A. N. Sherwin-White, who in his study of the Roman law as applied to the New Testament, made the point that so many Bible scholars fail to realise what, by comparable standards, are the excellent sources at their disposal. Sherwin-White's argument not only held a profound scholarship, but seemed to depend on where was placed the emphasis for proof. For instance, if the question is put: is there any reason why Jesus should *not* have fed the five thousand, then very likely the answer would be: no, there is none. If the emphasis is reversed, for example, is there any reason why Jesus *should* have attacked the Temple money-changers, it is possible to argue plausibly that there is no good reason. Depending therefore on the approach, whether a matter is initially perceived as positive or negative, the end conclusion must be very different. It was a valuable lesson to remember in trying to make sense of His life.

I began to grasp others. Among them was to view with some caution what may properly be called the *Dissimilar Test*. This relies upon a challenge: is a particular point or statement one that can be traced to Judaism, Jesus' first contact with faith, or to the early Church, which was founded on His faith? If so, it can be attributed to Jesus. Useful though such a yardstick is, to make it the prime or even the only way to try to establish a truth about Him, is a mistake: it narrows the field and distorts any view of Jesus by virtually removing Him from His times.

To try to set Him *in situ* – to place Him against the sacred places, the walls and gates, the mountains and valleys, springs and rivers, rocks and caves – would have been that much harder without studying the lucid and scholarly accounts by the great French rabbi-scholars, Shelomo Izhaki and David Kimchi; their commentaries set down some 600 years ago remain to this day as essential reading. So does the work of the Jewish historian Josephus. Born in Jerusalem shortly after Jesus died, his various treatises on the Jews have survived, including the indispensable *Antiquities of the Jews* and *Wars of the Jews against the Romans*.

More recently there is the work of Zev Vilney, lecturer in military history and cartography at the Military Academy of

Israel. He has made what must probably be an unsurpassed study of the land that Jesus would have known, drawing from the Hebrew Bible, Talmudic and medieval literature. His work made it possible for me to understand the life and traditions of Galilee at the time of Jesus and to evaluate the cultural conflicts of the Jews and the political position of Jerusalem, the actual layout of the city and its focal point, the Temple, and many of the major events in Jesus' ministry, the sites where He healed and preached, where the raising of Lazarus took place and, of course, the place of His Passion, Gethsemane and Golgotha.

While indeed it must still be said that every precise word and action of Jesus is probably irrecoverable by even the most exacting analysis, and that all we can speak of with total confidence is the Christ of faith, there can be no denying that a study of Gospel parallels can be invaluable. There are a number of such studies available. I drew upon the version prepared by the American Standard Bible Committee; it offers not only a full account of the non-canonical parallels but also cites the main non-Christian manuscript support. These extant sources were a further aid in establishing the probability of something Jesus said or did.

Those sources included the *Gospel of the Ebionites*, written around the middle of the second century, or perhaps slightly after, by the Ebionites, Jewish-Christians who believed that Jesus so fulfilled the Jewish law that God chose Him to be the Messiah; the *Gospel According to the Hebrews*, known as the 'Jewish Gospel', probably written around AD 120 in Egypt; the *Gospel According to the Egyptians*, written in Greek around AD 130–40 and circulated among Gentile-Christians in Egypt and not regarded as heretical at first in spite of its strong ascetic quality; the *Gospel of Peter*, written probably in Syria around AD 130; *Acts of Philip*, a fourth-century Gnostic work; the *Gospel of Thomas*, probably written around AD 140 and discovered in 1945 near the village of Nag Hammadi on the Upper Nile – written in Sahidic Coptic it is a collection of the sayings of Jesus, many showing a strong Gnostic influence.

The material led me down some extraordinary byways, not least the search for an answer to a question that has begun to intrigue many scholars: was Judas Iscariot the first and greatest villain of Christianity or has history misjudged Jesus' treasurer? In the popular mind he remains an infamous betrayer driven to a remorseful suicide. However, I encountered a growing body of respectable opinion that questioned whether the Apostle Matthew was right to say: 'It had been good for that man if he had not been born.'

In the spring of 1986 I travelled once more to Israel, this time to speak, among others, to Dr Robert Fleming. He is a Bible scholar, a social scientist who argues that any portrait of Judas as a mere reprobate is incomplete. Fleming is the director of the Tantur Ecumenical Institute, built beside the road between Bethlehem and Jerusalem. Students come from all over the world to be exposed to Fleming's ideas. Shortly before I arrived he had sent a ripple through conservative religious circles with his claim that Jesus was most likely older than His traditional thirty-three years. Fleming based his findings on a lengthy study of Syrian scripts dating from a census held in Judaea in 12 BC – and in a closely argued case concluded that was the year Jesus was born, making Him forty-two years old when He went to the Cross, an elderly man in those times.

'He was probably not entirely a fit man. In human terms Jesus could have been over his physical peak. There are no theological implications in revising His age. But it does help to explain why Jesus died so quickly.'

Such claims have placed Fleming among the *wunderkinder* of biblical revisionists. He is very much in the mould of a new kind of religious scholar, taking his students through the Wilderness, lecturing as he goes; inviting them to sit down and partake in what he insists is a faithful reproduction of the Last Supper in a replica of the original Upper Room. The Tantur Institute is a remarkably active and productive place in which a number of disciplines – theology, history and active ministry – co-exist under one roof. Some of Fleming's conclusions, such as the layout of the

354

original Upper Room, along with the social customs of Jesus' time, have found a place in this book – as indeed has Fleming's argument that Judas was not merely a money-grabber, motivated purely by the shallowest of motives.

Fleming's point is that Jesus would never have called Judas in the first place and given him such an important post as treasurer if Judas had been totally evil. In Fleming's portrait, Judas emerges as the outsider in a group of clannish Galilean-born Apostles – a man alone, driven in the end to betray Jesus because Judas actually thought that was the only way to bring about the Kingdom.

In Jerusalem, not far from Christ's final walk to Golgotha, I found support for Fleming's views from one of the most astute legal minds in Israel. Haim Cohn is a judge of the Supreme Court of Israel who has spent a number of years studying the popular Christian concept of Judas. The judge is the author of an influential legal study of the trial of Jesus – a work which he cheerfully admitted had attracted its share of criticism in Christian circles. I found it a persuasive and impeccably argued account – including his assessment of Judas.

'The whole Gospel portrait of Judas is so unlikely, so incongruous that it merits no credence. If Judas wanted to betray Jesus all he had to do was to denounce Him to the Romans as a rebel – and he would be certain of swift action. My own conclusion is that the prevailing portrait of Judas was included in the Gospels for purely theological reasons – a reminder that a Jew set in motion the death of Jesus.'

Mr Justice Cohn was a source of valuable guidance on the law and procedures – both Roman and Jewish – which operated at the time of Jesus, providing penetrating insights into the political and religious motivations of those involved in mounting and conducting the most famous law case in history. Through him it was possible to get a strong sense of the atmosphere in Annas' palace and the Antonia Fortress and, of course, obtaining that perspective of Judas.

The feeling that the treasurer may have been badly

misjudged was echoed by the Rev. Dr John Gosling, a noted Anglican theologian and adviser on Continuing Ministerial Education to the Diocese of Salisbury, England. He expressed the view that Judas' behaviour could be seen as that of a man making a final desperate attempt to implement the Kingdom by bringing Jesus into confrontation with the Roman and Jewish authorities. Dr Gosling argued that Judas might well have believed that in such a confrontation Jesus would have emerged victorious. It was a possibility that I felt had to be reflected in my own assessment of Judas.

What distinguished Judas from the other Apostles is that one act of final betrayal. Yet nowhere in the New Testament is a motivation for doing so ascribed to the treasurer. Both Jewish and Christian scholars continually reminded me that the Evangelical Gospels, by themselves, do not allow, or indeed are not meant to provide, a complete assessment of events. Extant to their testimony is a literature often forgotten or overlooked by Christians. The Vatican libraries alone have over 100,000 such volumes, many of them rarely consulted from one century to the next. Undoubtedly some of the most interesting include Jewish and pagan writing.

It was Duncan M. Derrett, Professor of Oriental Law at the University of London, who reminded me of the importance of that material. During my research he maintained a flow of challenging data. From it emerged the full horror of Roman and Jewish scourging and the precise manner of crucifixion. He also proved to be a brilliant scene-setter for the pre-trial atmosphere in the Sanhedrin, the relationship between Sadducees and Pharisees, the inter-tension between the Roman and Jewish administrations, including some highly useful glimpses of Herod Antipas. Above all, this distinguished lawyer provided a compelling assessment of why Jesus had to die.

'His doctrines were incomprehensible except in flashes to his contemporaries. Jesus was put to death by strangers for passing on a brand of wisdom which if it had been popular at the time would have stripped the powers that were of their authority and profits.'

It was a logical research step from Professor Derrett to those Jewish scholars who see Jesus as a rallying figure for the Zealots. At the forefront is Hyam Maccoby. He has gone further than any revisionist with his claim that Jesus was at the actual centre of the revolutionary movement in Judaea. It is not always easy to follow, let alone accept, Maccoby's thesis. But his Jewish sources deserve to be studied by any Christian. Through Maccoby I spent several profitable months reading Jewish history, including a remarkable document by Travers A. Herford dealing with the Pharisees; published in 1924 as a monograph, it remains unequalled. Some of the great names of Jewish Biblical scholarship – Israel Abrahams, Moses Aberbach and Herman L. Strack – became as familiar to me as their Christian counterparts. I am particularly indebted to Abrahams's *Studies in Pharisaism and the Gospels*, Aberbach's magnificent account of *The Roman–Jewish War (66–70 A.D.)* and Strack's *Introduction to the Talmud and Midrash*. Through them I began to see it was possible to give flesh and blood to the behaviour of Caiaphas and Herod Antipas.

Among my contemporary guides were Ze'ev Falk, Professor of Family Law, and R. J. Werblowsky, Professor of Comparative Religion. Both are on the faculty of the Hebrew University in Jerusalem, whose libraries are a treasure trove that allows for a fuller and, hopefully, truer record of Jesus to emerge. These two gifted men guided me to the tractates; a full list appears at the end of the bibliography.

Jewish scholars argue that many Christian theologians have developed an attitude which virtually ensures they live in what Professor Werblowsky called 'frozen Christology in which Jesus the man has no place. This attitude makes His trial that much harder to explain.'

Modern Jewish scholarship has also extrapolated from the writings of Suetonius, Plutarch, Cicero, Strabo and Virgil a clearer picture of Herod Antipas and his background. In this wealth of writing I encountered the first important clues about Pilate and Claudia Procula. The

357

Roman administration in Judaea came vividly to life in Suetonius' account *Tiberius* (XXX.11.2); Cicero's *In Verrem II* (12 and 11.2); Tacitus' *Histories* (IV.74.1); and Emil Schurer's masterful *The Jewish People in the Time of Jesus Christ*, translated into English in 1885 and still an indispensable source about Pilate and his wife and their life-style in Judaea.

Inevitably, the research trail led to Professor S. G. F. Brandon. His scholarship – and I must add in my case his encouragement – made it not only possible for me to trace more easily the public career of Jesus from His baptism by John, but also to accept that, though theologically necessary and politically convenient, a number of Christian versions of the trial of Jesus are misrepresentations of what actually happened. Brandon's work in this area of historical analysis is best seen in his *The Trial of Jesus of Nazareth*.

Brandon was the first to admit that there are theologians, philosophers and interpreters of the great legends and shibboleths of His life who want to crack the tough kernel of Jesus' very starkness and to grind to dust the acceptable core of His life. They are the ones who would say, in answer to Dr Robinson's question 'Can we trust the New Testament?' that, no, we cannot because the Gospels are only a record of faith.

One of the most sobering tasks I had to pursue was the work of those who are intent on stripping Jesus of anything which places Him beyond all mortals. There are, for instance, those who argue that Christ had actually married Mary Magdalene at Cana. There is, like so much in their revisionist world, a certain spurious plausibility to the claim: the incontestable fact remains that there is not a word in the New Testament to show that Jesus voluntarily renounced marriage. Therefore, runs the argument, why should Jesus' marital position be different from any other devout Jew of His time; that, after all, God's first commandment in the Torah is '*be fruitful and multiply*'. Indeed, the Old Testament, upon which Jesus had been nurtured, accentuated the importance of marriage – to the point where a Talmudic commentary of His days argued that failure to wed was a crime akin to murder; that from Genesis onwards it was written that '*it is not good that man should be alone*'; '*any man who has no wife is no proper man*'; '*he who is not married is, as it were, guilty of bloodshed; he caused the image of God to be diminished and the divine presence to be withdrawn from Israel*'.

Again, the Jesus-was-married school point out that the Apostle Luke confirmed that Jesus, on the threshold of manhood, was still an obedient son of Joseph and that within the prevailing Jewish culture betrothals were usually arranged by fathers. Joseph had made such arrangements, as the Book of Corinthians indicated, for the brothers of Jesus. Is it not possible, runs the argument, that Jesus shared the same Jewish belief in marriage as a sacred duty for Himself as well as others? If not wed to Mary Magdalene, could not His wife have died during those years before His public life began? Is it not significant that, when questioned about marriage, Christ endorsed the view in Genesis – '*for this cause shall a man leave his father and mother, and shall cleave to his wife and the twain shall be one flesh*' – instead of offering a new teaching? Is it really in the end, conclude the insidious persuaders, fantastic to accept that Jesus had been wed and widowed? There is a widespread tendency to accept in the arena of Christianity judgements and constructions that elsewhere would be rejected as utter fabrication.

Yet there are those who even argue that the climax of Holy Week, Good Friday, is really an elaborate sham: that Jesus arranged His own death; that the Romans and the Temple authorities connived in the plot; that the centurion had not pierced His side; that Joseph of Arimathea, another of the plotters, with the help of the women in His life, cut Him down – still alive – from the Cross at dusk and placed Him in the tomb; that later, under cover of darkness, He was taken away, His wounds tended, and that He lived for a further forty days before finally succumbing.

I discovered that a demented intellectualism – last seen

359

over a century ago in Europe – seems to be on the loose. The Vatican regularly receives solutions to the birth and life of Jesus. He was the product of an affair between Mary and a handsome Arab prince. She had been seduced by Joseph of Arimathea, which would explain his role after the Crucifixion. Joseph was Mary's uncle; their son the offspring of an incestuous union. There are claims, often supported by detailed genealogical charts, that Jesus had been a Tibetan, a Hindu, a Mongolian or a Mede. Some even insist he came from darkest Africa and was a Bushman. Zoologists and biologists write that the Virgin Birth is a scientific impossibility: parthenogenesis, as they prefer to rationalise it, is only seen in aphids and crustaceans.

If I was asked to put a name and date to when this revisionist onslaught began, I would answer without hesitation, Ernest Renan, 1862. That was the year the French theologian published his *Life of Jesus*; a volume that became not only one of the greatest religious bestsellers of the nineteenth century, but the springboard from which, in the next hundred years, others would follow with their arguments that references to angels announcing His birth and accounts of His miraculous curing of the sick are no more than fables; that events which bear out the Old Testament predictions, such as Jesus being born in Bethlehem, entering Jerusalem on a donkey, and His betrayal, should be rejected as wishful thinking, purely designed to bolster the myth that His life had been foretold. These statements, coolly and dispassionately argued, have opened a floodgate which still threatens to engulf traditional belief, sweeping away the Jesus of convention.

There are supposedly Christian scholars who account for Jesus' periodic bouts of fasting as proof He had a pathological fear of food, making Him the prototype for male anorexia. Others argue He is the original model for the Oedipus Complex, actually taking his mother to Heaven so they could be together eternally. Some claim that while in her womb He had experienced neurophysical trauma brought about by Mary having to explain to Joseph how she

360

had become pregnant. Jesus is accused of suffering from dromomania, tuberculosis and theomania, the sadly misguided belief He actually was God.

Emerging from this numbing morass of speculation, I began to see that my investigations must focus upon Jesus the Jew; that any assessment must be made within the framework of the faith Christ was born into and grew up with. Jesus had been raised in a circumambient world, already two thousand years old when He arrived, one where the Jewish identity was clear-cut and sharply divided from paganism. Jesus had existed, like any Jew, in a compartmented historicism. He and all those around Him were regarded by their fellow Jews as no more than part of a particular epoch, each charged for the moment as sole architects of Jewish destiny. For His fellow Jews that had been the world He, like them, had been expected to live in and, when their time came, to die from. It was one in which there was no possible Resurrection, and no possible hope of Eternal Life beyond the grave.

One happening – His trial – had led to all that changing. In the four Gospels the religious significance of that event is dramatically presented as an integral part in the foundation of Christianity. But the Gospels are narratives not theological treatises. Professor Brandon had argued that any evaluation of such a unique happening required judgement and criteria wholly different from those used in more conventional historical assessments of trials where religious issues had also been involved: the trial of Socrates, accused and condemned for introducing strange gods and corrupting the Athenian youth of 399 BC; the trial of Mani, the founder of Manicheism, a religion of vast influence in the second century AD; the trial of Joan of Arc in 1431, sentenced to be burnt at the stake for her claim that God had entrusted her with a special mission. While ample independent testimony existed in those cases, the Gospels offered the only Christian accounts of His trial and death.

But there is, as Brandon pointed out to me, that vast other literature of Christian apocrypha and non-Christian writings.

I read that, almost a full hundred years after His death, the first description of Jesus was discovered. It had been set down by a Roman officer called Lentulus stationed in Caesarea in the year AD 30. 'Nut-brown hair smooth down to the ears and from the ears downwards formed soft curls and flowed to the shoulders in luxuriant locks with a parting in the centre of the head after the fashion of the Nazarenes; a smooth clean brow and reddish face without spots or wrinkles; nose and mouth flawless; a full luxuriant beard parted in the middle. Eyes with an unusually varied capacity for expression.'

Two hundred years after Lentulus, another Roman, Origen, represented Jesus as a short, ungraceful figure with a lame right leg, a limp. A century later Epiphanius had created a towering Jesus, well over six feet tall, with a burnished complexion, aquiline nose, coal-black eyes and reddish hair. From then on it became open season for the length of His hair, the colour of His eyes, the shape of His lips and the prominence of His cheekbones. His would become the original facial melting pot: from it would come all the others: Face Resolute; Face Calm; Face Compelling; Face Compassionate and Face Tortured – all to be painted, sculpted and carved. There would be scholars who would insist it was deliberate that He had no discernible features and was virtually without biography; that He was meant to remain a figure physically and emotionally beyond human description – to ensure that the importance of His message would not be diminished by irrelevant detail.

Yet any investigation of the accounts of His trial can only end in one certain conclusion, one that Professor Brandon insisted was 'pregnant with suggestion concerning the real situation. The conclusion must be that all four Evangelists were horrified not only by the scandal of the Roman cross, but also that His chief opponents were the Jewish religious leaders. It was that handful of Jews who repudiated His claims to possess special authority, even going to the extent of ascribing his miraculous powers to daemonic forces. Thus, in His eyes, they also became the main enemy.'

362

Brandon was among those who continually urged I must pursue the apocryphal literature. While much of this material was written down probably between a hundred and three hundred years after the actual death of Jesus and therefore cannot be considered to be, in terms of historical documentation, any more perfect than the Gospels, the material does contain considerable data about Jesus that the Evangelical accounts either only allude to or ignore.

For instance, in the Prologue to the *Gospel of Nicodemus* – the Pharisee judge twice mentioned by John as a friend of Jesus (3:1 and 19:39) – there is a graphic account of one of the pre-trial Sanhedrin debates, with Caiaphas, Annas and Gamaliel clearly identified. Mr Justice Cohn told me he was under no illusion that this Gospel must have been written to supplement the canonical accounts, though the judge is sceptical of some of the claims made in the name of Nicodemus: he disputes, for instance, whether Pilate showed the faintest interest in Jesus' birth.

Through *The First Gospel of the Infancy of Jesus Christ*, translated in 1697 from Syriac, yet largely ignored because it had been part of Gnostic belief since the second century, a much clearer picture emerges of Christ's childhood and adulthood – the so-called 'unknown years'. There are details in this gospel of Jesus disputing with his schoolteacher, and later Christ performing His first miracle, lengthening a plank of wood that Joseph had cut too short; there, too, is the account of Jesus learning the craft of a dyer, which is why even today Iranian dyers honour Him as their patron. While it is clear there will always be a great divergence of opinion as to the place and importance of this and other writings, such as the *Epistle of Polycarp to the Philippians*, the *Epistle of Ignatius to the Magnesians* and an earlier one to the Ephesians, and the writings of Barnabas, a companion and fellow-preacher with Paul the Apostle, they do provide detail about rites and ceremonies Jesus would have participated in.

The sceptics, of course, distrust all such sources. Yet where it is possible to check them against non-Christian data or the contemporary background of Roman and Jewish society it is seen that the material *is* rooted in fidelity to fact. In his *New Testament Theology*, Jeremias argues that it is the 'inauthenticity and not the authenticity that must be demonstrated'. Dr Robinson, who set me off all those years ago on my investigation, went further.

'A Christian has nothing to fear in the truth. For to him the truth *is* Christ. It is large – larger than the world – and shall prevail. It is also a living and a growing reality. And therefore he is free, or should be free, to follow the truth wherever it leads.'

That seemed to me to be a very worthwhile leitmotif in pursuing my research.

The historical background came into that much sharper focus by personal research. It is one thing to read about Mary Magdalene; quite another to come across her tomb in a field where Magdala once stood; to stand in the synagogue where Jesus began His ministry in Capernaum; to follow the shore of Galilee as He once did; to walk the path where He was betrayed on the Mount of Olives; to retrace His steps through Jerusalem; to hear sounds and see sights that have not changed greatly from the time of Jesus.

There are many ways to see His land but probably the best is by air – in my case from the open door of an Israeli helicopter gunship rushing in from the sea south of Haifa to pass over a stretch of long sandy coast where Joshua, at the end of the Exodus, had led his people. They had found little peace as, from the sea, came the Philistines, pirates and booty-hunters, rapacious adventurers who spearheaded the Aryan invasion of this land in the twelfth century before Christ. They had been finally overcome by the Israelites. Then, some four hundred years before Rome was founded, and its dynasty of emperors conceived, another ruler, Pharaoh Rameses III had claimed all this land. Once more, the sons of Israel, among them the mighty Samson and the wise kings, Saul and David, rallied their people just as Abraham, Jacob and Joseph had done under earlier tyrannies – driving the enemy beyond the Land of Edom, a virtual wilderness to which the red-haired Esau had retreated to conquer his anger after Jacob had taken away his birthright. Only the name of Edom has been changed. Nor has the mountain fastness of the ancient Kingdom of Moab altered. Still visible is the peak from which Moses, close to death, had looked on the Promised Land he would never reach. There, too, is the craggy hill called Machaerus upon which Herod the Great had built a massive stronghold, one of many he erected across the land to subdue the people to the will of Rome. On that same hill, in that same castle, the King's son, the malevolent Herod Antipas, watched while his wanton step-daughter, Salome, danced and had rewarded her with the head of John the Baptist. The river in the middle distance: that was perhaps where Jacob had wrestled throughout an entire night with an angel. And beside the river, that winding track: it had been the road which had led from Alexandria to Damascus, a journey of months, a caravan route whose stopping places included Nazareth.

Tens of thousands of years before Christ had walked this ground nature had folded in on itself, crushing the limestone and other rock strata into new formations, while at the same time creating two fissures so deep that the Ancients believed they were the ante-rooms to Hell. Between these gigantic openings the earth collapsed, an inversion that over aeons gave it distinctive natural regions: Samaria, Galilee, Idumaea and Judaea, all occupied by the legions of Pompey. Rome, for easier administration, called it Judaea; a country they reckoned to be from north to south no more in length than a hundred and sixty Roman miles, about the distance from Florence to Rome, and at its greatest width to be eighty-seven miles, less than three days' march for a legion even over the roughest of ground.

Running the length of the country is a plateau ridge along which Jesus must have walked many times, the ground at the southern end still pitted with hollows of red silt, the residue from its creation: this is the Wilderness, a forbidding tawny-coloured vista, its shading suggesting the hide of a lion. It had been the first citadel of faith, where

Abraham had settled, where great Jewish kings had later ruled, where the true God was acclaimed – and which would be forever remembered as the scene of Christ's confrontation with Satan.

In the distance a glimpse of Jerusalem, its Herodian and Crusader walls clearly discernible and the gold dome of the Mosque of Omar offering a modest substitute for the Temple. The shimmering heat made the sun-baked limestone buildings appear dun-coloured. Abruptly, below was the ancient plain where Barak, another of Israel's great warriors, responding to the plea of the prophetess Deborah, had defeated Sisera and his heathen army. But the strict rabbis of Jerusalem had subsequently come to suspect the people of this area of not obeying Scriptural law with enough devotion.

This plain had all been part of the original Land of Canaan, a name chosen long before it was called the Holy Land or Palestine, let alone Israel. Canaan: from the Phoenician, *kinella*, the red-purple dye that was an important commodity for trading in the decisive time when the Israelites finally won this ground, and which, after their victory, they also named the Promised Land, a permanent reminder for them of the Covenant between Abraham and Yahweh, confirming them as His Chosen People and their right to live here in peace.

Then: the only true river in the country, mentioned more than two hundred times in Holy Scripture and about whose banks the Psalmist had sung, the Jordan. From its source in the north, it passes through wooded country once the home of the most industrious of all the tribes of Israel, the tribe of Dan. A few miles beyond, at one of the massive rock outfaces, Jesus had paused, and said to His devoted Simon: 'Thou art Peter, and it is upon this rock that I will build my Church.'

Beyond, the Sea of Galilee, no doubt even more breathtaking in the time of Jesus, when the trees had been more plentiful and a score, or more, white-walled villages and towns had rimmed the lake's harp-like shape.

In Christ's time the land to the south was to be avoided, an area of dark and deep valleys and canyons pock-marked with caves. In one such cavern David had bided his time to challenge and defeat Goliath near the Dead Sea. The lake is close to the Ghor, a fearful gash on the face of the planet, running two thousand further miles beyond this point. On ground near this rift had stood the cities of Sodom and Gomorrah. And somewhere nearby had stood a village where Judas Iscariot was born and from which he had made his way to that most pleasant of all the regions, Galilee. There he had met Jesus and through his actions remained inexorably bound to Him.

They both may well have looked like any of the men who today worship before the last fragment of the Temple of Jerusalem – that towering edifice of stones Christians call the Wailing Wall, where devout Jews stand and pray, rocking back and forth, remembering Moses and the miraculous crossing of the Red Sea and the manna from Heaven which had kept the Israelites alive in the desert and how, when they were safely delivered, God had told them that they alone could henceforth know Him as *Yahweh*, 'He who is'.

In Nazareth, the women's faces are mostly veiled, only the dark and darting eyes indicating awareness as they cross the main square – where in His day the local rabbis had pronounced punishments for infringements of the Law not serious enough to be referred to the Temple in Jerusalem. Mary, His Mother, had almost certainly come this way, bare-footed, perhaps to purchase new wicks for oil lamps or replacement straw mats which served as both seats and mattresses, spread over a floor of compacted earth. And, somewhere here, perhaps near the only fountain in Nazareth, and now dedicated to her – *ain sitti Miryam* – she had encountered the Angel Gabriel, whose revelation had left her deeply perturbed. I have often wondered whether the women moving slowly across the square, burdened with panniers and pitchers, would have reacted any differently. And had the Madonna looked like any of them?

Central to that question is the one that Dr Robinson put to me: can we trust the New Testament?

I believe we can not only trust it, but by also going back to all the other discarded literature our understanding and perception of why Jesus had to die will become clearer.

The bibliography which follows shows the road I travelled. My reading will almost certainly not be quite the same preference as anyone else's. I may have chosen books which are more radical over some matters and more conservative on others. But, then, there is nothing fixed or final in any account of His life. Yet, all the years of research have only strengthened my trust in the primary documents of the Christian faith – *all* of them. The undoubted scholarship of many of the authors in my bibliography did not give me faith – they only encouraged me that it had not been misplaced. In the end a Christian goes through life trusting. This book is an invitation to do so.

CHRONOLOGY

The most important happenings in the background and life of Jesus along with parallel events in general history. Compiled with the help of members of the faculty of the Hebrew University, Jerusalem; the Reubeni Foundation, Jerusalem; the Jerusalem Center for Biblical Studies and Research; the Archivio Segreto at the Vatican.

Date BC	Israel	Historical Parallel
1900 Circa	Abraham proclaimed new religion, so strict God must never be invoked by His name, Yahweh.	Hammurabi, King of Babylon, built new temple to moon god called Sin. Egypt's tenth pharaonic dynasty fell to Hyskos armies. Egyptian godhead contracted from nine to three – Ra, Holus and Osiris – but national faith still based on trinity concept of father, mother and son.
1700 Circa	Sodom and Gomorrah destroyed. Joseph died in Egypt.	Egypt liberated from Hyskos occupation. Pharaoh Akhnaton banned worship of all deities except Aton, the sun-god.

Date	Israel	Historical Parallel
1500	Jerusalem, already 1,000 years old, established as one of the great walled cities of the world, owing to fortification techniques of its Canaanite builders.	Hinduism emerged in India as major religion after centuries of developing from sacrificial cults.
1300 Circa	Moses, adopted son of Queen of Egypt and former viceroy of Nubia, finally persuaded Pharaoh Mernepath to 'let my people go'. The Exodus. Moses descended from Mount Sinai with Ten Commandments.	Assyria established itself as third-ranking power in world.
1200 Circa	Moses died after leading his people for forty years through Wilderness.	Philistines invaded Gaza, Ashdod and Sidon. The Trojan War began.
1180	Joshua led Israelites into Land of Canaan. Won major battle, defeating combined forces of five pagan kings.	Fall of Troy. Hector, brother of Paris, killed in single combat with Achilles.
1140	Famine in Canaan. Bethlehem among worst hit of cities. Samuel became leader of all twelve tribes.	Tomb of Rameses II looted near Cairo. The influence of Egypt as ranking power on wane.

Date	Israel	Historical Parallel
1130	Israelites began new series of wars against Philistines and Midionites. Gideon refused to accept kingship over tribes. Samson latest Jewish folk hero.	New Assyrian legal code established. Many tenets bore close resemblance to Torah.
1026	Saul became Israel's first king, crowned in small town of Silgal in eastern Benjamin. Israelites faced annihilation by Philistines. David-ben-Yishnai of Bethlehem slayed Goliath in War of Attrition.	Phoenician traders established business links with Europe.
1007	Saul dead. David crowned. Foundations laid for sacred belief that expected Messiah will only come from Royal House of David.	Brahmanism gained ground in India. Babylonia gripped by tribal warfare.
990	David drove Philistines out of Promised Land. The Holy Ark of the Covenant brought for first time into Jerusalem. The king's psalms written down.	Phoenician script introduced into Greece.

Date	Israel	Historical Parallel
958	Solomon king of Israel. First Temple dedicated. Queen of Sheba visited Jerusalem.	Hiriam, king of Tyre.
933	The Promised Land divided into two nations, Israel and Judah. Jerusalem remained loyal to dynasty of David.	Baalazar, king of Tyre. Greece completed domination of Aegean Sea.
900/800	The prophets: Amos, Hosea, Isaiah.	Greek migration and expansion. Shalmanaser III launched new period of Syrian aggression.
753	First Supreme High Court, Sanhedrin, established in Jerusalem; composed of priests, Levites and important laymen. High Priest appointed president. Court's power included trying cases of blasphemy and sedition.	Rome founded.
722	Northern Kingdom of Israel fell to Assyria. Judah remained intact, but tens of thousands gathered in Temple to mourn exile of 150,000 Jews from north.	Zoaraster in Persia.

Date	Israel	Historical Parallel
700/600	The prophets: Micah, Josiah.	Anarchy in Athens as Solon's constitutional reforms fail. Babylon invaded Egypt.
588	The prophet Jeremiah arrested in Jerusalem on charge of treason.	Dorian ban on all the works of Homer. Buddhism flourished in India.
586	Nebuchadnezzar captured Jerusalem. First Temple destroyed. Jews exiled to Babylon.	Delphi, home of the Oracle of Apollo, chosen as model for Pythian Olympiads.
538	Jews returned to homeland.	Babylon fell to Cyrus.
448	Rebuilding of Temple began. First Knesset opened in Jerusalem. The nation's leaders – 120 in number – pledged new nation would obey Torah: intermarriage forbidden; work on Sabbath banned; Temple offerings reinstituted.	Thirty-year-old peace pact between Athens-Sparta collapsed. Confucianism and Taoism continue to dominate Chinese spiritual thinking.
399	Ezra completed compilation of the Bible.	Death of Socrates. Sparta overrun. Alexander the Great established Greek superiority in Mediterranean basin.

Date	Israel	Historical Parallel
334	Greek forces occupied Judaea, Samaria and Galilee. Jews resisted introduction of Greek as equal language to Hebrew.	Rome established the social pyramid dominated by its small, warring, shifting ruling class, highly educated and motivated. Greek and Oriental scientists encouraged to come and share their knowledge.
332	Temple expanded in Jerusalem.	Alexander dead. Greek empire divided up, and weakened by, his generals.
300/200	The Ptolemies occupy Israel before being ousted by the Seleucids.	First Punic War (264–241) claimed annexations for Roman Empire. End of Second Punic War (218–201) saw large areas of Spain under Roman control.
165	Judas Maccabee liberated Jerusalem from Syrian occupation.	Antiochus IV, Tyrant of Syria, dead. Decline of Carthage. Fall of Macedonia. Unprecedented corruption revealed among Roman senators and consuls.
134	Yocham Hyracanus appointed High Priest of Temple and Sanhedrin. Deep-	Greece a Roman province. Third Punic War saw destruction of Carthage.

Date	Israel	Historical Parallel
	seated differences surfaced between rival parties of Sadducees and Pharisees over matters of faith and tradition. Violent demonstrations in Jerusalem.	
76	Queen Salome Alexandra first woman to rule nation. Sadducee influence in decline. The sect's leader, Diogenes, sentenced to death by Sanhedrin.	China added to her empire by occupying Korea. King Nicomedes III bequeathed his entire kingdom to Rome. Pompey defeated Mithridates.
63	Pompey entered Jerusalem. Temple desecrated.	Sixteen-year-old Roman–Parthian peace treaty broken by surprise Roman attack. Cicero Rome's leading lawyer. The Spice Route from East and trading links with China flourished.
44	Herod, the son of Antipater the Edomite, establishing reputation as leader Rome favoured to rule its newly named Judaea province.	Julius Caesar murdered on Ides of March.
40	Hasmonean King Antigonius rejected Herod ultimatum to	Treaty of Brindisi gave Octavian crucial hold in battle for

Date	Israel	Historical Parallel
	abdicate. Herodian forces, supported by three Roman legions, occupy Galilee and lay siege to Jerusalem.	control of Roman Empire.
37/27	Herod became King of all Judaea. Ordered Second Temple to be built. Began unprecedented rule of terror.	Elected divine emperor, Octavian changed his name to Augustus, one with ancient significance in pagan religion.
20	Herod Antipas born – the son of his father's fifth wife, the Samaritan, Malthace.	Augustus appointed unfailingly competent Agrippa as virtual co-regent and the degenerate Maecebas to watch over the army and empire's finances.
12	Census in Judaea and Galilee as part of empire-wide check by Rome for tax-evaders. JESUS BORN (?)	Augustus married off his witty, licentious daughter, Julia, for third time – to his step-son, Tiberius.
	Celestial phenomenon to be known as Halley's Comet, and 'Star of Bethlehem', seen from August to October. The Holy Child family fled into Egypt.	Roman expansion placed its forces on River Elbe, but empire's resources dangerously over-stretched. Augustus faced rebellion in Pannonia and had to abandon plan to conquer Bohemia.

Date	Israel	Historical Parallel
8	Herod Antipas, like all sons of Herod the Great, sent to Rome to complete education and gain knowledge of imperial policies, essential grooming as a potential successor to his father's throne.	Roman forces strengthened in Gaul in preparation for cross-Channel invasion of Britannia.
5	Herod Antipas returned home, Romanised, to be with his dying father.	Augustus claimed Armenia conquered, but his puppet government unable to control population.
4	Herod the Great dead. His kingdom divided between three sons. Herod Antipas made Tetrarch of Galilee. Continued father's tyrannical rule. The Holy Family return from Egypt to live in Nazareth.	Egypt main corn provider for Roman empire. Rioting in Spain during celebrations to mark another year of its incorporation into empire.

The Onset of the Christian Era

AD		
0	Jesus challenged the doctors of law at the Temple.	Herod Antipas' brother, Archelaus, deposed. Rome appointed first procurator to Judaea, Copenius.
6	Jesus among the actors at Sepphoris.	Annas appointed High Priest.

Date	Israel	Historical Parallel
14	Jesus in Nazareth, eldest son of growing family of brothers and sisters.	Augustus dead. Accession of Tiberius.
26	Joseph of Nazareth dead.	Pontius Pilate appointed procurator.
27	Jesus' cousin, John the Baptist, began to baptise on banks of River Jordan in autumn.	Rome reported to have record number of slaves, estimated as from one quarter to one third of entire population.
28	March: Jesus is baptised. Attends Cana wedding. In Capernaum.	Vast majority of Roman empire, including many of the most highly educated, reaffirm belief in astrology.
	April: In Jerusalem for Passover.	
	May: In Judaea. John the Baptist arrested.	
	June: Jesus in Galilee.	
	October: Returned to Jerusalem for Feast of Tabernacles. Then resumed His ministry in Galilee.	
29	April: John the Baptist beheaded. Jesus went from Jerusalem to Phoenicia and Iturea and back to Galilee.	Pilate informed Tiberius of execution. The emperor reminded his subjects of power of pagan

Date	Israel	Historical Parallel
October:	Went to Jerusalem for Feast of Tabernacles.	'saviour' deities who guaranteed life hereafter. Cults based upon magic rituals and sacramental banquets to purge human unworthiness flourished throughout empire.
Nov:	Preached in Peraea before returning to Jerusalem for Feast of Dedication.	
30		
Feb:	Jesus ministered in area adjoining northern shores of Dead Sea.	
March:	In Ephraim.	
April:	Arrived in Bethany. Entered Jerusalem. Last Supper. Captured, tried, scourged and crucified upon the bare mound of Golgotha. Finally succumbed some time late in the afternoon – fifteenth day of Nisan (later known as Good Friday, 7 April in the year 30 of Our Lord).	
		In the daily life of Tiberius and his subjects the most important event in the history of the world passed by all accounts unnoticed.

SELECT BIBLIOGRAPHY

Adam, K. *The Son of God*. New York: Sheed & Ward, 1934.

Akavia, A. A. *Calendar for Good Years: Comparative Calendar of All Chronological Tables from the Creation until the End of the Sixth Millennium*. Jerusalem: Mossad Harav Kook, 1975.

Albright, W. F. *The Archaeology of Palestine*. London: Penguin Books, 1956.

Allegro, J. *The Dead Sea Scrolls*. London: Penguin Books, 1956.

———— *The Sacred Mushroom and the Cross*. London: Hodder & Stoughton, 1970.

Allen, Richard Hinckley. *Star Names: Their Lore and Meaning*. New York: Dover Publications, 1963.

Amos, S. *The History and Principles of the Civil Law of Rome*. London: Kegan Paul, 1883.

Aron, R. *The Jewish Jesus*. New York: Orbis Books, 1971.

Barclay, William. *The Mind of Jesus*. London: SCM Press, 1960.

———— *Crucified and Crowned*. London: SCM Press, 1961.

———— *Jesus as They Saw Him*. London: SCM Press, 1962.

———— *The Master's Men*. London: SCM Press, 1970.

Bell, H. I., and Skeat, T. C. *Fragments of an Unknown Gospel*. London: British Museum, 1935.

Bishko, Herbert. *This Is Jerusalem*. Tel Aviv: Heritage Publishing, 1971.

Blinzler, Josef. *The Trial of Jesus*. Translated from the second revised and enlarged edition by Isabel and Florence McHugh. Westminster, Md: The Newman Press, 1959.

Bornkamm, Günther. *Jesus of Nazareth*. London: Hodder & Stoughton, 1973.

Bouguet, A. C. *Everyday Life in New Testament Times*. London: B. T. Batsford, 1954.

Brandon, S. G. F. *The Trial of Jesus of Nazareth*. New York: Scarborough Books, 1979.

———*Jesus and the Zealots*. Manchester: University Press, 1967.

Bultmann, R. *Jesus and the Word*. New York, Scribner, 1958.

——— *The History of the Synoptic Tradition*. Oxford: University Press, 1963.

Caillois, R. *Pontius Pilate*. New York: Macmillan, 1963.

Cohen, Boaz. *Jewish and Roman Law*. 2 vols. New York: Jewish Theological Seminary, 1966.

——— *Law and Tradition in Judaism*. New York: Ktav Publishing House, 1969.

Cohn, Haim. *The Trial and Death of Jesus*. London: Weidenfeld & Nicolson, 1972.

Craveri, M. *The Life of Jesus*. London: Panther Books, 1969.

Culican, W. *The Medes and Persians*. New York: Frederick A. Praeger, 1965.

Daniel-Rops, Henri. *Daily Life in the Time of Jesus*. London: Weidenfeld & Nicolson, 1962.

Daube, D. *Collaboration with Tyranny in Rabbinic Law*. Oxford: University Press, 1965.

Davies, W. D. *Christian Origins and Judaism*. Philadelphia, Pa: Westminster Press, 1962.

——— *The Setting of the Sermon on the Mount*. Cambridge: University Press, 1966.

Derrett, J. Duncan M. *Law and Society in Jesus's World*. Berlin/New York: Walter de Gruyter, 1982.

———*An Oriental Lawyer Looks at the Trial of Jesus and the Doctrine of the Redemption*. London: School of Oriental and African Studies, 1966.

Dodd, C. H. *The Authority of the Bible*. New York: Harper Torchbooks, 1960.

——— *Historical Tradition in the Fourth Gospel*. Cambridge: University Press, 1963.

Douglas, J. D. *The Temple: Its Ministry and Services*. Grand Rapids, Mich.: Wm B. Erdmans, 1958.

Driver, G. R. *The Judaean Scrolls*. Oxford: Blackwell, 1965.

Endo, Shusaku. *Silence*. London: Peter Owen, 1976.

Falk, H. *Jesus the Pharisee – A New Look at the Jewishness of Jesus*. New York: Paulist Press, 1985.

Ferguson, John. *Jesus in the Tide of Time: An Historical Study*. London: Routledge & Kegan Paul, 1980.

Flannery, E. H. *The Anguish of the Jews*. New York: Macmillan, 1965.

Flusser, D. *Jesus*. New York: Herder & Herder, 1970.

Foerster, W. *Palestinian Judaism in New Testament Times*. Edinburgh: Oliver & Boyd, 1964.

Fosdick, H. E. *The Man from Nazareth*. London: SCM Press, 1950.

Freyne, S. *The World of the New Testament*. Dublin: Veritas Publications, 1980.

Gibbon, E. *The Decline and Fall of the Roman Empire* (1776-88) (quotations are from Modern Library Edition). London: Penguin Books (no date).

Goldstein, M. *Jesus in the Jewish Tradition*. New York: Macmillan, 1950.

Goodspeed, Edgar, J. *The Twelve*. Philadelphia, Pa: The John C. Winston Company, 1967.

Grant, Michael. *The Jews in the Roman World*. London: Weidenfeld & Nicolson, 1973.

——— *The World of Rome*. New York: The New American Library, 1964.

Graves, R. *King Jesus*. London: Cassell, 1946.

Gross, W. J. *Herod the Great*. Baltimore, Md/Dublin: Helicon Press, 1962.

Guignebert, Ch. *The Jewish World in the Time of Jesus*. London: Kegan Paul, 1939.

Guilding, A. *The Fourth Gospel and Jewish Worship*. Oxford: University Press, 1960.

Guitton, J. *The Problem of Jesus*. New York: P. J. Kenedy, 1955.

Hall, G. Stanley. *Jesus, the Christ, in the Light of Psychology*, Vols 1, 2. London: G. Allen & Unwin, 1921.

Harnack, A. von. *The Sayings of Jesus*. New York: Putnam, 1908.

Harvey, A. E. *Jesus and the Constraints of History*. The Bampton Lectures, 1980. London: Duckworth, 1982.

Hengel, M. *The Atonement*. London: SCM Press, 1981.

Herford, R. T. *Christianity in Talmud and Midrash*. London: Williams & Norgate, 1903.

────── *The Pharisees*. Boston, Mass.: Beacon Press, 1962.

Hirsch, E. G. *The Crucifixion from the Jewish Point of View*. Chicago, Ill., 1892.

Hoenig, S. B. *The Great Sanhedrin*. Philadelphia, Pa: Dropsie College, 1953.

Hoever, Rev. Hugo, *Lives of the Saints*. New York: Catholic Book Publishing Co., 1967.

Hophan, Otto. *The Apostles*. London: Sands & Co., 1962.

Hunter, W. A. *Introduction to Roman Law*. London: Sweet & Maxwell, 1934.

Husband, R. W. *The Prosecution of Jesus*. Princeton, NJ: University Press, 1916.

Innes, A. Taylor. *The Trial of Jesus Christ*. Edinburgh: Clark, 1899.

Jacobs, J. *Jesus as Others Saw Him*. Boston, Mass.: Houghton, 1895.

Jennings, P. *Face to Face with the Turin Shroud*. Oxford: Mowbray, 1978.

Jeremias, Joachim, *Jerusalem in the Time of Jesus*. London: SCM Press, 1969.

Jewish Encyclopedia. 12 vols. New York: Funk & Wagnall, 1901–6.

Jolowicz, H. F. *Historical Introduction to the Study of Roman Law*. Cambridge: University Press, 1952.

Josephus. *The Jewish War*. Trans: G. A. Williamson, Rev. E. Mary Smallwood. Harmondsworth: Penguin, 1981.

Jowett, George F. *The Drama of the Lost Disciples*. London: Covenant Publishing, 1970.

Keller, Werner. *The Bible as History. Archaeology Confirms the Book of Books*. London: Hodder & Stoughton, 1956.

Kilpatrick, G. D. *The Trial of Jesus*. Oxford: University Press, 1953.

Klausner, J. *Jesus of Nazareth*. New York: Macmillan, 1925.

Lagerkvist, P. *Barabbas*. London: Chatto & Windus, 1952.

Loewe, H. M. J. *Render unto Caesar: Religious and Political Loyalty in Palestine*. Cambridge: University Press, 1940.

Maccoby, H. *Revolution in Judaea: Jesus and the Jewish Resistance*. London: Ocean Books, 1973.

——— *The Sacred Executioner: Human Sacrifice and the Legacy of Guilt*. London: Thames & Hudson, 1982.

Mackey, James P. *Jesus – the Man and the Myth – A Contemporary Christology*. London: SCM Press, 1979.

Martin, Ernest L. *The Birth of Christ Recalculated*. 2nd edn. Pasadena, Calif.: Foundation for Biblical Research, 1980.

McArthur, H. K. (ed.) *In Search of the Historical Jesus*. London: S.P.C.J., 1970.

Morrison, Frank. *Who Moved the Stone?* London: Faber & Faber, 1930.

Morrison, W. D. *The Jews under Roman Rule*. New York: Putnam, 1893.

Neil, William, and Travis, Stephen H. *More Difficult Sayings of Jesus*. London/Oxford: Mowbray, 1981.

Nweeya, Samuel K. *Persia: The Land of the Magi*. 5th edn. Philadelphia, Pa: John C. Winston, 1913.

O'Collins, Gerald. *Interpreting Jesus*. London: Geoffrey Chapman, 1983.

Olivier, E. *Mary Magdalen*. Edinburgh: University Press, 1934.

Olmstead, A. T. *Jesus in the Light of History*. New York: Scribner, 1942.

O'Rahilly, A. *The Crucified*. Edited by J. A. Gaughan. Dublin: Kingdom Books, 1985.

Oursler, Fulton. *The Greatest Story Ever Told*. Kingswood: The World's Work, 1949.

Parkes, J. *The Conflict of the Church and Synagogue*. New York: Meridian Books, 1964.

Radin, M. *The Trial of Jesus of Nazareth*. Chicago, Ill.: University Press, 1931.

Ramsay, William M. *Was Christ Born at Bethlehem?* Minneapolis, Minn.: James Family Publishing Co., 1978.

Reich, Wilhelm. *The Murder of Christ*. London: Souvenir Press, 1975.

Renan, Ernest. *The Life of Jesus*. New York: Modern Library, 1927.

Richards, H. J. *The Miracles of Jesus: What Really Happened*. London/ Oxford: Mowbray, 1983.

Riddle, D. W. *Jesus and the Pharisees*. Chicago, Ill.: University Press, 1928.

Rivkin, Ellis. *What Crucified Jesus?* Nashville, Tenn.: Abingdon Press, 1984.

Robinson, John A. T. *The Priority of John*. London: SCM Press, 1985.

Roth, C. *The Historical Background of the Dead Sea Scrolls*. Oxford: Blackwell, 1958.

Sandmel, S. *A Jewish Understanding of the New Testament*. Cincinnati, Ohio: Hebrew Union College, 1957.

Schoen, M. *The Man Jesus Was*. New York: Alfred A. Knopf, 1950.

Schofield, J. N. *The Historical Background of the Bible*. London: Thomas Nelson, 1938.

Schonfield, H. J. *The Passover Plot*. New York: Bantam Books, 1967.

Schurer, Emil. *The History of the Jewish People in the Age of Jesus Christ*. Vols I and II, rev. and ed. by G. Vermes. Edinburgh: T. & T. Clark, 1973–9.

——— *A History of the Jewish People in the Time of Jesus*. New York: Schocken Books, 1961.

Schurer, E. *History of the Jewish People in the Age of Jesus Christ*. Revised edn with new material by G. Vermes and F. Millar. Edinburgh: R. & R. Clark, 1973.

Schweitzer, A. *The Quest for the Historical Jesus*. New York: Macmillan Paperback, 1961.

────── *The Psychiatric Study of Jesus*. Boston, Mass.: The Beacon Press, 1948.

Sheen, Fulton J. *Life of Christ*. New York: Image Books, 1977.

Sherwin-White, A. N. *Roman Society and Roman Law in the New Testament*. Oxford: Clarendon Press, 1963.

Smith, Asbury. *The Twelve Christ Chose*. New York: Harper & Brothers, 1958.

Sox, H. D. *The Image on the Shroud – Is the Turin Shroud a Forgery?* London: Unwin Paperbacks, 1981.

Strack, H. L. *Introduction to the Talmud and Midrash*. New York: Meridian Books, 1959.

Stevenson, G. H. *Roman Provincial Administration*. Oxford: Blackwell, 1949.

Suetonius. *The Twelve Caesars*. Trans R. Graves. Harmondsworth: Penguin Books, 1957.

Tacitus. *The Annals of Imperial Rome*. Trans. M. Grant. Harmondsworth: Penguin Books, 1956.

Taylor, V. *The Life and Ministry of Jesus*. London: Macmillan, 1954.

Thurian, M., Brother of Taize. *Mary, Mother of the Lord, Figure of the Church*. London: Mowbray, 1985.

Toynbee, A. *The Crucible of Christianity*. London: Thames & Hudson, 1969.

Trevor-Roper, Hugh. *Tacitus: The Annals and the Histories*. London: The New English Library, 1966.

Trotter, F. T. *Jesus and the Historian*. Philadelphia, Pa: Westminster Press, 1968.

Van Paassen, P. *Why Jesus Died*. New York: Dial Press, 1949.

Vermes, Geza. *Jesus the Jew*. London: SCM Press, 1973.

────── *Jesus and the World of Judaism*. London: SCM Press, 1983.

────── *Jesus the Jew: A Historian's Reading of the Gospels*. London: Collins, 1973.

Vilney, Z. *Legends of Judaea and Samaria. The Sacred*

Land. Vol. 2. Philadelphia, Pa: The Jewish Publication Society of America, 1975.

—— *Legends of Jerusalem. The Sacred Land*. Vol. 1. Philadelphia, Pa: The Jewish Publication Society of America, 1973.

—— *Legends of Galilee, Jordan and Sinai. The Sacred Land*. Vol. 3. Philadelphia, Pa: The Jewish Publication Society of America, 1978.

Weber, M. *Ancient Judaism*. New York: Free Press, 1952.

Wells, G. A. *The Historical Evidence for Jesus*. New York: Prometheus Books, 1982.

Wight, Fred H. *Manners and Customs of Bible Lands*. Chicago, Ill.: Moody Press, 1953.

Wilkinson, John. *Jerusalem as Jesus Knew It – Archaeology as Evidence*. London: Thames & Hudson, 1982.

Wilson, I. *The Turin Shroud*. London: Gollancz, 1978.

—— *Jesus: The Evidence*. London: Pan Books, 1985.

Wilson, W. R. *The Execution of Jesus*. New York: Scribners Sons, 1970.

Winter, P. *On the Trial of Jesus*. Berlin: de Gruyter, 1961. Second Edition Revised and Edited by T. A. Burkill and Geza Vermes. New York: Walter De Gruyter, 1974.

Wolff, H. J. *Roman Law: A Historical Introduction*. Oklahoma: University Press, 1951.

Womack, David A. *12 Signs, 12 Sons: Astrology in the Bible*. New York: Harper & Row, 1978.

Zahrnt, H. *The Historical Jesus*. London: Collins, 1963.

Zeitlin, S. *Who Crucified Jesus?* New York: Bloch Publishing, 1947.

Zugibe, F. *The Cross and the Shroud*. New York: Angelus Books, 1982.

Other Gospels and Writings

(in the order they were originally set down)

The Gospel of the Birth of Mary
*The Protevangelion of the Birth of Jesus Christ by James the
    Less*
Thomas' Gospel of the Infancy of Jesus Christ
The Gospel of Nicodemus
The Epistle of Paul the Apostle to the Laodiceans
The Acts of Paul and Thecca
The First Epistle of Clement to the Corinthians
The Epistle of Barnabas
The Epistle of Ignatius to the Ephesians
The Epistle of Ignatius to the Magnesians
The Epistle of Ignatius to the Trallians
The Epistle of Ignatius to the Romans
The Epistle of Ignatius to the Philadelphians
The Epistle of Ignatius to the Smyrnaeans
The Epistle of Ignatius to Polycarp
The Epistle of Polycarp to the Philippians
The First Book of Hermas
The Second Book of Hermas
The Third Book of Hermas
Letters of Herod and Pilate
The Gospel according to Peter
The Acts of Andrew
The Gospel of Andrew
The Gospel of Barnabas
The Writings of Bartholomew the Apostle

388

The Gospel of Bartholomew
The Gospel according to the Egyptians
A Gospel under the name of Judas Iscariot
The Gospel of Philip
The Gospel of Thaddaeus
The Gospel of Thomas

389

The Tractates

Abodah Zarah
Aboth
Arakhin
Baba Bathra
Baba Kamma
Baba Metzia
Bekhoroth
Berakhoth
Betzah (or Yom Tob)
Bikkurim
Demai
Eduyoth
Erubin
Gittin
Hagigah
Hallah
Horayoth
Hullin
Kelim
Kerithoth
Ketuboth
Kiddushin
Kilaim
Kinnim
Maaser Sheni
Maaseroth
Makkoth
Makshirin
Megillah
Meilah
Menahoth
Middoth

Mikwaoth
Moed Katan
Nazir
Nedarim
Negaim
Niddah
Oholoth
Orlah
Parah
Peah
Pesahim
Rosh ha-Shanah
Sanhedrin
Shabbath
Shebiith
Shebuoth
Shekalim
Sotah
Sukkah
Taanith
Tamid
Tebul Yom
Temurah
Terumoth
Tohoroth
Uktzin
Yadaim
Yebamoth
Yoma
Zabim
Zebahim

Index

391

392

398

399